Harris & Ewing

SENATOR JAMES COUZENS

INDEPENDENT MAN: THE LIFE OF
Senator James Couzens

BY

HARRY BARNARD

WAYNE STATE UNIVERSITY PRESS   DETROIT

GREAT LAKES BOOKS

The publication of this volume in a freely accessible digital format has been made possible by a major grant from the National Endowment for the Humanities and the Mellon Foundation through their Humanities Open Book Program.

This book was originally published in 1958 by Charles Scribner's Sons.

Library of Congress Cataloging-in-Publication Data

Barnard, Harry, 1906–
Independent man: the life of Senator James Couzens / by Harry Barnard.
p. cm. — (Great Lakes books)
Originally published: New York: Scribners, 1958.
ISBN 978-0-8143-4396-8 (pbk.: alk. paper); 978-0-8143-3587-1 (e-book)
1. Couzens, James, 1872–1936. 2. Legislators—United States—Biography.
3. United States. Congress. Senate—Biography.
4. Michigan—Politics and government—1837–1950.
I. Title. II. Series.
E748.C87 B3 2002
328.73'092—dc21
[B]
2002069138

FOR PERMISSION TO QUOTE BRIEFLY FROM THE FOLLOWING SOURCES,
THE AUTHOR MAKES GRATEFUL ACKNOWLEDGMENT.

America in Midpassage by Charles A. and Mary R. Beard
(The Macmillan Company, 1939)
Inside U.S.A. by John Gunther (Harper and Brothers)
Letters of Franklin D. Roosevelt by permission of Mrs. Franklin D. Roosevelt
"Michigan Magic" by John T. Flynn (Harper's Magazine, December 1933)
Wild Wheel, The by Garet Garrett (Pantheon Books, Inc.)

Wayne State University Press thanks Frank Couzens Jr.
for his generous permission to reprint material in this book.

http://wsupress.wayne.edu/

CONTENTS

Book III: *The Senator* 139

Book IV: *The Independent Man* 211

FOR

Alfred P. Solomon

AND *Esther,* TOO

FRIENDS

AND

COUNSELLORS

FOREWORD

THE James Couzens in *Independent Man* was not the James Couzens I knew. I was his first grandchild, born in 1924, and probably because I was a first grandchild I received a lot of attention and many favors. My grandfather loved all of his grandchildren, and we loved him. We knew him as Daddy Jim.

In the summer, our family lived at Wabeek Farms, as did my aunt and uncle and their children, the Yaw family. On Sunday mornings I looked forward to my grandfather picking me up for a ride in his station wagon. He would show me his fields, the cows, the chickens, and the creamery. One Sunday he drove by the little cemetery on Middlebelt Road and told me that was where he would be buried. This was not where they buried him.

He had a smooth and effective way of correcting my poor manners. One day while having dinner at his home, he observed me trying to cut my meat with my elbows up in the air. He asked, "Are you trying to fly, Frank?"

Once he took us grandchildren to the Bloomfield Hills Country Club for lunch, as a treat. My grandfather didn't think that anyone should have to eat spinach, so he was really perplexed when we all ordered spinach. He didn't know how much we wanted to be like Popeye.

From the Senate he wrote to me in his beautiful handwriting. I did not fully appreciate those letters at the time. My mother, Margaret Lang Couzens Slattery, would see to it that I would write him back, usually when I was trying to listen to a Detroit Lions game. The writing had to be neat, the lines straight, and the spelling perfect. This required many rewrites, which decreased my appreciation for my grandfather's thoughtfulness.

Four generations of Couzens men. From left to right: James Joseph Couzens, Frank Couzens, Frank Couzens Jr., and James Couzens.

I truly looked forward to being with him; he was fun. On a couple of occasions, I was invited to go on a Great Lakes cruise with him, my grandmother, and my Aunt Betty. During each of two summers in the late 1930s Grandfather chartered a beautiful yacht. One was the *Buccaneer* and the other was the *Trudeon*. These yachts were too large to dock in most harbors. They would drop anchor and we would go ashore in one of the launches. Once we went ashore in Green Bay, Wisconsin, to meet one of my grandfather's colleagues, Senator LaFollette. This was before ship-to-shore radiotelephones; each yacht had a radioman or a signalman, and Morse code was the way communications were received and sent. We knew by flashing signal lights when to meet the Senator on shore, and Morse code radio transmissions were how my grandfather received the morning news and communications from shore. It was also very exciting, especially for a teen, to be in the Chicago harbor in 1934 the night John Dillinger was shot. We wondered the next day if the shots we heard in the night were the same that killed the infamous gangster.

We did not hear about my grandfather's business dealings or his Senate agenda. He loved his farm and his Ford station wagon. The lesson from Daddy Jim was, "Do it right," and "Fulfill your commitments." I am still working on these lessons.

Frank Couzens Jr.
January 2002

INTRODUCTION

INDEPENDENT MAN: The Life of James Couzens and I have been friends since 1958 when it was used in the preparation of my doctoral dissertation on Henry Ford. My copy cost $5.95. Present-day buyers pay more, but they, too, have made a sound investment.

Independent Man, a perfect title, has been out of print for many years (its publisher, Charles Scribner's Sons, does not know how long it has been unavailable or even the number of copies that were originally printed). Kudos to the Wayne State University Press for reprinting the only book-length biography of one of Michigan's most remarkable men.

Born in Chatham, Ontario, in 1872, Couzens moved to Detroit in 1890. Able, exacting, truculent, he had a don't-tread-on-me attitude reinforced by outspokenness and a terrible temper. On the job, wags said, when he smiled his annual smile, the ice broke up on the Great Lakes.

Couzens was a paradox. All business from his bump-toed shoes to his derby hat, he was a loving family man with compassionate, even tender, feelings toward children. His children and grandchildren called him "Daddy Jim." A capitalist multimillionaire, he had profoundly democratic instincts, and earned an unparalleled reputation as a radical. He was a dragon at the cashbox, but gave away most of his fortune. Although appreciative of publicity, he was tactless with the press, characteristically ordering the *Detroit News* to fire an offending reporter and forbidding the publication to "ever again mention the name of the Ford Motor Company."

Independent Man focuses on Couzens's careers with Ford, the city of Detroit, and the United States Senate, plus his embroilment in

Detroit's 1932–1933 bank crisis and the New Deal.

Couzens contributed as much to Ford Motor Company's early success, even survival, as Henry Ford. The two men did not partner by choice. They were tossed together when Ford's principal associate, coal dealer Alex Malcomson, assigned Couzens, a trusted employee, to watch over the Ford Company's business affairs. While Ford devoted himself to technical matters, Couzens ruled the rest of the firm. From the outset he deemed it good business to publicize Ford. "Our Mr. Ford made the first Gasoline Automobile in Detroit and the third in the United States" (both claims untrue), proclaimed one of his ads. Another declared that "Henry Ford has been the greatest factor in the development of the automobile industry . . . in the world." When given such bouquets, Henry kept the flowers. Within a few years Couzens could have echoed racing champion Barney Oldfield, "Ford and I made each other, but I did much the best job of it."

Couzens also initially credited Ford with having originated the company's famed five-dollar day in 1914. "It was quite natural that Mr. Ford should be credited with this project," he said, "because he was the head of the company, a majority stockholder, and it was to the benefit of the Ford Motor Company . . . to keep the name Ford much more before the public." After leaving the company, however, Couzens said of the plan, "I will say that I, personally, am responsible for it." Over the decades a spirited, futile discussion has ensued as to whether the larger credit belongs to Ford or Couzens. Suffice it to say, as historian Allan Nevins has noted, "The proposal would probably have been vetoed had Couzens violently opposed it, and could certainly never been approved without Ford's hearty support."

Couzens and his sister, Rosetta, owned 10.5 percent of the Ford Company from 1906 until 1919; Ford held 58.5 percent. The partners were not fond of each other, as indicated by a wide gap between them in formal photographs. By working in separate spheres, however, they avoided a major clash until 1915. That year, divergent views on America's World War I neutralism, war loans to the Allies, and national preparedness, prompted a showdown and Couzens's resignation from the company. In 1919 he sold his stock to Henry Ford for $28,308,857, receiving a higher share price than any other shareholder.

Before leaving Ford, Couzens accepted the chairmanship of the newly-formed Detroit Street Railway Commission, set up to force municipal ownership of the streetcar lines. During a bitter, seven-year fight, the privately-owned Detroit Union Railways raised fares from five to six cents. Couzens, by then Detroit's police commissioner, brought in the press to witness his refusal to pay the extra penny and be evicted from a car. The fare increase was rescinded, and Couzens gained in public favor. In 1922, by which time Couzens was mayor, the city acquired the rail company.

Couzens's rancorous police commissionership (1916-1918) paved the way to the mayor's office. Couzens's own car was stolen during his first month on the job. The populace also was amused, as well as alarmed, by the commissioner's insistence on strict enforcement of laws governing gambling, prostitution, and Detroit's 1,400 saloons. The cleanup campaign petered out, Detroiters being less amenable to marching orders than Ford workers. Of his campaign, Couzens summed up, "They wanted me to clean [the city] and not clean it." The commissioner was even hauled off to his own jail, after refusing to pay a $100 contempt-of-court fine.

Couzens enjoyed being in the public eye–albeit like a cinder, some said–and convinced himself that he was needed and electable as Detroit's mayor. Others disagreed. John Dodge did not think he could be elected "dog catcher or coroner." E. Roy Pelletier, ex-head of Ford advertising, refused to handle Couzens's publicity, saying it was impossible to "sell a man so lacking in good fellowship." Couzens nonetheless won handily, voters being persuaded by his promise to conduct himself "so that I have my own self-respect, regardless of whether people like me."

As mayor, the "maverick millionaire," as Couzens was called, continued to challenge accepted patterns of conduct and to provide bold, energetic leadership. At a time when the rapidly-growing city needed improved, expanded schools, sewers, streets, municipal hospital facilities, and other services, he drew up plans for the expenditure of $243,000,000, an astounding figure for that era.

Couzens's temper was not improved by the mayor's office. If he was not denouncing the Detroit Board of Commerce leaders as a "pack of curs," he was branding Detroit Edison's president a "liar," the latter epithet earning him ejection from City Council chambers. City Hall workers fumed when the mayor insisted that they start work at 8:30 A.M. and put in a "full day's work." Asked why he worked on holidays, when others were out playing, he replied, "I have to make good on this job." In Harry Barnard's view, he was "one of the few outstanding mayors in American history,"

Late in 1922, following Truman H. Newberry's forced resignation from the United States Senate, Couzens was appointed to that body by Republican Governor Alex J. Groesbeck. A constant thorn in the side of his party, Couzens summed up his political views with the statement, "I am a Republican, but not like Harding, Coolidge, and Hoover! . . . If being a Republican means kowtowing to the President, I do not care to be a Republican." A newspaper headline accurately pegged him as "James Couzens–One-Man Bloc." Hoover described him as "a very dangerous man."

Couzens repeatedly shocked fellow Republicans on issues ranging from liberalizing national prohibition laws to demanding the first investigation of the Department of Internal Revenue. When Secretary of the Treasury Andrew Mellon counterattacked by investigating Couzens's tax returns, the senator proved in court that he had overpaid $900,000 in taxes when selling his Ford stock.

In 1933 Couzens became embroiled in Detroit's bank closings. Many people and institutions were blamed for triggering the crisis and failing to solve it. Leading scapegoats were President Hoover, President-elect Roosevelt, the Reconstruction Finance Corporation, the Senate Finance Committee, Henry Ford, and the Communist Party. Couzens received far more criticism than anyone else. Many said that an RFC loan could have saved the Motor City's banks had not Couzens blocked an aid package, and that the senator balked partly because he hated Henry Ford and all other rich Detroiters. In refuting this thesis, Barnard asserts "if any one person forced the bank holiday this person was not Couzens, but Henry Ford." In 1934 Couzens's public reputation sank to an all-time low. Late in the year, Couzens's son, Frank, was elected to the first of two terms as mayor of Detroit. "That shows," the defensive father said, "that I haven't ruined the family reputation after all!"

The banking crisis was thoroughly aired in a grand jury investigation in 1933 and by a Senate subcommittee the following year. Couzens, who received extremely unfavorable press during the first probe, redeemed his battered reputation somewhat during the Senate inquiry. Interestingly, John Kenneth Galbraith, in his generally favorable review of *Independent Man* in the *New York Times*, is critical of Barnard's account of the banking crisis. "A biographer," he observed, "is a biographer and not a boxing ring second or a counsel for the defense."

Couzens admired Roosevelt from the time they first met immediately after FDR's 1933 inaugural address. "He's human," he said of the Chief Executive. Moreover, he often preferred Roosevelt's policies to those of his own party, especially with the coming of the New Deal. Indeed, Couzens anticipated the New Deal's public works programs, having publicly stated in 1931 that the government should "make work by building libraries, museums, highways, bridges, and schools" even if it meant tripling the federal debt.

Couzens's freewheeling independence eventually led to his political demise. He was anathema to Republican party regulars, and he had no political organization of his own. Couzens also alienated many voters by opposing such proposals as an ex-soldiers's bonus and the Townsend Old Age Pension Plan. Finally, in 1936 he supported Roosevelt's bid for reelection, heresy for a Republican. Michigan's Republican Party selected ex-Governor Wilber M. Brucker to run against Couzens in that year's primary, and Couzens's defeat was a foregone conclusion. In the long run, even in the short run, it did not matter. He was ailing, and had only two months to live.

Characteristically, Couzens remained independent to the last. When Franklin Delano Roosevelt arrived in Detroit on Oct. 15, 1936, to campaign, he offered to visit the senator at Harper Hospital. Couzens would not hear of it. Leaving his bed, he met FDR at the train station and accompanied him on a parade through Detroit's streets, at a rally at Hamtramck Stadium, and at a mass meeting at Detroit City Hall. Exhausted, Couzens returned to the hospital, where uremia aggravated his medical problems. A week later he underwent an operation, from which he did not awaken from the anesthetic.

If Couzens is less well remembered than he should be, it was the way he wanted it, for, with two exceptions, he refused to permit buildings or institutions to be named for him. By way of contrast, a list of Henry Ford-related nomenclature fills six pages of the *Ford Legend*.

Two buildings, two streets and a commercial enterprise have borne Couzens's name. Investing in downtown Detroit real estate in 1911, Couzens built the Couzens Building on Woodward Avenue. Its fate is unknown. In 1924 the name Couzens Residence for Nurses was given to a Couzens-financed ($620,000) dormitory at the University of Michigan in Ann Arbor. Although Couzens was indignant upon learning that the institution's regents had acted without his consent, he let the matter stand. Enlarged in 1960, five-story Couzens Hall went coed in 1970 and now houses 613 students, mostly freshmen. Its library lacks a copy of *Independent Man;* I have promised to provide one.

Couzens donated a comparable nurses's dormitory to Detroit's Harper Hospital in 1919. The name "The James Couzens Home" was proposed by hospital officials. When Couzens demurred, it was named for the head nurse, Emily A. McLaughlin. Today, six-story McLaughlin Hall is occupied by hospital office workers.

Hazel Park, a northern Detroit suburb, has a Couzens street, the origins of which are obscure. When Detroit's John C. Lodge Expressway (M-10) was extended in the early 1960s, the portion from the "Linwood Curve" to Eight Mile Road was named "James Couzens Expressway." Two decades later the state dropped the name "James Couzens" in favor of John C. Lodge Freeway. Signs on the Lodge's service drives are still marked "James Couzens" from Wyoming Avenue to Eight Mile.

In 1926, Couzens, desperate to be "active," organized the Couzens Ice Machine Company, capitalized at $1,000,000. Two factory sites were bought, one in Detroit, another in Wapakoneta, Ohio. Dealers were signed, literature printed, and sample machines displayed. At that point, Couzens, without explanation, abandoned the enterprise at great loss.

Couzens's greatest benefaction, the Children's Fund of Michigan, would have been named the Couzens Foundation if Couzens's associates had prevailed. The philanthropist not only rejected the name, but also stipulated that the Fund—established in 1929 with a gift of $10,000,000–spend itself out of existence within 25 years.

The Fund supported children's agencies and also initiated programs in underserved areas of children's medicine in the hope that they would attract private and/or government grants after the Fund's demise. Thus the Fund built and operated the Children's Hospital of Michigan, Northern Michigan Children's Clinic at Marquette and the Central Michigan Children's Clinic at Traverse City. For decades Couzens family members have maintained a direct interest in Children's Hospital. Margaret Couzens Slattery, the philanthropist's daughter-in-law, served as a trustee for 60 years, 16 of them as president and chairperson. Mrs. Slattery's son, Frank Couzens Jr., and Frank's daughter, Carol Marantette, are present-day trustees.

During its lifetime, the Children's Fund distributed $18,038,656, a sum which included the original $10,000,000 grant, an additional gift of $1,880,000 from Couzens, and income derived from principal. Couzens's total philanthropy, $30,000,000, approximated the sum he had received for his Ford stock.

Two of Couzens's residences remain in use. An Albert Kahn-designed home at 610 Longfellow Avenue, Detroit, in which the family lived from 1910-28, was given to his son Frank. Frank's widow, after moving from the house in 1962, gave it to the Maryknoll Fathers, who subsequently sold it. Today, a neighbor reports, it is a "terribly neglected private residence."

Couzens's last home, on his 800-acre country estate, Wabeek, was sold by the family in 1968 to Chrysler-Wabeek Development Company, a joint venture of Chrysler Realty Corporation and Arizona-based Del E. Webb Inc. Subsequent development produced the Wabeek Country Club, a 145-acre golf course, and hundreds of upscale houses and condominiums. The 12,000-square foot mansion, set on 2.23 acres at 3550 Wabeek Lake Drive, Bloomfield Township (its present address), housed a sales office from the late 1960s into the 1980s. Vacated for some years, it was restored by a Birmingham attorney, Leonard Hyman, and his wife, Virginia, and resold in 2000 as a private residence. Asking price: $3.8 million.

Couzens's imposing mausoleum vies with those of John and Horace Dodge and J. L. Hudson as Detroit's largest tomb. Set on a 15,526 square-foot lot—big enough to accommodate 200 burial sites—it commands the highest elevation in Woodlawn Cemetery, the Motor City's premier cemetery. The edifice, built of Barre granite, resembles a mini-Parthenon. Its twelve crypts will be filled with the future entombment of an unmarried Couzens granddaughter. The interior has a huge solid bronze crucifix, a beautiful altar, a prayer bench, and space enough for 15 to 20 persons to attend occasional masses (Mrs. Couzens was a Roman Catholic; her husband was not).

The mansion and mausoleum, believes Couzens's grandson, Frank Couzens Jr., were built mainly for the gratification of his grandmother, a member of a leading Detroit family. Still, one is bemused to find that Detroit's "man of the people" is entombed in a structure that cost more than $100,000 in 1921. In contrast, Henry Ford's grave is marked by a simple white marble stone in a small Ford family cemetery on Detroit's west side. Edsel Ford, the state's second most wealthy citizen, has a relatively modest tomb in Woodlawn.

Couzens is minimally remembered today, even by the global company he helped build. All the more reason to commend Wayne State University Press for preserving his memory with this reprint of *Independent Man,* which, as a reviewer for the *Nation* observed, "has not an unclear sentence from beginning to end." If he were alive, Couzens would ask no more—and demand no less.

David L. Lewis
Professor of Business History
University of Michigan

A NOTE ON THE AUTHOR

SURPRISINGLY, *Independent Man*'s first printing omits biographical information on the book's author; we'll remedy that shortcoming here. The son of an oculist, Harry Barnard was born with the surname Kletzky in Pueblo, Colorado, in 1906. After receiving a Ph.B. from the University of Chicago in 1928, he served from 1929 to 1957 as a Chicago newspaperman, University of Chicago research and press relations director, and Detroit advertising agency publicist. In 1938 and 1954 he authored biographies of two half-forgotten men, Illinois Governor John Peter Altgeld and President Rutherford B. Hayes.

Declaring himself a freelance writer in 1957, Barnard, who described himself as a "Jeffersonian-Altgeldian-Rooseveltian-Independent-Liberal-Democract," subsequently wrote five books, most notably *Independent Man* and *The Forging of an American Jew: The Life and Times of Judge Julian W. Mack* (1974). The Couzens book so favorably impressed John Shively Knight, publisher of the Knight Newspapers, that he invited Barnard to write an editorial-page column for his *Chicago Daily News*. The column, "Liberal at Large," was nationally distributed by the Des Moines Register and Tribune Syndicate. An active supporter of liberal causes, Barnard lived in Wilmette, Illinois, until his death in 1982. His papers are in the University of Wyoming's American Heritage Center.

PROLOGUE:

October 12, 1915

OCTOBER 12, 1915

WHEN the story broke, it shoved the European war dispatches into a subordinate position in newspapers all over the world. In London as well as in Copenhagen, not to mention New York, Chicago, St. Louis, and Los Angeles, this was true. The newspapers in Detroit put out extras with big headlines:

COUZENS LEAVES FORD!

Days afterward, from one coast of the United States to the other, the press continued to feature special commentaries and so-called "inside" stories about the man who left Ford.

There were stories, too, about the reasons (true, speculative, or imagined) for the startling separation that concerned the world's most conspicuous industrial enterprise—the Ford Motor Company of Detroit, U.S.A. If Henry Ford himself had quit, or had even simply disappeared, the sensation could scarcely have been greater.

"But none of the stories, then or later, of why it happened, came within one and one-half percent of the truth." So, years after, said John C. Lodge, the venerable ex-councilman and ex-mayor of Detroit. He was one of the very few people in all the world who knew both principals in the stories well enough to call the one "Jim" and the other "Henry." And Lodge believed that he at least had heard the "whole truth" from the lips of both "Jim" and "Henry"—but he wasn't telling, for he had been "pledged" not to tell.

Yet the whole truth was that no one really had told the whole truth—not "Jim" and not "Henry," not even when they had in fact tried to unburden themselves of the full story to old John Lodge. This is not strange. In such matters, the truth is almost always linked

3

with, and enveloped in, motives and aspects deeply psychological, things usually veiled—veiled most of all, perhaps, from the principals themselves. They can tell of the incident itself, the "what" of the occurrence. But they are not able to tell of all that really lay behind it—the "why." Such, clearly, was so in the case of James Couzens and Henry Ford—without either of whom the company that bore the name of Ford would never have been of interest to anyone outside of Detroit.

The "what"—the bare facts—may be pieced together briefly.

On the evening of October 11, 1915, Charles A. Brownell, who uneasily wore the title of advertising manager, had stepped, just before closing time, into the office of the Vice President, Treasurer, and General Manager of the Ford Motor Company.

Brownell, usually the opposite of a timid man, made his entrance with the attitude of caution and wariness customarily adopted by nearly everyone who went into that office. For Brownell had come to see "Jim"—though, to be sure, he did not refer to the Vice President, Treasurer, and General Manager of the Ford Motor Company as "Jim," but rather as "Mr. Couzens." His mission was to get Couzens' approval of the page proofs for the next issue of the Ford Motor Company magazine, the *Ford Times*. He was acting in accordance with a rule that everyone in the Ford organization understood in those days—that Mr. Couzens had to approve everything (or nearly everything) the company did, and of late this had applied especially to articles in the *Ford Times*.

Brownell handed Couzens a set of the proofs. In his characteristically quick way, Couzens thumbed through them, while Brownell held his breath. Nothing objectionable to Couzens turned up— until his eyes fell upon one particular article.

The effect on him of glancing at this article was an almost instantaneous—and characteristic—reddening, first of his neck and then of his face—danger signs that all who knew him well understood.

The article that produced this redness contained the substance of remarks previously published in the Detroit *Free Press* and credited to Henry Ford, remarks concerning the war in Europe and the "preparedness movement" in the United States.

The tenor of these remarks was distinctly "pacifist"—of the kind that led a little later to Ford's being persuaded to sponsor his celebrated *Oscar II* "peace ship" venture.

"You cannot publish this," Couzens told Brownell.

"But Mr. Ford himself—"

"You cannot publish this! Hold it over."

"But Mr. Ford said—"

"These are Mr. Ford's personal views, not the views of the company. This is the company paper. He cannot use the *Ford Times* for his personal views. I will talk to Mr. Ford tomorrow."

Brownell withdrew without saying anything more. He knew a decision had been made at the Ford company—when Couzens had made it.

After Brownell had departed, Couzens turned his swivel chair away from his flat-top desk and shut violently the roll top of his "aft" desk.

These two desks formed the nerve center of the Ford Motor Company. To them came the reports from the 6,700 Ford agents, the thirty-five Ford branches, the twenty-six Ford assembly plants, the forty-eight American banks, and the two foreign banks in which the Ford company millions were deposited. From these desks came the decisions that guided the company's affairs throughout its already vast empire in the United States and abroad, every place, in fact, except in the main shop and in the laboratory (Mr. Ford's particular bailiwicks)—and sometimes in these places as well.

Couzens got up briskly. He walked over to his clothes rack and planted a black derby firmly on his prematurely gray head. For a moment he stopped before the mirror over the wash basin to adjust his necktie knot to a precisely correct position in his high, stiff collar, flicked away some dust that may or may not have been on his jacket sleeves, thriftily turned off the office lights, and, in an instant, with his usual quick gait, left the office of the Ford Company for his home.

His movements that evening, down to the last gesture, were all routine for him. He had gone out of the Administration Building that same way night after night since it had been built. But, after arriving home, he went to bed earlier than usual that night, explaining to his wife, Margaret, that he had one of those headaches which his doctors called "migraine."

At ten o'clock the next morning, Henry Ford came into Couzens' office. "He was perfectly good-natured. He sat and visited awhile," Couzens later described the meeting.

The two "partners," as they were known, talked of Couzens' recent trip to California, of Ford's plan to attend the San Diego Exposition there with Thomas A. Edison. Then Couzens said to Ford, "I held up the *Times* because of your article in it about the war."

Suddenly, as if a match had been touched to gunpowder, the calm and friendly atmosphere in the office exploded.

Ford's geniality changed swiftly into something else—a belligerence not usually associated with Henry Ford in those days, an attitude he had certainly never before shown so sharply to Couzens, although others in the company already knew that Ford was capable of such a transformation. As Couzens himself said some time later, "Mr. Ford just flew off the handle . . . I was shocked . . . aghast."

Couzens did not recall in detail everything Ford said on that occasion. But he did remember Ford's having snapped:

"You cannot stop anything here!"

"Well, then, I will quit," Couzens replied.

Ford suddenly seemed to calm down.

"Better think it over," he said.

"No, I have decided," Couzens said.

"What will you tell the papers?" Ford asked.

"That we disagree about the war."

"All right, if you have decided," said Ford.

So these two—"Jim" and "Henry," who had been referred to in a business publication only a few weeks earlier as "The Damon and Pythias of the Ford Motor Company"—had separated.

And it all happened in less time than it takes to set it down.[1]

For some time a few persons in the automobile industry had known that there was trouble between the "partners," but no one ever assumed that matters would come to this. A Ford Motor Company without James Couzens would have then been as unthinkable as a Ford Motor Company without Henry Ford. Indeed, there were those who said that the Ford Company up to then *was* mainly Couzens. Of course, this was not true. Henry Ford could not be dismissed so casually. Conjecture about a Fordless Ford Motor Company is unrealistic. The Ford certainly was Ford's car, though, to be sure, C. Harold Wills, as well as certain other mechanics and designers including the Dodge brothers, John and Horace, had contributed to its creation. Similarly, the Ford ideas of factory production were more Henry Ford's than anyone's else, even though Walter Flanders, the Dodges, W. F. McGuire, Wills, Charles E.

Sorensen, and others contributed to their development and practice. Yet, indisputably, Couzens had played a role in the company that was decisive—as decisive as Ford's.

It was Couzens, for example, who had been responsible for the five-dollar-a-day wage plan which electrified the world in 1914. More than anything else, this plan gave the Ford Company its first international reputation. Ford himself once wrote (or had written for him):

"Ideas are of themselves extraordinarily valuable, but an idea is just an idea. Almost anyone can think up an idea. The thing that counts is developing it into a practical product."

And that was where Couzens figured in the Ford Company picture.

Norval Hawkins, the Ford sales manager in the halcyon days of the Model T success, once summed up the story quite accurately. "Mr. Couzens was a very remarkable man, as remarkable, in many ways, as Mr. Ford. Mr. Couzens was responsible for at least half of the success of the Ford Motor Company . . . Mr. Ford required just the type of man that Mr. Couzens was to occupy the front seat, and had Couzens been a less indefatigable worker, or a man who paid less attention to the details of that business . . . it might not have been as successful as it is today. . . ." [2]

Barron's, the financial weekly, said of Couzens in 1915:

"For twelve years he was with Henry Ford and it is an open question if the reverse order of the statement might not be fairly accurate. . . . The public thought of him all the time as entitled to equal credit with 'Henry' for the marvelous success of the motor enterprise."

John Wendell Anderson, one of the two Detroit lawyers who were among the original stockholders (and to whom it was worth literally millions of dollars, on the basis of a $5,000 investment, to watch the affairs of the company closely from the very start) said:

"It was due to his [Couzens'] efforts that the company became a success. The team work of himself and Mr. Ford contributed to its success to a much greater extent than either one of them could possibly have done alone." [3]

Many more such statements from those who knew how the company had been created and guided in its formative years could be compiled. But such compilation was not at all necessary in 1915— the very year, incidentally, in which the millionth Model T came off the assembly line at the Highland Park plant, a production and sales record that seemed incredible at the time—for the facts about Couzens' role in the company were widely known in the world of commerce and industry.

Then, suddenly, Couzens was out of the Ford picture.

Everywhere the question was asked: "What will become of the Ford Company?"

Some predicted that the Ford Company would go the way of hundreds of other motorcar manufacturing companies, the names of which only antiquarians in the field would now remember. Recalling what they knew (or thought they knew) of Henry Ford and his commercial views, they shuddered over what they *supposed* would be the future of the company. James Couzens himself, however, knew (or thought he knew) the answer to the fears expressed for the company. Just after October 12, 1915, he said:

"I hope I have assisted in so perfecting the organization of the company that my resignation will not make a pin's worth of difference. Mr. Ford agreed that his own resignation would not make a pin's worth of difference. The momentum of the business is too great . . ."

And this, of course, proved absolutely true. Indeed, as would be demonstrated around 1928, when Henry Ford was still clinging tenaciously to the Model T long after the public had begun to reject it, and again as demonstrated in another crisis period of the 1940's, the company had been built on such a strong foundation that not even Henry Ford himself could wreck it.

"What will Couzens do?" was another question widely asked.

He was then only forty-three. Financially he was worth anywhere from forty million dollars to fifty or even sixty million, depending on the value of his Ford stock and on investments he had made with Ford dividends and his salary. He was energetic and intellectually alert. In this respect, in fact, he was in his prime. But he had come to the end of his road—or so he thought. It seemed clear to others, however, if not to himself at just that moment, that a man who could walk out deliberately, as he had just done, on a business that was acclaimed "The Seventh Wonder of the World," undoubtedly would find another road, perhaps an even more rewarding and satisfying one. His role in the development of the Ford Company, important as it was, actually was but prelude for an even more important role on the stage of the modern industrial era—the motor age—which he had helped to usher into being in America.

BOOK ONE

The Money-Making Machine

CHAPTER I

THE BEGINNING

PROPERLY the story of James Couzens had its real beginning in the fall of 1870, two years before he was born. This was when his father stepped off a train in the windswept little town of Chatham, Ontario Province, Canada.

An immigrant tossed up by economic depression and also propelled by deep-seated inability to get along with his own father, this traveler, then twenty-one, had been en route to the United States from London, England. His goal was a better living than he believed he could achieve at home, for he was convinced that London in 1870 was "finished and had no future." [1]

To be sure, this precise-looking, sober-miened Englishman named James Joseph Couzens was not so dull as to believe with any strong faith that nondescript, tiny Chatham really promised a much better future for him than had London. The fact was that he had not even heard of Chatham in Ontario before arriving there by the slow train he had boarded at Levis, Quebec, where his ship had docked.

But he had rechecked the contents of his purse and concluded that the little funds he had left made it impractical for him to travel the fifty miles farther to Detroit, his original destination. So with British prudence he decided to stay right there at Chatham.

2

This was a mistake. Though not a man to admit error readily, he sometimes conceded this in after years, especially since his decision deprived his children, in particular his first son, of something that might have made a great difference: United States citizenship by birth.

However, he did have a sentimental rationalization to justify the error. He asserted later that he had rather fancied the idea of settling in a town, even an unattractive one, that bore the same name as the great naval-station city of Chatham in England, which was the home of the girl to whom he had become betrothed just before leaving London. But if this was a factor, one can be sure that not often afterward did James Joseph Couzens permit any such romantic notions to shape his conduct. Practicality was stamped all over him.

3

His training was that of an ordinary grocer's apprentice, and he knew his status. Yet in his manners and bearing there was a kind of special promise, a certain aristocratic air, a kind of self-assured dignity almost out of place, even somewhat humorously incongruous, in Chatham at that time, especially for an immigrant, job-seeking grocer's clerk. Years after he had left Chatham, people there still remembered this characteristic that had marked him when he first arrived. They also remembered the fact that, very early, he revealed an ingrained streak of belligerence (something he was destined to pass on to at least one son), the trait that had made his relationship with his father, a bailiff, less than tolerable.

He had a way of speaking that of itself set him off from others. He spoke in an especially polite and trimmed way. His style was not, to be sure, the cultivated one of Mr. Gladstone, the Prime Minister. But neither was it the cockney style of the submerged London masses. It was something in-between. And this was interesting, for he really had had only a little schooling.

He carried himself, too, with uncommon erectness. Clearly, he thought well of himself. Yet when he set about getting a job in Chatham, he made no pretense of seeking more than an ordinary one. He was satisfied to start at something even lower than what he had had in London and soon he was working as a handyman in a grocery owned by one Andrew Crow, a crude, shantylike establishment of the kind one associates with a general store at some crossroads in, say, Kansas, or in a mining camp in the Colorado territory of that same period.

4

Chatham, Ontario, did in fact seem just then like a Western outpost, a settlement in a state of arrested erosion. Years before, it had had a period of growth, even of excitement. It had been intended, by its original settlers, as a shipbuilding center for a Canadian navy because of its location on a river called the Thames. Hence its proud name, after the naval center on the Thames in England. But nothing came of the shipbuilding idea. As stated in a town chronicle, "Several gunboats were built, but it is questionable if they ever left the stocks." [2] In 1870, it was just a seamy settlement, quite as ordinary as its newcomer.

Yet the town had been brushed by history. During the War of 1812, the battle in which Chief Tecumseh had been killed was fought nearby. In this same war, a regiment composed largely of Chathamites helped to capture Detroit. Some years later people quipped that this was not the only time "Chatham captured Detroit." A second capture occurred, they said, when a man born in Chatham and named Couzens became its mayor.

5

In the 1850's, the organized Abolitionists in the United States selected the town as the end of the line for the Underground Railroad that helped slaves to freedom. In consequence, for a period, Chatham's population was comprised more of blacks than of whites. In search of material for *Dred,* her sequel to *Uncle Tom's Cabin,* Harriet Beecher Stowe visited there.

In 1858, John Brown held a meeting in Chatham for the purpose of organizing an armed invasion of the United States. Of course, nothing came of Brown's "Chatham Plan," and after the United States had fought the Civil War, most of the Negroes left town. The former Abolitionists ceased to visit Chatham—and also stopped sending funds to help the colony of black freedmen there. Then the town became as slow-paced and inconsequential as its meandering little Thames. When James Joseph Couzens settled there, it had acquired a nickname: Mudtown.

6

A year later, young Mr. Couzens, now wearing a beard, sent for the girl who had been waiting patiently in England for his summons —and a passage ticket.

Emma Clift, of the other Chatham, was the daughter of Thomas Clift, who had served in the Crimean war as a member of a commissary unit. After that war he had prospered moderately as a confectioner and may have sold some of his sweets to Charles Dickens, then living in Chatham, England. The war service of Emma Clift's father provided what was perhaps the one bit of "color" in the Couzens-Clift family history up to then. Moreover, Florence Nightingale had visited his regiment, led the soldiers in some singing, and asked Tom Clift to stand with her on his trunk while doing so. Emma's father liked to talk of that incident, as did some of his descendants.

Blue-eyed Emma Clift brought with her the "Nightingale trunk," when she made her own trip from Chatham, England, to Chatham, Ontario, to marry James Joseph Couzens.[3]

The couple set up housekeeping in a boxlike little brick "row-house" in "the cheapest and muddiest district" of the town. There, on August 26, 1872, a boy, blue-eyed and full-faced like Emma Clift Couzens, was born to them.

One thing only seemed remarkable about the birth of the couple's first child. James Joseph Couzens, Junior (as the boy was christened in the St. Andrews Presbyterian Church), was born with a caul, a fact, according to the old folk legend, that foretold special good fortune in life.

7

Young James grew up fully conscious of the supposed meaning of his caul. It was often a topic of conversation in the family and among the neighbors. His mother saved the caul, keeping it in a little silk sack that she made for it, and parted with it only when he married, presenting it to his bride, who also saved it.[4] After he had reached maturity, he scoffed at the superstition—"That nonsense!"—concerning his caul. Yet almost from the beginning of his life, his outlook toward the world, and his estimate of himself and his destiny, may well have been influenced by the story.

It is certain that for a boy who grew up in the forlorn neighborhood of Elizabeth and Grand in Chatham, he carried himself as if aware that a special destiny of fortune was his. Perhaps this was something acquired in part from his father. But, if so, it was more than just emulation. His pronounced assurance, apparent quite early, that he was an especially favored child of fortune plainly was one dominant factor that helped to make his later life so extra-ordinary, even startlingly so, in view of how and where it had begun. But that was all in the future.

That hot summer of 1872, when he was born, nobody in Chatham would have wagered twopence that the new baby out on muddy Grand Avenue would leave any special mark any place.

CHAPTER II

THE CANADIAN BOY

WHEN the boy was four or five, his father became a laborer in the soap factory of Lamont and Coate. He left the grocery trade because in Canada it lacked dignity, he later said. However, his real reason for the switch was the opportunity to earn a higher wage, which in that era meant one dollar a day.

Yet the family managed—even with self-respect. Nothing was wasted, ever. That this should be so was like a religion with James Joseph and Emma Couzens.[1] So their style of living was pinchedly narrow, but the boy developed into a sturdy, alert, good-looking youngster.

Very early, James Joseph, Junior, showed some positive characteristics. About the time he was learning to talk, his mother one day heard him making a great commotion in the backyard. Investigating, she learned that all the noise was his way of registering protest against a gust of wind that had blown down his alphabet blocks.[2]

2

A few years more and he made a decision about his name. He would not be known any longer as James Joseph Couzens, Junior. He insisted on being known simply as James Couzens.

It was not in him then, or ever, to be a junior to anyone. In his personal creed, indeed, this was to be a primary tenet—something to be remembered for future reference. To be sure, this decision about his name was a reflection of his attitude toward his father, an early declaration of independence from him.

For such a declaration, the elder Couzens gave him sufficient reasons. The townfolk considered his father a man who was amiable and cheerful enough, although highly dogmatic on religious matters pertaining to his Scotch Presbyterian affiliation. He was also known as the "soul of deference" toward his wife, perhaps because she "bowed to him in everything." Yet toward his first son, the father was strangely tyrannical and given to curious displays of the most violent temper, slapping and whipping the boy frequently. His son recalled later, "I have been panned ever since I was two years old." It was his father's conduct toward him that he had in mind.[3]

3

For such conduct on his father's part, there seldom was any realistic reason. For by no standard was the boy a delinquent. On the contrary, he was respectful to a fault and almost always obeyed to the letter any instructions given to him by either parent, even though he once said that all his life he felt an "unjustifiable resistance to people making me do things." [4] He thought he kept this "resistance" concealed, but apparently not so well concealed that his father did not suspect and resent this streak in him.

He was also tidier than most boys. He did willingly and well all the household chores assigned to him. Even his father took pride in "the punctiliousness" with which he performed the task of keeping the wood boxes clean. "He would pick out every piece of wood, each shaving, every bit of bark—that's the way he did everything," his father once said.[5]

4

Yet there is the record—the angry beatings, slappings, and endless emotional scolding from the dignified man whom the townfolk considered so amiable and polite.

It is clear that there was involved here an unusually strong case of tension between father and son. No doubt the elder Couzens never understood the cause of his flare-ups (significantly confined to his firstborn son). Nor was he able to restrain them. No doubt, too, just as lacking in understanding about the anxiety produced in him by his father, the boy often provoked the outbursts of "tyranny" without realizing that he had done so. But whatever the cause, the disturbance was certainly there, with all its consequent conflict. Inevitably it was to produce a defensive as well as aggressive youth, one destined to be in an almost constant state of resistance to most forms of authority, real or fancied. This side of his nature once came clearly into the open at school when, on very slight provocation, he yanked at the beard of the principal, getting himself suspended for the offense. He himself later said that he "guessed" he did that because the principal's beard represented "authority" to him.[6]

Yet, significantly, during his youth, he never rebelled openly against his father. Rather, he accepted, even courted, a great deal more punishment from his father than was necessary. As a sister, Alice, once recalled: "On many occasions, I tried to protect him from punishment by denying that he had committed little misdemeanors, such as running across the garden. But he would always contradict me, and would have nothing but the truth—and take his punishment." [7]

To Alice, these incidents denoted a penchant for telling the truth, even if the truth hurt. This was true, for he certainly had a penchant for truth-telling that hurt. But his sister's comments also reflected an aspect of his character that was more significant than his insistence on telling the truth. This was a tendency to court conflict and also, it seems, punishment, as if these were necessary to his existence. As would be said of him later, "He seemed always to need to wear the hair-shirt." [8] If so, the reasons for this must remain obscure. He himself often pondered his nature, but could not explain it. Probably much of the answer would be found in his attitudes toward his mother, as well as toward his father. But, except that he loved her, little is known for certain of his feelings toward the mild-mannered mother "who bowed in everything" to his father. He talked freely about other members of his family. But he reminisced very seldom of the blue-eyed Emma Couzens, his mother.

CHAPTER III

THE MONEY-MAKING MACHINE, I

BY THE time young James was seven or eight, his father's job at the Lamont and Coate soap establishment had become twofold. He manufactured the soap by the primitive, grimy process of steam-mixing wood ashes with discarded animal fats and he also acted as salesman. Once in a while, young James went along with his father on the selling expeditions. Chathamites remembered the sight. The erect, clean-faced, good-looking little boy sat pridefully, they thought, beside his bearded, incongruously dignified father on a one-horse wagon, taking in with intent eyes his first impressions of the world beyond the shabby area of Elizabeth and Grand streets.

On these trips, the boy naturally learned something about the customs and ethics of commerce. One custom called for housewives to save the wood ashes from their own stoves and fireplaces in order to trade them for free bars of soap if other bars were purchased. Some women tried thriftily to get more free bars than were coming to them. Young James Couzens listened with sharp and alert interest to the bargaining that resulted—his first bit of education on how to become a businessman; and he noted especially his father's satisfaction in not permitting a customer to get the better of him.

He learned also that people could be gullible. For example, some of his father's customers insisted upon buying the soap according to brand names on the wrappers, preferring his "Electric" soap to his "Gladstone" soap, or vice versa. They were sure the one was much better than the other. But James knew that both brands came out of the same odoriferous batch.

2

When the boy was nine, a great event happened to his father. The elder Couzens became a soapmaker on his own, establishing the "Chatham Steam Soap Works, James J. Couzens, Prop.," helped in this by an inheritance of about fifteen hundred dollars that unexpectedly fell to his wife on the death of her father.

Young James was well aware of the marked elation his father showed on becoming his own man, an independent entrepreneur, no less, in the great world of commerce and industry, a world in which the little "Chatham Steam Soap Works" was a substantial unit —at least in the eyes of its "prop."

Bearded James Joseph Couzens, Senior, the new independent man, began to walk with greater dignity than before. But so also did young James Couzens, *sans* the "Joseph" and *sans* also the "Junior," with ideas percolating in his well-shaped head, it may be assumed, of one day also becoming an independent man and heading some enterprise bigger and better even than his father's "Chatham Steam Soap Works."

This sudden economic rise in the world for the Couzenses of Chatham was accompanied by an appropriate growth in the size of the family. Two girls, Alice and Rosetta, were born. Later came two more boys, first Albert, then Homer. The fact of their existence naturally had an influence upon James, for a big-brother role now fell to him. Looked up to by four awed youngsters, he was now of lordlike stature in the family circle, his only rival for eminence being his father. Boyhood friends recalled, "He carried himself like a young lord." [1]

3

When this "young lord" was going on thirteen, the elder Couzens became a dealer in coal and ice, along with soap. He also began to manufacture cement paving blocks—some of which were still in use in Chatham seventy years later. Indeed, James' father had in fact become a real entrepreneur in Chatham, a status confirmed by his election as an elder of St. Andrew's Presbyterian Church.

Quite early, James concluded that making money was synonymous with growing into manhood, an idea that his parents and the general cultural climate in Canada, as in the United States, encouraged. Before he was nine, he was earning money on his own—ten cents a week for pumping the organ at St. Andrew's. When he wanted a saddle for the horse that pulled the soap wagon, his father told him to earn it. He should go out and sell soap, his father declared. This he did.[2] When gas street-lamps were at last installed in the neighbor-

hood, James scurried to get the job of lamp-tender. He obtained
the plum and was paid one dollar a month from the town treasury
for turning on four lamps each night and for keeping them clean.[3]
Of him, a town chronicler wrote: "In school, if a football or baseball
were wanted, he organized the drive, persuaded the youngsters to
chip in their dimes, nickels, and cents, and he made the ultimate
thrifty dicker with the storekeeper." [4]

4

His young mind obviously was much occupied with the power
that went with money. To impress his sisters and brothers, he did
an interesting and prophetic thing one day with his mother's "Nightingale trunk." Secretly he placed some coins inside it, then called
the youngsters together, waved his hand, and cried, "Presto!"—
revealing the coins. The trunk, he announced grandiosely to the
astonished audience, had been converted by him into a "Money-
making Machine." Its secret was known only to him.[5]

5

He had, said his mother, "big dreams."
Once he scolded her quite earnestly because he had been born
in Canada: "I can never be King of England, but if I had been born
in the United States, I could be President." [6]
From another boy such a remark might have been set down as idle
chatter. But his mother knew that he was serious.
She was often puzzled as to the source of such thoughts, and she
would become hurt when such things occurred as a neighbor complaining that James "deliberately snubbed" her daughter. The girl
had called hello to him from across the street, and he had ignored
her. But he had an explanation. "If a girl wishes to speak to me, she
should come across the street and do it properly." [7]
One of his schoolmates recalled most vividly his conduct on the
day that the pupils of his school, Central, were invited to attend an
entertainment program at the McKeough School. "In came the
Central pupils with Jim Couzens in the lead, and he proceeded to
jump from one desk to another. His idea was to get for himself the
choice of seats—and he took *the most direct way*." [8]
This, too, was prophecy.

6

For a time, he worked in his father's soap factory. But the smell and mess of the place offended him. Then too, working there meant working for his *father*, which he detested. Already he wanted to be on his own—especially in relation to James Couzens, Senior.

One day, during the summer after he had completed primary school, when he was only twelve, he saw a want ad for a book-keeper, placed in the local newspaper, the *Chatham Planet*, by a flour mill. A job like that would get him out of the soap works. So he applied for it, although, as he later admitted, he knew nothing about keeping books. Incredibly, he was given the position.

His father was not at all happy over this development. There was an emotional scene. But his father could give him no "good reason" why he should stay at the soap works if he could land the bookkeeping spot. So he took the job at the flour mill. He tackled it as though he really were qualified, and soon announced that bookkeeping was to be his career. Moreover, he said, he had no intention of going on to high school. He didn't need that—a waste of time, he said.[9]

But, as might have been expected, he was soon to sustain some severe blows to his ego. One came when he lost the bookkeeping job when his employers finally concluded that he was too young. Then, after he decided to enter high school after all, he failed to pass the entrance examination. His father was irate and heatedly ordered him to get back to the soap works. The "punishment" proved a spur for him to "bone up" for another try at the entrance examination. This time he passed.

At high school he was more studious and tensely so than he had ever been before. He spent less time than his fellows in idling with other boys in Market Square. Instead, he put in more time with his books.[10] He had not liked the taste of failure. It grated on his whole being. He "swore that it would never happen to him again." [11]

In his mind, too, was an anxious need for erasing the stigma he felt was attached to his failure on the bookkeeping job. So, after two years at the high school, he enrolled for a two-year course in bookkeeping at the Canada Business College in Chatham, to be properly prepared for "the next time." To pay his way while at this "college," he worked as a newsbutcher on the Erie and Huron. The railroad "never had a better one," recalled his superior, Bill Turtle. He was, said Turtle, a "hustler." [12]

7

It was inconceivable that such a "hustler," a youth whose anxious need for success gave him no rest, would long remain in the little town of Chatham.

He was bound to feel the lure of some bigger place—London, in Ontario; or Montreal, in Quebec; or even Detroit, only fifty miles away from Chatham. And just as inevitably, in view of his relationship with his father, he was destined to leave home as soon as he could. Only then could he—or his father and mother—have any real peace in the household: this was understood, though never expressed in so many words, by all three of them.

8

In 1889, when James Couzens was seventeen, a friend named Dickson went to Detroit, obtained a job with the Michigan Central Railroad, and wrote back that another job was to be had there. Young Couzens hurriedly packed up, and left at once to get it. But something went wrong. In a short time he found himself, unhappily, back home again.

A few months later—it was then 1890—he set off for Detroit again, and this time he stayed. On August 9, 1890, just as he was turning eighteen, he was hired as a car-checker by the Michigan Central in Detroit.

On the railroad his wage was forty dollars a month for a twelve-hour shift, seven days a week, and yet he was delighted. It was, he recalled, "great stuff" to be checking freight cars, even in weather so cold that the tacks which he carried in his mouth for affixing labels on the cars literally froze to his tongue. After each shift, he went to his room, in a place called the Amos House, feeling that he was "running the railroad." [13] Only when he had that kind of feeling was he ever content.

Most of all, however, he enjoyed the status of being on his own at last.

CHAPTER IV

THE NEW DETROITER

The place called the Amos House was a ramshackle, weather-beaten lodging and boarding place, favored by railroad workers employed at the "Junction Yards." Then, though not later, it was on the outskirts of Detroit. Its main attraction: low-priced meals. For the next three years, young James Couzens lived there, his steel-blue eyes more intently than ever focused on his goal: success.

It was noticeable that he did not mix much with the other Amos House boarders. He stayed out of their bull sessions and only rarely joined in the beer drinking that went on. Nearly everyone else there was called by some nickname. But not Couzens. His deadly serious manner about almost everything discouraged such familiarity.

He did make some friends. But these had to overlook or discount a "don't-tread-on-me" attitude that often became quite explosive. It was accepted, or at least expected, that if one made a remark that young Couzens disliked, or with which he simply disagreed, he would blurt out a stinging comment or retort. This seemed almost an instinct with him.

In appearance alone, he stood out from most of his fellow railroad workers. Even in his work clothes, he had a buttoned-up look. Instead of a car-checker, he could have been taken for an English bank clerk or even a divinity student, especially after he began to wear thin-rimmed spectacles.

From his always impeccable clothes to his neatly clipped, carefully brushed, blond hair, everything about him except his temper proclaimed disciplined orderliness, precision, and restrained tension. And always, in the taut mold of his forceful, open face, there was a warning that here was a man who spoke his mind.

2

By then, he had become a clean-cut youth of exceptional handsome-
ness. He was, indeed, a perfect specimen of the Anglo-Saxon type—
fair, well-built, with finely chiseled features. That girls would be
interested in the young transplanted Canadian, if he gave them half
a chance, could have been assumed. In Chatham, he had had one or
two friendships with girls, but none that were "serious," no doubt
because of his "don't-tread-on-me" attitude. In Detroit, he was in no
greater hurry to make any such alliance. He was not, however, altogether aloof in this matter. He did have a number of casual dates.
Some Saturday nights, he even unloosened the buttoned-up look
enough to attend the public dances at the Detroit Armory. On one
trip back to Chatham to see his family, he boasted to his brother
Homer: "I have so many girls in Detroit that I can take out a different one every night and not get back to the first one for two weeks."
But the brother gathered that this was mainly a boast.[1] Actually, his
major concern was getting on at the Michigan Central, keeping his
eyes open for all possible promotions.

3

He had come to Detroit at the proper time. In 1890, this city of
two hundred thousand was already on the threshold of its destiny.
Men in and near Detroit, at precisely this time, were beginning to
conceive, and even to make, something that was to propel Detroit,
in a span of ten years, to undreamed-of heights of activity and wealth:
the horseless carriage. By 1890, young Ransom E. Olds was working
at Lansing, Michigan, on just such a contraption, to be propelled
by steam. In this same year, on a farm at Dearborn, near Detroit,
another man, Henry Ford, was perfecting a two-cylinder gas engine,
fascinated with the idea of applying mechanical power to farm
chores.[2]

Not yet, to be sure, was the Detroit of the 1890's (more grim than
gay) entitled to its later favorite nickname: "Dynamic City." On the
contrary, in contrast to other cities of similar size, Detroit then
seemed the opposite of dynamic. It was extraordinarily backward in
(of all things) public transportation. After other American communi-
ties had been using electric trolleys for years, Detroit's streetcars were
still horse-drawn.

Car-checker James Couzens had to walk three miles over dusty or muddy unpaved streets from the Michigan Central yards to the near-est car lines. He was indignant about this—a fact to be remembered.

However, many of those factors destined to make Detroit truly dynamic were already present. It was a city of marked manufactur-ing ability. Its location on the river connecting it with the Great Lakes made the shipment of products and raw materials easy and profitable. Its stoves, railroad cars, wheels, seeds, cigars, and other manufactured items were known around the world. The Detroit River was already alive with freighters, barges, and steamers.

4

Hazen S. Pingree, a well-to-do, successful, and ebullient manufac-turer of shoes, was elected mayor of Detroit the very year young Couzens became a Detroiter. Later this fact would be of special and intriguing interest in respect to Couzens. For, although a wealthy industrialist and also a Republican (in the same ranks as William McKinley and Mark Hanna), this pugnacious Mr. Pingree conducted himself in such a manner that he was scorned by his fellow industrial-ists as a "socialist." Indeed, it was in this same year that Pingree, at times battling "special interests" alongside such progressives as Gov-ernor John Peter Altgeld, Illinois' "Eagle Forgotten," launched the stormy Detroit and Michigan political career that would be credited by one Michigan historian with helping to "lay the basis for the lib-eral movement in the Republican party which was carried forward more successfully by some of his successors," [3]—including one succes-sor named Couzens.

Pingree had burst upon the Detroit political scene just then as a "People's Mayor," denouncing tax-dodging corporations and fighting especially for improved public-utility service and lower rates for such service. Critics said he was "utterly lacking in tact and diplomatic gifts." [4] Nevertheless he became one of the *two* outstanding mayors in Detroit history.

Worth recalling is the fact that in 1890 Pingree started a movement for municipal ownership of public transportation, for which action he suffered social ostracism from his clubs and his church. During the panic of '93, Pingree increased the conviction of other businessmen that he was a socialist, or another kind of radical, by his insistence that unemployment relief was a function of government. He arbi-trarily allowed unemployed laborers to take over vacant lots for rais-ing food, mainly potatoes, and "Pingree's Potato Patches" became a national phrase, along with "Coxey's Army"—fighting words in the ideological disputes of that day.

5

The furor stirred up by Pingree's "radical" ideas, and especially the heated denunciation of them by leaders of his own party, made a strong and lasting impression upon young Couzens. What's more, even in the 1890's, though more from temperament than from any studied conclusions, Couzens harbored certain inchoate Pingree-like ideas of his own.

For example, he barked some uncomplimentary remarks to fellow railroaders about the low wages paid to stevedores on the river-front. And he stopped to listen when Single-Tax orators lectured groups of workingmen on Woodward Avenue. Later, he called himself a Single Taxer—"in principle." [5] During a streetcar strike in 1891, a stormy episode linked with Pingree's municipal-ownership program, he sympathized impulsively with a group of strikers he saw tossing bricks at a streetcar. Young Couzens hurled a few bricks himself.

In 1894 there occurred a national railroad strike, the one that resulted from conflict between Eugene V. Debs' "one big union" and the Pullman Sleeping Car Company. This brought the "social conflict," as editorialists then described labor-capital tension, quite close to Couzens of the Michigan Central R.R. Company, in the "Junction Yards."

He was not at all taken in by the overheated propaganda that pictured the Pullman workers and their striking railroad-worker sympathizers under mild-mannered Debs as "anarchists," "communists," or some other brand of revolutionists bent upon destroying America. Nor was he taken in by the same kind of clamor that churned around Altgeld in Illinois for protesting on constitutional grounds President Grover Cleveland's use of federal troops to break the strike—a clamor that soon also churned in Detroit around Mayor Pingree, who supported Governor Altgeld. Young Couzens assessed the outcries of "anarchy" for what they were. Remembering his own slim pay-envelope at the Michigan Central, he made up his mind that the strikers were just railroad men, like himself and his fellows, who merely wanted what he also wanted—somewhat fatter pay envelopes.

His unit of the railroad escaped direct involvement in the Pullman strike. But, in his talks with others at the yards, he did not make it a secret that his sympathies were with Debs' men. He was aware that if his attitude were "reported" it might cost his job, but his feeling was: If he thought so, why shouldn't he say so? Nobody was going to take that right from *him*.[6] This attitude he never changed.

6

Actually, he was neutral on the "union question," so far as he himself was concerned, for he was sure that the state of being a "worker" was only temporary for him. So the union question as such was not really a personal matter with James Couzens. Although at times he growled about the Michigan Central that "this road doesn't appreciate what we workers do," he worked faithfully for the railroad. And he worked superlatively well. "He was always on the job, worked his head off, never did any fooling around," a fellow worker at the railroad recalled.[7]

True, his record at the railroad was marred by a "letter of reprimand" on July 20, 1891. This made him "sore as Hell"—and the roar of angry protest that broke from him that day was considered memorable at the "Junction Yards." The fault, he felt, belonged to a fellow worker for having failed to awaken him, as he had requested, when he was taking a nap toward the end of a long shift. But there was no other black mark against him.[8] "I was," he boasted in after years, "the best God-damned car-checker on the line!" [9]

7

As if to point up the fact that he was a "man," after he became twenty-one in 1893, he went to his superintendent and asked for promotion. The job he wanted was that of boss of the freight office in the yards.

Before long the position was his, although this meant passing over a number of men who had been car-checkers long before he had begun working for the railroad. For the first time, he now had the responsibility of directing the work of other men, including some much older than he. He had no lack of assurance in the way he assumed that responsibility. He was not a popular boss and made no effort to be popular. Already he was a strict disciplinarian. Yet, though he did not win affection, he did win respect. "He never tried to shift responsibility upon others to shield himself; if he made a mistake, he would own up regardless of what the result might be," one of his men recalled.[10]

Nor did he pick on subordinates while kowtowing to superiors. "He was just as assertive with those above him." A superintendent, one Buchanan, once gave him a "calling down." Couzens talked back.

"You're fired!" said Buchanan.

"You can't fire me!" retorted Couzens.

He wasn't fired.[11]

8

At the freight office, for the first time he came into contact with patrons of the railroad, something he had in mind when he asked for the promotion. For he had concluded that it would take too long to realize his ambitions if he stayed in the railroad business. He hoped to get into something with a better and quicker future by meeting the businessmen who used the railroad.

Yet, of all the clerks in the freight office, he was most notorious for treating patrons "rough," especially when it fell to him to advise them about demurrage charges, a new tariff which had just been established by the Michigan Central and which was bitterly resented by most of the patrons. "The way Jim Couzens talked with these patrons on the telephone, giving them holy hell, was just astounding," recalled an associate at the freight house.[12]

With Alex Y. Malcomson, a coal dealer, he had had some of his more heroic rows over demurrage charges. But rather than resenting Couzens' blistering way of laying down the law to him, Malcomson admired it. Malcomson obviously concluded that here was an employee who really looked after an employer's interests. To the amazement of nearly everyone, Malcomson one day offered a job to Couzens.

In October 1895 Couzens went to work for the Malcomson Fuel Company as assistant bookkeeper, private car-checker, and all-around general factotum, for which he was to receive seventy-five dollars a month.[13]

CHAPTER V

THE COAL CLERK

In 1895, Alex Y. Malcomson was a restless, energetic Scot with a lean, though well-built, body and a long nose framed by mutton-chop whiskers that gave him the look of a successful merchant going full-steam ahead. And this was true—fortunately true, in a material sense, for the new office factotum, James Couzens.

Because of what the future then had in store, Malcomson was a figure who deserves to be remembered in the history of Detroit, for his own major role as well as for his influence upon the careers of some important and better-known Detroiters. Yet, curiously, so industrious a gatherer of facts as John Gunther, in 1947, wrote in his book *Inside U.S.A.:* "I would like very much to know what happened to a man named Alex Y. Malcomson. . . . It seems that he was a coal dealer, and Couzens was a clerk in his office. . . . I was unable to find anybody in Detroit who knew . . . about Mr. Malcomson." [1] In 1895, however, and for at least two decades afterwards, few Detroit businessmen were much better known in the city's commercial circles. [2]

2

Malcomson in the 1890's typified in many respects the enterprising American businessman more accurately than the Goulds, Wanamakers, or Vanderbilts. Lacking their capital, he, too, as one of his sons recalled, was "the plunger type, a man who did not hesitate to take chances." And he was constantly looking for chances to take. [3] Starting with a small grocery in Detroit, he switched to coal, soon bought out several competitors, merged them into his business, and laid plans to make his mark in higher reaches of Detroit business.

About two years before Couzens went to work for him, Malcomson, during a coal strike, had staged a business *coup* that was the talk of the trade. Most other dealers had no coal to sell and he had very little. But he learned that the Detroit gas company had a surplus and arranged to distribute the gas company's coal to consumers, on commission, at somewhat inflated prices. "He made a handsome profit," admiringly reported the *Detroit Free Press* a little later in a "puff piece" on Malcomson.[4]

3

Between Couzens and Malcomson there developed something more than an ordinary relationship. They were in emotional ways like father and son. At times, this was uncomfortable for Couzens, as well as for Malcomson, since it turned out that Malcomson had certain character traits that were strikingly similar to those of Couzens' own father. "He had a fiery temper and would blow up fiercely when anyone did something he considered wrong or stupid." [5] So one of Malcomson's sons recalled.

Couzens was often on the receiving end of Malcomson's outbursts. Once Malcomson called him a liar. Red-necked, then red-faced, Couzens flung his office keys at Malcomson and announced that he had "quit." Not until Malcomson had humbled himself by sending him a note asking him to return, did Couzens go back.[6]

There were other such incidents, enough to justify the comment, "How Malcomson and Couzens managed to remain affiliated is one of the mysteries of destiny." [7]

But they did remain together at the coal company for nearly eight years.

It could not have escaped Malcomson, who seemed himself to receive more gratification from the "game" of business than from the monetary rewards, that in trim, bespectacled James Couzens he had an employe who really did not work for pay, but from the love of work. He had what to any employer would have been a "find," what some would call a "jewel," a man to be kept at almost any cost.

True, young James Couzens, his eyes still firmly set on his old goal, one measured by monetary rewards, wanted what compensation was coming to him. It is also true that he intended to ask for and to get much more than he was then making. But it was clear that this transplanted Canadian, so fully trained in the philosophy of work by his Chatham parents, did his work because work was then his basic philosophy. And Malcomson, of course, liked that.

CHAPTER VI

THE FAMILY MAN

EVEN before leaving the Michigan Central, Couzens had found the girl he had been looking for. She was Margaret Manning, a widow's daughter, from a family fairly well known in Detroit. Her uncle was Aaron A. Parker, a banker and head of the White Star shipping line, which operated ships on the Great Lakes from Detroit. A nephew of hers, John C. Manning, later became one of the city's best-known newspapermen, the editor of the *Detroit Times.*

A good-looking young woman, possessed of a lively nature, Margaret Manning also had a practical outlook on life that suggested strength of character. Thus, this blue-eyed Margaret was good company, without being giddy—the only kind of girl in whom young Couzens, so serious for all his handsome appearance, could possibly have become interested. Probably more than he realized, she reminded him of his own mother, both physically and because of her serene manner—a factor that undoubtedly drew him strongly to her.

They had met through another girl, Margaret's cousin, whom he had been squiring casually on his days off. But soon after meeting Margaret, he stopped seeing her cousin. His bicycle, a prized new possession, began to be parked in front of the Manning residence with noticeable regularity.[1]

2

Not long afterward, he took a room in Margaret's home, for her mother had adopted the custom followed then by many families of renting extra rooms in their oversized houses to "suitable persons." Young Mr. Couzens certainly was recommended by Margaret as "suitable."

He began taking Margaret bicycling on Belle Isle—the way many romances started in the Detroit of that day. Sometimes wearing a derby, sometimes a cap, he talked to her earnestly of his hopes for rising in the world. He found Margaret a good, as well as a willing, listener. A few more months and it was understood that Mrs. Manning's lodger was Margaret's "young man." Finally, one afternoon in the winter of 1897, on the last visit of the season to Belle Isle, he proposed to her. As he expected, Margaret said yes.[2]

3

There was one problem: the Mannings were devout Roman Catholics. Actually, so far as Couzens was concerned, this was only an opportunity that he welcomed to deliver to his father another and quite final declaration of independence. For, although his mother accepted the religious situation calmly, his father, the Presbyterian elder in Chatham, was horrified by the idea that his son intended to marry a "Papist." He said he would never permit it. But Couzens firmly and coldly replied that he intended to go ahead with the marriage.

As for Margaret and her family, they, too, had a similar religious problem. For Couzens, although not a churchgoer (too much of that in Chatham, under the lash of his father, had cured him, he once said), had no intention of embracing Catholicism.

Bishop John F. Foley of the Catholic diocese of Detroit was a friend of the Manning family. He was consulted and suggested that Margaret's "Presbyterian young man" call on him. "The Bishop took a liking to him, and gave his approval to the marriage," [3] with Couzens agreeing, of course, that any children of the marriage were to be brought up in the faith of the Roman Catholic Church.

On August 31, 1898, when Couzens had just turned twenty-six, Bishop Foley celebrated the marriage sacrament at the Manning home.

They took the conventional trip to Niagara Falls for their honeymoon, after which they made their home with Margaret's mother. Couzens did not like staying on at the Manning home. But his income, still seventy-five dollars a month, made it the prudent thing to do. However, in agreeing to stay, he made a family rule: Margaret, for her part, had to agree that they would live within *his* income, no matter what it was. She was not to receive any money from her family. "He simply would not stand for it." [4]

4

A few months before his marriage he had gone to the federal building in downtown Detroit to attend to another matter of personal importance. This was to give up his status as a subject of Great Britain, by renouncing his allegiance to Queen Victoria, to become a naturalized citizen of the United States. He had intended to do this for some time, for he clearly never considered going back to Canada to live.

5

The War with Spain was then on. Though a puny affair, it nonetheless was a shot in the arm for business generally. The new prosperity directly affected Couzens, for in one of his periodic spurts of optimism, this time produced by the war activity, Malcomson had acquired a coal business in Toledo, the Crescent Fuel Company. Deciding that Couzens should be his manager in Toledo, he sent him there and raised his pay to one hundred dollars a month. For Couzens, this change held the promise of prosperity and even of some independence. But the bright prospect soon was overshadowed. Margaret became ill shortly after they had established themselves in Toledo, and Couzens was forced to ask Malcomson to let him resume the old job in Detroit so Margaret could be near her mother. Again they went to live with Mrs. Manning.

Then came a sadder occurrence. As part of their preparation for a child, they had arranged for a home of their own, renting, at twenty-one dollars a month, a "terrace" on West Grand Boulevard, just off Fourteenth Avenue. The child, a son, was born in the spring of 1899, but it died almost at once.

In the following year, Margaret gave birth to a second child, another boy, who turned out to be an extraordinarily healthy, bright youngster. They called him Homer. Then began for Couzens "the happiest period" of his life, as he himself described it. He became, in fact, almost a different man—at home. Whereas, to the outside world, he still displayed, like a trade-mark, his don't-tread-on-me manner, at home he relaxed almost completely, romped with the boy, and enjoyed being called "Daddy Jim." [5]

Margaret Couzens proved a perfect companion for him. He seemed, literally, to worship her.[6] With her he was the soul of affability and deference, just as his father had been to his mother. With nearly everyone else he still, constantly, asserted his spirit of belligerent independence. "He had a direct, blunt way of speaking to fellow employees and to customers. He expected to be obeyed without any question," said a stenographer at the Malcomson Fuel Company.[7] He was not much different in that job than he had been at the Michigan Central before his marriage, when "no one could tell him what to do." But he actually encouraged Mrs. Couzens to boss him, something that would have amazed his old railroad co-workers. He appeared to derive a kind of serenity from being bossed by Margaret. She even communicated to him, when she was with him, some of her own serenity. He was, recalled an intimate, "The perfect family man." [8]

6

In 1902 another son, Frank, was born. By then, he was much more than just a clerk at Malcomson's. Though without the title, he was really the manager, as everyone understood. Despite all his single-minded devotion to work, however, his income was then only eighteen hundred dollars a year. This was neither enough for his family's needs nor for his ego. The turn of the century seemed a time of prosperity for the nation generally, but little of it had drifted his way. Detroit was growing. Skyscrapers were going up. A new, although still quite infant industry, automobile manufacturing, had developed. Yet he seemed to be standing still. He considered taking up law and began reading law books at night. A lawyer's career appealed to him as one way of increasing his earning capacity, and also of meeting his greatest need—to be on his own.[9]

CHAPTER VII

THE FORD MOTOR COMPANY

SIMILARLY driven by ambition, Malcomson also was restless. He had lately invested some money in an icebox scheme, only to suffer a failure that cost him several thousand dollars. Couzens lost in the venture too, having put in $100.

In 1902 Malcomson eyed a new business, in connection with which he was seeing much of the spare, angular man named Henry Ford.

Malcomson had known Ford from the days when Ford had been employed as an engineer by the Detroit electric light company and had bought coal for the light company from Malcomson. After resigning that job in 1899, Ford continued to buy coal from Malcomson for his home.

By 1902 Ford had already been in and out of two automobile ventures. His first was the Detroit Automobile Company, formed by a group of Detroit businessmen to produce automobiles from a model that Ford had developed. Later Ford referred to his backers in this company as "a group of men of speculative turn of mind," whose "main idea seemed to be to get the money." [1] They had an agreement with him to build at least ten automobiles on a budget of $10,000, yet this sum "didn't pay for one." [2]

The main trouble apparently was that Ford was "a perfectionist." He could not bring himself to the point of letting the company go into production, for he kept wanting to make changes.[3] An illustration of this trait of Ford's occurred when Henry B. Joy, who later formed the Packard Motor Company, wanted to buy a car and was discouraged from doing so by Ford himself, who said his car was not yet good enough. Little wonder that the "men of speculative turn of mind" became impatient. They gave Ford, as it was put, "an opportunity to resign." [4] As some of these men went on to form the

company which became the Cadillac Motor Company, the first
Cadillac was, in a sense, really a Ford.[5]

In November 1901 the Henry Ford Company was incorporated,
organized around still another car designed by Ford and including
some of the men who had been in the Detroit Automobile Company. A company which most histories of Ford ignore, the Henry
Ford Company apparently turned out only one or two racing machines; then, as stated in a newspaper article, it died of inanition.[6]

So in 1902 Ford was at loose ends, but still hopeful. He had won
some fame as an automobile racer. But many called him a "nut,"
while some persons derided him as "Crazy Ford." [7]

Malcomson had about the same esteem for Ford the man as other
businessmen in Detroit at this time—that is to say, he did not esteem
him highly. The general attitude can be illustrated by an incident
which occurred when Ford was working on his first car. He had
to buy parts from Strelinger's hardware store, where his credit was
strictly limited to fifteen dollars. He wanted to make a larger purchase. "Fifteen is the limit," the storekeeper said.[8]

But Malcomson had made some careful inquiries about the kind
of automobile Ford had designed, a runabout with an opposed-type
two-cylinder motor in the rear. What he learned impressed him.
He began thinking about financing Ford's car. Ford was more than
willing. After many cautious talks, Malcomson decided in August
1902 to give Ford a third whirl at the automobile "game." But it
was Malcomson's idea to "promote" Ford's car by himself—no other
financial backers were to be in the scheme—and this appealed to
Ford.

Ford had calculated that it would take $3,000 for him to complete
a new model. Malcomson agreed to put up this amount, and also to
arrange for any further financing that might be necessary. Malcomson was to have a half interest in the car, and he and Ford "were to
share the emoluments and the profits of their joint venture equally."
There was to be no "Ford Motor Company"—only a Malcomson-
Ford partnership.[9]

That was the way the agreement was drawn up on the hot Saturday
afternoon of August 16, 1902, in the law offices of John Wendell
Anderson and Horace Rackham, two young members of the Detroit
Bar whose main client was Malcomson's coal company, for which
they handled, principally, the "bad accounts." [10]

2

And what about Malcomson's chief clerk? Couzens did not share his employer's enthusiasm for automobiles. Several times he had noticed Ford, then wearing a mustache, in the Malcomson office, and he knew that Ford was a customer. But he paid very little attention to him, not finding him then a man worth much attention. Back about 1892, when Couzens was still living at the Amos House, his path had crossed Ford's, for Couzens used to visit the gym of the Railroad Y.M.C.A. and, for a time, Ford taught a class in mechanics there to earn some extra money.[11] It is certain that Couzens would have paid no attention to Ford's class at the "Y," for he had not the slightest mechanical bent. "Malcomson used to take me out in his car sometimes and frequently he turned something on the dash board, explaining to me that he was changing the mixture," he once said. "I thought that he meant he was mixing water with the gasoline, and I continued to think so for a long time."[12]

But Couzens was greatly interested in Malcomson's new plans. They were bound to affect him, for he understood that Malcomson was prepared to pledge all his credit to get this automobile venture going. And if the automobile business failed, the coal business would go under too. But if the automobile venture succeeded, Couzens might find himself running the coal company, for Malcomson had already hinted that he planned to devote nearly all his time to the exciting new business. He had told Couzens that he would give him more responsibility at the coal office, a raise in pay, and a bonus of $1,000, if the coal office did a business of a certain amount in the next twelve months.[13]

3

There was another factor that brought Couzens directly into the picture. Malcomson wanted his dealings with Ford kept secret. He was afraid his credit with the banks would be injured if it were publicly known that he was backing anything "so risky" as an automobile venture.[14]

So Malcomson's money for the Ford project was placed in a bank in Couzens' name.

Malcomson also assigned to Couzens the duty of "checking up" on Ford's expenditures. "As Ford's bills piled up and finally went over the $3,000 limit, I warned Malcomson many a time,"[15] he said.

Before long, Couzens was so much a part of the project that Malcomson brought him into most of the negotiations for getting cars produced.

He was no passive onlooker. This came out explosively at a meeting with John and Horace Dodge. These brothers, later to be famous as motorcar makers in their own right, owned a machine shop and were brought in to make the chassis for the Ford cars, as they already were doing for Ransom E. Olds.[16] At a session with Malcomson, Ford, and Couzens, John Dodge asked for certain provisions in the contemplated contract.

"I won't stand for that!" Couzens declared.

Not many persons had ever dared to talk that bluntly to muscular, brusque John Dodge.

"Who in hell are you?" demanded Dodge.

"That's all right," Malcomson said, "Couzens is my adviser in this." [17]

4

When finally signed, the contract called for the Dodge brothers to produce, within a year, 650 chassis at $250 each—a commitment, in this one instance, of $162,500. Other parts, such as bodies, wheels, and tires, plus costs for promotion, brought the total of Malcomson's obligations to about $350,000.[18]

No such sum was in Malcomson's possession. He even lacked, in ready cash, the $10,000 which he had agreed to pay the Dodges, on account, once they started actual production.

Malcomson counted on "a perfect craze" for automobiles on the part of the public to carry him through safely.[19] He expected to sell the completed cars as soon as they were assembled, and then pay off his suppliers out of sales. He determined—a crucial decision—that a factory would not be needed, only a place for assembling the various parts, work for which even a barn would do. Everything would be made outside the assembly plant. *Thus no investment in machinery would be required.* By selling the cars for $850 (the price of the Cadillac) he figured on a profit of at least $95,000 on the first lot.[20]

On paper Malcomson's optimism seemed wholly justified. Soon, however, trouble developed. Couzens advised him that "Ford's bills" totaled $7,000, or $4,000 above the agreed limit. Then the Dodge brothers began demanding the $10,000 payment. Malcomson succeeded in stalling them for a time. But as the Dodge brothers grew more insistent, Malcomson decided to trim his sails somewhat. In November 1902 he moved to enlist some outside financial support after all. His plan was to sell some shares in his half of the partnership. He had new articles of partnership drawn up; these provided for a company to be called "The Malcomson-Ford Company, Ltd." [21]

"But everybody shied off from his stock," so Couzens said later,[22] and the original precarious arrangement had to stand—at least for a while.

5

In February 1903 Malcomson persuaded the Dodges to wait for their $10,000 until they had delivered some chassis. He boldly inserted large advertisements in trade papers concerning what he called "The Fordmobile," advertisements signed "The Fordmobile Company, Ltd." There was no such car and no such company. Both were merely reflections of Malcomson's desperate hope that this advertising would bring some advance orders for the car—and perhaps some cash in advance.[23]

He did get orders—but no cash.

As the date neared for the Dodge brothers to deliver the first chassis, Malcomson lost some of his nerve. He talked with the owners of the Daisy Air Rifle Company about having them take over his commitments, with the view of making the Ford car in their air-rifle plant at Plymouth, Michigan. He offered to give them half his interest.

There was some earnest talk of the car being called "The Daisy." But Ford objected and told Malcomson his car had to be called a "Ford." The plan fell through anyway, when the Daisy people decided against taking the chance. The whole business of making automobiles seemed too risky. Besides, one of the air-rifle company principals was interested in putting money in some land in one of the Southern states. Mississippi land seemed to him a much better bet than the Ford-Malcomson automobile deal.[24]

Then the Dodges issued an ultimatum. If Malcomson could not live up to his contract with them, they would produce and market the car themselves.[25]

Facing this threat, Malcomson decided he had to abandon the partnership idea entirely. He would have to make a clean breast of things to his bankers and organize a stock company after all. He called on John S. Gray, president of the German-American Bank of Detroit, who was related to him and whose bank did most of Malcomson's coal-business financing. Malcomson wanted two things from banker Gray. He wanted money—enough to pay the Dodge brothers —and he wanted Gray himself to join the company, for he believed that Gray's name would serve to attract other investors.

6

John Gray was aghast. Only a short time before, Malcomson had obtained considerable credit from Gray's bank for another merger, consolidation of the Malcomson Fuel Company with Jewett, Bigelow and Brooks.[26] Gray now suspected that he had cause to be worried about that loan.

"I want you to go out to the Dodge place this afternoon and see what is being done," Malcomson urged.

Gray went, but when Malcomson urged him to join in the venture, the banker refused.[27] "Invest in a horseless carriage?" he snorted. "Asinine folly!" Now it was Malcomson who seemed "crazy."

"Put up some money and I'll guarantee it to you any time within a year," Malcomson said.

"You mean if I am dissatisfied, at any time, I can call on you for the money?" Gray asked.

"Yes," said Malcomson.[28]

Under this arrangement, what did Gray have to lose? He agreed to put up $10,000 personally, but he still had profound misgivings despite Malcomson's "guarantee," never dreaming that what would later be known as "the fabulous Gray estate" was being founded by him that day.

7

On the strength of Gray's interest, Albert Strelow, who ran a carpenter shop, was persuaded by Malcomson to put up $5,000, and also to provide the shack in which the automobiles were to be assembled. Vernon Fry, a dry-goods merchant whom Malcomson knew as a fellow church member, was taken for a ride in Ford's runabout in an effort to interest him. He "was scared to death," but finally told Malcomson to put him down for $5,000 too. Charles T. Bennett of the Daisy Air Rifle Company then agreed to invest $5,000 as a personal matter, and the two lawyers, Anderson and Rackham, agreed to pledge $5,000 each.

To get his $5,000, young Anderson, who had studied at Cornell and graduated from the University of Michigan Law School—a spare, well-dressed barrister who parted his hair stylishly in the middle—wrote a glowing letter to his father, a physician in LaCrosse, Wisconsin. Dr. Wendell Anderson was "somewhat skeptical." But having a strong affection for his lawyer-son, he could not bear to turn down the touch.[29] Rackham, who always looked like something of a farmer, raised his $5,000 by selling a piece of Detroit land he had acquired. "What finally decided me," Rackham recalled, "was a bundle of letters, most of them bona fide orders for cars, which Malcomson and Couzens showed me." [30] C. J. Woodall, a junior clerk at Malcomson's, put up $1,000. And the Dodges finally said that, in lieu of the $10,000 owed them, they would take $10,000 worth of shares.[31]

8

And Couzens? In his and Margaret's bank account, he had just $400.

He told John Anderson that he intended to "beg, borrow, or steal" all the money he could, to be well represented in the venture.[32] But from whom?

His wife's mother had a nest egg of $15,000. He talked with her about a loan of a size that would have made him one of the biggest investors of all. There was a family meeting on the question. Mrs. Manning hesitated, for she recalled "Jim's icebox failure," the venture with Malcomson.

In the end, however, she agreed to a loan of some figure, but suddenly, at that moment, he decided that he could not bring himself to borrow from his mother-in-law after all. He simply could not be beholden to her in that way.[33]

9

There was his father in Chatham, but to borrow from him struck Couzens as being almost as distasteful. Yet he swallowed his pride and made the trip across the river to Chatham. He knew that, like his mother-in-law, his father had a nest egg, though not as much as $15,000. The elder Couzens had come a fairly long way from the time when he was a dollar-a-day laborer at a soap works. But he quickly and tartly demonstrated that he had no intention of parting with any of his funds, not even on a loan, for any such foolish enterprise as his son described to him.

"You should not even invest your own money!" the elder Couzens exclaimed.[34]

Rosetta Couzens had $300, saved from her earnings as a public-school teacher in Chatham. She was willing to lend that to her brother. But again, the father raised heated objections. Finally, Rosetta compromised and offered $150. "But he wanted it in even hundreds, so I gave him $100." [35]

Couzens returned to Detroit with the disappointing conviction that all he could invest was $500—his $400 and his sister's $100. Luckily, he found Malcomson in one of his expansive moods. Malcomson agreed to advance him $500 on his expected bonus, and also arranged for acceptance of a promissory note of $1,500. Thus, among the twelve shareholders—Alex Y. Malcomson and eleven disciples, so to speak—Couzens finally was recorded as a holder of $2,500 worth of stock.[36] In Couzens' view, there actually should have been thirteen shareholders, counting his sister Rosetta. But Ford objected strenuously to a woman being allowed in the enterprise— any woman—so Couzens carried Rosetta's one share in his own name.[37]

It irked Couzens that, except for the junior clerk, Woodall, he was low man on the shareholders' list, and it is probable that he suspected Woodall's interest was really a "blind" for Malcomson— a way for Malcomson to have a bigger interest than Ford. But there was no way for Couzens to improve his position at the time, and so he made the best of it, while making a mental note to correct this matter some time in the future.

10

On June 16, 1903, the Ford Motor Company was incorporated. Two days later, the twelve stockholders held an organizational meeting at the Russel House, a Detroit hotel.

Malcomson had expected to be chosen president. But that office went to banker Gray—an irony, in view of Ford's later attitude toward bankers—and Malcomson was named treasurer.

Ford was not even considered for president. Everyone concerned, even Ford, agreed that to have Ford as president would probably have been fatal to the financial rating of the new company. Instead, he was given the title of vice-president and general manager in charge of mechanics and production.[38]

The posts of business manager, in active charge of all business affairs of the new company, as well as of secretary, went to Couzens.[39] This was another disappointment for Malcomson, who had intended to be the business manager himself. His plan was to have Couzens run the coal office, but John S. Gray, still worrying about his bank's loans to the Malcomson Fuel Company, decided matters otherwise. "I am putting up my money because you are a good coal man," Gray told Malcomson. "You must stay in the coal business."

Malcomson argued that the coal business would be safe with Couzens in charge. He praised Couzens' extraordinary ability. "If Couzens is so good," said Gray, "then you can send him to the automobile business. He can watch that for you." [40]

Malcomson had no answer to this, and the decision that was finally made was in line with John Anderson's report on June 4, 1903, to his father in LaCrosse:

"Mr. Couzens . . . is going to leave the coal business, for the present at least, and devote his entire time to the office and management of the automobile business. And he is a crackerjack." [41]

CHAPTER VIII

THE BUSINESS MANAGER

As THOUGH by instinct the "crackerjack" paired off with Ford after the organizational meeting. Ford volunteered to take Couzens home in his odd-looking, tiller-steered runabout, and Couzens accepted the invitation. For the Ford Motor Company, this was the real beginning—and also for the two "partners," as, in due time, they would be called.

Up to that moment they had not had much to do with each other. "In the beginning, I did not esteem Couzens highly," Ford recalled.[1] As for Couzens, it has already been noted that he had no better opinion of Ford. Now things between them were different.

Ford had special reasons for seeking to cultivate Couzens. It obviously bothered him that his associates in the company were strong men who could out-talk him and, so long as he owned only a fraction more than a quarter of the stock, out-vote him. He felt the need of support, as he would often in the future. Only then could he function.[2] And Couzens seemed to be his man, for he would feel much less like a lamb among lions if Couzens were lined up with him. "He does his own thinking, no one could tell him what to do," Ford later said, and he appreciated that quality in Couzens—then.

For his part Couzens also was looking to the future. He seemed to recognize almost at once that his future lay more with Ford than with Malcomson. With Malcomson he would always have had to maintain a junior relationship, or leave him. But with Ford, he could expect a more equal relationship, even an equal one. Or so he thought. Besides, whether he realized it or not, he was psychologically attracted by Ford's apparent meekness, the easygoing ways that made him appear so different from Malcomson, the side of his personality that Ford usually showed at this time.[3]

2

As they bounced along that evening in Ford's car, both wearing derbies—Ford's somewhat at an angle over his birdlike face, Couzens' square, firm, and level on his solid head—they talked of their plans. Among other matters, they discussed the salary each might expect from the new company. Couzens suggested $3,000 a year for Ford, $2,400 for himself. Ford, the mechanic, wondered if $3,000 were not too much.

"No," said Couzens, the businessman. "This could be an important project." [4]

Ford's way of introducing to Couzens the matter of salaries was especially interesting: "What do you think we ought to ask from *those fellows?*" Couzens of course caught on to Ford's meaning. On one side there was to be Ford and Couzens; on the other, "those fellows." Already there was a division in the new company, and Ford also made some vague remarks, that June night, which caused Couzens later to believe he had said as well: "If this succeeds, I will go fifty-fifty with you." [5]

3

The next day the two managers began working together. The place was Strelow's barnlike carpenter shop on Mack Avenue, on which was painted a sign that read: FORD MOTOR COMPANY.

There were as yet no cars. There were only space and some unassembled parts. The motors and chassis were in a state of "being," at the Dodge brothers' machine shop. This, of course, was by design, for Malcomson's original idea was adhered to. The company was to make no pretense of being a manufacturing concern. It was to be only an assembling and selling organization. This was agreeable to Ford as well as to the others. "If the automobile craze goes to smash, I don't want my money tied up in walls and machinery," [6] Ford said.

But the "craze" did not "go to smash." The new business "moved along almost as by magic," as Ford remembered it. [7] The "magic" lay, in the main, in the public demand for automobiles—any kind of automobiles. It was a demand that no automobile manufacturer up to then had been able to satisfy.

Specifically, for the new company the magic lay in those advance orders Malcomson had obtained from his desperate advertising. "One dealer from Buffalo was here last week and ordered twenty-five. Three were ordered today, and other orders have begun to come in every day," Anderson reported.[8]

To assist in assembling the cars, C. Harold Wills, of the defunct "Henry Ford Company," a tall, dynamic, and resourceful man, was brought in to serve as a sort of foreman over about half a dozen hastily recruited mechanics.[9] Both Ford and Wills maintained a heroic pace in the assembly work to keep pace with the production activity of the Dodge brothers.

4

Speed was essential. In those days cars were sold mostly during the summer months, and it was already past the middle of June. Moreover, the new company's total working capital was only $28,000 to take care of payrolls, advertising, and the like, for others besides Couzens were represented in the final accounting only by promissory notes.[10] If the first season was muffed, this $28,000 would not be nearly enough.

Yet in "the factory" Ford and Wills labored no harder than did Couzens in "the business office." Most of the time he was on the job in the office and sales room of the plant from seven in the morning until after eleven at night.[11]

Couzens also played an important role in the production phase, for Ford's old perfectionism came close to endangering his third venture before it was even under way. Because he felt "they were not yet as good as he could make them," Ford held up shipment of the first cars. Couzens put his foot down—his first, but not his last, crucial act in the company. He insisted that the cars must go out so that money would come in.[12] He was not going to let Ford do to this company what he apparently had done to the Detroit Automobile Company. For a long time, the point has been made by automobile, and other, historians that Ford was very different in 1903 from the way he had been in 1902 in the matter of getting the cars out. In 1950, one such historian, Milo M. Quaife, commented: "How to account for this sudden change of attitude on the part of Mr. Ford is still a subject of speculation. As good a guess as any would be that he was now subject to the influence of such aggressive action as Couzens and John and Horace Dodge." [13]

5

To make doubly certain that there was no slip, Couzens even joined Ford and Wills in the manual task of getting the first cars to the railroad freight station. He helped to crate them and to nail the doors of the freight car. Then, putting back on his black, four-button jacket, he went to the bank to draw sight drafts on purchasers in Indianapolis, Minneapolis, and St. Paul, to whom those first cars were shipped on July 23, 1903.[14]

At last the new Ford company was on its way.

But once again, Ford's perfectionism threatened the venture. Shortly after the first cars had been delivered, complaints began coming in. Some of the cars would not climb even modest hills. Couzens knew by personal experience the validity of these complaints. When John Anderson's father came up from LaCrosse to visit the plant, Couzens volunteered to drive him to the railroad station. "On the way, he attempted to drive through a small park, but the car stalled at a little hill and after frequent attempts to cross the hill, Mr. Couzens was forced to detour around the block," said Dr. Anderson.[15] Ford was mortified and said that all shipments must be halted immediately.

Again Couzens took a firm stand. If necessary, mechanics should be sent to the customers to work on their cars, but he insisted that the cars must go out. "Stop shipping and we go brankrupt."

Couzens' judgment again prevailed,[16] and re-orders came in from the dealers.

6

The company's first "annual statement" was prepared by Couzens as of October 1, 1903. Sales from July 23 to September 30 totaled $142,481.72. Profits were estimated at $36,957.64.

In November 1903, on the basis of this showing, the directors voted for a dividend of 10 per cent. Couzens was given a new title, "Sales Manager," and his salary was increased from $2,400 to $3,000 a year. He was also authorized to employ a stenographer.

Another dividend, this time of 20 per cent, was voted at the first directors' meeting held in 1904. On the company's first anniversary, by which time a thousand cars had been sold, the directors celebrated with a dividend of 68 per cent.[17] Everyone in the enterprise had by that time taken out nearly 100 per cent. "Ford and I then declared our independence," Couzens commented later. They felt that they now had rights above the others. They were the producers; the others were "coupon clippers," and they intended that the distinction should be recognized.[18]

7

As the year 1904 was closing, the company moved to its own four-story building at Piquette and Beaubien Streets. For the first time, the company began to manufacture its own small parts.[19]

On June 16, 1905, a cash dividend of 100 per cent was declared. This was followed by another of the same size only one month later. Two hundred per cent in one year, nearly 300 per cent since the company had been organized only two years before! [20]

Perhaps "magic" was a factor, but it was not only magic. As put by one informed Ford Company employee: "Everyone worked like dogs, early and late, without regard to the hours of service or where they had to go to do it." [21] And Couzens was the pace setter. "In those days," said the *Ford Times*, "J.C. was the entire office management— he hired and fired—he kept the books, collected, spent, and saved the cash, established agencies, and dictated policy."

The company paper added that what Couzens did was too much "for most men but he did it." [22] Garet Garrett, a specialist in writing about business, who for many years paid great attention to the Ford Company, perhaps told the whole story best and most pungently when, in 1952, in his book *The Wild Wheel,* he summarized Couzens' role: "From the beginning . . . James Couzens had been the great he-person in the Ford organization. His gifts were four—a genius for the role of ringmaster in the arena of business, an immense store of energy, a terrible temper and leonine roaring pouches." [23]

CHAPTER IX

THE CLOUD

BY 1903, at least 145 other automobile firms had been founded in the United States. Already, despite the public's continued interest in motoring, most of them had disappeared. "Look at the constantly lengthening list of 'dead ones' in the automobile trade," the *Automobile Magazine* warned in December 1903. At that time the Ford car was not priced lower than a number of other cars—indeed, it cost more than some. Then what did the Ford Motor Company have that kept it alive?

In 1908, the *Ford Times* itself gave one answer: "While Henry Ford had the right car and inexhaustible confidence, push, and fight, it has been Mr. Couzens who has had to meet and solve those problems which daily confront every business enterprise and ruin or make it, according to the way they are met." [1]

How carefully Couzens looked after details is shown by some entries in a notebook he kept: "Boston says March telephone bill not paid, $6.69." "Mail Robbins check." "Get one bond for Block." "Philadelphia needs trouble-locater." "Radiator leaking." "Nuts on lamps hurt in cranking." "Cushion on rear seat not fastened." "Battery box off." "Wood-screws on fenders don't hold." "The gears on Buffalo K absolutely abominable." [2]

The production men heard about such things from him.

2

With dealers, if not with the public, he turned out to be a kind of supersalesman. Charles T. Bennett saw him in operation at the plant. "A man came in from a West Coast city to inquire about being a dealer. He had in mind ordering one car. Mr. Couzens asked him for the population of his town and when he learned the answer, said, 'For a town that size you ought to order 100 cars!' He talked the man into doing just that, and what's more, collected in advance for the ordered cars." [3]

He also demonstrated a keen sense for picking dealers and salesmen who would be hustlers like himself—men like urbane Gaston Plantiff in New York, knowing Louis Block in Philadelphia, hustling Tom Hay in Chicago, and ubiquitous Guy Herring in Des Moines, pillars of the Ford sales hierarchy for years. He personally selected all the Ford dealers and salesmen.

Couzens also made several innovations in organizing his sales force. Key sales points were manned by salaried employes rather than by independent agents. He called them branch managers, and they took instructions directly from him. William C. Durant of the Buick Company (later founder of General Motors) told him that such a plan would not work. "You cannot get a man to work for you as hard as he will work for himself." Couzens said: "We will pay him more than he could possibly earn for himself." [4] And for him, and the Ford Company, this plan worked superbly.

Other departures marked his management. He developed an incentive system. On top of their salaries, the managers received bonuses when sales topped certain figures. This was new for those days.

"If the Ford Company had begun with traditions, no one would know of that company today," Couzens said in 1921. "It made its success by striking out for itself and I imagine if we had only had more experience, we might have gone about our work differently. Certainly we should not have known that many of our most successful innovations could not possibly succeed!" [5]

3

Yet he was a cautious financial administrator. Extensions had to be paid for out of profits, not borrowed money. "It is easy to spend too much when money can be freely borrowed," he said.[6] He learned early not to speculate on materials.

"When we started business we were informed," he recalled, "that it was a safe rule to buy liberally on a rising market and to go slow on a falling market. . . . Time and again we tried it, and time and again we found that in the end we were no better off in price than if we had bought right along as we needed and at the market price. . . . The material speculator is as certain to be hit as the stock speculator." [7]

He set the company's credit policy. As stated in the *Ford Times*, it was:

"The Ford Motor Company never cuts a price, is never a party to a trade deal, does not consider anything but real money in selling cars, quotes no discounts or special allowances and would carry a thousand cars over rather than discount the price." [8]

4

He knew precisely how he wanted company affairs handled. Correspondence had to be taken care of on the dot. Accounts had to be kept precisely. Instructions had to be followed out to the letter. Contracts had to be fulfilled to the last comma. Infractions of such rules brought from him rebukes that made such infractions rare.

He was still a hard man to work for. Success did not soften him. He would remain as he was from now on by deliberate intention as much as by temperament. Like John D. Rockefeller, who once told members of a Bible class not to be "good fellows" because "good fellows end up in the poor houses," he earnestly believed that being a good fellow was incompatible with being a good businessman— perhaps a rationalization of his own temperament. "I am one of those who hold that it is not worthwhile to attempt to be popular. I should prefer to be a hard taskmaster—but a fair one," he once said.[9] "A floor walker in a big department store gets twenty-five or fifty dollars a week because he knows how to be pleasant and shake hands with the trade. But the man in the back room, who buys the goods and runs the business, gets $50,000 to $100,000 a year because *he* knows how *to run* the business." [10]

He prided himself on his fairness to an extreme—a fact that once cost a branch manager a tidy sum. About the time that bonuses were given out, this man wrote to Couzens to tell him what a good manager he was, with the bonus in mind, as Couzens understood. He wrote back: "I had put you down for $21,000 before I received your letter. Your letter has cost you $5,000, because it showed me that you did not trust me to treat you fairly. I have now put you down for $16,000." [11]

5

Indeed, he had become a businessman. He looked the part, too. He had filled out since the days when he had been a slender coal clerk, sitting on a high stool in the window of the Malcomson company. That rather tight look that had characterized his eyes before had now become one of firm assurance.

His face was rounder. He wore his hair, which was carefully parted down the middle, less closely clipped than before. There was about him now not so much the "don't-tread-on-me" manner as "be-careful-or-I-may-tread-on-you."

Milton A. McRae, the Scripps-McRae newspapers executive, met him about this time and made a mental note that "here was a comer," a man with leadership ability.[12] Others were puzzled by his aloof, outwardly cold manner. "In spite of all our meetings, I feel that I really do not know him . . . that there is something in reserve that I do not get at," said James Wilkie, the pharmaceutical merchant and Detroit civic leader.[13] But Ida M. Tarbell, the biographer and industrial historian, who saw him a little later, was not perplexed by his aloof manner. She catalogued him as a man who would leave a mark.[14]

He moved his family into a somewhat better residence on middle-class Frederick Street. In 1904 a daughter, Madeleine, was born. That same year, after paying off his promissory notes in the company, he prudently invested his Ford dividends in a house at 80 Chandler Avenue, for which he paid $7,500. Owner of his own home, father of three children, a key figure in a new industry, he was now, at last, beginning to fulfill the promise of the resourceful, independent boy of Chatham.

6

Yet there remained a cloud.

The company had been born under this cloud, for as early as July 1900 the owners of a certain patent had begun filing suits for infringement against various automobile manufacturers. Moreover, the validity of the patent had been conceded by Alexander Winton, then the leader in the industry. In March 1903 there was formed "The Association of Licensed Automobile Manufacturers," with the avowed purpose of forcing out of business anyone not licensed under the patent.

Not everyone would be licensed, either; the Association intended to practice discrimination.

Malcomson had gone about organizing the Ford Motor Company in ignorance of this patent, as well as of the existence of the Association of Licensed Automobile Manufacturers. In their own excitement, John Anderson and Horace Rackham, his lawyers, had not checked very well the patent status of the automobile, although Anderson later said that he had "made a very careful investigation, as careful as I thought a man could make, before I ventured my money in the Ford Motor Company." [15] Had they checked, it is most probable that they would have held back, and would have discouraged the others. So this, too, may have been part of the "magic." Not until a week or so after the Ford Motor Company was organized did any of the Ford promoters hear about the matter of the patent.

7

But then, this is what they learned: Back in the early 1870's, George B. Selden of Rochester, a lawyer with a mechanical turn of mind, a member of a prominent up-state New York family, had begun studying horseless locomotion. According to his son, he was inspired to do this by "some disagreeable experiences" with horses while serving with the United States cavalry during the Civil War.[16] His idea was to "construct a light-weight self-propelled vehicle with a large cruising radius, which could be operated by one man, not a skilled engineer." [17]

Selden at first experimented with a steam engine. Then he turned to the internal-combustion type. By 1879, he had progressed far enough to apply for a patent on this latter engine.[18] He had interested six financial sponsors, but "one of these men died suddenly; another went into bankruptcy; another became ill; still another met with an accident. The remainder changed their minds." [19]

Selden then determined to wait for the world to catch up with him. He contrived to postpone the issuance of a patent, but kept his application alive through a long series of "amendments." The patent was issued on March 5, 1899, after he had entered into an assignment of it to the Columbia and Electric Vehicle Company.

The owners of the Columbia and Electric Vehicle Company were a group of Wall Street financiers, including William C. Whitney, who were backing electric automobiles. Apparently they had no serious intention of producing cars themselves, but they intended to extract royalties from those who did—at the rate of 5 per cent.

Under the leadership of the Olds Motor Company, a group of Detroit manufacturers then formed a protective committee. They had a showdown with Whitney and the others of the Wall Street group. But instead of challenging the royalty principle, they merely took it over, after forcing Whitney and his associates to agree to reduce the royalty from 5 per cent to 1¼ per cent, of which only three-fifths would go to the patent holders. Two-fifths would go to their committee, which then would undertake to fight infringements and to police the industry.

Among the admitted, even boasted, aims of this committee was a restriction of production. Only manufacturers granted a license could produce cars, and these had to agree to limit the number of cars produced to a figure set by the committee. It was this committee that became "The Association of Licensed Automobile Manufacturers." [20]

Couzens first heard about all this a few days after the Ford Company was established, when John Anderson gloomily reported a conversation he had had with Frederic L. Smith, then head of the Olds organization and later president of the Association of Licensed Automobile Manufacturers. John Anderson, whose middle name of Wendell was an inheritance from the Wendell clan that included Oliver Wendell Holmes, Senior, may have then recalled that he was a descendant of the New Englander who owned the "Wonderful One-Hoss Shay" which Holmes immortalized for having gone to pieces all at once. He may have wondered if the Ford Company, with his investment and its prospects, might not go the same way.[21] For Anderson was convinced by his talk with Smith that he had invested "in a man's size lawsuit, instead of in an automobile company." He suffered "a feeling of gone-ness in his stomach." [22]

The seriousness of the situation became more apparent on July 26, 1903, when an advertisement appeared in the *Detroit Free Press* as follows:

NOTICE

To Manufacturers, Dealers, Importers, Agents and Users of

GASOLINE AUTOMOBILES

United States Patent No. 549, 160 granted to George B. Selden, November 5th, 1895, controls broadly all gasoline automobiles which are accepted as commercially practical. Licenses under this patent have been secured from the owners by the following named manufacturers and importers. . . .

No other manufacturers are authorized to make or sell gasoline automobiles, and any person making, selling, or using such machines made or sold by any unlicensed manufacturers or importers will be liable to prosecution for infringement.

ASSOCIATION OF LICENSED AUTOMOBILE MANUFACTURERS

No. 7 East 42nd Street, New York.[23]

A conference between Smith and the officers of the Ford Motor Company was held at the Russel House. In after years, Smith wrote: "By what miracle that flimsy patent was ever sustained . . . I know not."[24] But at this meeting, he politely, but firmly, repeated: the Ford Company could not stay in business unless licensed. For the Ford organization, he had only one kind of advice: they should go out of business. The Ford people were only assemblers, not manufacturers. Assemblers were not wanted.[25]

Nobody among Smith's listeners said anything for awhile. They had been told that a legal fight for carrying the matter to the highest court would cost at least $40,000, nearly as much as the total investment in the company. And there was no assurance that such a fight could be won. The patent lawyer in Detroit with the best reputation, Ralzemond A. Parker, whom they had consulted, had guessed that the chances of *losing* were high. Some of the Ford stockholders were for yielding to what appeared to be the inevitable. Others, Malcomson included, hoped for some kind of a compromise.

Banker Gray talked moodily. He lamented that now he could not even unload his stock on others because he could not "conscientiously" recommend the shares as being a good investment.[26]

Couzens broke the indecision and gloom. Following the pattern he had established as a boy in Chatham, as a freight clerk at the Michigan Central, and as assistant to Malcomson, he told Smith: "Selden can take his patent and go to Hell with it!"

"Couzens has answered you," said Ford.[27]

CHAPTER X

THE REALIGNMENT

AT THE next directors' meeting it was voted unanimously "to throw down the gauntlet, come what may." [1] Space in newspapers was purchased for denunciations of the Selden patent. These Ford advertisements assured prospective car buyers, "We will protect you." Then, to offset the Licensed Association, the Ford Company took the lead among independent firms in organizing a rival association, "The American Motor Car Manufacturers' Association." Formed at a meeting in New York, this association, for years afterwards a major factor in the industry, picked Couzens for its first president. [2] Thus he became the official voice of the opponents of the "monopoly manufacturers."

In the meantime, he dusted off his old law books and acquired others with which to begin reading law once more—patent law. Before long, he was able to talk on almost equal terms with the patent lawyers and often, at conferences, advised them on procedures and pleadings. [3]

When a trade publication asked the Ford Company for a public statement on its strategy, the answer was abrupt and to the point:

> We regard the claims made under the Selden patent as . . . entirely unwarranted and without foundation in fact. We do not, therefore, propose to respect any such claims, and, if the issue is forced upon us, shall defend not only ourselves but our agents and customers to the fullest extent . . .
>
> Yours Truly,
J. Couzens, Secretary [4]

Up to that time the Licensed Association had taken no legal action against the Ford Motor Company. But after the appearance of this letter, it acted. In the U.S. Circuit Court, Southern District of New York, two suits were filed at the same time: one against the

Ford Motor Company, another against its New York agent, C. A. Duerr & Co. A week later another suit was filed against a Ford customer, the O. J. Gude Company, to restrain it from even using a Ford car it had purchased.[5] So the legal issues were joined.

2

The ensuing battle was fought on the propaganda front as well as in court. New advertising barrages that specifically warned the public against the sale, purchase, or use of Fords were set off by the Licensed Association. Any "infraction" would lead to prosecution, these ads said. Fords were barred from the automobile shows held at Madison Square Garden. In reply, the Ford Company then advertised that it would put up surety bonds "to protect dealers, importers, agents and users from any attempt on the part of the TRUST to prevent you from buying the 'car of satisfaction.' " The American Motor Car Association, under Couzens' leadership, held its own annual shows—events that soon rivaled, at least in ballyhoo, the exhibits in Madison Square Garden.

The word "trust" was featured in much of the Ford advertising—shrewd exploitation of what was then becoming a popular political issue, thanks to President Theodore Roosevelt's "trust-busting" program.

On this issue of "monopoly," the Ford Company soon acquired an interesting and powerful ally, John Wanamaker. The great Philadephia and New York merchant, John Wanamaker, had fought a patent war with the so-called bicycle "trust." Now he looked forward to another and similar fight. Already handling Fords in his stores, Wanamaker began to feature them in his advertising. In January 1904 the Licensed Association filed suit against Wanamaker, and he hit back with full-page advertisements saying:

"Get a Ford car and enjoy it. We'll take care of the tomtoms. Don't give $600 to the Bogey man." [6]

3

All this uproar had an unanticipated result—perhaps the most important single thing that happened in the early days of the company. As Couzens said later, "The Selden suit was probably better advertising than anything we could put out." [7]

All the attention given to the controversy made the Ford car the best-known make in the land. Many persons bought Fords because they were the only automobile they had heard about. Others bought Fords because they hated "monopoly," or just to be contrary; still others because "Honest John" Wanamaker said they were good cars.

There was at least one other important result. Both Couzens and Ford came to feel great admiration for Wanamaker, who was then plumping a novel concept of business—that the purpose of business was to render "service to the public," that it was a duty of merchants to distribute products *at the lowest price possible.*

Both Couzens and Ford began to think and talk the same way. The influence of Wanamaker, indeed, may have been the central inspiration for the later, and world-celebrated, concept of the Ford Motor Company—that of producing and selling cars at low cost: the foundation of the mass-production system in heavy industry.

Undoubtedly, too, Couzens' attitude toward "big business" in general, as well as Ford's, was shaped in part by the Wanamaker influence, just as Pingree earlier had left an impression upon Couzens with respect to the labor problem.

Immediately, the fight engendered a crusading spirit on the part of the company and its dealers and salesmen. Ford advertisements reflected a spirit of pugnaciousness that was pure Couzens. A typical Ford announcement in *Harper's* said:

> We hear a lot these days about "hand-made" motor cars. It's funny, but these same concerns who, a year ago, prated of "quality, not quantity," as if the two were incompatible, now build 1,000 to 2,000 cars per year and still expect you to believe it is "hand work," "personal supervision," *and all that sort of rot. . . .*[8]

One day an Ohio Ford dealer telegraphed to Couzens: "My competitor wants to bet $500 that their machine will make a trip to Columbus and return quicker than the Ford Model S. Is it safe to bet?" Couzens answered: "Is it any credit for the United States to whip Venezuela? Take a bet like that with any car selling between $1,500 and $2,500."[9] This spirit paid off in sales, of course.

Yet the Selden cloud was to remain as a vexation and a threat until the courts finally decided the issue. As Horace Rackham observed, "The company could not determine what the future would be."[10]

Gray streaks showed up at Couzens' temples. He began to be tormented for the first time by massively painful migraine headaches. He consumed enormous quantities of aspirin. But he continued to push Ford sales just as if Selden really had gone to Hell with his patent.

And the company kept growing.

4

And Malcomson? In the light of his dominant importance in the formation of the company, it is a curious thing how little he figured in its affairs after the company was launched. This is not to be explained simply by saying that Malcomson was "too busy" at the coal office, nor by the assumption that he was content to let his former assistant take over completely. Nor is it to be explained by the fact that Couzens had demonstrated his ability to take over— true though this was. The fact is that in the genesis of the Ford Motor Company, Malcomson was doomed to play the role of a Moses, with Couzens his Joshua.

Like some of its cars, the Ford Motor Company very early developed "internal trouble." Ford's "those fellows" comment had borne strange fruit. There had come to the surface almost immediately a bad case of temperamental incompatibility. This arose not only between Malcomson and Ford, but also between Malcomson and John and Horace Dodge, and to an extent between Malcomson and Gray.

But it was most acute between Malcomson and Ford. After the first year, neither could abide the other. In the words of Rackham, "Both wanted to be boss." [11] And Ford, as soon would be apparent, was not at all the timid or lackadaisical man he had given the impression of being.

5

So long as the company appeared to be struggling, both Ford and Malcomson suppressed their true feelings, but the first appearance of prosperity brought a change. Directors' meetings became marked by explosive bickering. "There was much pounding on the table, and at times Ford's directors would get up and leave and refuse to come back." [12]

Couzens, not surprisingly, touched off some of these explosions. When Malcomson took an order for an automobile to be delivered to a friend at a discount, it was Couzens who insisted that there should be no discounts to anyone, not even to a friend of Malcomson. "He protested so vigorously that the other stockholders voted to compel Malcomson to pay the difference." [13] Malcomson considered this a personal affront.

In arguments between Ford and Malcomson, Couzens invariably stood with Ford, in accord with the understanding the two of them had reached on that June evening in 1903. Indeed, it became clear that Couzens was Ford's spokesman on all business matters, that if Ford kept silent, but Couzens spoke, it was really Ford, as well as Couzens, speaking. They began to seem like one person, and Malcomson resented this.

Couzens had begun to develop a deeper affection for Ford than he had ever had for Malcomson. Ford seemed to reciprocate that affection, although he did maintain a conscious line beyond which he would not let friendship carry him. Once, early in their relationship, he said to Couzens, "It is a mistake to make or have too strong attachments, because it weakens your will and your character." [14] Few persons ever heard them address each other in any way except "Mr. Ford" and "Mr. Couzens." Yet, T. J. Hay, the Chicago dealer, felt "they were like brothers."

Couzens saw that eventually either Ford or Malcomson would have to leave the company. If he himself wanted to stay, he had to choose sides. Actually, he had no choice, for Malcomson forced matters by his authoritarian and antagonistic attitude toward his protégé. Not long after the business was well under way, Malcomson flatly demanded that Couzens voluntarily return to the coal company.

Couzens refused.[15] At a directors' meeting later, Malcomson moved that Couzens be discharged as business manager.[16] The antagonism was out in the open.

6

There were five directors, each with an equal vote regardless of the amount of stock owned: Malcomson, Ford, John Dodge, John S. Gray, and John Anderson. If he could get two other directors to side with him, Malcomson would win his point about firing Couzens and establish his own supremacy in the company—even over Ford. Ford, of course, stood by Couzens. "I told Malcomson that I did not want him, but that I wanted his man Couzens," he later said.[17] And banker Gray stood by Couzens too.

John Dodge might not have cared too much for Couzens at that time. But, as he once said in court, he "really did not like Malcomson," [18] perhaps because, when the contract with the Dodge brothers had come up for renewal in 1904, Malcomson argued that the Dodges should reduce their price since their risk was less. Couzens had sided with the Dodges in that controversy,[19] and now John Dodge sided with Couzens.

Only John Anderson, Malcomson's lawyer, sided with Malcomson.[20] So Couzens remained as manager.

7

In September 1905 Malcomson raised another row at a directors' meeting because Couzens' salary was raised to $8,000.[21] Obviously, his objection was emotional. That year, the company had earned a net profit of $285,231.94.[22] The other directors voted Malcomson down. After that, even Malcomson had to concede that his own former clerk had supplanted him completely as the dominant businessman of the Ford Motor Company.

Which way the wind was blowing, how firmly the Ford-Couzens alliance had already jelled, was made evident even before this, when the Ford Motor Company of Canada was organized in 1904. In this corporation, Ford was president and Couzens was vice-president. But Malcomson was left out.[23]

In the parent company Malcomson was still treasurer, as well as a principal stockholder. But he really had little to say about policies. Ford and Couzens already had attained, substantially, their planned goal—independence from "those fellows."

Malcomson then did an astonishing thing. He formed another automobile company, the Aero, with himself as president, and set up a plant for turning out air-cooled "Aeros" not far from the Ford factory. Apparently his plan was to use his dividends from the Ford Motor Company for financing his own company, not only to add to his income, but also to show Ford, Couzens, and the others how an automobile company should be operated. Unquestionably, Malcomson took this step in anticipation of his complete separation from the Ford Motor Company, either voluntarily, or by being frozen out despite his large interest.

8

A procedure for freezing, or squeezing, Malcomson, as well as some of the others, out of the company already had been devised in the fall of 1905. This consisted of an interesting plan for organizing another corporation, "The Ford Manufacturing Company."

Ostensibly this second corporation was to make motors and other parts for the Ford Motor Company. Ostensibly, too, its creation was desirable for efficiency, as well as to make any expansion of facilities by the Dodge brothers unnecessary.[24] It was to be wholly controlled by the Ford Motor Company. But there was one important catch. Not all the stockholders in the parent company were to have an interest in the subsidiary. Malcomson, for one, was not to be included. Moreover, matters could be so arranged—for example, by the prices that the Ford Motor Company might pay the Ford Manufacturing Company for motors and parts—that the profits of the original company could be drained off into the subsidiary. Indeed, the subsidiary could swallow up the parent company.

The real purpose of the Ford Manufacturing Company was underlined by a comment made by Banker Gray. Vernon Fry had voiced to him his worries about the possible effect of the subsidiary on the parent company. "I have Mr. Ford's promise," said Gray, "that when they get things straightened out with Mr. Malcomson, the Ford Manufacturing Company is to be taken into the Ford Motor Company, just as if it had never existed." [25]

9

Not long after this plan had been devised, a resolution that formally requested Malcomson to resign as treasurer and as director was adopted by the board of the Ford Motor Company. "Moved by Mr. Rackham and seconded by Mr. Ford," this request was justified, for the record, on the ground that Malcomson's formation of another automobile company was "inimical to the best interest of the company." [26]

In the following week, The Ford Manufacturing Company was officially incorporated.[27] Later, a contract was entered into between it and the Ford Motor Company for it to supply ten thousand engines at a *price not stipulated*. And a building was fitted up for the subsidiary. Besides Ford and Couzens, the incorporators were the Dodge brothers, Rackham, Anderson, Bennett, and Wills.[28] Left out of the subsidiary were Gray, Fry, Strelow, Woodall, and, of course, Malcomson.

The morality of this procedure could be discussed and debated endlessly. Both Ford and Couzens unquestionably owed much to Malcomson. He was the real founder of the Ford Motor Company; he had given both men their start. However, it is doubtful if any of the principals in this drama looked at the matter at the time from the viewpoint of gratitude or loyalty—not even Malcomson. These were businessmen engaged in the game of business, playing the game according to the accepted rules. All played the game the same way and had the same objectives.

10

Malcomson put up a fight. In a letter to the board of directors, he indignantly refused to resign as treasurer and director. He denounced "such occurrences as the recent precipitate action of the board in doubling the manager's [Couzens'] salary, despite protest and without waiting for a full board meeting." Then he criticized bitterly the organization of the Ford Manufacturing Company. It was a scheme, he said, for causing "injury to those stockholders of the motor company that are left on the outside." He threatened a lawsuit to block the manufacturing company plan.[29]

His letter was ordered "placed on file." [30] It appeared that Malcomson had won a victory, for he did not resign as treasurer.

However, when the year 1906 opened, Malcomson was for all practical purposes, except for his ownership of stock, out of the Ford Motor Company. He was concentrating on his own company. And he issued an optimistic statement to the trade press: "We start in 1906, put up a factory and turn out 500 cars in one year. I believe that is a record." [31] It was better than the Ford Motor Company had done. He advertised his product as "The Car of Today, Tomorrow, and for Years to Come." [32]

In that optimistic mood, in May 1906, Malcomson made what later proved one of the great blunders in business history: he sold his one-fourth ownership of the Ford Motor Company to Ford. Couzens handled this deal for Ford.[33] His trump card in the negotiations was the existence of the Ford Manufacturing Company. Malcomson, of course, knew what that meant—that the profits of the Ford Motor Company could be siphoned out of it into the manufacturing company, to the point where Malcomson's one-fourth interest in the parent company could be made worthless.[34] Besides, Malcomson was fearful of the outcome of the Selden case.

He finally agreed to sell his one-fourth interest to Ford for $175,-000. Thus Malcomson, the real founder, in the phraseology of the principal Ford historian, was "jettisoned" from the company. Thus, too, for the first time, Henry Ford won a dominating interest in the company that bore his name. John Gray died in the following

July, and then Ford, also for the first time, received the title of president.

11

Later Malcomson made an effort to re-enter the picture. His two friends, Fry and Bennett, were indignant over the fact that the Ford Manufacturing Company was sold soon afterwards to the Ford Motor Company for $450,000. They decided to pull out, and it was Malcomson who bought their shares.[35] As a legal matter, it was highly questionable if these shares were salable to Malcomson, for each share bore the provision that if it were sold, it had to be offered to another shareholder—the provision that kept the Ford Motor Company a "closed corporation" for decades.[36] And Malcomson was not then a shareholder.

Ford and Couzens took the position that Bennett's and Fry's shares should have been offered to them, or to other shareholders, and that the sale to Malcomson was void. A new controversy with Malcomson ensued.

Couzens in the meantime had gone to Europe to set up agencies in England, France, Holland, Spain, Italy, Denmark, Germany, and Russia. In Denmark, he received a jubilant cablegram from Ford: Malcomson had conceded that the Fry and Bennett stock had to be sold to Ford and Couzens, at five dollars a share for the thousand shares.[37] The Malcomson "trouble" was over, forever.

A little later Couzens bought all of Strelow's shares for $25,000. He succeeded Malcomson as a director and treasurer, and then also assumed the title of general manager. The recorded ownership of the company stood:

Henry Ford	585 shares
James Couzens	110
Gray estate	105
John Dodge	50
Horace E. Dodge	50
J. W. Anderson	50
Horace Rackham	50

At last Couzens had attained his goal of moving up from the bottom of the list of shareholders.

12

After this the *Ford Times* contained as many references to "Mr. Couzens" as it did to "Mr. Ford." It seldom mentioned anyone else.

Everyone close to the company understood that they were the only ones who counted. Not a few understood something else. ". . . They used to tell it around the automobile shows and so forth that Couzens is the brains of the organization. Couzens is the front door. If you want anything you will have to see Couzens. This went on and on, without any inspiration from me. . . ." So Couzens himself said.[38]

Actually, that was how Ford wanted things. If anyone came to Ford about a business matter, he said: "See Mr. Couzens." [39]

Board meetings became perfunctory affairs. "I would not work for a company where the board did much interfering with actions or policies," Couzens said later.[40] In particular, he had in mind the Dodge brothers, and even Ford. The fact was, if the Ford Company then had a boss, the boss was Couzens.[41]

CHAPTER XI

THE MONEY-MAKING MACHINE, II

In 1907, business in America was generally in a bad way. Mark Twain said this was because Theodore Roosevelt, the President, was a "crazy man." Others said it was because of the financial manipulations by the "trusts." Whatever the cause, the country was gripped by economic panic. The stock ticker even reported that Wanamaker had failed, which, if true, would have been to many businessmen like doom itself. It wasn't true, but Wanamaker's store was in trouble and the bold merchant-king himself wrote in his diary: "Many people think the world is coming to an end so far as money and business are concerned." [1]

Detroit was not spared. Among others, Malcomson's Aero automobile company folded up, although not his coal business. To save Detroit's supposedly strong Union Trust Company (an institution to be recalled later) the hat was passed among Detroit capitalists. [2]

But the Ford Company was not fazed. Indeed, as other automobile companies went bankrupt, the Ford Company in 1907 chalked up its first million-dollar-profit year. In his private notebook, General Manager Couzens made a pleasant entry.

"Net earnings for 1907, $1,331,371.68. Total sales, $5,773,851.38. Percentage of commercial expenses to sales, 3⅖ per cent."

In the next year, Couzens called in the press to make a sensational announcement. The Ford Motor Company's capitalization was to be increased from $100,000 to $2,000,000, or twenty times, to finance its Model T. [3]

2

The Model T was an instantaneous, colossal success. Just why, nobody could explain. Ugly, noisy, often unpredictable, it had defects enough almost to outweigh its draconic virtues. In the beginning, it was not even cheaper than several other cars. For example, when first introduced, it cost as much as the Cadillac. Yet it caught on as had no other car. In all probability, the answer was that it came just at the right moment, when Americans suddenly decided that the automobile was really here to stay. The people wanted cars, and the Ford Company was able to produce them in undreamed-of quantities.[4]

"The first 'ad' appeared on Friday," related the *Ford Times*. "Saturday's mail brought nearly a thousand inquiries. Monday's response swamped our mail clerks, and by Tuesday night, the office was well-nigh inundated." [5]

As a consequence, Couzens directed that the first Model T's could be distributed only on a restricted basis. Before a dealer could get a Model T, he had to sell all previous models on hand.[6] Even then, only one Model T would be shipped to a dealer until all dealers had been so supplied, and then only if they could show bona fide sales in advance.[7] Nothing like this kind of "rationing" had ever been known before.

Quite as astonishing was the announcement of a new production policy. No longer were customers to have their choice in sizes, styles, or motors. The Ford Motor Company, henceforth, would make only Model T's, and only black Model T's. A famous quip attributed to Ford was: "The customer can have any color he wants, just so it's black!"

3

The true meaning of this development was explained by Couzens more clearly than by anyone else. "We standardized the customer. It was formerly thought that selling started with the customer, and worked back to the factory. We reversed the process." [8]

And the "standardized customers" responded with a deluge of orders. Within six months, agents had to be asked to stop sending orders, for the company's facilities were swamped.[9]

Back in April 1907 a fifty-seven-acre site in Highland Park, then a remote suburb of Detroit, had been purchased against a possible need for a larger factory. With the demand for the Model T straining production facilities at the Piquette Street plant, that day had come. What would previously have been a full year's production was being turned out and sold in one month.

Profits for 1909 totaled $4,452,602; sales, more than seventeen thousand cars. Plans were rushed for building in Highland Park "the largest factory in the state under one roof," where, for the first time in the history of the Ford Company, manufacturing was to be done on a large scale.[10]

Only a short time before, when the American automobile editor Fred H. Colvin, while in England, mentioned that the Ford factory was turning out as many as ten thousand cars annually, a British newspaper scoffed: "No manufacturer can possibly build that many cars in one year; and even if he could, he wouldn't be able to sell half of them." [11]

But in fact the Ford Company was already producing and selling, under Couzens' direction, almost twice that number.

4

There was, however, one flaw in the almost bewilderingly dazzling picture: the Selden patent matter. In 1909, this patent was sweepingly sustained in the Federal District Court at New York, where Judge Charles M. Hough ruled that it was "so fundamental and far reaching as to cover every modern car driven by any form of petroleum vapor." [12] It made no difference, the judge said, that Selden had contrived a delay of sixteen years in the issuance of his patent, from 1879 to 1895. "He did delay," wrote the judge. "He was not in a hurry. . . . Doubtless he appreciated that, if he was ahead of the times, it was wise not to let his patent get ahead too." But, the judge continued, "Selden did not overstep the law . . . the inventor may use his discovery, or he may not; but no one else can use it for seventeen years." [13]

This meant that the Ford Motor Company was liable to an accounting for its profits, and to being enjoined from producing any more automobiles.

However, in 1911, the Federal Circuit Court of Appeals, also at New York, decided that *while Selden had a valid patent,* Ford and other manufacturers were using an *"entirely different motor principle."* To the layman, this is confusing language, but it meant the Ford Company had not infringed Selden's patent after all.[14] And at last, the cloud over the Ford Company disappeared forever.

That year, the company produced thirty-four thousand cars and made net profits of more than $6,000,000.[15] Some years later, these figures might seem ordinary, but at the time they were colossal.

5

The Ford plant really went on a "production" basis. Approximately half of all the automobiles produced in America were being made there.[16] "Watch the Fords Go By" became a slogan that was familiar everywhere. In 1913, the Ford production schedule called for 200,000 cars. By then the assembly-line technique was perfected. And the money rolled in. Whereas profits had been $13,000,000 for 1912, for 1913 they had built up to more than $26,000,000 for the one year.[17]

Husbanding these great sums became a major responsibility for Couzens, along with his pushing of the sales force. He saw to it that the company's surplus was put out properly to earn interest. He initiated a financial plan that probably had no equal then in the business world: *Ford* monies would be desposited in banks for the specific purpose of being loaned to *Ford* dealers for buying more *Ford* cars. The banks charged the dealers regular rates of interest, and shared the earnings with the Ford Motor Company, to the enrichment of everyone concerned.[18] It was like a magic circle.

On just the replacement parts for old Fords, huge profits were made—$800,000 on parts alone in 1912, $5,000,000 in 1913. By 1915, parts accounted for nearly $10,000,000 in profits.

It is little wonder that John D. Rockefeller himself was astonished, or that a leading economist referred to the Ford Company as a "seventh wonder of the world." [19]

As Roger Burlingame has noted, Couzens and Ford (aided of course by some others, like Wills, Walter Flanders, and Hawkins, as well as Charles E. Sorensen, who then was still far down the ladder) had ushered the Industrial Revolution into a new stage of maturity, although neither of them realized it at the time, for they did little thinking in such terms. Because of them a whole new economic world had dawned.[20] In this era, the impact of what they had achieved was not unlike the impact of atomic energy in a later day.

6

Both Couzens and Ford, of course, became millionaires, and it happened to them before either was truly aware of it.

Naturally, their living arrangements had changed. Ford had long since left behind the modest house at 82 Bagley Avenue. By 1913 he and Mrs. Ford and their one child, Edsel, had moved into a massive, forty-five-room, castle-like residence called Fairlane, on a thirteen-hundred-acre estate at Dearborn.

In the meantime, Couzens had Albert Kahn, the industrial architect who had designed the Highland Park plant, build him a fine brick house at 92 (later 610) Longfellow Avenue. He also acquired a farm near Pontiac, Michigan, in the Bloomfield Hills section, and erected there a large white frame house for a summer home. He called the farm "Wabeek." It was an Indian word he found in the *Saturday Evening Post,* and it meant "the best place." "My favorite relaxation," he said, "is to go to Wabeek farm. I go about looking like a farmer, with no one to bother me. My cows don't talk to me, don't ask me questions, nor criticize my way of doing things." [21]

7

He did not forget his family in Chatham. In particular, he wanted to do something to make his mother's closing years more pleasant. He persuaded his father for her sake, if not for his own, to retire from the coal and ice business and come with his mother to Detroit to live. He presented them with a comfortable house in Highland Park, and otherwise saw that they lived pleasantly. Both of his brothers, Albert and Homer, and his sister, Alice, received "nest eggs" from him to help them toward financial independence. Rosetta, of course, needed no such help. That one share in the Ford Company —her one-hundred-dollar loan—had made her wealthy in her own right.

By then, his own family included four children, for in 1910 a second girl, Margo, had arrived. Later, the two sons, Homer and Frank, and two daughters, Madeleine and Margo, were joined by another girl, Edith Valerie, called Betty.

The youngsters formed an interesting group, all wholesome and apparently unspoiled by Couzens' sudden wealth. It was a long time before any of the youngsters suspected that "Daddy Jim" was of that breed, often discussed so admiringly in the newspapers of the period, called "millionaire."

8

Nor were his business interests limited to the Ford Company, vast as it had become. In 1908 he was elected a director of the National Bank of Commerce of Detroit. Before long, he was also on the directorate of the Old Detroit National Bank and of the Detroit

Trust Company. In February 1909 he became a banker in his own right, organizing the Highland Park State Bank, a banking subsidiary of the Ford Motor Company. He was its president. "I ran it from across the street, in my office of the Ford plant," he said.[22]

To the annoyance of other Detroit banks, he used his influence as general manager of the Ford Company to persuade other companies to keep deposits in "his" bank. If a company had money coming to it from Ford supplies, it would be told that the amount due had been deposited in the company's name in an account in the Highland Park Bank, whether the supplier wanted it that way or not. The suppliers usually acquiesced.

He accepted two more directorates in 1909: one in the Scotten Tobacco Company, and another in a new railroad, the Kansas City, Mexico and Orient—a variation of an old dream of John C. Fremont's, in which he became interested, because its promoter, A. E. Stilwell, was trying to create a new transcontinental railroad "without kneeling to Wall Street." [23] That appealed to Couzens' "Single Tax" and John Wanamaker-like ideas.

In 1911, he became a director of the Detroit Salt Company. He also went into the real-estate business, through the Highland Park Land Company. He invested in downtown Detroit real estate, and erected the Couzens Building on Woodward Avenue. He even entered the retail shoe business, as president of the Rogers Shoe Company, though this mainly was to help preserve the estate left by a brother of Mrs. Couzens.

As suited his status, he joined the Detroit Club and the Detroit Athletic Club. He contributed, although moderately, to the Republican party. The press played up the fact that he endorsed a Republican candidate for the Michigan Supreme Court. His comments on women's suffrage were solicited. He became active in the Detroit Board of Commerce and, in 1913, was its president. In short, he emerged as one of the biggest business names in Detroit, so outstanding indeed that a Canadian newspaper-writer soon would describe him as "this square-jawed, successful, masterful son of Chatham, Ontario." [24]

Definitely, he had arrived. The promise of the caul had been realized.

CHAPTER XII

THE CRISIS

YET the Midas touch left something to be desired for both Couzens and Ford. In spite of the riches that flowed in on them, in spite of all the doors thrown open to them, neither was really a happy man. Both illustrated a fact—that success often is harder to endure than failure, that it frequently carries with it the greater pitfalls for mind and soul.

Ford, who was a man of moods anyway, was often listless or dejected in the period between 1908 and 1913. He constantly talked about retiring and becoming a farmer. He spent little time at the plant. "He would come in maybe once or twice a week, and then just roam around," said an associate.[1] At one time, in 1913, Ford suggested that Couzens take his title—president of the company. "He said that he did not want to come to the office at all," Couzens recalled, adding, "I told him that we were getting along all right as we were."[2]

2

On two occasions, Ford even seriously contemplated selling the Ford Motor Company, once in 1908 and again in 1909.[3]

The first occasion was in connection with a merger plan set in motion by Ben Briscoe and William C. Durant, whose idea was to establish one big company, through consolidation of Ford, Buick, Reo, and Maxwell—then the leading producers. They had sounded out Couzens on that proposal before 1908. In his 1907 notebook, he had set down an interesting item:

Sell	$5,000,000 preferred 6% common?		Ford	$7,125,000
Bonus	2,500,000 common		Buick	7,125,000
Reo	7,125,000		Maxwell	6,125,000
		$35,500,000		

3

This tabulation summarized a tentative agreement: A $35,000,000 corporation was to be organized, shares to be distributed in proportion to the value set on each company in accord with Couzens' notation. Extra stock was to be distributed "mostly to the men who were doing the trade, as a consideration for keeping out of business and not lending their name to any other automobile." [4] This, specifically, included Ford.

Throughout the first six months in 1908, Couzens and Ford were in frequent conferences on the proposed merger, both in Detroit and in New York. An initial meeting was held at the old Hotel Pontchartrain in Detroit, where the principals discussed such questions as: "How was the (new) company to be managed?" "Who was to be the 'boss'?" "How were the different companies to be represented?" [5] Other meetings were held in the Wall Street law offices of Herbert L. Satterlee, attorney for Briscoe, and a brother-in-law of J. P Morgan. "We expected to get the capital to buy out Ford and to acquire other property and start the consolidation going from J. P. Morgan & Company," Satterlee recalled. "Fords and Olds were planning to get out of the business." George W. Perkins, a Morgan partner, selected a name for the new company—"The International." [6]

But these negotiations reached an impasse after Briscoe unexpectedly took the position that his company, Maxwell, was being undervalued. Ford then insisted that he had to have at least $3,000,000 "in cash," in addition to stock. This set off Ransom E. Olds, who declared that if Ford was to get cash, he wanted an equal amount. [7] Then Ford presented another problem. He would not, he said, agree to subscribe to stock in the International above his merger holdings. Durant summarized the development:

> This was a great surprise and the bankers who were expecting a large subscription from Mr. Ford were quite disappointed . . . Mr. Satterlee was quite put out and, after giving the matter a few moments thought, went back into the other room and very diplomatically stated that there had been a misunderstanding, that the matter of finance was entirely up to the bankers and when they had perfected their plan, another meeting would be called. [8]

The bankers never called another meeting. Durant went ahead to form a merger of his own, which became the General Motors Corporation. [9] And Ford and Couzens returned to Detroit to preside over the birth of the Model T.

4

Then, in September 1909, Ford heard about the adverse Selden patent decision and reacted gloomily. "He was in a very serious frame of mind," said Horace Rackham. Coincidentally, Durant was having trouble with his General Motors Corporation. Acquisition of a "going" property such as the Ford Motor Company would be "a way of getting out of a bad hole." [10] Could the Ford Company be purchased despite the Model T's success? Theodore McManus, the financial writer, told Durant that because of the Selden case it was possible. Later Couzens confirmed this, saying to Durant:

> Mr. Ford is very much concerned about the Selden patent suit and its outcome. The prospects of winning or losing the case are equal. To lose, means the payment of a very large sum of money. He is not a member of the license agreement and, on general principles, has opposed the right of any man to control this patent situation. General Motors, with its several companies holding licenses, would probably be able to make a very satisfactory adjustment with Selden if it owned the Ford Company.[11]

Durant had another talk with Couzens just before Couzens and Ford went to New York to discuss with lawyers the adverse Selden decision. "I told him frankly that the General Motors would like to acquire the Ford Motor Company and asked him if he would talk the matter over with Mr. Ford," said Durant.[12]

It was arranged that Couzens and Durant would see each other again in New York. They did so at the Hotel Belmont on October 5, 1909.[13] Ford did not meet with Durant this time, for he was "sick in body and disturbed in mind," as Couzens later recalled,[14] and he told Couzens to carry on the negotiations. When Couzens and Durant were talking, Ford was lying on the floor of his hotel room, suffering from lumbago.[15]

5

Part of the new proposal was that Couzens would increase his holdings in the Ford Motor Company from 11 to 25 per cent, so that he would own a porportionate share in the new General Motors. For the most part, this was to be Couzens' compensation. Ford was to have his payment in cash. He was to retire entirely from the automobile business, although with the right to engage in making tractors.[16]

Couzens told Durant:

> Mr. Ford will sell the Ford Motor Company for $8,000,000 giving me the privilege of purchasing 25 per cent of the company's stock, which I am prepared to take over, as part compensation for service rendered. The balance of the purchase price, the remaining three-quarters interest of $6,000,000 to be paid for as follows: $2,000,000 cash at the time of the sale, the remaining $4,000,000 at 5 per cent interest due on or before three years. Mr. Ford to have his proportion of the annual profits on the stock which he carries until paid for and delivered.[17]

Couzens then returned to the hotel room and reported on this proposal to Ford. "Tell him he can have it, if the money's all cash!" Ford shouted from the bathroom. "Tell him also, I'll throw in my lumbago!"

"He's gone. He's coming back tomorrow for an answer," said Couzens, adding the question: "You want to let it go for that?" meaning $8,000,000.

"What do you think?" asked Ford.

"I'd say yes," said Couzens.

"If we get cash," Ford said.

"Cash, or the answer is 'no,'" agreed Couzens.[18]

But later a part-cash, part-notes proposal was agreed upon.[19]

Durant received a written option for the Ford Company.[20] On Sunday, October 24, 1909, both Ford and Couzens met Durant secretly at the Ford plant to check the inventory.[21] Two days later the General Motors board of directors formally ratified the purchase agreement.[22] All that remained was for Durant to raise $2,000,000. Frank A. Vanderlip, president of the National City Bank, agreed to get the money for him. But when the loan committee of the bank vetoed Vanderlip's plan, Durant failed to act upon the option.[23] And the Ford Motor Company was again saved by bankers, although somewhat obliquely.

6

The question may be asked: Aside from his concern over the Selden matter, what was troubling Ford so profoundly that he would have abdicated? Undoubtedly some of the explanation is to be found in the peculiar status Ford then held in his own company.

Until the success of the Model T, the Ford Motor Company was really more Couzens than Ford. The important aspects of the company were business, sales, and financial matters. Not until after the Model T came out did production matters begin to come to the fore. It was no wonder that Ford spent little time in the office that went with his title of "president." There was little for him to do there. One executive of those days remembered only one occasion when Ford spent many hours in his office. Ford was toying with the idea of preparing a book, and was dictating his ideas to a stenographer. The subject was birds.[24]

7

Couzens was no better satisfied with his own role in the company. His association with the Ford Company, rich as it had made him, had become a source of frustration, for the Ford Company would always be just that—"the Ford Company" and not "the Couzens Company"—no matter how important he was within it.

In view of Couzens' whole temperament it is plain that this was becoming emotionally intolerable. His frustration was apparent in his resistance to letting himself mellow in disposition. He was still much the way he had been as a boy in Chatham and as the young freight clerk at the Michigan Central—assertive, often testy, and aloof. When some acquaintances from Chatham came to visit him at the Ford plant and greeted him as "Jim," he turned a cold stare upon them. "They call me Mr. Couzens around here," he said.

When Cyril Arthur Player, then a Seattle newspaperman, approached him at a hotel to get material for a story that would help publicize the Ford Company, Couzens snubbed him: "Newspapermen! Nothing to say!" In the Ford office one night with T. J. Hay of Chicago, he embarrassed a clerk by saying: "See that gentleman there—the only man in the organization who can't get his work done when it should be done, in the daytime!"[25]

A dealer in Denver, thinking Couzens would be pleased, wrote that he was preparing a certain report at night, and in longhand, in order to get it in on time. His response was a curt note: "You should get your work done on time and have your letters typed. We haven't time to read letters written in longhand."[26]

No wonder that nearly everyone in the organization trembled at the message: "Mr. Couzens wants to see you."[27]

His testiness, especially with representatives of suppliers who called on him to sell goods to the Ford Company—and invariably failed to get orders by the conventional salesman's flattery and "good-fellowship"—became proverbial and gave rise to numerous stories, some true, some apocryphal. One of the more famous of these tales concerned his reaction to jokes about the Model T. It was said that when the *Detroit News* devoted an article to these jokes, Couzens sent the editor a letter saying: "Sir: I hereby forbid you ever again to mention the name of the Ford Motor Company in your publication" and withdrew all advertising from the paper, an order which Henry Ford later cancelled.[28] This story, circulated for years, was generally accepted as a true reflection of Couzens' temperament, though it never happened.

Clearly, Couzens was not a happy man. On the contrary, he was a profoundly discontented man—an unhappy multimillionaire.

8

On top of whatever ailed him temperamentally, he began to be concerned about the possible bad effect of his wealth, a worry resulting as much as anything from a reawakening of a social conscience, although he had not revealed this much since the days of Pingree. Except for his admiration of Wanamaker, he seemed to have suppressed this conscience while engaged in making a success of the Ford Company. Now it was coming to the surface.

There was a revealing occasion in this connection when his daughter Madeleine happened to read an article in a newspaper about his and Ford's suddenly developed fortunes. "Whew, that's a lot of money we have!" He answered her solemnly: "But it doesn't belong to us. . . . It's a trust. It's a responsibility, and a tough one." [29] He really believed this, though the idea would have shocked a good many of his business friends.

He kept his children on modest allowances. Both he and Mrs. Couzens deliberately conditioned them to avoid any conspicuous display of wealth. "I am always annoyed at any sort of display and have fought against that for years," he told them.

He took seriously, more than ever, the duties of fatherhood. "It does not pay to waive all discipline because then no character is developed. Resistance to temptation is developed by discipline." [30] Hewing to that line, he was more stern as the children approached their 'teens than he really wished to be, even with the handsome older boy, Homer, whom he doted upon particularly. He once apologized for this. "I am not very demonstrative," he wrote, "but

I think and keep on thinking of you, and I am perhaps more concerned or interested than a parent who is more demonstrative. . . ." [31]

He strove to build in his children a large measure of emotional
self-discipline. To Madeleine he once wrote a revealing letter:

> The measure of your happiness will depend largely on how you
> show yourself outwardly. To surrender to every trial or disappoint-
> ment only weakens your resistance and drives friends and sym-
> pathizers to the position of unconsciously hindering your recovery
> rather than aiding it. Your outward cheerfulness will help you and
> help your friends to help you. So buck up, and be my dear little
> Pal and chum again. . . .[32]

But he himself found it hard to "buck up" under the discontent
that gnawed at him. He was able to deaden his discontent somewhat by continuing to drive himself almost savagely in work. Work
was both a medicine to him and a drug. "I am never happier," he
once said, "than when I am working at top notch, and the only
reason I let down at all is to be able to work at top notch the majority
of the year." [33] However, by 1913 he faced a crisis in his discontent
so acute that even this medicine failed. To a large extent, this crisis
was precipitated by a drastic change in his relationship with Ford.

9

In the earlier years, he and Ford had been inseparable companions.
Not only had they worked together harmoniously, but there was also
a certain display of friendship between their families. "Henry Ford
submitted to me in everything as far as the business, sales, and
finances were concerned. . . . He was the most perfect working
companion I have ever known," Couzens once recalled.[34] But after
the golden flood of profits had set in, Ford was no longer "the perfect working companion."

No longer did the two "partners" see as much of each other as
they had in the past. As early as October 1912 Couzens informed a
dealer in England, who had inquired about Ford, "I have not been
able to visit with Mr. Ford very much . . . but I hope and believe
he had a most excellent time this summer." [35] In view of their former
close companionship, this comment and the almost impersonal
manner in which it was made certainly struck a new note. The fact
is, the "partners" did not wish to see much of each other any more.

They were beginning to rub each other the wrong way.[36] The same thing was happening that had happened with Malcomson.

Couzens' temperament, notably his desire for independence and achievement, was, of course, one root cause. But in the main, what had happened was that Ford no longer "submitted" to Couzens in everything. Ford had worked through his own discontent by determining to be more aggressive in the company. He shoved aside thoughts of retiring. To Garet Garrett, Ford made a significant remark: "I own fifty-eight per cent of the stock, and I can do with the company what I like, can't I?" [37]

Also, there was the impact on Ford of the success of the Model T. In view of the way the company had leaped ahead once the Model T took hold, Ford could hardly be blamed if he believed that it was his Model T alone that had made the company. In the words of Allan Nevins, "Success had given him a feeling that he was almost infallible." [38] Besides, Ford was never as disinterested in business affairs as he had let on. He had his own ideas about how a business should be operated, as he had demonstrated back in the days of the Detroit Automobile Company.

Of course, many of Ford's ideas could not be put into practice unless plenty of money were available. By 1913 the company had more money than it knew what to do with. There was no longer any reason for Ford to hold back in expressing his ideas or insisting that they be put into effect. He now encroached at times even on Couzens' domain. With increasing frequency there now occurred such incidents as this: The manufacturer who supplied many of the wheels for Ford cars came to Couzens for renewal of his contract. Couzens declined to renew unless the price were lowered. Ordinarily that would have ended the matter, but the manufacturer went to Ford, and Ford signed the contract himself.[39] Couzens was angered. The period of "See Mr. Couzens" obviously was over.

Ford also had shed the apparent meekness that had attracted Couzens in their earlier association. He was now almost as symbolically authoritarian, in Couzens' eyes, as had been the bearded school principal in Chatham, and as had been both his father and Malcomson. When this would become absolutely clear to Couzens, the outcome could be predicted.

There was as well another force at work. Mrs. Ford, "The Great Believer," as Ford called his wife, had begun to dislike Couzens. Possibly this was merely the reflection of a loyal wife's defense of her husband's good qualities. In any event, there is evidence that Mrs. Ford began to resent Couzens' assumed influence over her husband and also the general publicity to the effect that Couzens was the "man behind Ford." Couzens said that he knew of the talk against him at the Ford home.[40]

In short, many cars had flowed from the Ford plant since that June evening both had ridden home in Ford's tiller-steered runabout and talked of what salaries they would get from "those fellows."

10

Still another change in their relationship occurred. Ford had taken to scoffing at the importance of the financial and sales end of the business. All that was necessary, Ford felt, was to keep lowering the price of the car, and sales and management would take care of themselves. He began vetoing carefully worked-out sales and promotion campaigns that Couzens had approved. In talks with associates, he even belittled Couzens' contribution.[41]

Once Ford became indignant when he was asked by an employee to sign a printed form as a receipt for some item he had requested. The form was part of a system that had been installed with Couzens' approval. Ford asked to be shown all of the forms on hand, took them into the yard of the plant, poured gasoline on them, and burned them.[42] Whether Ford realized it or not, this act bespoke contempt for much of Couzens' role in the company.

For his part, Couzens began to lose much of the respect that he had had for some of Ford's mental processes. He continued to recognize Ford's indisputable shrewdness and the validity of Ford's "common sense" judgments on many things, especially on mass production. But he found himself shocked by certain points of view taken by Ford, like Ford's anti-Semitism and such absurd statements as: "If you will study the history of almost any criminal, you will find he is an inveterate cigarette smoker."

One of Couzens' first real jolts came over the way Ford reacted when Walter Flanders resigned as production superintendent to join the competing E-M-F Automobile Company across the street and subsequently "raided" the Ford Company for personnel.

"If you say the word, I will have his head knocked off," said Ford.

"What do you mean?"

"Oh, I have a couple of fellows who will beat him up."

"Oh, no," said the shocked Couzens. "We will stand this without that." [43]

This incident set Couzens to "thinking" about Ford. He concluded: "Mr. Ford was not one man, but two men." [44]

As early as 1907, Couzens had received a jolt of another kind, as later he had reason to recall. He had told Ford of the trouble the company had obtaining sufficient currency because of the business panic that year. A few days later, Ford announced a solution: "I am going to build a vault and take our money out of the banks and put it in the vault, so that we can pay our men in cash without having all this trouble with currency." Couzens said to him, "But this money is not in the banks! You can not think that money is in the banks?"

"Certainly it is there," replied Ford.

Even after Couzens gave Ford a painstaking explanation of the credit system, he felt that Ford still wanted to try out his scheme "even if it would wreck the country if everyone followed suit." [45]

On at least one occasion, Couzens delivered a lecture to Ford for certain of his public utterances: "Look here! You are in a very prominent position. You should think over some of these things before saying them!" Ford did not like that.

"Mr. Ford does not want to be influenced or argued with. He wants to tell people what to do and have them do it," Couzens later said.[46]

II

Something even more important happened to Couzens in 1913. He had passed forty, and apparently had come to a kind of climacteric in his life, a change for which, as yet, he possessed no adequate philosophy. All of a sudden, the foundations of his very existence seemed to drop out from under him. Until now, his existence had meant the struggle to establish himself economically. By 1913 he suddenly realized that this struggle was over. Psychologically, nothing could be more devastating to the ambitious man. It was like going blind—or suddenly seeing for the first time. Like many another businessman, he had measured the worth of the struggle by money, and now it dawned on him that he had all the money that he wanted.

"You know," he said later, "there comes a time when the fun of making money is all gone. Say what you will, every man deep in his heart must acknowledge that. . . . The battle is won; the goal is achieved; it is time for something else." [47]

The idea of continuing to devote himself merely to making more money began to produce in Couzens "a kind of nausea." [48] The recognition struck him with shattering force that there could be something more important in the world than producing Ford cars— or dollars.

12

If not more money, what, then, did he want? He wanted—indeed, he needed—the constant sense of achievement. This was central with him, and it was being denied him.

The conviction tormented him that everything ahead for him in the Ford Company would be repetitious. Ironically, he, the general manager, was in the same position as the mechanic in the plant who spent his days endlessly turning "Bolt No. 2" on the monotonous assembly line.

The years of climbing had been stimulating. The Selden fight had been a challenge. The establishment of agencies all over the world had been exciting and broadening. But from the way the company was going in 1913, he found himself believing that almost anyone could direct it without anything serious going wrong. In this, of course, he was right. The framework of the Ford Motor Company had been solidly built.[49] As its later history was to demonstrate, only a major catastrophe could wreck it, or keep it from growing still larger, if only from its own momentum. The Ford Company could even climb back to first place in production and sales, as in the 1950's, after having slipped far down in the 1930's, and do this despite the great resources of the giant that General Motors had become after Durant lost it.

As Couzens pondered the solidity of the company, he concluded that for him to stay on would mean accentuation of the trouble between himself and Ford, which he would regret. It would also mean something just as unpleasant—a coasting on past achievement, which could only heighten his feelings of frustration. "I seemed to have no interest in life for awhile," he said. "I had achieved what I started out to do." [50]

CHAPTER XIII

THE FIVE-DOLLAR-A-DAY PLAN

REALIZATION that he faced a crisis in his life plunged him into a state of self-examination, doubt, discontent, and indecision. He was at a dead end. He had to give his life a new purpose, or throw the balance of it away in dissipation, in absorption in trivialities, or in activity that bored him. He suffered from sleepless nights, and complained of not feeling well. His doctor recommended that he go away for a rest.[1] He knew, however, that his trouble was not merely physical. "Be assured," he wrote to a friend, "that when you see me you will think there is nothing on earth the matter with me, that I am only four-flushing." [2]

His trouble was really a result of inner conflict which could be cured only by making a decision. In July 1913 he took the first tentative step:

"Notified Mr. Ford of my desire to resign, have office downtown, or have year's absence." [3]

Thus did he record in his little notebook the fact that a new James Couzens was ready to emerge. His money-making period was nearly over. No longer could he tolerate a career that was in such contradiction to his primary personality trait—a desire for independence. He had to be James Couzens—not merely Couzens of the Ford Motor Company.

2

He certainly felt, although often tentatively, that he had to separate himself from Ford, especially since Ford, who was also apparently going through some kind of climacteric, continued to conduct himself in ways that depressed Couzens. For example, in 1912 Ford had reacted violently on his return from Europe to finding that C. Harold Wills and others in the plant had put together an improved Model T. They had worked up a model with longer and lower lines—almost streamlined—apparently thinking that Ford would be pleased. Instead, Ford went into a rage, ordered the car taken outside, and he "himself helped knock it to pieces." [4]

Among other things, this incident showed that Ford's *real* trouble was that he could not bear having anyone beside himself play a part in the design of the car that bore his name—not even when they improved it. The Ford had to be *his* and his alone, and so must the company—an attitude that inevitably led to antagonism, if still largely suppressed, toward Couzens.

Couzens sensed Ford's personal problem and there were times when he went far out of his way to cater to him. Thus, not long after Ford had gone into his rage over the improved Model T, Couzens became involved, for Ford's sake, in a heated controversy with young Roy D. Chapin, president of the Hudson Motor Car Company. In the September 28, 1912, issue of the *Saturday Evening Post*, the Hudson company had published a double-page advertisement which stated, among other things, that its Howard E. Coffin was "the foremost engineer in the industry." This was certainly a harmless puff, the sort of claim Couzens would ordinarily have ignored. But instead of ignoring it, Couzens sent Chapin one of his characteristically blunt letters, demanding "to know" how Hudson could claim Coffin to be "America's foremost automobile designer" whereas "I have learned from many sources which are considered reliable, and which I think you will admit are reliable, that Mr. Ford is considered 'America's foremost automobile designer.'" [5] This led to an acidulous exchange of letters that merely added to Couzens' reputation for cantankerousness. But, obviously, his real motive had been to please Henry Ford.

At times Ford was appeased, but not permanently.

3

Two events made Couzens postpone action on his decision. First, the Dodges, also distressed by Ford, had served notice that they planned to bring out their own car, the Dodge, and that they would cease making parts for the Ford Motor Company. This produced a crisis for the Ford Company. Out of loyalty, Couzens decided he should stay on. Then, while he was talking this matter over with Ford, Couzens was offered an interesting assignment. At the suggestion of John Dodge, Mayor Oscar B. Marx of Detroit asked him to accept the chairmanship of the Detroit Street Railway Commission, only recently created by the city to attain, at last, Hazen

Pingree's goal of municipal ownership of the streetcar lines.[6] Couzens jumped at this opportunity, and soon became so engrossed in the municipal streetcar problem that he began to feel that he could solve his discontent without leaving the Ford Motor Company.

By sheer aggressiveness, he scored a dramatic victory over the streetcar corporation. When the corporation refused to settle a dispute with the city over fares, he issued an ultimatum: "If you do not take this proposition, we will stop your cars and I will supply one thousand Ford automobiles to replace the service." The corporation gave in.[7]

As a result, when the year 1914 opened, Couzens seemed more settled in the Ford Company than ever before, for he had also become vice-president, the post that John Dodge had given up.

4

He was not, however, the same Couzens. As he groped for a way to give his life a new direction, he began obviously to look at the Ford Motor Company from a different perspective. Up to then, the company had been merely a money-making machine. In Calvin Coolidge's phrase, its "business was business," and nothing more. Now Couzens began to view the company as a possible social instrument, particularly in regard to "the labor problem." Not for some years had he given much thought to his youthful ideas about wages and the general position of the workingman. Now those ideas occupied much of his thinking.

At his clubs, he began to get the reputation of an "argumentive fellow" on economic subjects, for he questioned the ideas then common among successful businessmen. In part, he was bent on deflating some swollen egos. It pleased him to tell other wealthy manufacturers bluntly that they were "successful," not because of "superior brains," but because of a direct, or indirect, government subsidy, or because their labor was "sweated."[8]

In May 1911 as a member of a committee of the Detroit Board of Commerce, he went to Washington to testify on the effects of the Payne-Aldrich Tariff Act. He was for revising it downward. So unorthodox was his testimony that Oswald Garrison Villard, editor of the liberal *Nation*, hunted him up at the New York automobile show shortly afterwards "to see what kind of a freak he was."[9] Couzens, co-head of the great Ford enterprise, had taken a position on a great and controversial public issue that, surprisingly, was the same one taken by Senator Robert M. La Follette of Wisconsin,

Louis D. Brandeis and other outstanding progressives and liberals of the period.[10]

5

In one major respect, however, Couzens was not yet unorthodox at all. Wage rates were no higher at the Ford plant than at any other automobile plant. Indeed, for certain skills, they were even lower at Ford's, where janitors were paid as little as seventeen cents an hour.

In 1911 he did not question the prevailing idea at the Ford plant that workers should be obtained for the lowest possible wage rates. But by 1913 he began to examine the concept—in this way responding to the temper of the times.

Woodrow Wilson, who had just been elected President, talked of "the new freedom" and "industrial democracy." William Jennings Bryan, still a symbol of revolt for "radical" Democrats in the 'nineties, was in Wilson's cabinet. Many businessmen were dismayed. On the inauguration of Wilson, John Wanamaker gloomily wrote in his diary: "The first entry under the reign of a Democratic president . . . I am unpatriotic enough to want a habitation in Sicily or Italy for the next four years!" [11]

But Couzens was interested in the Wilsonian reforms, even sympathetic. He had not voted for Wilson; he had supported the Bull Moose candidacies of Theodore Roosevelt and Hiram Johnson. Now, as president of the Board of Commerce, he invited Bryan to make an address to the board on "The New Era." Through him, too, Miss Jane Addams, of Chicago's Hull House, appeared as a Board of Commerce speaker.[12]

He read crusading, or "muckraking," magazines like *Everybody's* and *Collier's*, which exposed the methods of the "trusts," and while he read them, he remembered the Selden patent fight, a personal symbol of his opposition to monopoly. He began subjecting all businessmen, especially the most publicized, like Rockefeller, to critical scrutiny.

6

His real awakening was emotional. During the winter of 1913 the Ford Company ordered some temporary layoffs of factory workers. He knew that the vast majority of laid-off men could not have any savings. "All winter," he recalled, "I sat in my office on the second floor of the Ford Building and every time I looked out the window,

I saw a sea of faces looking up. There were men shivering in the cold with their coat collars turned up." This sight haunted him, he later said.

Another incident occurred that especially distressed him. A crowd of jobless men had stormed the Ford employment office, and the police had turned a fire hose on them although they were already shivering from the cold.[13] He was upset for several days afterwards. In addition, I.W.W. organizers, seeking to unionize the Ford workers, were saying things about the Ford management that troubled him, albeit he "wanted no truck" at this time either with the I.W.W. or even with milder forms of unionism.[14]

He discussed with Ford the idea of instituting a pension plan. He later said that this occurred to him because of a sentimental interest in an old man to whom he had given a job in the stationery-supplies office a few years back. This man, named Bruce, once a schoolteacher in Chatham, had begged for the job at the Ford plant after having been forced to retire as a teacher. Now, in 1913, Bruce was hobbling around as a watchman, but really was too infirm to work at any job. Couzens was on the point of ordering a pension for the former teacher. Then he rejected the whole idea as being contrary to his own concept of independence.[15]

Ida Tarbell came to the plant at just this time to gather material for a book. Couzens discussed his notion of Bruce's pension with her. "He says that he thinks it degrading . . . but he also said that something had to be done," Miss Tarbell wrote. "His idea was that the solution should be something which would enable the man to take care of himself. He said: 'We have no right in this country to allow conditions that make pensions necessary. I hate the word.' "[16]

If not a pension, what then? Profit-sharing, or higher wages, or both? He did not know. But he was sure that employers, including himself, owed a greater duty to their workers than they had accepted. In his conversations, he dwelt especially upon the influence of luck in the economic fate of individuals. He felt keenly that "time and chance" had been important in his own case, that it was accident that brought him into contact with Malcomson, and also with Ford. He recalled his married life, his wife's illness, and the death of their first child, and found himself identifying himself with workers in economic trouble. People who considered him "cold" and "unfeeling" would have found this hard to believe, but this is the sort of man he was becoming.[17]

7

At the Ford factory, meanwhile, certain practical, economic facts were being explored. The most acute problem of the company was how to increase productivity without increasing unit costs. The famous assembly line had been installed, but this by itself failed to provide a complete solution.[18] It dawned on certain Ford executives that something had to be done to "improve" labor, as well. They observed that the workers resisted the speed-up. All too often, Ford workers quit for other jobs, just after they had been well broken-in. Quite a large number were discharged by foremen. The result was an enormous—and costly—turnover in the labor force.[19]

This turnover was first spotlighted by a lawyer who had been told to "look around and see what he could do" about improving efficiency. After noticing how often men were being hired and fired, the lawyer began studying the factory payrolls. In telling of his findings, Ida Tarbell recorded:

> At the end of three months he had some figures. The manager of the factory said they couldn't be true. One day, Mr. Couzens asked the lawyer what he was doing, and he showed him the figures. They were alarming enough to startle even a stand-pat manufacturer—to a man like Mr. Couzens . . . , they were a shock and a condemnation. They showed that to keep a force of 12,000 men, Ford's was hiring 60,000 a year. What did it mean? How could it be corrected? . . .[20]

Couzens issued a revolutionary order as a result of the report. Foremen were to be stripped of their authority to fire. No employee anywhere in the company was to be discharged unless Couzens or Ford approved. Even then, no employee was to be fired until he was tried out in some other department, since it had been discovered that many men applied for jobs for which they had no training. "They, of course, say they can do anything. . . . Anyone of us would do the same if we were out of a job," Couzens told Miss Tarbell.[21] Wage studies were then made to "classify" labor according to various skills, with varying rates. As a result, wages were raised 15 per cent. More studies were made and another revolutionary step was taken. The working day was reduced from ten hours to nine.

Conditions improved—but not enough.

8

One evening near Christmas in 1913, Couzens was at home reading a magazine "of socialist tendencies," as he described it—probably it was *Everybody's*. He came across an editorial item that seemed to have a bearing on the labor problem at the Ford plant. The editor was commenting on a letter from a reader who had asked why, "if it believed in socialism, the magazine did not practice what it preached in its own affairs." The editor answered that progress had to be universal, that until everyone changed, a single person or company could not change and survive. "That," said Couzens, in telling Miss Tarbell about it, "was an asinine answer!" [22]

To B. C. Forbes, Couzens himself told what followed. Forbes wrote:

> An idea flashed through his head. Why shouldn't the Ford Motor Company take a decided lead in paying the highest wages to its workers, thus enabling them to enjoy better living conditions? The company was making money hand over fist and could, therefore, afford to do something worthwhile.[23]

The next morning Couzens told Henry Ford that the basic minimum wage at the Ford plant should be five dollars a day. He decided on five dollars because "it's a good round number," he told Ida Tarbell.[24]

9

Ford raised objections. "We pay as much as anyone pays," he said.

"But we're responsible for those men," Couzens said, pointing to the men outside looking for jobs, "because we don't pay them enough to live on. . . . We should give our people wages that permit them to save against the time when we have no work for them." [25]

Couzens mentioned to Ford the incident of the fire hose. "Do you know that a Russian woman, an anarchist, has been talking to those unemployed men and advocating that you be assassinated?" [26] He also pointed out to Ford that the I.W.W. had been making efforts to "organize" the Ford plant. "Do we want a union to tell us what to do?" he asked.

He recalled to Ford their talks about pensions and the difficulty workers had in surviving periods of unemployment. The solution, he said, was to pay the workers enough so that they could "accumulate something for hard times." [27] "We should raise the minimum for all employees to five dollars a day and charge the difference to our profit account." [28]

10

Ford continued to object, but Couzens renewed his arguments. Then he put the whole matter to Ford in the form of a dare. Ford

answered that he did not take dares.[29] But Ford did consult his
production assistants, including Peter Martin, the general superintendent. They could not see the point of an increase as large as
Couzens proposed. Rather, they thought of increases in terms of
"twenty-five cents" or "fifty cents." [30] In this connection, Theodore
McManus, in his authoritative *Men, Money and Motors* [31] wrote that
Ford came back to Couzens with the following argument: "Martin
says he is willing to pay three dollars a day. That five dollars a day
will cause trouble. That other firms . . ."

"I know how Martin thinks," interrupted Couzens. "He thinks
if we pay five dollars a day it will cause a general disturbance in the
labor market. That we will be flooded with requests for jobs. What
if it does? And, what if we are? We'll get the pick of the workmen
and you know, as well as I do, that a good workman is worth five
dollars a day.

"You and I have talked this over enough—not this plan, exactly,
but some similar plan—and each of us realizes that the division of
our earnings between capital and labor is unequal and that we ought
to do something in the way of relief that is suitable for others. You,
yourself, have often said that is what we should do."

"Well," Ford said, "I'll go back and talk with Martin."

Couzens pressed for a decision. He knew, he said later, that if
he didn't get Ford to consent at that time, he would probably never
be able to get the plan through. "If we talk of anything more than
forty-eight hours, we never do it." [32]

Ford came back next with the suggestion that minimum wages
for everyone be increased to three dollars and fifty cents a day.

"No, it's five or nothing," said Couzens.

"Then make it four," said Ford, adding that Martin would agree
to that.

"No," insisted Couzens, "five or nothing." [33]

And then, Couzens added: "A straight five-dollar wage will be the
greatest advertisement any automobile concern ever had."

As E. G. Pipp (to whom Ford told this) stated: "Couzens did not
have to say that twice to Ford." [34]

II

At just this juncture, Horace Rackham came into the office. "The
three of us make a quorum," Couzens said. "Let us consider this a
meeting." [35]

The results are in the Ford Company minutes:

Present: Henry Ford, H. H. Rackham, James Couzens. It was stated by the officers that a plan of better equalizing the company's earnings between the stockholders and the labor of the company be inaugurated. The plan was gone over at considerable length, but briefly it carried with it, in addition to wages, sums to make the minimum income of all men over 22 years of age $5.00 for eight hours work, and that other increases were to be made to men getting above the minimum wage, to maintain the same rate between the minimum, intermediate, and maximum wages.

After considerable discussion, it was moved by Director Rackham, and supported by Director Couzens, that such a plan be put into force as of January 12, 1914, which plan, it was distinctly understood, would approximate an additional expenditure for the same volume of business of $10,000,000 for the year 1914. Carried unanimously.[36]

12

It was Couzens, about this time described by a visiting writer as a man with "the keen, 'unwinking' blue eyes of the old gladiator," [37] who made the announcement to the press. The following April, in *Everybody's* magazine, Garet Garrett put down his version of the scene: "Henry Ford was there, with an air of restless detachment from the business at hand, and stood silently by a window [in Couzens' office], while Mr. Couzens read the statement he wished the reporters to publish." [38]

The statement was an oddity because of the way it reflected an obvious effort to divide credit for the plan evenly between Couzens and Ford.

It was also the best description ever made of the famous wage plan, which, because it doubled wage rates at one stroke in a great factory, was indisputably one of the major events of the era, both in its immediate and in its later impact upon the economic structure of America. His statement was:

> The Ford Motor Company, the greatest and most successful automobile manufacturing company in the world, will, on January 12, inaugurate the greatest revolution in the matter of rewards for its workers ever known to the industrial world.
>
> At one stroke it will reduce the hours of labor from nine to eight, and add to every man's pay a share of the profits of the house. The smallest amount to be received by any man 22 years old and upwards will be $5.00 per day. The minimum wage is now $2.34 per day of nine hours.
>
> All but 10 per cent of the employees will at once share in the profits. Only 10 per cent of the men now employed are under 22, and even every one of those under 22 will have a chance of showing himself entitled to $5.00 per day.

Instead of waiting until the end of the year to make a distribution of profits among their employees in one lump bonus sum, Mr. Ford and Mr. Couzens have estimated the year's prospective business and have decided upon what they feel will be a safe amount to award the workers. This will be spread over the whole year and paid on the regular semi-monthly pay days.

The factory is now working two shifts of nine hours each. This will be changed to three shifts of eight hours each. The number employed is now about 15,000 and this will be increased by 4,000 or 5,000. The men who now earn $2.34 per day of nine hours will get at least $5.00 per day of eight hours.

This will apply to every man of 22 years of age or upward without regard to the nature of his employment. In order that the young man, from 18 to 22 years of age, may be entitled to a share in the profits he must show himself sober, saving, steady, industrious, and must satisfy the superintendent and staff that his money will not be wasted in riotous living.

Young men who are supporting families, widowed mothers, younger brothers and sisters, will be treated like those over 22.

It is estimated that over $10,000,000 will be thus distributed over and above the regular wages of the men.

"The commonest laborer, who sweeps the floor, shall receive his $5.00 per day," said Henry Ford.

"It is our belief," said James Couzens, "that social justice begins at home. We want those who have helped us to produce this great institution and who are helping to maintain it to share our prosperity. We want them to have present profits and future prospects. Thrift and good service and sobriety all will be encouraged and recognized."

"If we are obliged," said Mr. Ford, "to lay off men for want of sufficient work at any season, we propose to so plan our year's work that the lay-off shall be in the harvest time; July, August, and September, not in the winter. We hope, in such case, to induce our men to respond to the calls of the farmers for harvest hands and not to lie idle and dissipate their savings. We shall make it our business to get in touch with the farmers and to induce our employees to answer calls for harvest help.

"No man will be discharged if we can help it, except for unfaithfulness or inefficiency. No foreman in the company has the power to discharge a man. He may send them out of his department if they do not make good. The man is then sent to our clearing house, covering all the departments, and is again repeatedly tried in other work until we find the job he is suited for, provided he is honestly trying to render good service."

"We shall still pay," Mr. Couzens said, "we are quite sure, good, handsome dividends to our stockholders, and will set aside reasonable amounts for additions and improvements and assembling plants in other parts of the country. And after that it is our hope to be able to do still better by our employees. We want them to be in reality partners in our enterprise.

"Believing as we do, that a division of our earnings between capital and labor is unequal, we have sought a plan of relief suitable to our business. We do not feel sure that it is the best, but we have felt impelled to make a start and make it now. We do not agree with those employers who declare, as did a recent writer in a magazine, in excusing himself for not practicing what he preached, that the movement toward the bettering of society must be universal. We think that one concern can make a start and create an example for others. And that is our chief object.

"The public need have no fear that this action of ours will result in any increase in prices of our products. On the contrary we hope to keep up our past record of reducing prices each year.

"We may have to make changes in our plan. If hard times should befall us we may have to reduce or modify our distribution of profits. But the outlook now is such as to justify this distribution for the present year."

"We believe," said Mr. Ford, "in making 20,000 men prosperous and contented rather than follow the plan of making a few slave drivers in our establishment multi-millionaires."

13

The appeal of the plan to workers—not to mention social reformers—was instantaneous. Mechanics from all over America streamed to the Ford factory for jobs. The employment office was swamped.

It developed later that the wage plan included some naive, although well-intentioned, interference in the lives of the Ford workers, such as the following:

Employees should use plenty of soap and water in the home, and upon their children, bathing frequently. Nothing makes for right living and health so much as cleanliness. Notice that the most advanced people are the cleanest. . . .

Improved garbage cans, of which there are several good types available, should be used. The can should be covered at all times, especially during the summer time. . . .

From 12 years of age to 18 is especially a time when (children) should be guarded well, and not allowed to contract habits and vices injurious to their welfare and health. . . .

Do not spit on the floor in the home. . . .

A double purpose is served under the profit-sharing plan. First, to provide money for future needs; second, to foster self-control. The second is the more important of the two, because, having that, the first is quite assured. . . .

> Avoid, as much as possible, making purchases upon the install-
> ment plan. . . .
> A good understanding should be had between husband and wife
> as to expenditures and savings. . . .
> Cases have been brought to the company's attention indicating
> that some young men, in order to qualify as profit-sharers, have
> hastily married without giving serious thought to such an impor-
> tant step in their lives. Seldom does such a marriage prove a happy
> one. If they would give more thought to the uncertainty of business
> affairs and the certainty of the obligations and responsibilities as-
> sumed in the marriage vows, there would be less work for the divorce
> courts. . . .[39]

The company sent investigators to the homes of the workers to see
how their beds were made, check their bank accounts, and advise
them on their most intimate affairs. This, of course, was paternal-
ism.[40] Couzens deplored this later, although at the time he defended it as "simply an effort to show our people how to take care of
their money, how to live and how to get the best out of the increase."[41] He knew the plan "paid off" for the company. He quoted
with approval a Ford worker: "I work for what I get. When I get
three dollars a day and work ten hours, I make 300 bolts. Now, when
I get five dollars a day and work eight hours, I make 900 bolts."[42]

14

Ford at the time received all the credit. The reason for this was
explained by Couzens himself:

> It was quite natural that Mr. Ford should be credited with this
> project because he was the head of the company, a majority stock-
> holder, and it was to the benefit of the Ford Motor Company that
> he should be credited with it; because it gave it a personal touch
> which was greatly beneficial in an advertising way and kept the
> name Ford much more before the public, and this is great adver-
> tising. . . .[43]

In 1915, he bluntly wrote: "When you get down to the wage
scheme which we started at the Ford Motor Company, I will say that
I, personally, am responsible for it."[44]

It is significant that Ford never claimed, over his signature, that
the wage idea was his. He certainly played his part. As Couzens
frequently said, the wage plan could not have gone into effect without Ford's approval, but Couzens was its sponsor.[45]

CHAPTER XIV

_____

THE FINAL BREAK

THE wage plan proved a good temporary palliative for the tension
between Couzens and Ford. Ford enjoyed being interviewed for
magazines, newspapers, even books. Both Couzens and he obtained
pleasurable excitement from watching how the paternalistic side
of the plan worked, and eagerly followed reports on what was being
done to make certain that the workers "deserved the big envelope."

While Couzens was in California, a glowing report on this aspect
of the plan was sent to him by Klingensmith, now his assistant. "I
wish you could be here [Klingensmith wrote] just to see the enthusiasm among the investigators on this welfare work. . . . You need
have no fear that this branch of this work which you started will have
the very best of attention. . . . Mr. Ford has been at the office
practically every day . . . and is very enthusiastic over the work
and puts a lot of enthusiasm into the people in realization of the
possibilities of this profit-sharing plan." [1]

Especially was Couzens pleased because his predictions as to the advertising value of the plan were justified. Sales leaped upward. As
a consequence, he pushed expansion plans, particularly those for
Ford assembly plants in other cities. "The plans for Atlanta are
practically completed. The many questions re Pittsburgh are being
worked out. Indianapolis goes out for bids today. They have started
the plans for Cincinnati and have gotten out a preliminary sketch
for Cleveland." So Klingensmith summarized progress.[2]

Once again, Couzens became the busy, absorbed executive. The
attitude of other businessmen had a stimulating effect on him, for
nearly all other American industrialists and financiers denounced
the plan.[3] Garet Garrett recalled:

> The Board of Commerce was in a panic. Smaller manufacturers,
> outside the motor car industry, had been serving notice that they

95

were leaving Detroit, and several of them did. The owner of the
barber shop at the hotel told me that he would have to go out of
business; even barbers would be wanting five dollars a day. . . .[4]

"Consternation" was the word Alfred P. Sloan of General Motors
used to describe the reaction of industrialists generally.[5] The program at Ford, they said, was bound to "disaffect the working class." [6]
The Ford management was described as being in the hands of men
who had lost their minds.[7] Bankers issued instructions to their loan
officers "to watch the credit of 'any customers doing business with
Ford.' " [8]

Couzens became even more interested in seeing it through. "This
is the most interesting subject in the world to me. It is one I can
spend more time and more thought on than any other thing I ever
came in contact with," he told a friend.[9] Indeed, he became a
veritable crusader for a fairer distribution of the profits of industry.

To E. D. Stair, then publisher of the *Detroit Free Press,* he wrote:
"It is my sincere judgment that even if a company made only six
per cent, it should divide three among its employees. This would
follow out to the betterment of all concerned." [10]

2

In the following winter, despite the prosperity at the Ford Company, Detroit was gripped by a severe depression, as a result of the
war abroad. Thousands of men tramped the streets in a vain search
for employment. So serious was the situation that the Board of
Commerce organized a committee on unemployment.

Couzens, who a short time before had been president of the board,
watched this committee with increasing skepticism. Its main purpose,
it seemed to him, was not to find jobs for the men but to direct them
to charity. Three days before Christmas, Couzens strode into a
Board of Commerce meeting to speak his mind—

> You fellows sit back, smug and complacent, and don't give a damn
> what becomes of your workmen.
> You go down to the Board of Estimates and ask for high-pressure
> systems to preserve your plants from fire; you ask for more patrol-
> men to guard your property; but what do you do for your work-
> men? . . . You kick them into the street, and that's all there is
> to it. . . .
> The situation is up to the employers of Detroit. These unem-
> ployed are sent to charity for assistance, when they want work. . . .

It is not the man's fault he has not had enough wages to carry him over a period like this. Many absolutely refuse to line up with those seeking charity. They are a part of commerce just as much as we are. Then what in hell have they to do with charity?

They are just as human as you and I, but they are not as well taken care of. You can't give these men work during the summer and then discharge them in the winter while you take your golf sticks and go to California, and do your full duty. . . .[11]

He incurred the lasting enmity of a good number of Detroit businessmen as a result of that outburst, one that anticipated by forty years the acceptance by the automobile industry, and particularly by the Ford Company under Henry Ford II, of a form of guaranteed annual wage system. The *Detroit Journal* referred to his as a "commercial Savonarola," and what many Detroit businessmen called him was unprintable. But his outburst did provoke the formation of a new committee that obtained jobs for hundreds of unemployed workers.[12]

3

All this eased his relations with Ford. But, again, the easing was only temporary. True, in the fall of 1914, he told newspaper reporters that "perfect harmony" existed in the company. "Sometimes Mr. Ford will drop into my office, as he did this morning, and we will discuss things for an hour or two. Again, we may not see each other for a month. But all of the time every part of the immense organization is running smoothly in its own groove." [13] However, within six months after the wage plan had been put into effect, the old trouble between him and Ford came to the surface again. As put by one Ford biographer, "Relations between Mr. Ford and his general manager became more and more strained." [14] Plainly, all that was needed for a final break to occur was some appropriate "incident."

In August 1914, it appeared that such an incident had occurred. The war in Europe had caused runs on banks and Ford began talking of withdrawing his personal funds from the Highland Park State Bank—Couzens' bank. Couzens assured Ford that his money was safe where it was. Ford seemed to accept that assurance. He agreed not to make a transfer. But he ordered the withdrawal anyway.[15] Couzens flared up, and sent the following telegram:

August 5, 1914

HENRY FORD,

HARBOR BEACH, MICHIGAN

IN THESE STRENUOUS TIMES MEN INVARIABLY SHOW THE KIND OF STUFF
THEY ARE MADE OF. WE ARE MAKING ARRANGEMENTS TO TRANSFER YOUR
MONEY TO THE DIME BANK.

JAMES COUZENS [16]

To his secretary, Henry S. Morgan, Couzens talked about resigning
right then. "You may have to choose soon between continuing with
the Ford Motor Company and staying on with me," he told Morgan.[17]

4

Still the break did not come—this time because of a profound
personal tragedy. On the afternoon of August 8, 1914, he had cut
short a golf game at the Bloomfield Hills Country Club—later he felt
that it was a kind of premonition that caused him to forego the full
eighteen holes—and thus he was at his Wabeek residence in time to
receive a telephone call that sent a chill through him. An automobile
listed as belonging to the Couzens family had overturned on a road
near a small lake close to Wabeek. The driver, a boy, had been
pinned in the water beneath the car. With Margaret, Couzens rushed
to the scene. They found their worst fears confirmed. Their elder
son, Homer, was dead in the Model T Ford they had given to him
on his fourteenth birthday.[18]

That evening, although obviously near the breaking point, Couzens
insisted that the family sit at the dinner table as usual. "We must not
give in to our feelings," he said. Klingensmith called at the house,
and Couzens took him in to see the body. "Wasn't he a fine big boy?
Wasn't he a fine big boy?" he kept repeating. But there were no tears.
He simply refused to let them come.[19]

Yet he was a man distraught, and he remained so for months.
He thought a motor trip would help, and set out on one with the
family, but he soon turned back. Work, endless work, was all that
made any sense to him. So he clung to the Ford Motor Company, regardless of how things stood between himself and Ford.

5

But the break was not to be avoided. Ford had begun issuing various pronouncements on the war and its meaning for the United
States, statements that increasingly irritated Couzens. He would never
permit his factory to produce war material, not even if the United

States was involved, Ford said in one statement. In another: "To my mind, the word 'murderer' should be embroidered in red letters across the breast of every soldier." [20]

Now, Couzens then was also, in a sense, a "peace advocate." In a newspaper interview in October 1915, he said: "Mr. Ford and I are one in our desire for peace. . . . I was born in Canada, but I am absolutely neutral." [21] When William Howard Taft, Hamilton Holt, Alton B. Parker, and others formed a "League to Enforce Peace" Couzens joined and contributed $5,000.[22] So something deeper than just Ford's Peace views was involved.

6

Milton McRae, who was a friend of both men, tried to patch things up. He suggested to Ford that he employ "a public relations counselor," hoping that such a counselor would steer Ford along a different path. Instead, Ford engaged a "peace secretary," a newspaperman, who, with Madame Rosicka Schwimmer, later came up with the plan for his famous "peace ship," the *Oscar II*.[23] On October 11, 1915, there occurred the conversation between Couzens and Brownell about the *Ford Times*. It was followed the next morning by the decisive meeting between Couzens and Ford.

7

Klingensmith described the incident as he saw it develop:

> On the day that Couzens quit, I saw Ford go into Couzens' office, and then come out, and walk down the corridor. A minute later, Couzens called me into his office. "I've just resigned from the Ford Motor Company. There's my resignation, right there."
> His face was red, from anger and agitation. He pointed to a sheet of paper on which he had written his resignation from the Ford Motor Company, to take effect immediately.
> He had written it out in longhand, and given it to Ford, but Ford had left it on Couzens' desk.
> "I decided," said Couzens to me, "that I had had enough of his God damn persecution."
> Then Couzens put on his hat, and walked out of the office. He went downtown and notified a newspaper friend.[24]

The newspaper friend was Jay G. Hayden, then secretary of the Street Railway Commission (later chief of the Washington Bureau of the *Detroit News*.) "About eleven o'clock in the morning," recalled Hayden, "he came busting into the board room. I thought *I* was to be fired. 'I've just resigned from the Ford Company and I want your help,' he said to me.

" 'On what?'

" 'I want to give the story to the papers before Ford does, but I don't want to give it out myself.' "

Hayden then went over to the Book-Cadillac Hotel and called the various newspaper offices.[25]

To Louis B. Block, Ford dealer in Philadelphia, Couzens made an observation that largely explained the whole matter. "A man sometimes gets to the point where his freedom of thought and independence is greater than all else." [26]

8

Years later Couzens learned that Ford had come into his office that morning to provoke his resignation. As Ford himself said to E. P. Pipp, a managing editor of the *Detroit News:*

> It's like this. I have had a check kept on him, and he has been at the plant only 184 days during the past year. He has been in California and now plans to go to Asheville. I don't believe in absentee control. If Jim is on the job, I'd rather have his judgment than anybody else's judgment, but Jim's judgment off the job isn't as good as somebody else's on the job. If a man has a job with us, he must stick to it. . . . I got to thinking about it, stayed home two or three days to figure it out, and came over to the plant to make an issue of it. Jim sprang the thing about the article in the little magazine. Fine, I thought, that's a dandy way out of it, so I stood pat.[27]

All this was merely a rationalization on Ford's part. There never could have been any valid criticism of Couzens on the ground that he was not on the job. If anything, he had worked too hard at it. The truth was that Ford had determined to take over, to deal with Couzens as he had with Alex Malcomson, and the determination had coincided with Couzens' own inevitable decision to be on his own.

BOOK TWO

The New Public Man

CHAPTER XV

THE JOB-SEEKER AGAIN

EVEN after his break with Ford, Couzens remained a director in the company, and continued to take an interest in the "social experiment" in the Ford organization. He continued to make crusading speeches to other businessmen. Before the Windsor (Ontario) Board of Trade, he denounced businessmen who paid low wages to girls and then headed "committees to save women from prostitution." "I have no use," he said, "for the man who works a lot of girls at $3.50 and $4.00 a week, and then puts on a frock coat on Sunday." [1] He had in mind a millionaire merchant who was known for paying low wages to female employees and whom he ordered out of his house when this merchant called on him for a contribution to a home for wayward girls.

He also retained the presidency of the Highland Park State Bank. That activity, his Wabeek farm, his investments, and his post as head of the Detroit Street Railway Commission should have been sufficient to keep him contentedly occupied. Instead, he became restless and fidgety.

It seemed for a time that the Street Railway Commission by itself would provide a cure for what he considered his idleness. During the previous year, in August 1915, he had stirred up the old Pingree municipal ownership issue, informing Jere C. Hutchins, the president of the Detroit Union Railways, that the city should buy the D.U.R. lines. Hutchins had been astounded when Couzens called him on the telephone to make the suggestion. "It has seemed to me that the people are satisfied with conditions as they are!" Hutchins said.

"Not at all!" Couzens said. "What is wanted is municipal ownership. What do you want for the lines?" [2] So he forced the issue—and a municipal election on the question.

2

A referendum on the question was set for the following November. Couzens threw himself into the campaign to get Detroiters to vote in favor of the proposal. Victory would mean a satisfying and ready-made job for him, for he would be the manager of the city-operated streetcar system if the referendum proposal carried. With his own funds he financed the printing of literature that supported the purchase of the system. He directed the lawyers in a fight against an effort to have the referendum barred by a court injunction, one asked for by Clarence Burton, the Detroit historian. "I don't care about the merits of this or any other plan," said Burton. "I want the courts to say that municipal ownership of street railways is illegal and can never be had in this city." [3]

The injunction suit was killed, and the issue went to the voters as scheduled, with Couzens the principal speaker at mass meetings organized behind the proposal. On the whole, his speeches were effective. The spectacle of a multimillionaire arguing for municipal ownership caught the imagination of the city and it seemed the answer to the main argument of the D.U.R., that the plan was "socialistic."

But he had naively committed one serious political error. Shrewd Jere C. Hutchins had refused to set a price on the D.U.R properties. Couzens determined to go ahead with the referendum anyway. If the people voted to buy the lines, the price was to be set later by the judges of the County Court.

Coached by Hutchins, the opposition immediately raised a powerful cry: "Couzens is asking the city to buy a pig in a poke!"

Couzens tried to counter this move by announcing that if the price eventually set by the court was not satisfactory, he, personally, would re-purchase the lines for $40,000,000, higher than any figure the company had ever set on its property. But the "pig in a poke" cry deterred even old-time followers of Pingree from actively supporting him.

Another handicap was a matter with which Couzens himself was not involved—at least not yet. The city administration then admittedly was corrupt. The police department, especially, was notoriously graft-ridden. "Do you want such an administration to run the streetcar lines?" the opposition demanded. Couzens had what sounded like an effective answer. "The opposition tries to befog the issue by talking of graft. Well, speaking of graft, how about private business?

There is more favoritism, more politics, and more graft in private business—and I should know—than in any city government in America. If you can't run your lines and keep out graft, you are a poor lot of citizens. What does the D.U.R. care about you? All they care about is your fares. The streetcar line is by nature a monopoly, and you should own it." [4]

But this argument was not enough. The referendum lost by three thousand votes.[5]

"I'm in a mess," Couzens told Jay Hayden that night. "Now I have to get a job." [6]

The following spring, out of sheer desperation, he organized another bank, the Highland Park State Bank of Detroit (later the Bank of Detroit), and became its president. At first, he was delighted with the new bank. "I never experienced such joy in my life as I did the day of the opening," he told John W. Anderson. But soon he was forced to recognize the bank for what it was—just another money-making machine. He was still looking for a "job," a new career.

3

The streetcar question apart, it seemed inevitable that he would find his career in public affairs. Milton McRae had been urging him for some time to go into politics. Indeed, in 1913 he had advised Couzens to accept the Board of Commerce presidency with that in view.[7] And Couzens clearly was interested even before leaving Ford.

He had set his sights high—on national politics. Thus, after the failure of the streetcar referendum, he "considered" becoming a candidate for United States Senator, and some of the newspapers began printing items to the effect that his wealth made him a natural contender against Senator Charles E. Townsend in 1916.

But he dropped the idea when it became obvious that he could not hope to unseat Townsend. Instead, he served as treasurer of Townsend's re-election campaign.[8] He believed, naively, that this was the way to break into politics.

In that same year, 1916, he dabbled in the preliminaries of the Presidential campaign that developed into the contest between Woodrow Wilson and Charles Evans Hughes. To Charles B. Warren, the Republican National Committeeman, he wrote: "I am keenly interested in the success of the Republican Party this fall." To prove his interest, he sent Warren a four-thousand-dollar check for the party campaign fund.[9] Out of gratitude for this contribution, the party designated him as a Hughes elector, even though he had been active in an unsuccessful boom on behalf of Theodore Roosevelt and had sat conspicuously on the platform at a Detroit meeting for "T.R." He was a delegate to both the state and national Republican conventions, in opposition, incidentally, to a group from Michigan that was booming Henry Ford for the Republican nomination for President.[10]

4

Before voting time, however, it was a local election that became more important to him. Mayor Marx, a Republican, was seeking re-election, and was handicapped by his lax police department. Marx's secretary, Edward T. Fitzgerald, called on Couzens to ask him if he would be interested in becoming commissioner of police.[11] The political strategy was obvious: If Couzens became Commissioner of Police, the Marx regime could be salvaged.

"It came to me like a flash," Couzens later recalled, "that here was my opportunity." He said he was interested, but on a condition. He had to have a "free hand without political interference of any kind." [12] There followed talks with Marx and John Dodge. On September 28, 1916, Marx announced that Commissioner John Gillespie had resigned and that Couzens had taken his place, a substitution that saved the election for Mayor Marx—and launched Couzens upon his new career.[13]

CHAPTER XVI

THE POLICE COMMISSIONER

IN THE words of Detroit's semi-official historian, George B. Catlin, he "immediately began making history" as Commissioner of Police.[1] Owing to that penchant of his for saying what he thought, he started off with a storm. During an interview with the newspapers he was asked to give his policy on law enforcement, particularly in regard to the state law forbidding the sale of alcoholic beverages on Sunday. Instead of repeating what every other police commissioner had said —that, of course, he would enforce all laws—he was frank. He said that he had not "made up his mind," and added:

> Certain laws are debatable. It is debatable whether it is right for a man to have a glass of beer on Sunday. It is not debatable that when a rich man may have his glass of beer in his club or elsewhere, the poor man is entitled to the same privilege. Whether either should be permitted is the question. There are in statute books and among city ordinances so many obsolete and absurd laws that it would be foolish for an official to announce that he intended to enforce the law strictly.[2]

He soon learned that it was more foolish for a police commissioner to be so forthright. "Can Detroit hope for much from a man who, even before he takes the required oath of office, announces in the public press that the enforcement of the public law in some regards is to him a debatable matter?" inquired Judge William Connolly, the Democratic candidate for mayor.[3]

"Is Couzens going to enforce the law passed by the people in Lansing, or just a little of it here and there, as it appeals to him personally?" asked one newspaper.[4]

A newspaper in Grand Rapids commented: "It would seem as though it is about time for the state authority to take Mr. Couzens and the whole Detroit outfit by the ear." [5]

Ministers denounced him from their pulpits.

2

For once, he was indecisive, as a statement he issued showed. "Neither wets, drys, ministers, politicians, nor the public have any reason to become panicky because I have not determined what policies are to be enforced as yet. I do not intend to be driven into a panicky condition. I know I shall not be." Which of course meant that he really was "panicky"—for him.

Then he made a wise decision—to conduct a personal survey of police conditions in Detroit. Emulating Police Commissioner Theodore Roosevelt of New York some twenty years before, he prowled around the city, night and day. Without revealing his identity, he talked to policemen, to saloonkeepers, to streetwalkers, and to ordinary citizens. He later recalled:

"I found conditions far worse than the public dreamed they were. The real inside conditions were never known to the public. . . . The town was wide open . . . gamblers ran as they pleased; hundreds of houses of prostitution were scattered around, and 1,400 saloons ran all day and all night and on Sundays." [6]

He then made the only decision possible for him: *All laws would be enforced.*

To Police Superintendent Ernst Marquardt he sent the kind of order he might have issued as general manager of the Ford Motor Company:

> Effective at once, I want every man in the department instructed to absolutely enforce all laws twenty-four hours of the day, whether on or off duty. . . . From now on, I want every law and ordinance complied with, and this includes specifically the prevention of crime of all kinds, and the proper regulation of laws, ordinances, rules, and regulations governing traffic, saloons, pool rooms, and every other thing that will bring about a clean and decent city. . . . No excuses will be accepted. [7]

3

There was first amazement, then amusement over this order. It was considered by the "wise ones" ludicrous as well as fantastic. A police commissioner of a metropolitian city issuing a command actually calling for complete enforcement of all laws!

To be sure, it was fantastic, in a sense. And of course the Couzens order was not fully obeyed, for the city was not the Ford Company. Yet it did bring some results, enough to cause "wise ones" to hold their breath. For example, his order called for the enforcement of the ordinance against saloons being open on Sundays.

People had said that nobody could enforce the Sunday law, that the politicians would not permit it. But Couzens enforced the law.

He soon learned, however, that types of lawbreaking other than violation of the Sunday rules were not so easily uprooted, not even by the strongest, most Couzens-like general order. "I discovered," he said, "that there was a vast difference between running a government department and manufacturing automobiles. . . . When they asked me to clean up Detroit, they didn't mean it. They wanted me *to* clean it up and *not* clean it up. They wanted me to make it nice enough for the reformers and let it stay rotten enough to appease the bums." [8]

4

His goal, he now said, was "a disciplined city." [9] No one before him had ever seriously tried to discipline Detroit, not even Pingree. The temperament of the city had never encouraged such efforts. The city's nonconformism was shown even in the way Detroiters operated their automobiles, for at that time practically no traffic regulations were enforced. Perhaps symbolically, during Couzens' first month as police commissioner, his own automobile was stolen, to the great delight of his ill-wishers, whose number by then had greatly increased.

The politicians formed an almost solid opposition. Most of the city's forty aldermen were openly hostile. "Why give Commissioner Couzens everything he wants?" an alderman cried at a council budget meeting. "To let him hang himself!" jeered a colleague. [10]

5

On one occasion, Mayor Marx openly tried to frustrate him. When Couzens wanted certain legislation at Lansing to strengthen the police department, the mayor had a representative at the capital to lobby on the other side—against his own police commissioner. [11] "I learned all the emotions of public service when I was commissioner of police," Couzens wrote later to Arthur H. Vandenberg, then editor of the *Grand Rapids Herald*. He had in mind such headlines as these:

"COUZENS FAILS EVEN TO REGULATE MOTORISTS" . . . "POLICE KEEP RIGHT ON WITH THEIR BUNGLING"

... "VICE DENS FLOURISH IN HEART OF DETROIT" ...
"COMMISSIONER COUZENS HASN'T MADE GOOD."

This hurt. But he concluded: "Nearly all public men who did
their duty had to endure about the same sort of stuff. A man can't
set himself up as a target if he doesn't want to be hit." [12] So he held
to his goal doggedly. "He made life miserable for everybody in
Detroit who violated any statute, ordinance, order, edict, enactment,
provision, rule, regulation, or section thereof," said the writer
William Hard.[13]

6

He announced that he was determined to abolish the so-called
red-light districts. This caused a group of reputable citizens to
descend on him to argue that his policy would lead to worse evils.
He answered that they should go to the state legislature and get
prostitution legalized; until then, he intended to enforce the law.
"But our families!" protested the citizens. "They would misunder-
stand our motives!" "Well," he replied, "if you think you can con-
vince me that prostitution is all right, you should have no trouble
with your families." [14]

Still another group of citizens visited him to save the red-light
areas. They said they were interested "only in Detroit's welfare."
To these Couzens displayed a little black book and read off some
automobile license numbers. "Are those your license numbers?"
he asked. Some of the callers admitted that they were. "Well," said
Couzens, "I have a mind to publish these numbers!" Then he told
his dismayed callers that the numbers had been taken down by investigators from cars found parked in front of some of the more
flashy brothels in the city! [15]

In dealing with traffic regulation, he succeeded in stirring up an
even bigger storm than he did by his frankness on the red-light
districts. After becoming convinced that elimination of all parking
in the busiest downtown streets was necessary, he issued an order
to that effect, although warned by the city's law department that
his order exceeded his authority. Business leaders assailed him as
a "czar." Former Mayor Philip Breitmeyer counseled open rebellion.[16]

The stir was such that the order had to be rescinded. But the very
impulsiveness of his action so dramatized Detroit's need for some
traffic control that shortly afterward the city council enacted legisla-

tion along the lines that he had intended to establish. Thus he became the father of the city's modern traffic code.

7

His biggest storm—actually a serio-comic episode worthy of Gilbert and Sullivan—began in March 1917, when he decided to bring into the open a half-secret scandal involving a municipal judge. "Judge Albert Sellers," he announced to the press, "is giving blanket releases to professional bondsmen with the names of prisoners to be filled in as the occasion arises." [17] The judge sneered at him. "Police Commissioner Couzens should quit his job and go home."

Couzens then issued an order that henceforth the police department would ignore Judge Sellers' releases unless they had been issued in a regular court session.[18] Then the city settled back to await the inevitable collision. It came very soon afterward when Couzens' order was enforced in the case of two women arrested as streetwalkers. Judge Sellers had issued the pair his usual prearranged releases. Couzens' police officers refused to honor the releases. So the judge issued a contempt citation against Couzens.

Haled into court, Couzens was given the choice of paying a fine of $100 or serving a thirty-day sentence in jail. He refused to pay the fine and was taken to jail.[19] Of course the city howled, either in indignation or with delight. The city's multimillionaire police head locked up in his own jail! Not even Teddy Roosevelt had endured such an experience in his similar efforts to clean up a crime-ridden city.

Couzens did not remain long in his own jail. But the incident did win for him the favorable public opinion that a bad press had denied him. He carried this fight with the judge to the State Supreme Court, and won a decision that outlawed the practice of giving blanket releases.[20]

8

For a time this civic comedy made him a hero. But his troubles were not over. That spring the United States entered the European war. The city filled up with "floaters." Crimes increased—and Couzens was blamed. The *Detroit News*, usually his supporter, said: "The present condition cannot continue. If Mr. Couzens is responsible even in part, it is preposterous that he be kept in his place. . . . Certainly the stubborn pride of any one man or any group of men cannot be permitted to result in perpetuation of this reign of terror." [21]

The situation really was impossible. There was one face-saving avenue of escape open to him—to take a war job in Washington, and thus get out of the police "mess." Just at this time, General George W. Goethals, then Acting Quartermaster General of the Army, invited him to Washington to talk over a proposal that he become head of a new motor-truck division of the war department.[22] This was the result of a recommendation Milton McRae had made to the Secretary of War, Newton D. Baker, that Couzens be brought into the national picture in some wartime capacity. He and Goethals got along very well. Goethals' greeting to him was: "So! You are Couzens! They tell me you are a hell of a hard man to get along with. Well, I am too!" [23]

But while Couzens was negotiating with Goethals, the politicians at home had the City Council pass a resolution requesting his removal. The resolution said that the crime wave was a result of his "incompetency," and directed Mayor Marx to remove him, "in order to restore confidence in our city and for the protection of our homes and our loved ones." [24] Couzens immediately returned to Detroit to face his opponents. "The politicians want me to quit because I will not grant them special privileges. They can't remove me," he announced.[25] He was not removed.

CHAPTER XVII

THE ODD CANDIDATE

"THE first thing you know, Jim, you will be a national character. Remember that Theodore Roosevelt started his career as police commissioner of New York City. Incidentally and confidentially, let me tell you that William Alden Smith will not be a candidate for United States Senator again two years hence. What's the matter with Jim Couzens for his job?" [1] So Milton McRae had written him in November 1916.

Couzens was skeptical then. "It is one thing to receive an appointment to a public office, and another thing to get elected. I make such a poor public showing that I doubt if I could be elected." [2] By 1918, however, on the basis of his eventful record as police commissioner, he began to believe he might be a successful candidate after all. [3]

In April 1918 the *Detroit News* reported "a real Couzens boom for the Senate" was "getting definite," but that there was an odd fact about it. The Couzens "boom" was being openly promoted by John Gillespie, the discredited former police commissioner. The *News* commented: "The boys think that Mr. Couzens as a police commissioner would make a wonderful United States Senator. They have taken him to their bosoms to get him off their backs." [4]

2

To Couzens patriarchal Senator Smith then gave some "candid" advice. He would make "a good senator," but he would "find great difficulty in being nominated and elected." For he had never done anything to get the party obligated to him. "And that was a hard handicap." [5]

Deciding this was sound, Couzens withdrew his name from the senatorial race, in which the contenders by then included Commo-

dore Truman H. Newberry, Governor Chase S. Osborn, Editor
Arthur H. Vandenberg—and Henry Ford. "I have been advised by
counsel," Couzens said, "that my continued ownership of Ford Motor
Company stock disqualified me for the Senate because the Ford
Company is engaged in making war materials for the government." [6]
Of course, this reasoning also applied, as Couzens well knew, to Ford,
though Ford ignored the thrust and became an active candidate
for the senatorial nomination, not only as a Republican but also
as a Democrat.

That same year, Detroit had adopted a new charter, mainly in
order to get a strong chief executive—something previous charters
had prevented.[7] Shortly after the "strong mayor charter" was adopted,
Couzens made an announcement—he would stand for mayor. His
aim, he said, was to be the first of a new line of powerful mayors
who would give Detroit the kind of government it needed.

3

At first his announcement provoked amusement among the political experts, even those who were friendly toward him. They said
about him exactly what had been said of Hazen S. Pingree: one so
lacking in political tact and diplomacy could not be elected mayor
of Detroit. John Dodge assured him that he could not be "dog
catcher or coroner." E. Roy Pelletier, a former Ford Company advertising manager, laughed when Couzens asked him to handle his
campaign publicity. Pelletier did not think it possible to "sell" a
man so lacking in "good fellowship." [8] Mayor Marx thought "nothing
was funnier," was certain his police commissioner would make one
of "the oddest" candidates in political history.[9]

The *Detroit News* said:

> They say he is arrogant, bull-headed, uncompromising. They say
> he has no consideration for other people's feelings. They say he
> would rather refuse a favor than grant one. According to their lights,
> they are right. Toward the special-favor seeking politicians, Mr.
> Couzens looks that way because he feels just that way.[10]

The *News* then suggested that Detroit ought to have precisely
that kind of man as mayor.

4

He started his campaign by making a curiously candid admission.
He was not a candidate by "overwhelming requests of my friends,
or anything of that sort." He was a candidate solely because he

"personally" believed that he would make "a good mayor." The new charter said the mayor was to be "the chief executive officer of the city." He would be precisely that "without the assistance of any political boss."

He drafted a lengthy platform, its most important plank being a statement on the old Pingree issue of municipal ownership of the streetcar system. "My plan," he said, "will be to proceed to condemn the property of the street railway company so the city may get possession as soon as possible." [11]

5

Unintentionally, the streetcar company gave him a tremendous political assist. For the D.U.R. picked just this time to raise fares on the so-called "Pingree lines" from a nickel to six cents. According to the company, wartime inflationary costs forced them to do this, and probably the increase was justified. But in a political sense, it was ill-timed—for the D.U.R.

Taking advantage of this blunder, Couzens immediately announced that he would institute court action to block the increase in fares. Then Edward T. Fitzgerald, Mayor Marx's secretary, who was working for Couzens, came up with an even better idea. He recalled that in a similar situation in 1895, Mayor Pingree had boarded a streetcar, offered the old rate of fare, and had been thrown off the car. Detroiters had rallied to Pingree's support.[12]

Fitzgerald persuaded Couzens to copy Pingree. So in the morning on August 7, 1918, three weeks before the primary, Couzens boarded a Fort Street streetcar, dropped only a nickel in the fare box and proceeded to a seat. "Just a minute!" called the conductor. "The fare is six cents."

"I won't pay it," said Couzens.

"You'll pay six cents or you will have to leave the car," said the conductor, following the instructions issued by the corporation.

"I'll do no such thing!" said Couzens. "I insist on my rights."

The conductor stopped the car and announced it would not proceed unless Couzens got off. Other cars piled up behind and traffic was blocked, but Couzens refused to get off voluntarily. The conductor pushed him off while newspaper reporters and photographers stood by to record it all.[13]

6

The stunt was eminently successful. Indeed, it was too successful. Hundreds of other Detroiters followed his example. The streetcar company met the rebellion by stopping all cars, with the result that there was rioting all over Detroit. Of course, many citizens were outraged. And among them was John Dodge, Couzens' successor as president of the Street Railway Commission. Dodge accused Couzens of "encouraging the thousands of Bolsheviki and Anarchists in the city." "He ought to be put in jail!" Dodge cried.[14]

Although Couzens too was dismayed, he shrewdly said nothing, counting on the rioting to subside. When it did subside, most citizens decided that he had won a victory for the car riders, for the company abandoned the increase in fares.

In the primary, Couzens led all the other candidates, running ahead of Judge Connolly, who had Democratic party backing, ahead of Ex-Commissioner Gillespie of the Marx-Republican machine, and ahead of Divie B. Duffield, a respected lawyer who had drafted the new city charter.

The following November a runoff between Couzens and Connolly was held. Again he defeated Connolly, and became Detroit's new mayor. Of considerable additional interest to him then—and of great importance to him later—was the fact that the same night's election returns showed that Ford, running as a Democrat, in the senatorial election, had lost a bitter contest with Commodore Newberry, the Republican candidate.

CHAPTER XVIII

THE STRONG MAYOR

"I AM by nature somewhat more destructive than constructive,"
Couzens had said back in 1915 in a burst of self-analysis.[1] What he
really meant was that he received pleasure out of challenging accepted patterns of conduct that did not jibe with his own strictly
disciplined moral code. This is the way he had performed his job
as police commissioner, and as mayor he followed the same course.
"I will conduct myself so that I have my own self-respect, regardless
of whether people like me," he announced.[2]

He was aware of what some people said about him, that he "had
ice water" in his veins, as he once put it.[3] He was caricatured as
"King James." He felt that he was "probably the loneliest Mayor
any big city ever had," because he did not "grant favors." [4]

But he proved to be the answer to Detroit's wish for a strong
executive. Actually, even in the opinion of some who had professed
a desire for a non-political mayor, he was too strong—stronger than
Pingree, stronger even than big-fisted old Zach Chandler, mayor of
Detroit in the 1850's and later a boss of the national Republican
party in the time of U. S. Grant and Rutherford B. Hayes.

2

He did not share the view that a man in public office must, if
possible, act in an ingratiating manner toward everybody. Rather
he conducted himself in accord with his own code. He might have
ingratiated himself, for example, with Senator William Alden Smith.
President of the Grand Rapids Savings Bank as well as owner of the
influential *Grand Rapids Herald*. Senator Smith had asked him, as
"a great compliment to me," to place a deposit in the Smith bank.
This would have been a nice gesture on Couzens' part, especially
since he wanted Smith's good will, as well as that of Vandenberg,

Smith's editor. But Couzens bluntly turned down the request. "I cannot afford to carry any money on deposit," he wrote Smith, citing local taxes.[5] The incident was but one of many that caused his friends to bemoan his "political dumbness."

Just as typical was his response when an employer telephoned him one day for a police squad to "chase away some strikers," complaining that the pickets were calling him names.

"What are they calling you?" asked Couzens. When the man told him, he replied: "Oh, I've heard you call your workers the same names!"

He refused the request.[6]

3

He began almost every day by handing over to his secretary a list of automobile license numbers to be sent to the police department—license numbers on cars which he himself had observed breaking traffic laws as he drove to City Hall.[7]

He did not even hesitate to lay down the law to newspapers, as in the following letter:

November 1, 1921

Detroit Journal
Detroit, Michigan

Gentlemen:
One of your delivery wagons deliberately parked double just west of Wayne on Congress this morning. The car was left unattended, blocking traffic. This kind of disregard for law must be discontinued, otherwise the driver will be arrested.

Very truly yours,
JAMES COUZENS, Mayor.[8]

4

Because he always said forcefully just what he thought, regardless of diplomacy, he stirred up even more tempests as Mayor than he had as Police Commissioner. When the Detroit Board of Commerce opposed his plan for improving a municipal hospital, objecting to the expense, he let fly the statement that the Board leaders were a "pack of curs." [9]

He threw the City Council into an uproar by shouting "Liar!" at the president of the Edison Company during a discussion of utility-company profits, and found himself "banished" from the council chambers because of the outburst. In answer, he announced that he would seek the impeachment of the respected and venerable presiding councilman, James Vernor, the ginger-ale magnate, who had ordered Couzens to "mind his manners." [10]

He even provoked a near fist-fight with an old friend in the council, John C. Lodge, being too quick, as he himself later admitted, to voice the charge of "sell-out." [11]

He antagonized nearly all of the medical profession in Detroit and Michigan when, over the protests of the medical societies, he invited Dr. Adolf Lorenz of Vienna to Detroit to use the Lorenz treatment on children with infantile paralysis. When the doctors refused Dr. Lorenz the facilities of the private hospitals, Couzens opened the municipal hospitals to him, the while denouncing the doctors for "un-American intolerance." [12]

5

Well-wishers urged him to exercise greater restraint, to be more affable, even with his critics. His old hero, Pingree, had not been affable, he answered. "I recognize the desirability of composure . . . but sometimes it takes an explosion to cause action to be taken to prevent a repetition of what causes the explosion." [13]

But while his temperament provoked a great deal of controversy, it produced much positive good for the city of Detroit. He completely transformed the shabby atmosphere that had prevailed in the municipal offices. After his first ten months in office, an unfriendly newspaper had to concede that he had brought into the City Hall "business dispatch, confidence, and decorum. . . . Since the first floor front of the City Hall became his home, scandal has become a lost word in the municipal lexicon. Not a hint of bossism, bargaining, political debt-paying."

The Board of Commerce, with which he was almost continually at loggerheads, also had praise for his non-political administration. "Couzens' favorite campaign phrase was 'I'll reward no friends and I'll punish no enemies.' He kept his word. His appointments were made on merit—he paid no political debts," said its official publication.[14]

City functionaries of long standing who had never before seen any mayor in their particular bailiwick, now saw Couzens frequently. The first person to enter the City Hall and the last to leave, he almost literally wore out stenographers with the amount of correspondence that he insisted on handling.[15]

Veteran officeholders were astonished to discover that when he called something to their attention, he expected to hear that the business had been transacted immediately. "If he did not get a report promptly, we got a request for a report; that had never happened before in the City Hall." [16]

On a holiday, a subordinate found him at his desk as usual, and asked, "Why do you work when everyone else is out playing?" "I have to make good on this job," he said.[17]

6

From the time he had come from Chatham twenty-eight years before, Detroit by then had grown fivefold in population. It was then a city of nearly a million persons, the fourth city in America. Since 1915, it had doubled in area, mainly under the pressure of the automobile industry he had helped to build. Yet only slight efforts had been made to keep even the basic municipal services in line with the city's growth. In 1919 the city still had the same sewer and water installations that had been insufficient when Detroit was half the size. Schools were overcrowded, with thirteen thousand children on half-time schedules. Public hospital facilities, parks, and playgrounds were lacking. The main thoroughfares were narrow, traffic-choked, and studded with bottlenecks and deathtraps.[18]

Most glaring of all was the city's continuing deficiency in streetcar transportation. Always a source of annoyance to Detroiters, as Couzens well knew from his own first days in the city, the streetcar system was then abominable, and even the streetcar corporation admitted as much.

7

To change this, Detroit had long needed bold, energetic leadership that would be able to win the people's confidence. Couzens did not hesitate to recommend the expenditure of millions of dollars for the needed schools, sewers, hospitals, and street improvements. Convinced of his honesty and ability, the people followed his guidance, and it was his good fortune that within a week after his election, the Armistice came, bringing an end to wartime restrictions on materials needed for rehabilitating and extending the city's services.

In his first three years as mayor, Couzens directed planning for the expenditure of approximately $243,000,000—an astounding figure in that period.[19]

Under his leadership, Detroit became, in government as well as in industry, the "city dynamic." [20] Indeed, it would be years (in fact, not until Fiorello H. LaGuardia, a strikingly similar sort of man, became mayor of New York) before all America was to know another such aggressively constructive mayor of any city in the land.

He eschewed all partisan politics, except when he secretly tried to play a part in the 1920 Republican Presidential nominations. He favored the nomination of the old Bull Mooser, Senator Hiram Johnson of California, then still reputed an insurgent. Couzens personally paid all of the expense, about five thousand dollars, for establishing a Hiram Johnson campaign headquarters in New York.[21] The nomination went to another senator, Warren G. Harding, who soon invited Couzens to visit him at his home in Marion, Ohio, to "discuss the coming campaign." Couzens declined. He was too busy, he said. But his real reason was that Harding, darling of the Old Guard, was not his kind of man.

CHAPTER XIX

THE PEOPLE'S MAN

IT WAS not merely because Couzens was a "builder mayor," nor even because he was so conspicuously honest and aggressively non-political, that he became one of the few outstanding mayors in American history. In all probability, his "disgraceful contemporary," as he called Mayor "Big Bill" Thompson of Chicago, outdid him in the field of public improvements.[1] And, even in those days, there were other mayors who were honest and non-political. But Couzens was outstanding primarily because he stood for liberalism and intelligence during a period—the aftermath of World War I—that was characterized by reaction.[2]

He frankly favored not less government action, but more government action whenever he was convinced of the social need—and this was a full decade before Franklin D. Roosevelt's "New Deal." Indeed, when there was a nationwide coal strike in 1922, he went so far as to advocate government ownership of coal mines.[3] When an acute shortage of homes in Detroit developed at the beginning of his term, he announced that he favored having the city government appropriate funds for home building, an early suggestion that there should be "public housing." "I do not believe private initiative and capital are able to cope with this situation," he announced. "Meanwhile, Detroit cannot wait. We must have accommodations for these people. . . . I do not see why we cannot float a $5,000,000 bond issue of five-year bonds to aid workers in getting homes. . . . Workers would get their homes nearly at cost, and the city would get the money cheaper than private interests could get it."[4]

He did not drop the idea until lawyers had convinced him that the city could not go into the home-loan business without changing the state constitution.

2

In 1919 and again in 1921, Detroit was hit especially hard by severe postwar unemployment. Like Pingree, Couzens insisted that the city assume responsibility for relieving distress, and also for providing jobs on public works. So many jobless men were put to work in the streets department, he once said "the streets were almost disgracefully clean." Just as openly, he dispensed doles from the city treasury to needy workingmen's families.[5]

Also like Pingree, of the "potato patches" of the 1890's, he was called a "socialist." His answer was: "Human beings cannot be permitted to starve because of political theory."

3

Significantly—and oddly, perhaps, to some—only one other man in the nation received as much attention in the field of unemployment relief as did Couzens. This was Herbert Hoover, the Secretary of Commerce in Harding's administration. Then a symbol of liberalism in Washington, Secretary Hoover caused President Harding to call a White House conference on unemployment in September 1921, to which Couzens was invited.[6] As chairman of this conference, Hoover declared: "There is no economic failure so terrible in its import as that of a country possessing a surplus of every necessity of life in which numbers willing and anxious to work, are deprived of these necessities. It simply cannot be if our moral and economic system is to survive."[7] Couzens was delighted with Hoover's viewpoint, especially since Hoover specifically endorsed the program for which Couzens had been called a socialist in Detroit. Later, Hoover visited Detroit and was an overnight guest at the Couzens home on Longfellow Avenue. Couzens found Hoover to be "a hard man to entertain socially."[8] But there then began, if not a friendship, an association that seemingly foretold harmonious relations in the future, if their paths should happen to cross again.

4

As an advocate of freedom of speech in America, Couzens was even more commanding on the municipal scene. In New York City, Mayor John Hylan announced a ban on "unlawful assemblages" which his police took to mean all meetings of radicals. Emma Goldman, the anarchist, was hounded from city jail to city jail. There was a demand for rough treatment of strikers and all "labor agitators." In most cities, the police complied with enthusiasm. But not in Detroit. Despite all the postwar hysteria about "Bolshevism," Couzens determined to uphold democratic procedures.

A test came in the winter of 1919. "Big Bill" Haywood, then the most publicized radical in America, was billed for a meeting in Detroit. A statement authorized by the state headquarters of the American Legion declared: "If Mayor Couzens and the police department do not intend to prevent Haywood from speaking here, the American Legion will." [9]

Couzens' own police commissioner, Dr. James Inches, urged that the Haywood meeting be suppressed. Dr. Inches argued that if the Legion intended to break up the meeting, in his opinion the only solution was to keep the meeting from taking place.

But Couzens said this was cowardice. "As long as Haywood conducts himself within the law he can speak." [10] The Legion backed down; Haywood made his speech. And Couzens himself was there to see that he did.

5

Not long after this, A. Mitchell Palmer, Wilson's Attorney General and also a candidate for President to succeed Wilson, staged his so-called "red raids" all over America.[11] In later years, even conservatives came to view this activity as a shameful, unnecessary "witch hunt." In 1930, before the Harvard Law School alumni, Chief Justice Charles Evans Hughes spoke "with deep concern about inflammatory appeals to prejudice made by district attorneys and about the browbeating of witnesses . . . in every part of the country." [12] Yet, at the time, with the exception of a few senators like La Follette, almost the only official voice to be raised in America against the Attorney General was that of Mayor Couzens. When he learned that his own Detroit police department had cooperated with Palmer's agents, and with an assistant U. S. district attorney in Detroit named Frank Murphy in seizing and jailing supposed, or even real, "reds," Couzens ordered the practice ended.[13] "I am not sure that there is any reason for these raids," he said. "I won't be stampeded by federal officials." [14] He wasn't, and, at least officially, Detroit resisted the general hysteria.

6

Just before Palmer began his movement to "stamp out Bolshevism," Couzens prepared a noteworthy statement for the Newspaper

Enterprise Association. He branded propaganda about "Bolshevism" a disguised effort to halt social progress, the same position vigorously taken in Kansas by another enlightened Republican, William Allen White of the Emporia *Gazette*.[15] Couzens went on:

> The makers of dictionaries in the future are likely to have a hard time defining the term "Bolshevism" as it is being applied in America today.
> The word is a vague definition applied to almost anything that disturbs our social viewpoint.
> In the typical American metropolis of Detroit, we are confronted with every phase of the [war] reconstruction problem. But we have not found it necessary to throttle free speech nor to interfere with the lawful expression of radical ideas. Criticism of government is absolutely needful. I am convinced that to attempt to bottle it up is highly dangerous. Are we to stifle every symptom of thinking by shouting Bolshevism? . . .[16]

Published in newspapers throughout the country under the heading "Don't Bottle Free Thinking!" this statement indicated a further step in his maturing as a public man, one who, often without realizing it himself, had become a people's man. Like Pingree of his own city, like Altgeld of Illinois, like La Follette of Wisconsin, like Tom Johnson and Brand Whitlock of Ohio, like Brandeis of Massachusetts, and others, Republicans and Democrats, who fought for people's rights, he was following a long-standing American tradition of progressivism and freedom.

CHAPTER XX

THE BATTLE FOR M.O.

IRONICALLY, no one in the Detroit of that period was more often called a "Bolshevist" than Couzens himself—mainly because of his battle to establish municipal ownership of the city's streetcar lines.

He had flatly declared in his inaugural message that Detroit needed to run its own public transportation system. His blue eyes never looked more like steel than when he said: "Unless the Detroit United Railway agrees to reasonable terms by which the city takes over its city lines, I will be ready to adopt war measures." If necessary, he added, he would submit a purchase plan "every six months, until one was adopted." [1] For his one idea was to put over municipal owner-ship, no matter what it cost him. [2]

Even so, against his deepest personal inclination, he began with a compromise. He had concluded long before that the best procedure would be for the city to build competing lines, "start small like the Ford Company did," deny any more franchises to the D.U.R. while letting the old franchises expire, and then sit back to watch the municipal lines crush out the company lines. But he let the members of his Street Railway Commission, three amiable businessmen, persuade him that such a course meant a fight which, they said, would be "bad for Detroit." They induced him to go to the voters in a referendum in April 1918 with another purchase plan—to buy the D.U.R. lines for $31,500,000, a price to which the D.U.R. had agreed. They also persuaded him to conduct only a mild campaign, keeping himself in the background. His commissioners argued: why stir up the people when the company had agreed to sell and all the Detroit papers were in favor of the purchase? [3]

2

The compromise turned out badly. For one thing, the D.U.R., which had ostensibly agreed to the sale, had in fact prepared reams

of literature against the proposal and distributed this material at
the last minute.[4]

But more serious opposition came from Henry Ford. In 1915
Henry Ford had unqualifiedly endorsed Couzens' M.O. plan in a
front-page interview in the *Detroit News,* saying: "It is one of the
safest business propositions I have ever heard of. I will gladly work
under James Couzens in the street railway matter." [5]

True, Ford's newspaper, the *Dearborn Independent,* had carried
an item, just after Couzens' election, that had belittled Couzens'
streetcar program. But Ford personally had sent a copy of the paper
to Couzens accompanied by this message:

"While I have bought this paper, I am not taking active management until January 1st, 1919. I do not agree with this article in any
way. My sentiments are to help you in every way." [6]

But despite this, during the last week of the streetcar campaign,
Ford, acting through Charles E. Sorensen, then general manager
of the Henry Ford and Son Tractor Plant, let loose a resounding
blast against the Couzens plan. Everyone understood that while the
statement ripping into Couzens' plan (which soon was posted all
over Detroit in handbills and printed in full-page advertisements)
bore Sorensen's signature, it was really Ford's. Indeed, Ford had
admitted to E. G. Pipp that he intended "to keep Couzens from
getting his way." "He seemed to feel unusually peevish toward
Couzens that day," recalled Pipp. Pipp reminded Ford that previously
he had supported Couzens' efforts toward municipal ownership.
"I have a right to change my mind," snapped Ford.[7]

3

The Ford statement injected a wholly new argument into the
streetcar controversy: electric streetcars are out of date; the "coming
thing" is gasoline-propelled cars; Henry Ford is developing the new
type of car; hence the city of Detroit would be paying $31,500,000
to the D.U.R. for "junk." [8]

Of course, the Ford gasoline streetcar was pure fiction, or little
more than just an idea. In the words of Jay G. Hayden, "The announcement was plainly designed to scuttle the purchase proposal." [9]

Couzens boiled with anger. "What Mr. Couzens said regarding
Mr. Ford could not be presented in these polite columns," the
Detroit Saturday Night recalled later.[10] Ford came back with a

barbed statement filled with sarcastic references to Couzens' "lack of mechanical knowledge." [11]

Had this exchange continued, it would doubtless have dawned on the majority of Detroiters that the "Sorensen statement" was really an expression of personal feeling and had nothing to do with the merits of Couzens' streetcar plan. As it was, the time was too short for the public to catch on.

As a result, thousands of Detroiters, who otherwise were for M.O., voted against Couzens' plan because they were taken in by the Sorensen statement. So Couzens lost his second M.O. referendum.[12]

4

The *Detroit News* analyzed the defeat as having resulted from Couzens having been, for once, too soft. The people were fed up with inadequate transportation and wanted the D.U.R. treated roughly. "What they want is to hang the D.U.R.'s hide on the fence." [13]

Couzens agreed, and bided his time for another occasion when he could again raise the M.O. issue. It came when a strike, two months later, halted all streetcar service. He decided that the strike, ostensibly for higher wages, was really a collusive affair between the D.U.R. management and the unions to get further rate increases.[14] On the second day of the stoppage, he issued a decisive statement:

> The moment has arrived to finish up our dealings with the D.U.R. I reached that conclusion last night. That conclusion was confirmed when I left my farm at 5:55 this morning and came to town and saw how comfortably we were getting along without the D.U.R. . . . We will order the company off the non-franchise lines and put our own equipment on the tracks. . . . By fall, we can have cars sufficient to have a fair-sized system of our own running, or to have forced the D.U.R. to turn over its property at junk prices.
>
> If the Council will cooperate, I am willing to let this end all relationship with the D.U.R. once and for all. We have been grasped by this lying corporation until it seems to me that they have made their final grasp.[15]

And to this he appended—as if in answer to critics of his "impulsiveness"—a personal note:

"I have reached this conclusion under no pressure and after no moments of excitement, but after thirty-six hours of quiet thought."

An ominous postscript, that—for the D.U.R.

5

Then the D.U.R. knew it was in for a battle to the finish. It promptly settled the strike, after Couzens had directed his city attorneys to seek a court order placing the company in receivership for failure to render transportation service.[16] Then, suddenly, the company discovered that it wanted to build numerous extensions that it had previously refused to consider. Just as suddenly, it discovered that it could increase wages without charging for transfers.[17] It started a discussion of subways, and even offered to surrender its city lines to another company, keeping only its interurban properties. Or it would deal with the city on a service-at-cost basis —anything, in fact, to keep the people from accepting the Couzens proposal for a rival municipal line.[18]

Most of the members of the City Council backed away from a showdown, saying that it would be better to try to get improved service and, perhaps, a subway, than to start another fight. Couzens' own street-railway commissioners, all personal friends who had been appointed because they supposedly favored his program, also backed away. They said that instead of municipal ownership, Detroit should adopt the so-called Taylor Plan, a service-at-cost scheme under private ownership which was being tried in Cleveland.

"Well, gentlemen," Couzens said to them, "if that's your conviction, I'll have to ask for your resignations." [19]

He then announced a referendum for April 1920 on a bond issue of $15,000,000 for the establishment of a competing independent, city-owned streetcar system.[20]

Against this plan, the D.U.R. enlisted an army of orators and sundry propagandists. The Board of Commerce and a special group of business leaders, led by Alvan Macauley and Henry B. Joy, both of the Packard Motor Car Company, joined the D.U.R. in its fight.

Even the three friends who had been Couzens' streetcar commissioners openly opposed the proposal.[21] Aided by utility companies in other cities, the D.U.R. let loose a flood of literature that literally clogged the Detroit post office. It was estimated that the company spent $500,000 to defeat the plan.[22] Joining in the attack were not only those interests opposed to "socialism," but also those eager to see a personal setback for Couzens. As Jay Hayden has recalled: "For years, he had been stepping on sacred toes. If he won this battle, it was clear that he would be even more firmly entrenched. The myriad of interests that he had thwarted moved as one in a supreme effort to stop this man." [23]

But, luckily for Couzens, just at this time Ford had set his heart on buying out all of the minority stockholders in the Ford Motor Company. There had been a good deal of jockeying on Ford's part to get the other stockholders, including Couzens, to sell out without knowing who wanted to buy. Couzens had held out until he could discover who was behind mysterious offers being made by various brokers. He found out that the buyer was Ford himself when Edsel Ford, in September 1919, came to his home and put all the Ford cards on the table.[24] Unless Couzens agreed to sell, some of the others would hold back. Couzens was the key to the whole transaction.

At the session with Edsel, Couzens agreed to sell, although he insisted on getting a higher price for his stock than the others in recognition of his part in the creation of the company. John Anderson, for one, endorsed this proposal, saying to Stuart Webb, one of the negotiators: "If there is anybody in that organization who is entitled to a little bit more than anyone else . . . it is Mayor Couzens. It was due to his efforts that the company became a success." [25]

The deal was closed for $30,000,000 for his stock, of which $29,-308,857.90 was for himself, and $691,142.10 for his sister Rosetta.

Apparently out of gratitude, Ford then made a truce with Couzens that culminated in a curious letter which Ford had his secretary release to the *Detroit Saturday Night*—to correct some "rumors":

> The relations between Mr. Ford and Mr. Couzens during his association with the Ford Motor Company, or afterward, have at no time been strained. Both men have ideals wherein they are desirous of serving the people in the best and most beneficial way, and each has chosen his method of doing so. I believe as well that neither one of these men would hesitate to cooperate with the other if the resulting benefit was for the best of the people.
> Very truly yours,
> E. G. LIEBOLD,
> General Secretary to Henry Ford.[26]

Ford now forgot the Sorensen's "gasoline car" and came out for the M.O. plan. This time more than 63 per cent of the voters approved Couzens' program for municipally owned and operated streetcars. Couzens immediately gave the order to begin excavation work for the new M.O. lines—thus starting, at last, to carry out the program first proclaimed as far back as the 1890's.[27]

CHAPTER XXI

THE "DAMNABLE OUTRAGE"

PROBLEMS remained, however. The D.U.R. launched nine different lawsuits to try to invalidate the referendum. One suit was even based on the point that the paper used for the ballots was too thin.[1]

Steel for the rails was needed, and no major steel company would submit bids. The bonds voted in the referendum had to be sold, and investment brokers boycotted them.

Couzens arranged for the steel by making a personal plea to James A. Farrell, president of the U.S. Steel Corporation. He met the boycott of the brokers by buying many of the bonds himself, and by using certain municipal funds for buying others. Lawyers argued that the procedure was illegal,[2] but he went ahead—and was sustained by the courts. Meanwhile, construction went on.

The tracks of the new municipal lines had to cross D.U.R. tracks at several points. As the law was then understood, the D.U.R. had the right to prevent this. Consequently, there occurred another of those civic comedies with Couzens as script writer.

At midnight on Saturday, January 8, 1921, some two hundred city workers, under secret orders, converged at the intersection of St. Jean and Mack Streets. Policemen ringed the intersection to keep out "intruders," and under their protection, the workers proceeded to saw and hack the D.U.R. rails in two. As expected, the D.U.R. general manager arrived with a court order commanding that the city work be halted. He was arrested and taken to a police station on Belle Isle, where the drawbridge to the island was lifted, so that no one could get to the park to serve legal orders for his release. By the time the manager was freed, the crossing had been achieved and city streetcars began running across the D.U.R. lines.[3]

There was an appeal to the courts. D.U.R. attorneys said that the midnight crossing was "an abominable, damnable outrage." [4] The

lower courts agreed and ordered the city not to use the crossing, but
—and this was the important thing—the city was not ordered to tear
up its tracks. The case was appealed to the Supreme Court of the
United States. The D.U.R. retained as its counsel none other than
Charles Evans Hughes, then marking time between two terms in
the highest court, but even he was not able to save the D.U.R.
In effect, the Supreme Court rendered a decision which supported
fully the "damnable outrage." [5]

2

One more effort was made by the D.U.R. to destroy the municipal
lines. It submitted to the voters a proposal that the city lines be
merged with those of the D.U.R. in a new private company to operate on the service-at-cost principle. This plan offered a number of
attractive concessions to the public. But Couzens presented a counter
proposal—for the city to take over certain D.U.R. lines on which
there was no franchise and which the D.U.R. had no choice but to
sell. In the campaign that followed, the D.U.R. issued a threat. If
its proposal were not accepted, it would take all its cars off the streets.

"We will not be intimidated," [6] said Couzens, and the voters
supported him in sufficient numbers to kill the D.U.R. proposal
while they approved his own proposal.[7]

However, unless the city system could operate on certain D.U.R.
routes—notably those on such main thoroughfares as Woodward
Avenue and Fort Street—the city's position still was not yet satisfactory. Couzens then asked the D.U.R. to sell its lines on those two
main streets, but, as usual, the D.U.R. refused.

Then it was Couzens who made a threat: He would tear up the
D.U.R. tracks—a weapon that no other mayor of Detroit had ever
seriously considered using—if the voters approved. In an election
of November 1921 the people again stood by Couzens, voting the
ouster authority, at the same time re-electing him mayor for a
second term.

3

Couzens then prepared for the kill, forcing the company to permit
city cars to operate over its lines, with an interchange of transfers.
In effect, he achieved by this a unified car system for the city.[8]

Knowing it was licked, the D.U.R. then presented him with the
proposal that the city lease its lines.[9] He refused; his goal was to

purchase, not to lease, and he knew he had the corporation in his power. A meeting of the D.U.R. stockholders was called. Having purchased a share of stock to qualify as a shareholder, Couzens himself occupied a front seat. He listened to the discussion, and then stood up. Unless the D.U.R. agreed to sell to the city *all* its municipal lines at the price he had already specified, he would carry out his threat to tear up the tracks on Woodward Avenue and Fort Street. "This issue must be settled now, in February," he added.[10]

4

On the last day of February 1922 the D.U.R. surrendered.

That April, Couzens presented the voters with an agreement by which the city would acquire the D.U.R. city lines for $19,850,000. It was approved—and a month later the D.U.R. lines became a part of the municipal railway.[11] The long battle for municipal ownership in Detroit was won at last. Probably no one but Couzens could have won it. Considering the stakes, the obstacles, and the bitterness of the opposition, he had, by his "bull-headedness," scored a victory that was unique in the annals of American politics in his or even later eras.[12]

CHAPTER XXII

THE REWARD

Couzens' satisfaction at having established the nation's largest mu nicipally owned railway was "sweeter," he said, than anything he had ever achieved in business.[1] Best of all, he had demonstrated beyond any question that he was his own man. The *Detroit News* commented:

> The only way to dictate successfully to Mr. Couzens about anything would be first of all to throw him into a deep well and then to fill up the well with scrap iron and paving bricks. After that, it is assumed that if you told him to stay there, he might do it.[2]

This was precisely the reputation he wanted.

2

Would he now be content to rest on his laurels? Would he be satisfied to continue as Mayor of Detroit, to run for that office again, and then call matters quits? No one who really knew him could have thought so. Close to fifty then, he was still subject to the drive of ambition that had always marked him.

The truth was that he had never given up the idea of being United States Senator from Michigan, the highest office to which he could aspire in view of his Canadian birth, and he seldom forgot that this was his ultimate goal. In November 1922 there would be another senatorial election.

Henry Ford had unexpectedly precipitated a political issue that made it altogether reasonable for Couzens to expect to capture the Republican nomination from Senator Charles E. Townsend. For Ford had placed with the Department of Justice evidence that Senator Truman H. Newberry had expended large sums of money in the 1918 campaign. On the basis of this, Newberry had been convicted of violating the federal corrupt-practice act in a lower court. The

United States Supreme Court had overruled the conviction,[3] but the
issue had been kept alive.

In January 1922 the Senate took up a resolution to expel Newberry. On one side were the Old Guard Republican senators; on the
other, insurgent Republicans, led by La Follette of Wisconsin, and,
of course, the Democrats. Senator George W. Norris of Nebraska
made a powerful, sarcastic speech against Newberry, which began,
"Mr. President, they had a public sale up in Michigan . . ."[4] This
resolution was defeated, but this did not end the matter. Instead, in
the 1922 elections, "Newberryism" became an issue against every
senator up for re-election who had supported Newberry.[5] This was
particularly true in Michigan, for Senator Townsend had defended
Newberry.

3

Here was a situation that seemed made to order for Couzens. No
other nominal Republican in the state so definitely represented the
antithesis of "Newberryism." Besides, when he had stood for re-
election in the mayoralty campaign the previous year, 1921, he had
demonstrated that he was a political force of the first magnitude in
Michigan on his own, regardless of party machinery. If his first
election as mayor could have been passed off as a freak, this was not
so in 1921, for all of his shortcomings, real and alleged, had been
fully aired, and all the people he had offended by refusing to be a
"good fellow" had opposed him. "You are too mean to people to
be re-elected," his friend Jay Hayden had told him.[6]

The business elements generally had been against him. "They opposed my activities at every turn," Couzens himself said.[7] Yet he
was handsomely returned to office. "He hasn't a soul with him—
except the city of Detroit," said one observer.[8]

4

His health, however, finally determined that he would not enter
that senatorial race after all. From the first year of his mayoralty,
his physical condition had become a cause for concern. Just after
his initial municipal-ownership victory, marked by the heavy speaking program that had clearly overtaxed him, he began to be conscious of a stiffening in his left knee. Severe rheumatic pains attacked
him. His leg was placed in a cast and he was forced to hobble about
with a cane.

Then his tonsils, considered a possible cause of his trouble, were removed. For a man of his hitherto perfect health—except for headaches—he was remarkably slow in recovering from the tonsilectomy. The stiffness in his leg and the pain persisted. Later, he began to suffer from severe abdominal pain.

He was operated on again, this time for the removal of a gallstone. After spending two months in Florida, he seemed to have recovered his health. But soon he was again operated on, this time for bladder trouble. His condition became so desperate that it was reported he was dying.[9] He staged a comeback, only to be subjected to still another operation two months later, this time for an infection resulting from the previous operation.

When he finally did get back on his feet, he was by no means an invalid. Back at his desk in City Hall, he took on even more activities, adding the active managership of the street railway lines to his general duties as mayor. He was proud of the way he could still drive himself. "I get up at 6:30 every morning and hustle to get out of the house at 8 o'clock. I make straight for my office at the street railway headquarters and stick on the job there until noon. Then I change from being general manager of the traction system . . . and get on the job as Mayor. . . . I have never worked so hard in my life." [10] But the made-to-order opportunity to be a United States Senator had slipped by—so he thought.

5

Actually, the "Couzens luck" was running with him again.

Almost as soon as he had reconciled himself to a long wait before he could have another chance at the senatorship, the news came that Commodore Newberry intended to resign from the Senate. His colleague, Senator Townsend, had been defeated by a Democrat, Woodbridge N. Ferris. Very correctly, Newberry interpreted Townsend's defeat as a rebuke to himself. He also foresaw that when a new resolution for his expulsion came up in the Senate, it would certainly pass. Therefore, on November 18, 1922, he prudently resigned—"lashed from the Senate," in the words of Mississippi's Senator Pat Harrison.[11]

Governor Alex J. Groesbeck, known as a progressive Republican, then described the kind of man he would appoint to the vacancy. He would be "aggressive, and capable of taking care of himself on the floor of the Senate . . . something besides a mere dispenser of patronage," one who would be against "so-called standpatism" and "have the capacity and courage to do things that will advance the state and national welfare, regardless of personal and political considerations." This seemed to fit Couzens to a T, except for one thing. The appointee naturally had to be a Republican. Couzens professed to be a Republican, but was he?

6

It was widely known that he placed an individual's stand on public questions ahead of party regularity. Back in 1918, in response to a request for a campaign contribution on behalf of Republican Congressional candidates, he had told Fred W. Upham of Chicago, treasurer of the Republican National Committee:

> I must confess that I am not so much a party man as I am for individuals, and, in declining contributions to their campaigns, I have stated that I would have to know for whom the campaign was being conducted. . . . There are Democrats that I would rather vote for than some Republicans, though I am a Republican.[12]

Governor Groesbeck was warned against the Couzens "temperament." The *Detroit Times*, then owned jointly by William Randolph Hearst and Arthur Brisbane, commented: "The principal objection to Mr. Couzens seems to be that he is temperamentally unfitted to work on a job where he is surrounded by men equal to him in authority. He is a lone hand player." [13]

On Saturday, November 25, 1922, Governor Groesbeck called on Couzens at his home, obviously for a confidential "feeling out" sort of conversation. Couzens reiterated that he was a Republican, but he frankly said there was not much about the party's program at that time that he approved. The Governor really felt the same way, and so this was not against Couzens in Groesbeck's view. As for patronage, Couzens said: "I hate the very sound of the word." Couzens made one concession that Groesbeck accepted as satisfactory: he did "believe" in "party government." [14]

7

Groesbeck had said that he would definitely announce his choice on the 27th. The 27th passed and Groesbeck was silent. The press began to mention other available men. Among them were E. D. Stair of the *Free Press*, Ralph Booth of the Booth newspapers, and Marion L. Burton, president of the University of Michigan.

As for Couzens, he went about his affairs as usual. He had planned to spend Thanksgiving Day in New York City with Madeleine, who was at school there. Besides, Frank Couzens had married Margaret Lang of Kitchener, Ontario, the previous October 22nd; the newlyweds would also be in New York, and Couzens wanted to see them. He did not see fit to change his plans.[15]

Only a few hours after he and Mrs. Couzens and Madeleine had settled themselves in the Hotel Belmont on November 29, 1922, there was a telephone call from Governor Groesbeck. He had been appointed to the Senate as Newberry's successor.

BOOK THREE

The Senator

CHAPTER XXIII

THE ONE-MAN BLOC

HE WAS a marked man in the Senate from the very beginning. His career in industry as well as in municipal government, plus his wealth and his reputation as a fighter formed a combination that caught the public fancy.

One news service, unaware of his Canadian birth, sent out during his first month a story to the effect that he was "a natural candidate for President in 1924." "If the Democrats pick Ford, the Republicans are sure to seize upon Couzens as the only man who has a chance to beat him," said the story.[1]

Indeed, he rivaled in public attention, quite successfully, that distinctive feature of the year 1922—the "flapper." [2]

2

The Washington newspaper writers as a group immediately liked him, in particular such journalists as Thomas L. Stokes, Paul Y. Anderson, and Ray Tucker. Many senators were cautious in permitting the press to quote them, but not Couzens. Consequently, he was often good for a "story." The journalists, especially those of a liberal bent, flocked to his office. On the basis of one such meeting in his first week, William Hard wrote: "He is a perfectly non-political type of person . . . comes close to being the perfect independent." [3] This was sound prophecy.

3

He never mastered the art of oratory. For the most part, parliamentary procedure was a complete mystery to him. But he worked hard at his new career, attended every committee meeting, unless ill. He naively attempted in the beginning to function in the Senate as an executive, and never fully reconciled himself to the fact that this was impossible. Indeed, quite early in his career he remarked to a colleague: "This senator thing is not my line, and I probably won't be here long. There is too much talk, talk, talk." [4]

"He goes for the point like a bullet. He's a man of strong likes and dislikes. He's far from patient. Riled, he manifests it with plenty of vigor and urgency. Called to order, he effervesces like a shaken-up bottle of soda water. If you have business with Senator Couzens, make it snappy. He's there to transact it, and he's very accessible, but he doesn't want a conversation to drool along. . . . Efficiency, efficiency. That's Senator Couzens." So one observer wrote. [5]

In those first weeks, he spent considerable time searching in books to try to learn what a senator should do and be. [6] Finally, he gave up the study—and decided to be himself.

4

When he was sworn in by Vice President Calvin Coolidge on December 7, 1922, to become "a real live senator," as he wrote Madeleine, Harding was still President. The Secretary of the Treasury was Andrew W. Mellon. Many believed he functioned as the real power of the Harding administration. Charles Evans Hughes was Secretary of State. Herbert Hoover still headed Commerce. William Howard Taft was Chief Justice.

In the Senate itself, there was still Henry Cabot Lodge of Massachusetts, a link with an era long past. The venerable Mr. Lodge's celebrated whiskers were fading somewhat, but he remained the grandee of the Old Guard, symbolizing a strong hold on the government by old line conservatives. As faithful lieutenants in the Senate, Lodge had James Watson of Indiana, Reed Smoot of Utah, David Reed of Pennsylvania, George Moses of New Hampshire, and Simeon Fess of Ohio, all fervently devoted to the policies that President Harding had termed "normalcy." [7]

With Wilson's party largely in a state of coma after the defeat of James Cox and Franklin D. Roosevelt for President and Vice President in the 1920 election, [8] the Old Guard leaders, for all practical purposes, were the Senate of the United States throughout the first half of the Harding era. [9]

5

It is true, however, that by 1922, the Republican stalwarts found themselves confronted with a challenging force, even so. In the Senate then were men, mainly Republicans from the West, who appeared to have been infected with the virus of Populism which many believed had been annihilated in the first Bryan campaign of 1896. These included Senators Robert M. La Follette, Sr., of Wisconsin, George W. Norris of Nebraska, Hiram Johnson of California, William E. Borah of Idaho, and, to some extent, Albert Cummins of Iowa, Arthur W. Capper of Kansas, and Charles L. McNary of Oregon. As the result of a kind of political dust storm in Iowa, the 1922 elections had even turned up a supposedly peculiar Republican who was pictured as a cross between John Peter Altgeld of Illinois and Nicolai Lenin—Senator Smith Brookhart, whose middle name was "Wildman."

Under Old Bob La Follette's magnetic personal leadership, these men had formed a Progressive bloc to make war on the clique around Harding, the "curious crew," as Senator Norris called them.[10] Senator Moses called this progressive group "Sons of the Wild Jackass," with Couzens to be included in the epithet.[11]

This group contrived at times to stir up heated controversy. They inveighed against domination of government by big business and flayed Wall Street and the power trust. They championed the cause of the western agricultural areas, which somehow did not share fully in the blessings of Harding's "normalcy." They opposed the administration tax policies. And finally, they turned the spotlight on evidence of corruption that made the Harding regime comparable to that of President Grant, uncovering a scandal, in the Teapot Dome oil leases, that rivaled any governmental venality the nation had known before.[12]

William Allen White thought he saw in this Progressive bloc, mainly Republican, a movement "that portends revolution—not noisy, bloody and disorderly . . . but a nice, decent, and dangerous revolution that will take a long forward trek toward economic justice for those who have been hankering to see something smash something."[13] This was optimism, for the basic calmness of the over-all political scene was really little disturbed just then. It would be ten years before the "nice and decent revolution"—that of Franklin D. Roosevelt—was to come.

6

Couzens himself was anxious for action. He gave a hint of this by his behavior when he was sworn in by Coolidge. When his name was called, he loped down the aisle so swiftly that retiring Senator Town-send, supposedly his escort, had to hurry to catch up.[14]

But the general listlessness of these early 1920's was a definite handicap to him. His nature demanded that he strive to be outstand-ing, to leave his mark. The criticism which had been voiced to Gov-ernor Groesbeck that Couzens was a "lone handed player" was ac-curate, and therefore he could not wholly identify himself with any group in the Senate and gain satisfaction from the activities of the group—much less his party. He had to be on his own. He was at his best when tackling major problems, as in the case of the streetcar issue in Detroit. But the Senate as a whole was slow then in facing up to major problems.

7

As might be expected, he became an almost constant thorn in the side of his own party. His enemies never said anything more accurate about him than that he was a Republican "in name only." He himself later summed up his partisanship: "I am a Republican, but not like Harding, Coolidge, and Hoover!" Inasmuch as these three were the titular heads of his party throughout his senatorship, a fair question would have been: "Republican? What kind?" A news-paper headline of the period came closest to pegging him properly:

JAMES COUZENS—ONE-MAN BLOC [15]

Curiously enough, despite his progressive record as Detroit's mayor, he did not immediately commit himself as to which group he would line up with. But which group *could* he line up with? The Old Guard, under Lodge? The Progressives, under La Follette?

One of the first things he did was deliberately to insult Senator Jim Watson of Indiana by pretending to him that he had never heard of him before and asking him what party he belonged to. A Re-publican organ in St. Louis reflected Watson's reaction by observing: "Evidently, this new specimen of the political fauna from the wilds of Detroit intends to make it plain that he was formerly associated with Ford by trying to out-Ford himself in arrogance. It is safe to predict that he will fade away from Washington just about the same way as Multimillionaire Senator H. A. W. Tabor of Colorado." [16]

8

Couzens' first vote as Senator was in opposition to a ship-subsidy bill, which the Harding clique supported with great fervor. This bill was an outgrowth of World War I, during which the government had acquired a great merchant fleet operated by the U. S. Shipping Board. The Ship Subsidy Bill of 1922 provided that the vessels "be turned over to private companies on generous terms and that substantial appropriations be voted to help them operate on a comfortable margin." [17]

Although it is debatable how well this jibed with the popular idea that the government should get out of business, it certainly was good business for the companies that were to get the ships and the generous subsidies, estimated at $850,000,000.

Along with Brookhart, Couzens caused this bill to be shelved in the Senate just when its passage appeared near. For he and Brookhart obtained enough signatures to a round robin to get the subsidy measure taken off the calendar in favor of a farm-relief measure.

This ship-subsidy issue had been prominent in the 1922 Congressional elections, a number of members having been defeated primarily, it was said, because they had favored it. Now the Lame Duck Congress was given its orders to pass the bill before the new members took their seats—a maneuver that inspired Senator Norris later to begin his long and finally successful fight for the so-called "Lame Duck Amendment" to the Constitution.[18]

Harding made a personal appearance before Congress on behalf of the subsidy.

It was no wonder that the Couzens-Brookhart action produced a sensation. As stated by the *Baltimore Sun:*

> This was the most novel experience the Senate has had in many years. Here were two senators who had hardly acquainted themselves with the methods of getting in and out of the Senate chambers and yet they had become leaders in fact in the subsidy fight, if not in name.[19]

The staunchly Republican *Philadelphia Public Ledger* headlined the incident:

POLITICAL CHAOS NOW
REIGNS IN WASHINGTON [20]

9

That Couzens in his first week had helped to incite all this seemed to mean that he, too, was an insurgent Progressive. Additional evidence along this line appeared when the Senate began considering an offer by Henry Ford to buy the Muscle Shoals, Alabama, facilities (later the basis for the Tennessee Valley Authority). This offer, which had enormous popular support, was almost accepted by Con-gress.[21] Couzens asserted bluntly that neither Ford nor any other private individual ought to have the government-owned nitrate and power development, but it should be held by the government for the benefit of the public.

In this, of course, he shared the view of Senator Norris, "father of TVA", who at just this time issued a report that called Ford's offer "the most wonderful real estate speculation since Adam and Eve lost title to the Garden of Eden." [22]

Couzens felt so strongly on this issue that he gave it as one reason for giving up his interest in the Bank of Detroit just before he took the oath as senator. "I am going to fight Mr. Ford on Muscle Shoals and I don't want my stand to embarrass the bank," he told the direc-tors of the bank.[23]

His attitude helped to bring about a sharp decline in Congressional sentiment for the Ford offer, and helped to save Muscle Shoals for the later T.V.A. As the *Detroit Free Press* put it: "That Senator Couzens, former business partner to Ford, is opposed to the offer . . . has convinced Republican leaders that it would be a mistake to put the Ford offer before the Congress." [24]

Even so, Couzens' vote on the Ship Subsidy Bill, his outcry against the Ford offer, was not yet a safe indication of his political thinking. He had acted against the subsidy bill merely upon impulse. Later, he said, "If it is the business of the United States to see that we have a Merchant Marine, then we ought to assume the responsibility and not transfer it to private interests, augmented by taxes." [25] But in December 1922 he had merely been annoyed that the business of the Senate had come to a stop while senators orated for days on the ship-ping bill.[26]

10

Political success is often corrosive of political principles. When the rebel, the iconoclast, the independent, finds himself in a position of high influence, there is a tendency to retract the horns, to prove that, after all, he is "safe" and "sound"; a kind of self-reformation of the reformer occurs. With some, this change lasts only a short time; with others, the weak ones or the opportunists, it becomes permanent.

Couzens experienced this change temporarily. He demonstrated at the outset an unwonted sensitivity to the charge that he was not a "regular Republican." It was commented upon that his social com-panions, at lunch and at golf, were all of the Old Guard, men like

Frederick Hale of Maine or the steel millionaire Lawrence C. Phipps of Colorado.

When he was in the company of Progressives like Norris, "he developed streaks of orthodoxy," one observer noted.[27] Another, in talking with him, suggested that he would naturally be classified as a Progressive, citing his record as mayor of Detroit, but Couzens on this occasion was evasive. "I don't want to be classified at all," he said. "If this bloc you call progressive is for something I believe in, then I'll be with them, but I'll not commit myself to any group. The standpatters are not always wrong." [28]

11

Early in his Senate service, he cast a vote that was odd for a man considered a "Bolshevik" back home.

Senator J. Thomas Heflin of Alabama, a lesser figure of the species of "Pitchfork" Ben Tillman and Tom Watson, had made a remark, during debate on an agricultural credit bill, which the Old Guard took as a special slur. He was in the Senate, Heflin said, to "represent the people . . . not the bond sharks, the big financiers of Wall Street." [29] Senator Lodge especially was outraged, asserted that Heflin had violated the Senate rules against impugning the motives of colleagues, and demanded that Heflin be refused further use of the floor. Vice President Coolidge so ruled. A vote was taken—and Couzens voted for suppression of Heflin.[30]

In one respect, this vote could have been deemed praiseworthy, even for a Progressive. For Senator Heflin could by no means represent personally a cause worth a Progressive's martyrdom. In the words of a quite moderate observer: "Congress had its quota of strong men, weak men, and fools, and foremost of the fools was . . . Heflin . . . the national idol of the Ku Klux Klan." [31]

Yet, in a larger view, the silencing of Heflin was an attack on free and open debate, a principle Couzens always championed.

12

Heflin turned on Couzens. He said sarcastically that he knew the explanation for Couzens' vote. It was his money. He had heard it said that, though Couzens was a multimillionaire, he was progressive. "I said, 'Say that to me again and say it slow.' . . . Mark what I tell you. . . . When the big interests are attacked, you will see him go over and take his place with the bellwethers of the standpat party.

"I saw him do it this morning—my good friend Couzens of Michigan, parading himself down here as a Progressive, and this morning he walked right over and sat right down under the whiskers of the Senator of Massachusetts." [32]

Although another man might have laughed, Couzens characteristically lost his temper. He stood up in the aisle to answer Heflin, "his posture that of a bulldog." In angry tones he made a demand that startled everyone. The Senate reporter should be instructed to read the record of the remarks just made by Heflin, because, he explained, Wadsworth of New York had advised the Senate at an earlier time that Heflin had edited certain remarks he had made about Wadsworth.

"I do not propose to give him the opportunity to go in the night time, in the dark, and change the references he has made to myself. If Senators are free to get up here and tell the galleries and the American people that the motives of a senator of any state are to be questioned, we might as well stand up here and call everybody thieves and liars!" [33]

There ensued a scene which was, according to the *New York Herald*, "reminiscent of Socialist outbreaks in the Reichstag, the French Chamber of Deputies, soap-box events in Union Square and Hyde Park, London." [34] Undoubtedly, this was an exaggeration, but by dropping the pose of a dignified Roman Senator as soon as he was attacked, Couzens certainly had transformed the Senate into something resembling the rowdy Detroit city-council meetings when he was mayor.

Nine senators were on their feet at once, all clamoring for recognition and arguing loudly one way or another about Couzens' request. The upshot of all the furor was that both Couzens and Heflin withdrew their remarks. Couzens found himself praised by a group whose praise he would not appreciate for long—the clique around Harding, to whom Big Tom Heflin was especially obnoxious. The Old-Guard press hailed him as "a hero." Couzens was all right after all, they decided.

13

But at just this time he also gave Harding and the Old Guard newspapers cause to regret his presence in the Senate. For he had deliberately attacked Harding's leadership on the subject of government ownership versus private ownership of the railroads.

In a special message to Congress, Harding had referred to the government's administration of the railroads during the war as "folly." For the railroad brotherhood's newspaper, *Labor*, Couzens prepared a sharply critical statement on the President's message.[35] He also carried on the attack in an address before the Philadelphia Real Estate Board.[36]

He did not commit himself definitely in favor of government ownership, but he made it plain that he resented the idea that government ownership was evil *per se*. In this same address, to make the point that private business could be worse than government, he ripped into the Lincoln Motor Car Company for the profit it made on its contracts to produce Liberty airplane motors during World War I.[37]

He strongly refuted the propaganda line put forward by *The Railway Review*, that those who even considered government ownership of the railroads were subversives, in league with "the most dangerous organizations of radicals in the country." But, as the Kansas City *Star* said:

"Couzens has the background of many years of successful business experience and . . . is the wealthiest man in the Senate. It will be difficult for foes to brand any plan he puts forward as coming from a 'wild-eyed radical.' " [38]

The Progressives were exultant. "Jim Couzens is one of the greatest men in Washington!" Senator Brookhart exclaimed.[39] La Follette and Norris paid him an unprecedented compliment, for a first-termer. They backed him, though unsuccessfully, for chairman of the Senate Committee on Interstate Commerce.[40]

14

It was inevitable that Couzens and Harding should eventually be at loggerheads. They were antithetical figures: Harding, the prince of good fellows, had, in the words of William Allen White (who liked him), "the harlot's virtues";[41] Couzens was the epitome of the rigidly ethical. Indeed, at their first meeting there was an air of suppressed hostility.[42]

Just at this time, Harding appointed James G. McNary, a Texas banker, to the office of Comptroller of the Currency. Couzens, as chairman of a subcommittee of the Senate Committee on Banking and Currency, had the duty of investigating McNary's background. When a banker himself, he had adhered to certain rules which he considered basic: A banker must not borrow from his own bank, nor must he permit associates in his bank to make loans to themselves.[43] To his amazement, Couzens came upon evidence which indicated that Harding's choice for Comptroller had violated these rules in an extravagant fashion as president of his bank in Texas. Couzens was advised for example, that "for a period of more than five years, Mc-Nary was a continuous borrower from the bank of which he was president. . . . At one time 88 per cent of the capital and surplus funds . . . was loaned directly to the officers and directors." Couzens immediately went to the White House to tell Harding to withdraw the McNary appointment.[44]

Harding, however, adopted the position that McNary's background, instead of disqualifying him, proved him "a very practical man," the kind "needed as Comptroller of Currency." [45] Couzens stood firm. "I agree with you that Mr. McNary is a very practical man. I am afraid he is too practical to be the kind of disciplinarian that the Comptroller of the Currency should be." [46]

Despite Couzens' opposition, Harding insisted that the Senate confirm McNary. He was angry that Couzens had made public the Senate committee's findings on McNary, evidence obtained in "executive session." To have made it public was "in violation of the long-established conception of wise procedure," he wrote Couzens.[47]

The strongest possible pressure was brought on the Republican leaders in the Senate to push the nomination through, for McNary was an important cog in the Republican organization of the Southwest, described by William Allen White as the party's "field agent" in Texas and New Mexico.[48]

On the last day of the session, Couzens, carrying on a singlehanded fight, threatened to filibuster unless the McNary appointment were withdrawn. He so informed "Jim" Watson, Harding's floor leader.[49] Rather than see other legislation lost, Harding yielded, and the appointment was withdrawn. Daniel R. Crissinger of Marion, Ohio, Harding's home town, who later became Governor of the Federal Reserve Board, was named instead.

15

That a Republican senator could be responsible for such an affront to a Republican President revived a familiar question. Was Couzens a Republican? He himself raised the point in a talk at Bay City, Michigan. "I would like to be considered a member of the Republican party. . . . But, if being a Republican means kow-towing to the President, I do not care to be a Republican." [50]

From then on, he was the old Couzens. No one would ever again be able to say that he sat under the whiskers of Senator Lodge or any other standpatter. He dropped the pose of not knowing the difference between the Progressives and the Old Guard. To a reporter for *Nation's Business,* who inquired about statements that he was a radical, Couzens said, "Yes, I'm radical as hell when I see an evil that ought to be ended." [51]

To the *Saturday Evening Post* he became "The Scab Millionaire." [52]

CHAPTER XXIV

THE PLAIN-SPEAKING STATESMAN

IN THE summer of 1923, a full-fledged boom was under way to nominate Henry Ford for President of the United States. Ford was set to run on either major party ticket, but preferably the Republican, judged the most likely to win. To a later generation, one nursed on the picture of Ford as a man above politics, or even against politics, this movement would seem unbelievable. Ford himself later denied that he had Presidential ambitions.

But it is indisputable that the boom had his approval.[1]

An article signed by Ford entitled "If I Were President," appeared in *Collier's* magazine August 8, 1923. Allen Benson, prominent in the Socialist Party, wrote a laudatory biography of Ford as part of the boom. Besides, Ford as much as admitted to Couzens that he was a receptive candidate. On one occasion, at a wedding, "with just the inflection of seriousness to make me realize that he meant every word," he even discussed with him the possibility of having him in his cabinet.[2]

A good deal of joking went on in the press about the Ford-for-President movement. But the reality of the Ford boom was no joke. Even Senator Norris, the Nebraska liberal, greatly admired Ford at the time, and perhaps would have suggested him for President.[3]

That summer there was also much discussion, pro and con, of the desirability of modifying the national laws, adopted during World War I, prohibiting sale of intoxicating beverages. Both subjects—the Ford boom and prohibition—were too hot for most public officials to discuss openly with any forthrightness. The passions they generated were too strong. But Couzens, though he hadn't planned it that way, was soon doing precisely that.

2

That June he was visiting in Ottawa, while on a motor trip with his family. A newspaper reporter there asked him to comment on the liberal Quebec liquor laws, "I think they are fine," he said. "I think the United States might with good grace adopt some of them. If our constitution were easier to amend, I believe the Volstead act would be repealed." [4] Somewhat embroidered, these comments were telegraphed to newspapers in the United States—on the same day that President Harding, on a "voyage of understanding," spoke in Denver in spirited defense of prohibition. "I am convinced," Harding had said, "they are a small and a greatly mistaken minority who believe that the Eighteenth Amendment will ever be repealed."

The result of this divergence of views between Harding and Couzens was a newspaper sensation:

HARDING DEFENDS DRY LAW:
COUZENS ASKS O.K. ON BEER

The results could have been foreseen.[5] Couzens was denounced by the prohibitionists all over the land, but especially in Michigan. The Anti-Saloon League, the most powerful pressure bloc of the day, went after him in full cry. He was called a "traitor to America," a "betrayer" of his party, his state, and his nation, and of all decent people. The Anti-Saloon League served notice it would seek his defeat in 1924 if he had "the gall" to become a candidate to succeed himself.[6]

He hit back at the Anti-Saloon League. It was, he said, an organization that sought "to dictate" who should hold public office on the basis of one issue, "disregarding all other problems." "They are out to elect a man who will go to Congress and do what they want, no matter whether he is a bum, an anarchist, or what not." [7] These were fighting words, and other politicians shuddered at his daring—or folly.

To the amazement of other politicians, he gave a half dozen speeches in this vein. *Time*, a new magazine, ran his picture on its front cover as if to cheer him on. But for the few who praised him, hundreds denounced him.[8] "Mr. Couzens Destroys Himself," the *Christian Science Monitor* headlined. "It is a pity. There were possibilities in Couzens as a public man that now may never be tested, for his political future is, alas, behind him." [9]

With this din in his ears, Couzens took himself and his family off to Europe for the balance of the recess between Congressional sessions, wiser perhaps, but not chastened in spirit.

On his return from Europe he made some interesting comments about European conditions. La Follette, Borah, Norris, Johnson, and Wheeler, on foreign affairs, were largely "isolationist," to use a term which became current only in the 1940's. It was then almost a hallmark of a Progressive to turn one's back on Europe and Asia. But with remarkable insight, Couzens warned:

> Germany is decidedly unhappy, with sixty-five or seventy millions of people, the majority of whom are in great distress. . . . The extreme isolationists [in America] have forbidden or intimidated the United States from having a voice in world affairs. We cannot go on that way. We have got to stand up and be counted, for or against these various proposals for settling the economic conditions in Europe.[10]

He also advanced a program. The United States with other powers should establish "a receivership for Germany," to put its affairs in order. Ultimately, he hoped, there would develop a "United States of Europe."

While in Paris, he copied into his notebook a statement by Victor Hugo. "I belong to a party not yet born, but which will be born in the Twentieth Century. This party will have its principle in a United States of Europe." He read this to newspaper reporters, pronouncing it a "sound idea." [11]

3

While Couzens was on the ocean, Harding's death had occurred. Promptly on his return, Couzens wrote a letter of advice, based on his observations in Europe, to the new President, Calvin Coolidge. Coolidge should abandon "the Harding isolationism," he said. He hoped, he wrote, that Coolidge in his first message to Congress, would "express a very strong, energetic, forward position on foreign relations."

At that time, the principal "isolationist" in the Senate was Hiram Johnson. Johnson was and remained Couzens' friend. Nevertheless, Couzens now bluntly told Coolidge: "I do not think that we are going to get anywhere in any way by trying to placate Senator Hiram Johnson." [12]

4

Couzens also made a number of public comments at this time that caused some observers to suggest that he had gone over completely to the camp of "noisy radicals," notably La Follette, who was being accused of wanting "to undermine the Constitution and the Supreme Court." For he was outraged just then by a decision of the court against federal regulation of child labor, a decision which set off a revival of the movement Theodore Roosevelt and Albert J. Beveridge had sponsored a decade earlier for permitting Congress to overrule the court.[13] La Follette sounded anew a call for "curbing the court" and Couzens was instinctively in agreement. To the press, he said: "I am for bringing about a change which will not permit the Supreme Court to declare acts of Congress unconstitutional by a majority of one. I would have at least a favorable vote of two-thirds of the court necessary." [14]

To Editor Arthur H. Vandenberg in Grand Rapids, who was alarmed by his comments, he wrote:

"The point I want to raise . . . is that the interpretation of the Constitution is made by human minds, and I do not believe the opinions of five human minds should offset the interpretation of the Constitution of the United States made by hundreds of Congressmen and four members of the Supreme Court. . . ." [15]

Vandenberg attempted, by long letters, to change Couzens' views, arguing that Supreme Court decisions ought to be considered sacred. Any proposal to let Congress "nullify" a court decision would "emasculate" the court and turn Congress into a "despotism," he said.[16] He sent Couzens copies of editorials he had written in the *Grand Rapids Herald,* including one that bitterly denounced the Scripps-Howard newspapers, as well as the *Detroit News,* for supporting the La Follette proposal to permit Congress to overrule the Supreme Court.

It was all very well, Couzens came back at Vandenberg, to be "theoretical" about such matters. But he could not see how "a decent man" could defend a Supreme Court decision that condemned children to labor in factories and mines. "I am not out looking to stir up trouble, where trouble does not exist," he wrote. "I cannot help, however, before concluding, raising the question of how many thousands of children may be suffering because of the Supreme

Court. . . . May it not be that we are prone to let these things go, rather than risk a change? Does not the doctrine of 'leaving well enough alone' sometimes impose a lot of hardship, which we do not truly visualize?" [17]

5

As for Ford, who had been granting some interviews to Dr. William L. Stidger, a Methodist minister later associated with Boston University, for publication in newspapers and in a book on Ford's Presidential aspirations, the *Detroit Times* on October 25, 1923, published this:

> DR. STIDGER: What do you think of the stand that your friend Senator Couzens is taking on the prohibition laws? He is in favor of going back to five per cent beer and light wines.
>
> FORD: He knows he is wrong about it. Mr. Couzens knows better. He knows that in the Ford motor plant booze never did anybody any good, and he is taking a backward step when he stands for five per cent beer and light wines. *Jim Couzens knows better than that.* Maybe he feels he is striking a popular chord.

Couzens considered Ford's remarks about him an attack on his integrity.[18] A week later, Couzens, for the first time in his career, publicly gave vent to his anger at Ford.

He began a speech before the Republican Club at the Hotel Statler in Detroit with an apparently general discussion of the need for truthfulness in public affairs. "Parties and public men have not always been truthful," he said. Then he said he was "forced" to discuss a man who "exemplified" this. "The example is our chief Democratic politician, Henry Ford, who recently gave a newspaper interview, so it is reported, and he has not denied it, differing with me on the amendment I suggested on the Volstead act." He denounced Ford in particular for ascribing political motives to Couzens' suggestion that the Volstead Act be modified. He went on:

> It comes from poor taste from a man who is so politically ambitious as Mr. Ford and who has never gotten over his peevishness because of his defeat for United States senator on the Democratic ticket. A man who has perhaps made more unfulfilled promises than any man in America should be more guarded in challenging the motives of other people. . . .
> If Mr. Ford wants to be president—and it is quite evident he does —because he has filed his name, or at least permitted it to be filed,

in the Nebraska primaries—why does he refrain from announcing himself as a candidate? The reason, it appears to me, is that he is afraid, realizing that the probable outcome would be as great a fiasco as his "Peace Ship" . . .

Mr. Ford for president? It is ridiculous. . . . If the American people ever stop to analyze Mr. Ford's experience and his qualifications for the presidency of the United States, he will never even get started. It is my hope that they will stop and think.

I say this not only because I want to save Mr. Ford from the greatest humiliation that could befall him. But I want equally to save the United States from the humiliation it would suffer.[19]

A good many persons had been saying precisely these things privately. Republican leaders generally were pleased that Couzens did so publicly. In his syndicated column from Washington, Mark Foote wrote: "Republican politicians howled with delight. President Coolidge is said to have pulled a wry Puritanical smile. . . . Politicians who had never been able to discern any good points in James Couzens now declared him a great man." There also was some comment on the fact that just before leaving Washington for Detroit to make his speech on Ford, Couzens and his wife dined with the Coolidges.[20]

6

He did not return to the subject of Ford's Presidential ambitions. He had not really relished attacking his former associate openly. Moreover, the Ford boom suddenly petered out, after Ford and Coolidge had a meeting at which Coolidge seemed to agree to support Ford's ideas for Muscle Shoals.[21] After this meeting, Ford said to reporters: "Muscle Shoals? Where is Muscle Shoals?" [22]

Ford did not answer Couzens. And before long, curiously enough, he and Couzens seemed better friends than they had acted for a long time.

Besides, Couzens was soon involved in an heroic controversy with Secretary of the Treasury Andrew W. Mellon, who more than any other individual embodied the dominant philosophy of the Republican party in this era.

CHAPTER XXV

THE MILLIONAIRES' WAR

EARLY in November 1923 the *New York Times* sent a telegram to Couzens in Detroit: "We will appreciate it if you wire us collect your views on Secretary Mellon's propositions to reduce income taxes." [1] Quite innocently, this telegram directed him on a course that touched off one of the most explosive political controversies of his generation.

Couzens had not planned things this way. Indeed, he answered the *Times* noncommittally. "It would not be wise," he said, "for a Senator to commit himself in advance to a proposal of this kind. The matter will naturally go to the Finance Committee and no Senator should commit himself until he hears the arguments and recommendations of the Committee." [2]

Only a few days earlier, in a speech before the Detroit North End Republican Club, he had mentioned the Mellon proposals in passing. He seemed to favor them. In any event, he did not denounce them. "There is going to be a suggestion before Congress," he said, "that the surtax be reduced from fifty to twenty-five per cent, and a hurrah goes up that it is all in favor of the rich. Well it does not make much difference who it is in favor of, so long as the Government gets its proper taxes from each and every individual." [3]

But what were "proper taxes?" The *New York Times* telegram set him to thinking about this in specific terms. He was aware, of course, that Mellon's proposals, widely acclaimed in the press, were close to being canonized doctrine of the Republican party. For this was the era in which Andrew Mellon was hailed as "the greatest Secretary of the Treasury since Alexander Hamilton." In the words of one observer: "Anyone who disagreed with Andrew Mellon on taxation was a menace to constitutional government." [4]

Promptly on returning to Washington the following December, Couzens summoned a stenographer and dictated a letter to Secretary

Mellon. By asking Mellon some pointed questions—his habitual manner—he hoped to clarify his own thinking. He set down the claims made for Mellon's proposals—that the current high wartime surtax rates were retarding business; that the government would get more revenue, not less, from lowered rates; that high surtaxes were driving vast sums of capital into tax-exempt securities and thus retarding industrial investment, etc.—and after each argument, he asked for "proof."

Now, Mellon, a multimillionaire financier and industrialist in his own right, was a man of mild appearance. He was "self-deprecating, gentle and smiling," William Allen White said.[5] But this appearance was deceptive. Actually he was as self-assured and nearly as aggressive as Couzens himself.[6] He was used to being treated with the utmost respect, even by those who did not like him, even by Democrats. Yet here was Couzens, a Republican, challenging his views on taxation, views considered to be his great contribution to public service, or so Mellon interpreted Couzens' letter.

2

Mellon responded with a letter that displeased Couzens violently.[7] As he afterward told Vandenberg, "Whatever has been the outcome of my first correspondence with Mr. Mellon, has been due entirely to Mellon's own arrogant desire to 'lord it' over all of us who dared to question him."[8]

He was not alone in that opinion. David Lawrence, an admirer of Mellon, conceded that "Mr. Mellon rubbed the Michigan senator the wrong way."[9] Even Mark Sullivan said, "Although Secretary Mellon is one of the gentlest of men, and Senator Couzens one of the most truculent, I think the former is a little more responsible than the latter for the beginning of the row."[10]

What Mellon ought to have done, said Sullivan, was to "dump a couple of barrels of figures on Mr. Couzens." Instead, he wrote Couzens a letter "that sounded a little resentful."[11] In effect, Mellon told Couzens that he ought to leave such matters in the hands of a man who understood them.

3

Couzens replied caustically. He accused Mellon of seeking to impose his views on the nation to the exclusion of everyone else. "I dissent," he wrote, "from permitting one individual doing the diagnosing and prescribing the remedy. I propose to engage in this diagnosis myself and perhaps have some voice in the decision." [12]

Mellon sent back a reply, but not one calculated to placate Couzens:

> It is reported in the newspapers that all your capital is now in tax exempt securities, and I have not seen any denial from you. This means, if it means anything, that you pay no income tax. . . . Must a system of taxation which permits a man with an income of over $1,000,000 a year to pay not one cent to the support of his Government remain unaltered? [13]

This was a jab at Couzens in a sensitive political spot. It was a fact that the bulk of Couzens' money was in government bonds. He never denied it. His usual reply to critics on this was: "In reality, I prepaid my tax by investing my money in municipal, state, and government securities at a very much less return than I would receive if I had invested in mortgages, railroads or industries." [14] Then, too, he had switched his investments from private securities to government bonds because, as he once explained, he wanted to insulate himself against pressures that might be exerted through ownership of stock in companies or banks. But he could never get people to understand these considerations, as he himself conceded some years later in urging that tax exemptions on government securities be abolished. [15]

To Mellon, Couzens rejoined: "So long as you have entered into the record of my securities, will you please tell what your securities are, how much you own of them, and how much you will benefit by the reduction of surtaxes as proposed by you?" He followed with barbed references to a well-known fact: much Mellon money was invested in the distillery business. Is money used for making whiskey more "useful" than money invested in public improvements? he demanded. [16]

Ordinarily, cautious men in politics might have dropped matters there—assuming they had let things proceed this far. But neither Couzens nor Mellon was cautious. They kept up the exchange, sending each other a sufficient number of letters to make a good-sized book, and each contrived that much of this correspondence should become public.

In one letter, Couzens cited his own experience as evidence that Mellon's proposals would "help the rich." It was ironic, in view of what was to come, that he recalled that when he sold his Ford Company stock to Henry Ford, he paid an income tax of $7,229,161.75 for the year 1920. "If your proposal had been law, I would have saved nearly four million dollars; so I do not see where the country gains by creating these enormous savings for those well able to pay."

He wound up by urging that Mellon engage in a public debate on the matter, "where both of us will be forced to rely upon our knowledge, rather than upon statisticians who can make figures tell any kind of a story, or upon lawyers who can argue from any side." [17]

Couzens soon found himself thrust into the role of the nation's leading opponent of "Mellonism." Though he had not intended this, he accepted the role, while the public enjoyed a dramatic spectacle: two multimillionaire public officials at war.

Couzens cleared his decks for action by abruptly accepting the resignation of his secretary, Walter Dorsey, whom he had inherited from Senator Newberry. Trained in the old school, Dorsey felt that Couzens "ought not have criticized Mellon." [18] Then, at the suggestion of Jay Hayden, Couzens took on a new secretary—John Carson, a Scripps-Howard reporter with a flair for fact-finding and crusading who, years later, was appointed to the Federal Trade Commission by President Harry S. Truman. With Carson's help, Couzens prepared for a real assault on Mellon.[19]

4

On February 21, 1924, he struck at Mellon in a way that startled everyone. He introduced a Senate resolution calling for an investigation of the Bureau of Internal Revenue.[20]

This bureau had never before been subjected to investigation, though its financial and political powers were obviously enormous, a fact that Couzens was to point up when he said: "Give me control of the Bureau of Internal Revenue and I will run the politics of the country." [21]

Almost before Mellon and the Old Guard were aware of what had happened, the Progressive bloc, joined by some Democrats, had lined up behind Couzens' bold resolution, and it had passed.[22]

With the aid of John Carson, Couzens was soon making public some interesting material. Over the protests of Senator Watson, chairman of the committee, and Senator Richard Ernst of Kentucky (a personal friend of Mellon), Couzens had obtained from the Bureau of Internal Revenue its files on thirty-eight corporations in which Mellon was at that time, or had been previously, financially interested.

These files revealed that certain of the firms had received large tax rebates. They also revealed, through various memoranda, that the Bureau had gone out of its way to treat these corporations with special deference, if not with favoritism.[23]

Mellon denounced the revelations as "nonsense." The rebates were merely routine. The companies in question were entitled to what they had received. He professed to be unconcerned. But Mellon was obviously fuming, and began to look for a politically safe way to bring the Couzens "nonsense" to an end.

One way to stop the investigation was to get Couzens out of the Senate. Couzens soon found himself a guest at the White House, where an attractive offer was made to him by President Coolidge— the ambassadorship to the Court of St. James. But Couzens' answer was, "I won't be kicked upstairs." [24]

5

Governor Gifford Pinchot of Pennsylvania, the old Bull Moose Progressive, then entered the picture. An ardent "dry" and an equally ardent political enemy of Mellon's, he gave Couzens some material which suggested a scandalous situation in the Bureau of Internal Revenue with regard to prohibition enforcement.[25] But it would be useless, Pinchot said, to go into this, or even into income-tax matters, unless the committee had the services of a lawyer experienced in investigations. He had a name ready—Francis J. Heney of California, a La Follette follower who had handled the public-lands scandal investigation during the Theodore Roosevelt administration.

Indeed, Pinchot had already consulted Heney by telephone.

Heney was interested, but there was a stumbling block—Heney had to be compensated. Was Couzens aware that his resolution for the investigation had omitted any mention of retaining and paying for counsel?

For the first time, Couzens realized that he had omitted such a provision. But he quickly came up with a solution. "I will pay Heney out of my own pocket!" he told Pinchot.[26]

At the next meeting of his committee, Senator Watson raised vigorous objections. For a Senator to use his own funds for such a purpose was highly irregular, he maintained. But the two Democratic members of the committee sided with Couzens, and Heney was retained.[27]

Watson immediately communicated with Mellon and also with President Coolidge, as he later told the Senate.[28]

A conference of administration leaders was hastily summoned.

For months, these leaders had been disturbed over Senate investigations in general. The Teapot Dome investigation was then in progress. There was also an investigation of the Department of Justice and one of the Veterans' Bureau under way. Ahead was the 1924 election. The thought of Heney being set loose on prohibition enforcement, as well as tax administration, was appalling to the Old Guard. Watson was surprisingly candid about this. With Heney conducting an investigation, backed by Couzens and by Pinchot, Mellon's old enemy, there would result, said Watson, "a saturnalia of vituperation and aspersion unequaled hitherto in the political annals of America!" [29]

6

On the heels of the leaders' conference, Mellon sent Coolidge a solemn communication. The Couzens investigation, it said, was merely an effort to "vent some personal grievance," but its effect would "threaten the institution of government itself." "A private individual is authorized to investigate generally an executive department of the government. . . . If the interposition of private resources be permitted to interfere with the executive administration of government, the machinery of government will cease to function." [30]

Coolidge then promptly dispatched Mellon's letter to the Senate, incorporating it in a special message of his own:

> It seems incredible that the Senate of the United States would knowingly approve the past and proposed conduct of one of its committees which this letter reveals. . . .
>
> Under a procedure of this kind, the Constitutional guarantees against unwarranted search and seizure breaks down, the prohibition against what amounts to a Government charge of criminal action without the formal presentment of a grand jury is evaded, the rules of evidence which have been adopted for the protection of the innocent are ignored, the department becomes the victim of vague, unformulated and indefinite charges; instead of a Government of law, we have a Government of lawlessness.
>
> Against the continuance of such condition, I enter my solemn protests and give notice that in my opinion the departments ought not to be required to participate in it. . . . It is time that we return to a Government under and in accord with the usual forms of law of the land.
>
> CALVIN COOLIDGE [31]

7

Obviously, this was not a Presidential message calculated to please senators. Even regular Republicans in the Senate were angered. Only a short time before this, Coolidge, in a confidential chat with Chief Justice Taft, had referred to senators as "cowards," [32] but he was to learn now that some senators could strike back, even at him. Tom Walsh of Montana, in charge of the Teapot Dome inquiry, called the Coolidge message "the most arrogant sent by an executive to a parliamentary body since the days of the Stuarts and Tudors." Reed of Missouri called it "such an insult as one branch of the government could not accept from another." He presented a resolution to have it expunged from the records.[33]

Carter Glass, who had been Wilson's Secretary of the Treasury, declared that Coolidge had "impeached the probity of the Senate . . . charging it with subterfuge and insincerity." Glass added: "This message, this letter of the President and of the Secretary, constitute the most extraordinary breach of official etiquette that has ever occurred in the history of the Republic." [34]

8

Clearly, Couzens had found himself with ardent allies, but he himself was not among the senators who replied to Coolidge from the floor of the Senate. For several weeks before this, he had been suffering from intense abdominal pains.[35] On the very day of the Coolidge blast, he was laid so low that once again his family feared he was dying. His son Frank and Dr. Hugo Freund were called from Detroit. Soon he was at Johns Hopkins Medical School Hospital in Baltimore for another operation, his fifth in four years. Mark Foote published an appropriate comment: "It was an irony of fate that just as Senator Couzens was cited by the President for 'throwing the government into disorder,' he should be sorely stricken and taken to a hospital. . . . Thus the Michigan senator, whose worst enemy would not accuse him of running away from a fight, is not able to fight back. . . ." [36]

Just before he was placed on the operating table, good news was brought to him. The Senate had defeated a resolution by Jim Watson for squelching the investigation. It was to proceed, this time with authority to employ counsel at Senate expense. Couzens had to make one concession. Heney could not be retained, but was to be replaced by another lawyer acceptable to all members of the investigating committee.[37] But he had the satisfaction of knowing that he had scored a smashing victory over both Coolidge and Mellon.

9

After his recovery, he returned to the investigation. Senator Watson had in the meantime had the good grace to resign as chairman of the committee, and Couzens succeeded to that post, which, according to all precedent should have been his from the outset.

Beginning in December 1925, Couzens issued a series of reports that were revealing documents, particularly with regard to tax allowances permitted corporations that had engaged in military production during World War I.[38] They showed that such companies had obtained "refunds" running into many millions, on the basis of Treasury interpretation of tax and defense acts. One such report, issued in December 1924, listed refunds, among others, of $4,590,585 to the Gulf Oil Company (a Mellon concern); $3,378,000 to the Standard Oil Company of California; $5,000,000 to the Sinclair Consolidated Oil Company; $1,638,375.87 to the Kennedy and Springer Corporation.[39]

The following January, Couzens' committee issued a report which estimated that "improper amortizations" on World War I production facilities, between July 1, 1921, and April 30, 1924, had cost the federal treasury nearly $460,000,000. Among the firms cited were the Aluminum Corporation of America (Mellon), $15,589,614; the United States Steel Corporation, $55,063,312; the Bethlehem Steel Company, $22,103,942; the E. I. DuPont de Nemours Company, $15,369,123; the Federal Shipbuilding Company, $10,849,786; the Midvale Steel and Ordnance Company, $9,336,440; and the National Aniline Chemical Company, $9,912,140.[40] Among other beneficiaries of Treasury rulings, the report showed, were various persons prominent in Republican affairs, and publisher W. R. Hearst.[41]

These refunds were all legal. But this was Couzens' main point. His purpose was to show what loopholes existed in the tax laws, and with what leniency the Bureau of Internal Revenue had secretly been interpreting the laws, often without the general public having any inkling of what was going on.

It was said at the time, and later, that "nothing came" of Couzens' revelations. In a sense, this was largely true. His reports did not completely reform the Bureau of Internal Revenue. In World War

II, large "amortizations" on war production were again permitted, and in many cases they were probably no more justified than those revealed by Couzens' committee.

But his inquiry did end the secrecy. In 1929, in consequence of his reports, an executive order issued by President Hoover provided for publicity on all Treasury refunds of more than $20,000.[42]

In addition, his inquiry resulted in the creation of the Joint Committee on Taxation of the Senate and House, which, for the first time, placed at the disposal of Congress a continuing staff of experts on a legislative subject—a major reform in Congressional history.[43] In Ray Tucker's phrase, this was Couzens' personal "monument."

10

There was, however, a surprising, even shocking, sequel. On March 7, 1925, Mellon brought a tax action, in the name of the Treasury, against Couzens.[44] It charged that Couzens had underpaid approximately $10,000,000 in taxes due from his profits on the sale of his Ford Motor Company stock back in 1919. All of the other former Ford stockholders were also sued. But Couzens was the real target of the action.

Later it developed that this incredibly vindictive counterattack was an indirect outgrowth of both the Newberry case and Henry Ford's lawsuit against the *Chicago Tribune* in 1916. In connection with the Ford suit, a *Tribune* reporter, in 1922, had suggested to Senator Watson that an investigation be made of the income-tax payments made on the Ford stock sold to Ford. A memorandum purporting to prove that not enough taxes were collected was handed to Watson, who in turn handed it to the Bureau of Internal Revenue. The memorandum was checked by the Bureau and found unsubstantiated. When Senator Newberry was being prosecuted by Ford, the same information was produced by Senator Watson.[45] Again the Government rejected the matter.

Now, in connection with Couzens, this old and discredited memorandum was remembered by someone, who called it to Secretary Mellon's attention. And it was on the basis of this that Mellon took action against Couzens.[46]

11

There followed a legal battle before the United States Board of Tax Appeals that lasted three years. Joseph E. Davies (later the

United States ambassador to Moscow) joined Arthur J. Lacy, Clarence E. Wilcox, and C. J. Huddleston, Couzens' personal attorneys in Detroit, in the defense battery. Perhaps no other tax action by the federal government was ever so vigorously prosecuted—or defended. In taxation history, it was a *cause célèbre*.

The upshot was a complete vindication of Couzens. For it was brought out that in the government's own files were documents that cleared him of the least suspicion of tax evasion. They showed, in fact, that his tax return on the Ford stock sale had been subjected to investigation on various occasions and that each time it had been decided there was no basis for reopening the matter. The action was flagrantly political.[47]

The decision was that he had paid not too little tax on the Ford stock sale, but too much—that instead of owing the government $10,000,000, he was entitled to a refund from the government of more than $900,000 as overpayment.[48] Indeed, not only the financial angle, but the whole matter redounded to Couzens' advantage. For the proceedings exposed to the public, for the first time in an official way, much of the inner history of the Ford Motor Company, and this history revealed what few realized—that Couzens was as much responsible for the fabulous Ford Company success as Henry Ford. A typical newspaper headline throughout the world read:

COUZENS THE MAN BEHIND FORD SUCCESS

Politically, this was all to the good for Couzens. Moreover, as one journalist noted, "this denouement was crushing for Mellon," for it placed the High Priest of the Administration Temple in "the role of a shyster prosecutor." [49]

CHAPTER XXVI

"*THE LA FOLLETTEITE!*"

By THEN, Couzens' political creed had matured. It was not conscious Progressivism, in the La Follette sense, though most of the time he did stand close to La Follette. Nor was it simon-pure insurgency, in the style of Brookhart or Magnus Johnson, the Minnesota whirl-wind, though much of the time, certainly, he was an "insurgent" in the Republican ranks. His political principle was almost purely and simply the principle of Independence—the old-fashioned American habit of dissent. "I can't help it," he once exclaimed, "that the Progressives generally are in agreement with me!" [1]

The closest he ever came to formulating any definitive political philosophy was in a letter to a newspaper editor:

> I want to do what I can to see that life is not made a burden for the many and a holiday for the few. I want to do that which will contribute the greatest good to the greatest number. That has been and will be the basis for my work in public life.[2]

In practical political terms, his position of independence always presented him with a problem. It naturally cut him off from any political organization, in particular the old-line Republican cliques in Michigan, headed by such leaders as Charles B. Warren. These never wanted him on any terms. Because, almost as a matter of honor, he scrupulously avoided building a personal organization, as La Follette and others had done, it was asking for an apparent miracle to expect him to get elected to remain in the Senate. "Bullheadedly," Couzens did not believe this. In 1924, when his appointed term was finished, he set out to prove he was right.

The 1924 election was the crucial one in his Senate career. In the primary, he was opposed by the Anti-Saloon League, as could have been expected. But he was also opposed by the chambers of commerce, the manufacturers' associations, and (because Mrs. Couzens was a Catholic) by the Ku Klux Klan, then at its peak of influence. The various state Republican factions put up candidates against him, notably Hal H. Smith, an attorney for the Michigan Manufacturers Association, and Federal Judge Arthur J. Tuttle, who declined, thriftily, to resign as judge to join the race.

Former Congressman Joseph W. Fordney undoubtedly expressed the sentiment of the dominant party leadership:

"Senator Couzens is a wolf in sheep's clothing. He is not a Republican. He is a Socialist. Anyone who is for President Coolidge should not be for Senator Couzens." [3]

2

The major 1924 campaign issue centered on Senator La Follette. When La Follette, following Coolidge's nomination, announced he would run for President on a Progressive platform, the big question in the Republican primary in Michigan became loyalty to Coolidge and the Republican party. The Republican leaders, and the party press, attempted to submerge every other question, especially after Senator La Follette, together with the railroad brotherhoods, issued strong endorsements of Couzens.

The partisan press set up a statewide commotion. If Couzens were not a "La Folletteite," it was up to him to denounce La Follette, the editors said.

This Couzens refused to do. He insisted that he, and La Follette too, had as much right to the Republican label as Coolidge or Andrew Mellon. Besides, he admired La Follette's courage, unquestioned integrity, keen analytical mind, and great oratorical ability.[4]

In May 1924 the Old Guard tried to smoke him out. Burt D. Cady, chairman of the Republican State Central Committee, sent Couzens a letter which asked him to sign a pledge that he stood for "the principles of the Republican party" and that he would support any candidates nominated by the party. Couzens rejected any such pledges. He was "always prepared" to tell how he stood on any principle. He would do so, but it would have to be "in my own way" and "at the proper time," not by the signing of a partisan "pledge." [5]

3

In Grand Rapids, Editor Arthur Vandenberg was worried. He admired Couzens' independence, he said, but feared his defiance of the party leaders would cost him the nomination. If Couzens would only come out strongly against La Follette, Couzens would be all right. The situation certainly seemed critical, for the Republican state convention had just then handed Couzens an unprecedented snub, convening without even extending him an invitation to attend. In effect, he had been read out of the party, in so far as this could be done.

Vandenberg met with Couzens and they had what both described as "a delightful talk." [6] But Vandenberg got nowhere with his attempts to persuade Couzens to disavow La Follette and at the same time declare himself for Coolidge for President and Charles G. Dawes for Vice President in any statement he planned to make of his own candidacy. Instead, when he announced his candidacy, appropriately enough on Independence Day, Couzens took the occasion to denounce what he considered an effort by the state political organization to dictate to him. He would not be controlled "by party bosses," said his statement. It included no statement at all on the Presidential election.

As for pledging himself to support the party's principles, he asserted that he could be a Republican without approving the state and national platforms. Platforms, he said, too often are designed "to fool the people." To which he added:

> I claim to be a Republican as much as though I abjectly said I will follow President Coolidge. Nothing in the Constitution requires that I say "yes" to everything that the President, whoever he may be, proposes. I consider the fact that Congress refused to be dictated to and controlled by the President as a strong element in the safety of our Republic.[7]

4

Vandenberg and other conservatives were, of course, saddened and dismayed, though Progressives generally hailed his defiance of the state machine. La Follette was delighted, and immediately offered to come to Michigan to help Couzens campaign for the nomination.[8] Hiram Johnson, equally jubilant, telegraphed to Couzens that he had demonstrated "independence and courage . . . the two qualities most feared by those who would exploit government for selfish purposes." [9] Taking note of reports that Coolidge and Mellon were working for Couzens' defeat, Johnson said:

> The fact of the matter is your offense, like that of some of the rest of us, was your position on the Mellon Tax Plan. . . . Mr. Mellon and his Tax Plan were the test of progressivism, and also the acid test of our conservative brethren. The gentlemen who bebelieve that government is for the few . . . could forgive any other action than opposition to Mr. Mellon and his tax scheme.[10]

The *Detroit News* carried an amusing comment:

> The political situation is somewhat confusing. . . . President Coolidge is for Senator Couzens, provided Mr. Couzens is for President Coolidge. Mr. Mellon is not particularly for Mr. Couzens. Senator Couzens is somewhat against President Coolidge and somewhat against Senator La Follette, but not enough against either one to be for the other.[11]

5

Vandenberg kept peppering Couzens with arguments against La Follette, most of which amounted to the allegations that La Follette was either a "radical" or a "hypocrite."

Couzens did not pretend to possess Vandenberg's ability for full-blown rhetoric. But he certainly held his own in their exchange. "What I do not understand," he told Vandenberg, "is the intolerance such a finely-educated and clear-thinking gentleman as yourself has for Mr. La Follette." "Even Christ was a radical," he reminded Vandenberg, and enclosed an editorial from the *Detroit News,* which said, "It is idle to pretend that La Follette or the Conference for Progressive Political Action are opposed to American institutions in any particular. Even those who disagree most strongly with La Follette admit his honesty, his loyalty and his courage."

"This *Detroit News* piece," said Couzens, "comes much nearer meeting my views than the editorial which you wrote." [12]

In August, Vandenberg did wring a concession from Couzens. He personally would vote for Coolidge for President. He reasoned that he might as well, since there was no chance that La Follette would win. There certainly was no difference, in his view, between Coolidge and the Democratic candidate, John W. Davis. But Couzens refused to call for a Coolidge victory or to repudiate La Follette. Vandenberg and his newspaper had to be content with endorsing Couzens' nomination on the basis of his unenthusiastic commitment to cast his personal vote for Coolidge.

6

Hysteria in the Republican ranks over the La Follette uprising reached a climax in September. The Republican campaign managers expressed a fear that La Follette would get enough electoral votes to result in a draw, necessitating a decision by Congress as in the case of President Rutherford B. Hayes in 1876.

This, they said, might conceivably lead to the selection of Governor Charles W. Bryan of Nebraska, brother of William Jennings Bryan, the Democratic candidate for Vice President, as "Acting President." In the words of a careful scholar of the campaign, the prospect of "Brother Charlie" becoming President "was an anomalous situation carefully nurtured by Republicans to frighten voters away from the La Follette candidacy." [13]

In Michigan, Couzens' opponent, Hal Smith, of the manufacturers' association, immediately raised the cry: "How does Couzens stand?" He demanded that Couzens state whether he would vote for "Hell and Maria" Dawes for Vice President, or for "Brother Charlie," should the issue reach Congress. In Grand Rapids, Vandenberg professed great alarm. To Couzens, the whole matter was "fantastically silly." Besides, he had no intention of committing himself in advance to a "standpatter" like General Dawes.

He conferred with Governor Groesbeck. So far as he knew at the present time, he told the governor, he "probably" would vote for Dawes. But "whether I would be of that mind next December is another question." How could he say in advance? He did not think the matter was a real issue. He would not make any statement, and he telephoned Vandenberg to that effect.[14] Vandenberg was beside himself. All might be lost if Couzens persisted in his attitude, he insisted.[15] But Couzens stuck to his position. In a letter to Vandenberg he wrote: "It would be perfectly stupid to promise something today and then next December find that to carry it out would be the height of folly. . . . For example, suppose Mr. Dawes went crazy or became unbalanced in any way between now and December; certainly then he should not be put in the office of President." [16]

Afterward, he explained that he "resented" being "hounded" on the Dawes-Bryan matter, whereas nobody raised that question with his primary opponents. "It makes it seem as though I were some outcast and begging to be taken in," he told Vandenberg. "I assume you understand how I feel about that. So long as I feel that way, the office would never induce me to surrender."

To which he added:

> I have seen a number of editorials that the country is going to the bow-wows if any one of the three candidates for President is elected. We go through all these tortures and excitements, each side claiming if the other side gets into control, the country is done for. Yet we go on, decade after decade, no matter who is in the White House. . . . In other words, I cannot get excited over this question.[17]

7

Couzens turned out to be right in saying there was "nothing to get excited about." Despite his "irregularity," sentiment ran so strong for him that Hal Smith retired from the race at the last moment. Smith urged his supporters to vote for Judge Tuttle in the primary. But Couzens had a counter in that game, for it was apparent that many Democrats planned to cross over into the Republican primary to vote for him. In August, William A. Comstock, the Democratic state chairman, declared: "Couzens is really a Democrat, only he doesn't know it!"[18]—something that would be said of President Dwight D. Eisenhower a generation later by newspapers like the *Chicago Tribune*. E. D. Stair's *Detroit Free Press* set up a constant barrage against Couzens on one theme: He was a "Socialist . . . La Folletteite." It called for all Republicans to rally behind safe and sound Judge Tuttle. But the primary resulted in a resounding Couzens victory. The best part, Couzens wrote to Vandenberg, was that the result "freed me of any obligation to serve the organization Republicans or to be with them."[19]

In the election itself he was supported by La Follette Progressives, by Socialists, and by many Democrats, as well as regular Republicans who had no other place to go. He was returned to the Senate for his first full term by a majority of enormous proportions, a victory all the more remarkable in that, although his independence had alienated him from the regular political organizations of his party, he had refrained from building any real personal organization. This would have meant making use of patronage in one way or another, and this he never would do. So his senatorial destiny, as he wished it, was to stand or fall on his record alone.

CHAPTER XXVII

THE CRITIC OF COOLIDGE

"WHAT I hope for is that there will be enough aggressive Republican representatives in the next Congress to make the party stand for something better than it has in the past," Couzens had told Vandenberg during the campaign.[1] His hope was ill-founded. For the landslide that kept Coolidge in the White House had crushed not only the Democratic party—forever, some mistakenly said—but also the La Follette movement. In Charles A. Beard's phrase, the era of the "golden glow," was on. Less than a year later, Senator La Follette died.

Couzens, in addressing the Brotherhood of Locomotive Firemen and Enginemen the following day, paid La Follette's memory one of the finest of tributes.

> Yesterday we lost, I think, the greatest American of our age. No man stood up for so many years against the abuse, the misrepresentation, and the lies of the big press and of capital more fearlessly or more unflinchingly than did Senator La Follette. We may not always have agreed—any of us—with all he did or said, but none there are, who, having a proper appreciation of his noble attributes of mind and heart, could fail to admire him. . . . The few who dare, must speak, and speak again, to right the wrongs of many. I think Senator La Follette typified that thought more than any man who has ever been in public office.[2]

The Old Guard under Coolidge and Mellon had conspired to deprive La Follette of his committee chairmanships as punishment for his third-party heresy, and now they looked askance at Couzens for his praise of La Follette. Some charged it to his "idiosyncracy." But as often happens history provided a sequel. In 1955, on the one hundredth anniversary of Old Bob's birth, at an observance arranged by the Wisconsin State Historical Society, Chief Justice Earl Warren

of the Supreme Court of the United States, a Republican appointed
to the Court by a Republican President, Eisenhower, stood alongside
one of La Follette's surviving colleagues, Editor William T. Evjue
of the liberal *Madison Capital-Times,* and paid tribute to La Follette
in almost the same phrases used by Couzens in 1925.[3] Had he lived,
even Vandenberg would probably have been there—thirty years later.

In 1957, a bipartisan committee of the United States Senate included La Follette among five Senators—along with Clay, Webster,
Calhoun, and Robert A. Taft—to be considered as "immortals" of
the Senate.

2

No one emerged to take La Follette's place in the Senate during
the 1920's. Neither Couzens nor Norris had his precise qualities. La
Follette's son, Robert, Jr., who succeeded him and with whom
Couzens always had a kind of father-son relationship, carried on his
policies, but he was too young.

Besides, for many of the old farm bloc, the attraction of insurgency
had begun to wane. Hiram Johnson, for example, began to reflect
the views of Hearst more and more and to make a narrow isolationism, rather than progressivism, his standard. William Allen White
commented: "The country is in a Coolidge mind." [4] And Senator
Norris recalled: "Those were dark days and years, when America
seemed lulled into indifference." [5] No wonder; prosperity seemed
to be everywhere. The political atmosphere was becalmed.

When squalls did develop, Couzens was usually at their center—
or nearby.

There was, for example, the controversy at the beginning of
Coolidge's new term over the nomination of Charles B. Warren of
Detroit as Attorney General. Stone had been appointed to the Supreme Court, "kicked upstairs," some said, for his embarrassing
integrity. This was the same Warren whose Detroit Board of Commerce committee on unemployment relief Couzens had so severely
criticized in the hard winter of 1914–1915—and whom he had
"buttered up" with a $4,000 contribution to the Republican party
in 1916, when he considered himself a "regular" Republican. But
now Couzens had different ideas about Republican leadership, and
joined progressives of both parties in opposing confirmation of
Warren.

3

Ample reason certainly existed for Couzens' opposition to Charles Warren. As Couzens knew from personal experience, Warren had long been associated with the so-called "Sugar Trust," as attorney and also as principal owner of sugar-corporation shares. In 1911, when a Congressional committee investigated the trust, he was one of the figures called and later even placed under indictment. Indeed, this case was still pending in March 1925 when Coolidge sent his name to the Senate. As Couzens, along with Senator Tom Walsh of Montana, emphasized in Senate debate, this meant that as head of the Department of Justice, Charles B. Warren, if confirmed, would be in a position to dispose of his own anti-trust case.[6]

To Couzens, this appointment by Coolidge was another McNary case. Just as he had opposed Harding in that appointment, he now opposed Coolidge. As the Republican senator from Warren's home state, Couzens' stand was crucial. When the Judiciary Committee, following custom, requested his expected approval of Warren's nomination, he declined to give it. "Mr. Warren is an able and shrewd lawyer," was all he would say.[7]

Tremendous pressure was exerted to win him over to Warren. For by then Warren had become an important contributor of Republican campaign funds. Harding had sent him to Tokyo as United States Ambassador, and he had served Coolidge well as a floor leader in the Republican convention of 1924.[8] Warren himself made a personal appeal to Couzens, on the basis of "old days" and local patriotism. The Michigan and Detroit bar associations flooded Couzens' office with telegrams in Warren's behalf. Coolidge himself exerted all possible White House influence.[9] In the judgment of William Allen White, Coolidge, who had all the facts about Warren, "was stubborn to his own hurt and without much principle involved." [10]

To his face Couzens told Coolidge that he simply "could not stomach" Warren as Attorney General. There was no use in pressuring or cajoling him.

On the original Senate vote, there was a tie. Vice President Dawes might have broken the tie in Warren's favor, but he was absent, supposedly taking a nap in the Hotel Willard. By the time Dawes was summoned, the confirmation was rejected.

Then, obtusely, Coolidge re-submitted Warren's nomination. This appalled even Chief Justice Taft, who wrote to his son, Robert, in complaint about Warren's "subterranean methods." [11]

Couzens was subjected to another barrage. More appeals to his "loyalty to Michigan" were made. The *Michigan Manufacturer and Financial Record* snapped: "No emotion or joy over the promotion of any citizen of Michigan seems to enter his mind." [12]

But he remained adamant. He frankly told Warren that he might support him for some other post, but not for Attorney General. The public had a right to an Attorney General "above any kind of suspicion," he said.[13] On the second vote, Warren was rejected 46 to 39, and Coolidge had to admit a galling defeat.[14]

During the debate over Warren, the Senate also had been the scene of considerable acrimony when the Republican caucus determined to discipline Senator La Follette and Senators Brookhart, Frazier, and Ladd, who had supported La Follette's candidacy for President. The penalty was refusal to recognize them in committee assignments as Republicans, hence cause them to lose all committee memberships.[15] Couzens was on the point of entering into that debate, on the side of La Follette, when he found that he himself was the object of "discipline." For this was the moment Secretary Mellon selected to file against him the $10,000,000 tax case. It was a safe guess that Mellon had obtained the President's permission for the action as retaliation for Couzens' stand against Warren.

4

Couzens himself broke this news on the Senate floor. "Mr. President, I want to point out that all party discipline is not administered in the Senate. Party discipline is administered throughout the states and party discipline is administered in the Departments of the Government here. . . ."

Whereupon he told his colleagues of the tax suit, and read into the record the complaint filed against him. The action, he said, was taken because "the senior senator from Michigan has not been regular, and because he has persisted in endeavoring to eliminate rottenness in governmental departments, no matter under what administration it may occur." [16]

Immediately there was a new furor, one that almost overshadowed even the Warren controversy, as various senators rose to denounce the action against Couzens, and others as stoutly went to the defense of Secretary Mellon.

Senator Ernst was among those who went to Mellon's defense, and brought against himself from Couzens the charge that he had played a part in filching certain papers from the committee's files.

This accusation caused Senator Ernst to make an outburst destined for parliamentary anthologies. "I want the chair to tell me," he cried, "whether there is any way under the rules that I can call a fellow senator a willful, malicious and wicked liar!"

Carter Glass had just taken the floor, and thought Ernst was referring to him. "I want to know whom he is calling a liar!" Glass cried.

"That's just what he can't do; he can't call anybody a liar here," ruled the presiding officer, Joseph T. Robinson, to the amusement of the whole chamber.[17]

Couzens told the Senate that he considered the Mellon action an effort to intimidate him in the investigation.

"Will it have any effect upon the further investigation of the Bureau of Internal Revenue?" asked Kenneth McKellar of Tennessee. "It will have a most vital effect," answered Couzens. "The Senator from Michigan will be more energetic than ever in prosecuting the investigation!"[18] It did not displease him that a few months later Kentucky voters unseated Senator Ernst in favor of Democrat Alben W. Barkley, later Vice President under President Harry S. Truman.

5

Another squall developed when Coolidge disapproved of legislation for raising salaries of postal employees. Couzens fought for the legislation. Economy at the expense of human beings was false economy, he maintained.

Coolidge called Couzens to the White House. The result was an encounter that left the President sputtering with anger.

"A postman cannot raise a family on $1,500 a year," said Couzens.

"In Northampton, Massachusetts, you can have a first-rate house to live in for $30 a month," answered Coolidge.

"That's no argument!" snapped Couzens. "All of our postal employees can't live in Northampton, Massachusetts!"

"I had an uncle in Northampton," continued the President. "He sent his children through high school and college and he never made more than $1,500 a year in his life."

Couzens banged his fist on Coolidge's desk. "That's the trouble with you, Mr. President!" he roared. "You have a Northampton viewpoint, instead of a national viewpoint!"

The interview came to an abrupt end. Couzens had gone to the White House in the first place mainly to urge the appointment of

Governor Groesbeck for Attorney General, but never even got to that.[19] A conservative Vermonter, John Garibaldi Sargent, was appointed to succeed Harlan Stone.[20]

6

Couzens also bitterly criticized the administration for its treatment of General William "Billy" Mitchell, who was ousted from the Army in 1924 because of his advanced views on aviation power.[21]

He was openly contemptuous of the U.S. State Department then headed by former Senator Frank Kellogg, whom some called "Nervous Nellie," for its refusal to permit a member of the British Parliament, Shapurji Sakatvala, a Communist, to enter the United States to attend a conference of the Inter-Parliamentary Union, an early instance of what, in a later era, would be called lowering an "iron curtain." "The idea that this great United States is afraid to let one man come into this country just because he believes in a form of government different from ours is the greatest joke imaginable. Are we afraid of one man among our one hundred million?" Couzens asked.[22]

In 1926, he stirred a storm in Detroit over a similar issue. The industrial department of the Detroit Y.M.C.A. had invited William Green, president of the American Federation of Labor, to talk there. The board of directors of the "Y" ordered that Green's appearance be cancelled. Couzens was so indignant that he advised the Detroit Community Fund, to which he was a leading contributor and which helped support the "Y," that unless the ban on Green were withdrawn, he would not make his annual contribution. At the same time, he resigned in protest as honorary chairman of the Community Fund.[23]

All along, in the meanwhile, he kept up a constant fight with Secretary Mellon. In March 1928 he introduced a resolution calling upon Mellon to resign from the cabinet, charging him with "contempt for the law."[24] Mellon did not resign, but there was another fine fight.[25]

7

But by and large, these actions did little to disturb the national calm. The Bull Market was on in earnest. "Don't sell America short!" Arthur Brisbane wrote day in and day out in the most widely syndicated newspaper column of the period. Though some economists (later) would conclude that precisely in the period 1925–1927 things happened in the economy in America, and abroad, which assured disaster ahead, almost everyone was in an euphoric state. In the phrase of John Kenneth Galbraith of Harvard, in looking back at 1925 through 1929, from the vantage of 1955, the Coolidge Bull Market was a "remarkable phenomenon." [26]

True, there were some happenings which even to the layman did not seem to blend wholly with assurances of good times without end. In England there had been general strikes. In Italy there had occurred the Fascist march on Rome. In Germany the Weimar Republic was tottering, despite a Dawes Plan and a Young Plan. Even in the United States, there had occurred the Sacco and Vanzetti case, revealing that, seemingly, down underneath, there was not the confidence in the social order that most of the nation's leaders professed to have. Yet, the over-all atmosphere was one of satisfaction on the part of nearly everyone.

The independent man in politics does not flourish in such an atmosphere. Nor does the man of action in public life. There was not much business of importance before the Senate. So when his committee for investigating the Bureau of Internal Revenue had finished its work, Couzens found time hanging heavy on his hands. He began to suffer acutely from ennui. In this mood, he wrote self-analytically, and with considerable insight, to his daughter Madeleine:

"With no physical disabilities for twelve whole days, I still am not contented. What a queer character. . . . Strange incongruities to exist in one human being." [27]

CHAPTER XXVIII

THE RESTLESS STATESMAN

HE KNEW what was missing. Back in the time when he was mayor, a group of newspapermen one day asked him for a definition of success in life. "Contentment and peace of mind, something that comes from within you," he said. "I sometimes think that I will never find them for myself."

He certainly tried to find them. His whole career, in one sense, was a monument to that search. But aside from the material results, what he had attained was not contentment, he said, but "the forgetfulness that comes from work." [1]

Now in the slow pace of his senatorial duties, in the Coolidge period of the "Golden Glow" even this balm was denied him and he was often wretched about this.

2

There was, of course, the outlet of Washington social life. He did participate in this social whirl, and with enjoyment—much more than he cared to admit. "Invitations" naturally poured in on him and Mrs. Couzens, because of themselves, but of course also because of their wealth—and the lovely daughters.

On their part, they did considerable entertaining in the various handsome residences they occupied while in Washington. First, they lived in the former Newberry house on Massachusetts Avenue. Then they moved to the former Senator Freylinghuysen place on Sixteenth Street (later the site of the Hotel Statler). But Couzens was so sensitive to even slight traffic noises at night that, in spite of all those rooms, he had to fix up a bedroom for himself—in a clothes closet. So they moved to still another Washington residence in the gladed Rock Creek area.

They were frequently at the White House on social calls—remarkably frequently, considering Couzens' status as an insurgent. But there, too, he found that wealth was a door-opener, as he had discovered in Detroit in the early days of the Ford success. Besides, perhaps oddly, Calvin Coolidge liked the Couzens society if not the Couzens politics. It would be stated that Coolidge was so impressed with business success—"The business of America is business," he had said about this time—that he could forgive Senator Couzens' political irregularities, even against himself, in view of the Couzens wealth. And the Couzenses, as did everyone, enjoyed having easy entree to 1600 Pennsylvania Avenue.

Besides, while he never came to like Coolidge's political and social views any more than Coolidge came to agree with his, Couzens also developed a certain real affection for Coolidge, the man, enjoying especially his unostentatious, even homely, ways. They got so that they could discuss divergent views frankly, without a blowup. "I admire Coolidge," Couzens wrote to Vandenberg. "I do not believe he admires the sycophant who bows, scrapes and dances to please him. There are men of that kind, but I do not think he is, and certainly I could not be that kind of a fellow even if I were told I had to be to enter the Kingdom of Heaven." [2]

3

He found pleasure, too, in his daughters, observing with fatherly pride their maturing. He and Madeleine developed an especially tender relationship that was wonderfully satisfying. After having finished her course at the Bronson school in New York, she delighted him especially by undertaking to do what he himself once had wanted to do—study law.

As a student at Washington College of Law, she followed closely the legislation in which he was interested, and frequently was to be found in the visitors' gallery of the Senate listening to the proceedings. Madeleine and he, walking to and from the Capitol, became a familiar sight, and their walks together were among his most cherished activities.

When Madeleine was away, he wrote to her in a warm, affectionate way that probably surprised even himself, considering his reputation for being cold-blooded. He once told a friend that he had trouble all his life "to say what I feel in my heart." [3] But this was not true between himself and Madeleine.

In one letter he wrote:

You are well and happy, so I am pleased, although no one but myself knows how much I miss you. Something keeps you in mind every hour of the day and in many of my dreams. I miss seeing you in the Senate gallery and I miss your cheery welcome when I come home. All this even though I have a loving wife and two sweet and loving daughters still with me. . . .[4]

At this time he joined the Burning Tree Country Club and became one of the most avid and best-known golfers in Washington.[5] He also developed intimate friendships with other senators, most of all with Charles L. McNary of Oregon (the 1940 Republican candidate for Vice President with Wendell L. Willkie), and with Pat Harrison of Mississippi, Frederick Hale of Maine, and Hiram Johnson.[6] This camaraderie was something he had never permitted himself in his earlier years.

However, in none of this outwardly pleasant life did he find the complete cure for his restlessness. He simply had developed no philosophy that permitted him to accept, let alone welcome, a calm existence. He did much thinking and reading—the *Nation* and the *New Republic* being his favorites among magazines. But actually the contemplative life was foreign to him.

He kept religion at arm's length, perhaps, as he once said, because "there was so much religion at home in Chatham." So nearly all he had to fall back upon, since he could not indulge in just pleasure, was his old formula, "making good."

4

Twice he came close to returning to the business world. Just after his election in 1924, Joseph P. Tumulty, who had been Woodrow Wilson's secretary, informed him that the *Washington Post* could be purchased from E. B. McLean for $6,000,000. To own a newspaper in the capital appealed to Couzens. He became seriously interested, and Tumulty was eager to act as broker.

However, McLean's well-known eccentric ways—oddities that finally caused him to be committed to a sanitarium—were a stumbling block. He refused, for example, to submit any kind of financial statement. Nor would he answer a series of specific questions concerning the property that had been drawn up for Couzens by Jay Hayden. He stubbornly took the attitude that if Couzens wanted the *Post*, he should buy it without asking questions. The farthest he would go was to give a "warranty" that the newspaper was "profitable." Couzens then refused to have any further dealings with Mc-Lean and gave up entirely the idea of acquiring the *Post*.[7]

In 1926, he actually launched another commercial enterprise of his own—the Couzens Ice Machine Company, which he capitalized at $1,000,000 for the purpose of producing mechanical refrigerators. His principal motive, he said, was to assure a fitting career for Frank, then in the house-building business in Detroit with John P. Frazer. There was an impulsiveness about this whole matter which indicated how desperate he was to be in "something active." When Wilcox, his lawyer, warned him that it might be wise to check the status of patents on mechanical refrigerators, he brushed the warning aside.

"Nonsense. We'll go ahead and fight out the patent trouble later, as we did in the Selden case."

It was also suggested to him that there be more testing done, but he vetoed this too.

"If we did that in the beginning of the Ford Motor Company, we never would have gotten any place. The thing to do is to start production and make improvements later."

Two factory sites were purchased, one in Detroit, and another in Wapokeneta, Ohio. Dealers were signed up. Literature was printed. Sample machines were displayed in stores. Then, just as the company was preparing to go into production, he suddenly called the whole thing off, at an enormous loss.[8]

5

He had been studying the installment purchase system. Installment buying and selling were bad for people morally, encouraging them to live beyond their means, and even worse for the nation economically, he concluded. He became something of a crusader on this view, made several speeches about it, and also contributed several magazine articles in which he warned that the system was bound to lead to a crash [9]—one of the few warning signals sent up during this era of euphoria. And he had been advised that it would be impossible to market the Couzens refrigerator except on the installment plan. Rather than do that, he determined to kill the enterprise entirely. At least, this was his excuse.[10]

It was just as well. Frank, himself now a father, with one of his sons named James Couzens II, did not need to have his career mapped for him. He was already shaping a future quite satisfactorily, incidentally moving along a path paralleling his father's, for in 1928,

Frank became a member of the Detroit Plan Commission. Later he became a commissioner of the municipally owned Detroit Street Railway.

By 1929, Frank was to be a figure of status in his own right in municipal politics. A statement issued by him on the mayoralty campaign that year attracted wide attention. "You see, I have competition in the family already," Couzens told Madeleine.[11]

6

Having decided against re-entry into business, Couzens turned to personal projects. It had been logical for some time that he should erect a permanent, year-round residence at Wabeek. Soon after he called off the refrigerator project, he became engrossed in building a new Wabeek residence, completed in time for it to be the scene of Madeleine's marriage in January 1928 to William R. Yaw. He undertook still another construction project, an office building in the town of Birmingham, Michigan. There he established his personal office (and, a few years later, the Wabeek State Bank, created mainly for handling his own financial affairs). It was no longer necessary, he said, for him to keep an office in Detroit. By having his headquarters at Birmingham, he would not be disturbed by people "wanting favors or to sell him something." [12]

In the country-squire existence that he began to lead at Wabeek, there were gratifications in abundance for him. He took to spending a great deal of his time in the outdoors. He enjoyed puttering around the estate and superintending farming operations at Wabeek, although it exasperated him constantly that he could not make the farming side of it pay. The feeling of being a great landowner—Wabeek by then was expanded to some 800 acres—pleased him. Then in 1929, he launched a project that filled some of the more basic requirements of his restless nature and won for him a measure of peace that had come from nothing else. This was his creation of, for the era, one of the nation's most important philanthropies, the Children's Fund of Michigan.

CHAPTER XXIX

THE MAGNIFICENT GIFT

BACK in 1915, Couzens had written to a friend: "You are quite right, I have more money than I am entitled to. I am just commencing to take time to learn how to separate myself from some of it." [1] That year Henry Morgan, his secretary, persuaded him to visit a small home for crippled children in Detroit maintained by a Blanche Leuven Brown, herself a cripple. He could not get the sight of these children out of his mind. Almost before he knew it, he became the principal financial backer of the Brown home, giving it $10,000 in 1915. And from then on, he began to become a "giver."

In 1918, he made an interesting alliance. A young man named Byers H. Gitchell, later a figure in department-store merchandising, had been talking to him about certain social improvements needed in Detroit. Gitchell had been secretary of the Board of Commerce at the time Couzens was its president. Like Couzens, he had resigned because he felt this commercial group was not "getting behind the real things that should be done for the city." [2]

To Couzens, Gitchell now sketched an almost pioneer concept of city planning—better homes for workers, more parks, improved educational opportunities, better hospital facilities, and more integration of various organized charities. If he could afford it, Gitchell added, he would like to devote his energies to developing such a program—this at the time Couzens was thinking of standing for Mayor.

"All right," said Couzens. "Go ahead. I'll pay your salary!" [3]

One result of this was the creation in 1918 of "The Detroit Patriotic Fund," forerunner of the Detroit Community Fund and Community Chest. Couzens was its leading contributor, his gifts averaging $150,000 a year. For several years he served as president of the fund and was the dominant influence in its administration. [4] It was he, too, who was chiefly responsible for having brought to

Detroit, from the Cincinnati Council of Social Agencies, William J. Norton, a hardheaded yet progressive and liberal-minded Maine-born social worker, to serve as founding director of the Detroit Patriotic Fund—thus beginning for himself, as well as for Detroit and Michigan, an important relationship.

2

In 1919 Couzens gave a $650,000 nurses' residence to Harper Hospital of Detroit. In that same year, as a birthday present to Mrs. Couzens, he made a gift of $1,000,000 for the furtherance of what by then was his great hobby, the helping of crippled children. This donation was really an outgrowth of his interest in the Brown home. He had become a member of a committee (along with Alex Y. Malcomson) for converting the Brown home into a scientific institution.

Largely on his initiative, it was merged with the Michigan Hospital School.[5] Later, he was instrumental in effecting a merger of this Michigan Hospital School with the Children's Free Hospital of Detroit. When this was achieved, in 1922, and there came into being the Children's Hospital—the word "free" was eliminated as "distasteful," at his insistence—he donated an additional $1,000,000, which was used, among other purposes, to create the hospital's famous countryside branch at Farmington.

3

He liked to say that helping children was a matter of "absolute justice," not sentiment, as he once wrote to Norton.

But no man could have been more sentimental than he over the plight of deformed youngsters. He suffered actual pain at the sight of a crippled child, or even if he merely read about such a child. Morgan once sent him a pamphlet describing the work of an organization for helping cripples. Before returning it, Couzens wrote on it:

"I'm glad you showed me this, but it has spoiled my day." [6] And this at a time when other leading Detroiters insisted he was "cold-blooded" and "unfeeling."

In 1924, he donated still another residence for nurses, this time to the University of Michigan, at a cost of $620,000. In this same year, he established a $100,000 fund for making loans to physically handicapped war veterans, primarily to help them "make a start in a self-supporting business in a manner which will enable them to maintain their self-respect." [7]

The idea for this came to him after a crippled war veteran had come into his office at the Senate and asked for a loan of fifty dollars. Couzens had abruptly turned down the veteran, saying a casual loan "would do no good." But after a sleepless night he set up the $100,000 fund.

4

His great philanthropy, however, was the Children's Fund of Michigan.

Over a long period, he had discussed his plans for this with Dr. Freund, his personal physician, with Norton, and with his lawyer, Judge Arthur J. Lacy, formerly of the Court of Domestic Relations, then with John Anderson's firm.[8] He reached his decision to act just after Madeleine's first child, Margot Yaw, was born. A letter to her gave a hint, but only a hint, of his decision. She had asked him to come to Detroit from Washington to see his new granddaughter sooner than he had planned.

"I want Frank to be there when I come to Detroit," he wrote. "I have something important to do and want Frank present." [9]

The "something important" was the Children's Fund.

Its purpose was told in the carefully selected words of the trust instrument:

"To promote the health, welfare, happiness, and development of the children of the State of Michigan primarily, and elsewhere in the world."

He started the Fund with an irrevocable gift of $10,000,000. Later, in November 1934, he added $1,880,700. Counting income as well as principal, the gift resulted in the expenditure, as of its final reporting date, May 1, 1954, of $18,038,656.36. In later years, after other wealthy men had seen the desirability of establishing welfare foundations (also after money values had become inflated) this sum perhaps would not seem extraordinarily remarkable. But at the time, his gift was sensational and amounted to one of the fifteen largest publicly listed charitable trusts.[10]

For him, the Children's Fund represented a broadening of his interest in the welfare of children. Though still greatly concerned with helping physically handicapped children, he now desired to do his part for the benefit of children generally. In 1935, he summed up his views:

> I know of no greater obligation resting upon the adults of a civilized nation than the application of their love for their children

in those practical, organized ways which guarantee that each generation . . . will have progressively greater opportunities of arriving at manhood and womanhood better equipped for life's contest than their predecessors had.

Science contributes year by year a constantly enlarging stream of knowledge of how to keep the body well, how to cure sickness, how to train the mind for more efficient performance, and how to mold the character for strong and resourceful struggle against odds. It is a major business of adult mankind so to organize this growing fund of knowledge and so to apply it that more and more children will be able to start the race of life without handicaps and on even terms.[11]

5

He stipulated that all of the money in the Children's Fund must be expended within twenty-five years after May 1, 1929, and that, on the average, at least $700,000 was to be distributed each year. Permanent foundations, while pleasing to the vanity of men who wanted their names remembered in perpetuity, tended to defeat their purpose, he felt.

He also made it clear that the least possible portion of the Fund was to be used for buildings of any kind. Not monuments to himself, but effective activity for children, was his goal.

Indeed, he leaned over backwards in this. When he donated the nurses' home to Harper Hospital, he refused to permit it to be called "The James Couzens Home," as was proposed by the hospital board. "He would not hear of it," related Dr. Stewart Hamilton, director of the hospital. He asked that the home be named after the then principal nurse of the hospital, Emily A. McLaughlin, in tribute to her service in France during World War I.[12]

He was positively indignant upon learning that the University of Michigan authorities had designated the nurses' home he had given that institution as "The Couzens Residence for Nurses." [13]

He held to this principle always. In the notes of Arthur J. Lacy, who, with Clarence Wilcox, handled the legal matters involved in setting up the Children's Fund, there appears this:

> We tried to induce Senator Couzens to call this the Couzens Foundation, but he refused to have his name included. He said the fund belongs to the children. . . . He said it is not where it comes from, but where it is going that is important.

He insisted too, that there be no racial or creedal discrimination of any kind. "I have never felt justified in contributing to any particular creed, color, or race, and I am anxious to see that all are treated alike," he once said.[14]

He participated directly and actively in all that the Fund did so long as he lived. He had himself designated as chairman of the board that was formed to administer the Fund. No detail in planning or execution was too small to command his interest, as the work of the Fund progressed. He wrote "voluminous letters from Washington" about it to its officers.[15]

6

The original board of trustees, of which Frank Couzens, as well as himself, was a member, was carefully chosen by him. All were men who knew his views, who were definitely interested in social welfare—Lacy and Wilcox, McPherson Browning, a Detroit banker, Dr. Freund, and Norton.

Dr. Freund, a physician of unusual social and psychological insight, was exceptionally well qualified to be Couzens' adviser in this field. Aside from the experience that came from a large medical practice, he was well grounded in public-health work, having been a member of the Detroit Board of Health for a number of years, under Couzens as well as other mayors. He was interested in research. Perhaps most of all, Dr. Freund concerned himself with the general problem of mental health, and he was a doctor interested in social conditions. He was named president of the Fund and much that the Fund accomplished bore the impress of his broad and informed interests.

Norton was well acquainted with Couzens' views because of their close association with the Community Fund. A true humanitarian, yet levelheaded and practical—outstandingly so among welfare workers—Norton was precisely the man for operating director. Couzens "drafted" Norton to serve as executive vice-president and secretary. At first this was on a part-time basis, with Norton continuing with the Community Fund. Then Norton made the Children's Fund his full-time career. He and Couzens made a superb team.

7

The Children's Fund adopted and followed two main policies from the beginning. It decided to support selected activities of already existing agencies in the children's field. It initiated activity of its own in more or less neglected fields, but always with the thought that this activity ultimately would be carried on by some other agency, preferably by state or local governments. Thus, the work of the Fund would go on, even though the Fund itself was to cease existence after twenty-five years. In this respect the Fund was a trail blazer.[16]

Michigan was a backward state with respect to public-health work in rural areas when the Fund was established. Numerous counties had no public-health facilities at all, not even the minimum services for inspecting water supply or controlling communicable diseases. To correct this lack became a major objective of the Children's Fund. Its approach was to offer financial support to selected counties, by which health officers, nurses, dentists, and sanitary inspectors would be employed, provided the counties established health districts.

The Fund constructed and undertook the operation of two children's clinics outside Detroit—the Northern Michigan Children's Clinic at Marquette, and the Central Michigan Children's Clinic at Traverse City. Serving large areas, these clinics made available medical services including orthopedic treatment of cripples, that previously were unknown to rural children. It also maintained a laboratory, mainly in the field of biological chemistry, where scientists launched studies in problems of nutrition and of growth, with the view to finding means of improving the physical well-being of children everywhere. This laboratory, in which the offices of the Fund were located, was constructed adjacent to the Children's Hospital, in accord with Couzens' plan that ultimately it should be a gift to that hospital, so that its work would continue after the Fund had expired. The executive headquarters and laboratory building were deeded to Children's Hospital when the fund was liquidated on April 30, 1954.

In Detroit there was established the Children's Center, staffed by psychiatrists, psychologists, and psychiatric social workers, who specialized in treating maladjusted children. With the cooperation of the state, a similar center was established at Lansing, Michigan, to bring the value of mental-hygiene work to the attention of the state at large. In addition, the Fund sponsored a program for acquainting teachers in the public schools with advances in the understanding of juvenile personality problems.

Some twelve years later, the Michigan legislature authorized the State Hospital Commission to establish three child-guidance clinics

—at Muskegon, Kalamazoo, and Saginaw. This meant that the Children's Fund had played a vital role in fostering acceptance of a progressive step in public health, and that its work in an important field would go on. Indeed, it had sparked many such activities and encouraged gifts in its field by other persons and foundations.

Couzens himself once summarized accurately its work:

> New services for health, new implements for self-discipline, and an enlargement of scientific knowledge have come into being with our assistance. And we have entered practically into the lives of hundreds of thousands of children to their happiness and advantage.[17]

8

Nothing that he had ever done—not his role in the building of the Ford Motor Company, nor the winning of public office—gave him more real pleasure. A tabulation of all his contributions—counting the Children's Fund—showed an interesting total, approximately $30,000,000, or precisely the sum he had received for his Ford Motor Company stock.[18]

The mail he received from all over the nation from persons pleased by his gift "has been terrific, like a cyclone," he told Madeleine. "I have taken the trouble to personally answer each letter." [19]

In the following June, while at his desk in the Senate, he wrote her an interesting personal letter.

> I just happened to observe that I was getting older and shrinking up. When I went shopping for some shoes and stockings the other day, my sizes had to be reduced. Socks for me for years were ten and a half, but now I have to have size ten. . . . Keep well and keep your temper and disposition sweet; it pays immensely, in spite of the fact that I have not practiced it! [20]

If he was getting old and "shrinking up," this by no means indicated an easier, more relaxed time ahead for him. Actually, one of his most active periods lay just ahead. For a vast change was to occur in the American scene—and there was work aplenty for a public man with a sensitive conscience.

CHAPTER XXX

THE "DANGEROUS MAN"

His Children's Fund gift was cited in many quarters as proof of the healthy working of the American economic system. By coincidence, however, the system was just then on the eve of a great spell of sickness, the first symptom of which was a pronounced rise in unemployment.

Nearly everyone dismissed this trend in the latter days of the Coolidge Bull Market as something that would pass. Secretary of Commerce Herbert Hoover had been elected President in the previous November. During his campaign he had said hopefully: "We in America today are nearer to the final triumph over poverty than ever before in the history of the land." [1]

Couzens was not so sure of this. Indeed, as early as 1924, he wrote:

> Notwithstanding the abundance of everything in this country, we never seem to have devised a way to create security for those "have nots" who are willing to work. . . . I have unbounded concern for the family man who has no security in a job. This is the one outstanding problem to be solved.[2]

In 1926, when he was studying the installment-buying question, he said, "I am sorry that so much publicity is given to universal prosperity that does not exist." [3] In February 1927 he told Frank Couzens, "Times are not too good and it is my impression that they will be worse before they are better." [4]

During Coolidge's last days in the White House, Couzens warned the President that danger existed in the widespread stock-market gambling, especially in banking securities.[5]

On the Senate floor he sharply criticized the Federal Reserve Board for encouraging "a great orgy of speculation." This, he said, was a "dumb" policy that could only end in disaster.[6]

2

Early in 1928 along with "Young Bob" La Follette, he persuaded
the Senate to authorize an investigation into unemployment. As
chairman of the Committee of Labor and Education, he took charge.
The result was a Senate report that became a significant document,
a kind of American "Beveridge Report," which called attention to
the need for unemployment insurance and old-age pensions.[7]

In one respect this document was historic. It endorsed a principle
that was not to become part of the doctrines of progressivism in the
United States until after World War II—that, under democracy,
men have a *right* to self-supporting employment. In the main, this
doctrine was Couzens' personal contribution. His report said:

> No one will question that every man is entitled to the opportunity
> to provide for himself and his family. That is a fundamental right
> and society cannot consider itself successfully organized until every
> man is assured of the opportunity to preserve himself and his family
> from suffering and want.

The report also said:

> Cyclical unemployment has been like the plague; it has come and
> gone at regular intervals until it has been accepted as a necessary
> evil by some who should know otherwise. . . .
> We do not believe any more that it is necessary for the baby to
> have diphtheria and rickets and other "diseases of childhood."
> We have found and are finding methods of preventing these dis-
> eases. We should recognize also that there is an obligation on all
> society to attack, unceasingly, the problem of unemployment.[8]

His report included two recommendations of great significance
later:

> The government should adopt legislation without delay which
> would provide a system of planning public works so that they would
> form a reserve against unemployment in times of depression. States
> and municipalities and other public agencies should do likewise.
> Future consideration might well be given to two questions, the
> effect had on unemployment by industrial developments such as
> consolidation of capital, and the necessity and advisability of pro-
> viding, either through private industry, through the states, or
> through the federal government, a system of old-age pensions.[9]

And all this, of course, before the "New Deal" and the social security program that came with it. As a Senator, he was again the trail-

blazing industrialist that he had been in 1914 when it was he who pushed through at the Ford Company the $5-a-day plan and also, as in 1915, had urged upon the Detroit Board of Commerce a policy which, in effect, meant a guaranteed annual wage.

He engaged in a good deal of correspondence with key industrialists throughout the nation upon these problems. To a businessman in Connecticut, who had objected that relief funds did not get at "fundamentals," Couzens wrote:

> That is true, but . . . relief has got to be had while we are attacking the fundamentals. I, for one, am unable to see the suffering that goes on while we are trying to find the basis of permanent relief.[10]

This was in May 1929—before "the Great Crash."

With George W. Johnson, the shoe manufacturer, he carried on a correspondence in which he championed a favorite idea. Industry must undertake payroll-stabilization plans for ending seasonal and cyclical unemployment. "That means," he said, "the arousing of the consciousness of the employer to the necessity of doing for his employees what he does for his plant and his stockholders." When Johnson argued that it was necessary to go slow, to learn by experience, Couzens agreed. "But we must not let too many people suffer while we are gaining this experience." [11]

It was then, in 1925, that he began to speak out strongly for a proposal which other progressives were not to espouse seriously until a quarter-century had passed: The guaranteed annual wage for industrial workers.

In short, he was for scrapping the old-style wage system entirely, and substituting the annual salary for all men and women in industrial employment. Especially did he recommend this for the great automobile industry, which he had helped to found.

3

The stock market collapsed in October 1929. The *Commercial & Financial Chronicle* called the result "the greatest stock market catastrophe of all ages." [12]

President Hoover, however, assured the country that all was really well. "The fundamental business of the country . . . is on a sound and prosperous basis," he said.[13] But this was whistling in the dark. The "great depression" was on,[14] though *The Literary Digest* called it a "prosperity panic." [15]

In the following December Couzens addressed the annual dinner of the Michigan Manufacturers Association at Detroit. By then the depression had unmistakably set in. Fifteen years almost to the day after his memorable address on unemployment before the Detroit Board of Commerce in 1914, he repeated almost word for word what he had said then about the irresponsibility of employers toward their workers. By failing to act, the manufacturers were, in large part, to blame for the unemployment, he said, adding that low wages had reduced the needed purchasing power of the people.

He chided the business leaders for opposing increased taxes for unemployment relief and for their slogan, "No government interference in business!"

> You can prevent these high taxes. You can prevent bureaucrats from interfering with progress and development of business. You can prevent officials from sending out forms by the bushel for you to fill out and return—if you will solve these problems yourselves. Government does not interfere with business until business itself has created the necessity.[16]

Now he was no longer bored. Once again he was the crusader, constantly plumping for what he saw was the only sound solution of the unemployment problem—adoption, by basic industries, of the annual wage for factory employment. And he was more realistic in assessing the causes and the extent of the "crash" than nearly everyone else in the land.[17]

4

In 1930 he stood again for re-election. Then it was not much of a handicap that he had not gone along with Coolidge. Indeed, by 1930, this was almost in his favor, even with Republicans.

A suggestion of the change in the land was personified in Vandenberg. Back in 1927 the quiet Senator Ferris had died, and Vandenberg was appointed to the vacancy. Now himself a senator, Vandenberg was not so completely Hamiltonian as he had been in 1924, when he was so certain that La Follette intended to undermine America. At first, he and Couzens did not get along well in the Senate. "I did not want you appointed. I think you are too conservative," Couzens frankly told Vandenberg just after he was sworn in.[18]

But by 1930 Vandenberg was more sympathetic toward even mild "La Folletteism," although he would never come to be styled a progressive himself.[19] Frank R. Kent said that Vandenberg took on "a progressive coloration . . . largely to keep Jim Couzens off his back." [20] If true, this was a straw in the wind indicating that even among orthodox Republicans the old order was giving ground. It had to, for this depression was vastly more severe than any the nation had known.

5

So it was no surprise that Couzens this time won renomination, easily defeating the highly popular former Bull Mooser and ex-Governor, Chase S. Osborn. The Democrats had no more heart to campaign against him now in 1930 than did the troubled Old Guard Republicans. They considered not even putting up a candidate against him. Thomas E. H. Weadcock, a former Congressman, who finally did consent to run as a Democrat, polled only 139,814 votes in the election. Couzens received 520,247.

This vote of confidence—with many of the regular party leaders backing him, at least passively—did not cause him to change his style as the Senate's gadfly. The *Baltimore Sun* in March 1931 carried an item that showed that he was still the old Couzens.

> He likes Hoover personally and politically [wrote Frank R. Kent, with tongue in cheek] and has consistently voted against him in the Senate only because Hoover happened not to think the way he thinks. Actually, Couzens thinks he has been helping Hoover. It would be interesting to know what Mr. Hoover thinks.

One of the early votes Couzens cast against Hoover was on the appointment of Charles Evans Hughes as Chief Justice, to succeed Taft. Back in 1916, Couzens had taken his first tentative step into the political arena as an elector pledged to Hughes. Now he joined organized labor in opposing Hughes for Chief Justice because, he concluded, "Hughes is too conservative." [21]

6

As unemployment continued to rise in the nation as a whole as well as in the Detroit area in particular, Couzens hammered consistently away at two ideas—the unemployed must be given relief; businessmen were to blame. What had happened, he felt, had remarkably confirmed his long-standing opinion that leaders of business were no supermen, and that the much-publicized superiority of the successful was largely myth. As noted by one Washington writer, he, the multimillionaire, talked more and more "in a way to make a conservative's blood curdle." [22]

More people listened now to Couzens, fewer to Andrew Mellon.

Indeed, by then Mellon, with his world apparently going to pieces, had become, as Thomas L. Stokes wrote, "an uncertain little man . . . lonely and tragic." [23]

Couzens' targets now were the leaders of big business, the bigger the better, in his view. One target became Albert H. Wiggin, chairman of the governing board of the Chase National Bank of New York. Wiggin had made the front pages by suggesting two principal "remedies" for the depression: scale down the war debts owed the United States by foreign nations, and reduce wage standards in the United States generally. Sympathetic toward the first suggestion, Couzens was wrathful concerning the second:

> When it comes to a cut in wages and calling upon labor to accept such reductions, it seems wholly unreasonable, in view of the fact that one of the difficulties that brought about this depression, and in my opinion the major one, has been unequal distribution of the earnings of industry between capital and labor. . . . This should not be considered, even though the suggestion comes from a great financial giant such as Mr. Wiggin.[24]

He challenged the Chamber of Commerce of the United States to present a program for relieving economic distress, issuing in 1931 a bitter statement which lambasted business leaders for opposing social-security legislation—they called it the "dole"—without offering a constructive substitute. He took the chamber to task for its propaganda against "government interference with business" and its scary pronouncements about the evils of "a dole."

> Congress is warned against a dole; it is warned against unemployment insurance and old age pensions. When capital is idle, it continues in many cases to receive dividends and interest, but I have heard no complaint registered that anybody has been offended because it was a dole. Why is a dole to men and women more offensive than a dole to capital? [25]

7

In 1928 he had supported Hoover's election. To be sure, he was not so active for Hoover as Vandenberg. But he had gone out of his way to make a few speeches for Hoover's election. Remembering Hoover's leadership in the Conference on Unemployment in 1922, Couzens believed that Hoover was something of a progressive, a view that many, even the liberal *New Republic* magazine, had shared. He considered Hoover a competent executive, a man of strength, the "Great Engineer," who knew how to act in time of crisis. Moreover, Hoover had once described himself as an "independent progressive" who objected "as much to the reactionary group in the Republican party as . . . to the radical group in the Democratic party." [26]

But Hoover was a disappointment to Couzens. The first glimmer came when Hoover failed to replace Mellon. Couzens had understood from Senators Brookhart and Borah that Hoover had promised not to reappoint Mellon. The promise was kept, technically. Hoover did not reappoint Mellon—he simply let him carry over.[27]

Then, Hoover asked Couzens for a memorandum on reforming the Bureau of Internal Revenue. Couzens prepared a lengthy one —and nothing happened, except the executive order on publicizing refunds of more than $20,000.[28]

His disappointment soon turned to disillusionment and, finally, into bitter antagonism.

It did not help matters that Hoover, as President, impressed Couzens as being ponderous and authoritative, the very kind of personality least palatable to him.[29]

8

Hoover did not conceal an antipathy on his part toward Couzens. He frequently went out of his way to single him out for criticism. Couzens was "a very dangerous man," Hoover once told a White House visitor, according to a report that Couzens himself received.[30]

This was sad, for Hoover, as well as for Couzens, and for the country too; for undeniably Hoover was a man of great ability, and the country would have benefited had he and Couzens been able, with others, to work harmoniously together toward meeting the problems of the depression. But between them, as the phrase "a very dangerous man" indicated, was a great gulf, not only temperamentally, but also in social outlook, and this was tragic for the nation in its larger implications, for it meant a policy of drift, or government by doctrinaire slogans, when obviously what was required was practical action along the lines that Couzens was urging, in broad policy if not in detail.

CHAPTER XXXI

THE CRUSADER AGAIN

THEIR first major clash was on the old question of Muscle Shoals. For Hoover held to the same view on Muscle Shoals that Coolidge had advocated, that it should not be operated as a government power project, but should be turned over to private power companies, if developed for power at all.[1] In his very first message to Congress, Hoover denounced the idea of government ownership of Muscle Shoals with a characteristically unfortunate phrase, calling it "degeneration."[2] This was galling to Couzens and he said so.

Early in the administration, he also broke with Hoover over another issue carried over from the Harding and Coolidge days—that of the railroads. Then chairman of the Senate Committee on Interstate Commerce, he had begun an intensive study of the railroad problem. In principle, he favored a program of consolidations, for getting rid of unnecessarily competing lines. But at the same time, he was against combinations which would mean "killings" on the part of speculators in railroad securities and the perpetuation of "watered" capitalizations. He was also on the alert against a program that would "solve" the railroad financial problem at the expense of the railroad workers.[3]

While Couzens' committee was engaged with this problem, Hoover came out with a proposal for consolidating all railroads east of the Mississippi into four systems.[4] Couzens criticized Hoover's program. It was solely "a proposal to help the railroads out of their financial difficulties," rather than a program that considered the railroad problem in its larger aspects, he said. He added that the Hoover program would result in fewer jobs for railroad workers at a time when unemployment was becoming a major problem.[5]

Hoover defended his program and, in doing so, attacked Couzens. "If Senator Couzens blocks it, that will add sensibly to our depression difficulties," he said.[6]

Supported by the railroad brotherhoods, Couzens made sure that the Senate did block the Hoover plan. "A victory very pleasing to me," he wrote to Madeleine.[7]

Reflecting Hoover's attitude was the observation made twenty years later by a friendly Hoover biographer:

> The radical bloc in Congress, led by Senator Couzens of Michigan and supported by the Democrats, defeated the proposal. Their evident purpose was to keep the railway industry demoralized in the hope that eventually the government would have to take them over. Socialism was in the air then, as it is today.

This, of course, proved nonsense of a type that would have been especially irritating to Couzens.

2

On the soldier's-bonus issue, Couzens again broke with Hoover. Normally, he was as opposed as anyone else to "veterans' raids" on the Treasury, for he had none of the politician's fear of the so-called veterans' vote. But he felt that with the government failing to provide adequate depression relief generally, prepayment of the Soldiers' Bonus, as provided by the bill in Congress, was a practical, if inefficient, way of getting funds to needy citizens who happened to be war veterans.[8] Hoover, however, took the position that this would seriously impair the federal credit. He cited Secretary Mellon as his authority on this.

Couzens was scornful. If the outlay for the bonus would bankrupt the nation, he asked, what was there to the earlier argument that Mr. Mellon was "a wizard" in his conduct of the finances of the country? He unburdened himself in the Senate of a sarcastic thrust at both Hoover and Mellon:

"In view of the great Secretary Mellon being alleged to have served under three Presidents, I desire to point out that the fact is that three Presidents have served under the Secretary of the Treasury." [9]

When Hoover vetoed the Bonus bill, Couzens was lined up with the senators who re-passed the bill over the veto.[10]

3

He was especially outraged when Hoover advocated a national manufacturers' sales tax on all commodities "except necessary food" and possibly "some grades of clothing," as a way to balance the budget.[11]

The sales tax was a "monstrosity," a levy that mainly hit the poor, Couzens declared. "When we scratch down below the surface of this question of a sales tax, we find an effort to get rid of the income tax." "Whenever anyone mentions a general sales tax I become irrational," he once wrote.[12]

He was a leader in the revolt in Congress that blocked enactment of the sales tax.[13]

To his personal lawyer, Arthur Lacy, who that year was unsuccessful Democratic candidate for governor of Michigan, Couzens commented acidly on senatorial colleagues who had voted against an amendment of his to forbid the sales tax and to substitute a 10 per cent increase in surtaxes on large incomes. "What I think of some of my colleagues who voted against my proposed amendment could hardly be dictated to a female stenographer. 'Wealth' certainly has an enormous number of friends, even among those who are not wealthy. It seems that practically every publisher, nearly every lawyer, nearly every public official and nearly everyone who has the public ear is on guard, in defense of 'wealth.' " [14]

4

But it was over unemployment relief that he found himself in sharpest division with Hoover. In principle, he believed, with Hoover, that the federal government should not undertake direct unemployment relief and that relief funds should be distributed by the state and local governments. But he parted from Hoover by vigorously taking the view that relief by whatever means, had to be made available even by federal handouts, if the need existed, precisely his position during the depression of 1921 as mayor of Detroit. The victims of the depression could not be fed and sheltered on political philosophy, he asserted.

To Couzens, the spectre of jobless men, the sight that had caused him to initiate the five-dollar-a-day plan at the Ford Company, still was a haunting thing. That his and Young Bob La Follette's 1928 report on unemployment, urging a social security program, was gathering dust did not surprise him. But he did expect Hoover, whose reputation as a public figure was built largely on his humanitarian zeal for getting food to the people of Europe during and after World War I, would come up with some imaginative program for relieving similar distress in America. Yet Hoover even opposed a proposal for appropriating $20,000,000 to the American Red Cross for assisting the poor in drought areas with food. The President took the position that it would violate the "American way" and desert the principle of "private charity" if the Red Cross received support from the government.[15] To Couzens, this was carrying "rugged individualism" to absurd lengths.

In August 1931 Couzens was one of several senators who urged Hoover to call a special session of Congress to enact legislation for federal funds to be distributed through municipal governments. He acted after Mayor Frank Murphy of Detroit advised him that the city was unable to raise funds to provide unemployment relief, that at least $10,000,000 was needed to tide Detroit over the winter.

"We have played ostrich enough," Couzens said. "Families cannot be allowed to starve." [16]

But Hoover refused to call the special session. In his view, the suggestion had come from "radicals." "We cannot legislate ourselves out of this depression," he said.[17]

Couzens was all the more angry over this because he had just had a personal experience with appeals to private relief. To meet the situation in Detroit, he advised Mayor Murphy that he personally would contribute $1,000,000, if other wealthy men of the city would contribute an additional $9,000,000. Not only was the $9,000,000 not forthcoming, but at a meeting called by Mayor Murphy, Couzens was criticized—for having made such an "embarrassing offer." [18]

In November 1931, over the radio, Couzens spoke out vigorously against Hoover's tendency to minimize the seriousness of the depression. "Conditions today seem to indicate the bankruptcy of business genius and leadership in this country," he said. He criticized leaders who "take refuge inside their storm cellars of wealth and tell those on the outside not to be alarmed, because the country has always pulled through and will do so again." [19]

5

By the time Congress convened in December 1931 conditions had become much worse. Even Hoover then admitted that extraordinary measures were needed and proposed the creation of the Reconstruction Finance Corporation, by which the government would make available millions of dollars to banks and other financial institutions. Although reluctantly, he went so far as to recommend that the RFC be empowered to loan up to $300,000,000 to states and municipalities for relief expenditures, if these local units were unable to sell bonds on their own account in the regular market.[20] Indeed, here was the real start of the later New Deal. But such concessions by Hoover came too late.

As 1932 moved forward, the worst fears of Couzens and others came to pass. Unemployment in the United States reached, according to some informed estimates, the unprecedented total of 17,000,000 persons. Banks by the hundreds failed. The Insull empire in Illinois collapsed.[21] Farmers in some instances threatened to hang judges who foreclosed mortgages, in others halted the shipment of farm products to the cities because of the ruinous prices.[22] In Chicago, the city police were alerted and held in stations to be prepared for rioting. To save the banks there, the RFC loaned $90,000,000 to Charles G. Dawes' bank, just after Dawes resigned as RFC president.[23]

6

Detroit in particular was shaken. For Couzens, this was doubly jolting. He had helped to make Detroit the great industrial center that it had become, one that had attracted thousands of workers. Now, it seemed, it had all added up to a social disaster.

Although only a few knew it, the banking structure of Detroit was in a state bordering on collapse. More obvious as to Detroit's distress was the fact that the Ford plant closed down.

With amazement, Couzens read the startling news. Ford had even abandoned the five-dollar-a-day plan! No longer was it true that "the commonest laborer who sweeps the floor shall receive his five dollars a day." Instead, the minimum rate for common labor was cut to fifty cents an hour, or four dollars a day.[24] In May 1932, 80,000 unemployed workers gathered in Cadillac Square, in front of the Detroit City Hall, for a demonstration to demand action by the government. Not long after this there occurred a riot at the Dearborn plant of the Ford Company in which four men were killed.[25]

A number of magazines and newspapers carried sober articles that discussed whether or not America was on the verge of revolution, and how a revolution might be staged.[26] Dwight P. Morrow, a House of Morgan partner turned United States Senator from New Jersey, wrote: "Most of my friends think the world is coming to an end." [27]

Couzens' reaction to all this was more indignation. In his view, many of the individuals who then talked of the "need" for a Mussolini, or who were fearful of a revolution, were the very ones who had produced the crisis.

7

His attitude in this respect was considerably reinforced by the results of an investigation, begun in December 1931 by the Senate Finance Committee, with his participation, which examined procedures used by American banking and investment firms in the floating of foreign loans. A legislative result was the Johnson Act of 1934, which barred the sale in the United States of the bonds or securities of any foreign government which had defaulted on the payment of its debts to the United States.[28]

Still another result, indirectly, was one of the most important reforms of the future New Deal, divorcement of investment affiliates from commercial banks. But what interested Couzens primarily was not the foreign-relations aspect of this branch of the securities field, but the morals and patriotism of the investment bankers. Thousands of Americans had their savings wiped out by defaults of the foreign governments whose bonds they had purchased on the endorsement of leading investment firms. By 1932, more than a billion dollars worth of foreign bonds, issued by Brazil, Bulgaria, Chile, Colombia, Ecuador, Greece, and El Salvador, among others, had become all but worthless. Couzens wanted to know if "world conditions" alone were responsible, or if, in truth, investors had been swindled.[29]

The investigation confirmed his suspicions, he felt. It brought out that the bankers in certain cases had literally forced loans on foreign countries, so eager were they for the profit from floating the resultant securities in the American market. In some cases, the bonds were sold to American investors after the State Department had warned that the issuing governments were shaky, politically as well as financially. Instances were uncovered showing that some of the most respectable banking houses of the nation were not above using peculiar, if not illegal, methods.[30]

Couzens was especially indignant when it came out that Charles E. Mitchell of the National City Company not only personally profited to the extent of $4,418,732 in bonuses for his operations during the years 1926–1929, but also managed, by the device of selling some bank stock to a member of his family, to avoid paying an income tax in 1929.[31] His National City Company, as said by Thomas L. Stokes, spurred on its stocks salesmen "by contests, just as if they had been selling soap or vacuum cleaners." [32] Also, to keep up the "morale" of its officers, as Mitchell testified, it maintained a "management fund," out of which the executives received extra compensation on the basis of the earnings of the company. Couzens wanted to know if this system of "splitting" earnings did not cause "a lack of care in the handling and sale of securities to the public."

"I do not recall seeing it operate that way," said Mitchell.

"You wouldn't," retorted Couzens scornfully.[33]

8

It was no wonder that Couzens was even more contemptuous than ever of the big financiers. He now regularly raised questions about RFC help to big banks, such as the Dawes bank in Chicago. To him, the RFC operations smacked of bailing out "banksters" and preserving their undeserved gains, at the expense, he feared, of the general taxpayers. In July 1932 he proposed a full-dress Senate investigation of the RFC, but was appeased by the establishment of a select committee with the authority to confer with RFC officials.[34]

The bankers, he felt, were the very men who, while aided by the RFC, opposed, with cries of "no dole," every proposal to help the little people of the land who were out of jobs through no fault of their own. The conviction grew upon him that millions were out of jobs actually, in large part, through the fault of these same financial giants. No wonder, too, that their talk of the need for a "dictator" irritated him.

He was naive in taking up temporarily with an economic fad called "Technocracy," and for this he was held up to ridicule.[35] But at least he did not make common cause with those who welcomed a dictatorship for America. Back in 1917, in a discussion with a Detroit lawyer, he had conceded that democracies were often inefficient, but said: "Democracy will never be efficient. . . . As long as we believe in democracy, we will have to pay the price, and I for one am willing to do it." [36] He had never changed. Not dictatorship, but more democracy was the answer, he felt, meaning not simply political democracy, but economic democracy, through more equal distribution of security and income. As he wrote a little later to the editor of the *United States News*, when asked to comment on an article by David Lawrence, that said the great need was a greater dissemination of knowledge among the people, "This dissemination of knowledge, I believe, has brought our people to the conclusion that there has to be something besides the dissemination of knowledge, and that is the wider dissemination of this world's goods, so that the masses may have some economic security." [37]

9

In the summer of 1931, he began to work in that direction himself. Recalling the recommendations in his 1928 "Report on Unemployment," he announced that he hoped to introduce legislation for a national unemployment-insurance law, one that also would provide for old-age pensions, despite frequently expressed opposition by President Hoover to any such government program. The *Detroit Times* commented editorially: "He means to work most of the summer with a view to urging immediate legislation in the next Congress. . . . With Couzens working for unemployment insurance and old age pensions, these two reforms appear less remote of realization than they once did." [38]

About this same time, Ray Tucker, the Scripps-Howard writer, dropped into his office. They fell to discussing Hoover's objections to spending large enough sums of government money to diminish unemployment. Couzens told Tucker that even if it meant tripling the federal debt, the government ought to "make work by building libraries, museums, highways, bridges, schools, and so forth, even if they returned no income."

Tucker was astonished by the boldness of the idea, and asked him if he, a businessman and millionaire, would stand for quotation.[39]

"Sure!" replied Couzens.

"So fantastic was the suggestion at that time," recalled Tucker, "that I got an eight-column banner in the New York *World-Telegram*." He thought that Franklin D. Roosevelt, then Governor of New York, might have obtained from that story inspiration for his public-works program after he became President.[40]

Of course, Couzens got nowhere with his "fantastic notions." Such reforms, he knew, would have to wait for a new administration.

He had lost all vestige of hope in Hoover, though events were pushing Hoover also in the direction of federal action.

CHAPTER XXXII

THE END OF AN ERA

AHEAD was the 1932 election. Basically, this election among other things was a referendum on the Hoover policies on the depression in general, on unemployment relief in particular. Including many Republicans, the people plainly were angry with Hoover, rightly or wrongly. Even so stanch a regular Republican as Frank O. Lowden, the former Governor of Illinois who had come close to getting the Republican nomination for President in 1920, instead of Harding, deserted Hoover, though mainly on the farm issue. When he appeared in Detroit, Hoover was booed—something that rarely has happened to any President in office—and Secret Service men in Detroit feared for his life.[1] To Thomas L. Stokes, this experience was Hoover's "Calvary." [2]

The Democratic candidate was Governor Franklin Delano Roosevelt of New York, who in 1920 had been defeated for Vice President in the Harding landslide.

Couzens liked Roosevelt's speeches. Indeed, when Roosevelt made his famous "Forgotten Man" speech, and was attacked for it as a "demagogue" by former Governor Alfred E. Smith, it was Couzens who defended Roosevelt in the Senate. "I'm awfully tired of hearing men accused of demagoguery because they speak out for the little fellow," he said.[3] It did not escape him that Roosevelt's speeches were built largely around ideas which he had long championed in Detroit, as well as in Washington. Moreover, he sensed intuitively that he and Roosevelt held a similar view as to the causes of the depression. This was that the depression was in reality a moral, rather than economic, breakdown, that ethical conduct by the business leaders would have prevented the crash.

Neither Roosevelt nor Couzens was much of an economist. But both thought they knew what was "wrong" and "right" in the distribution of the good things of the world and they were for wider distribution.[4] Both would be assailed as socialists, or some other breed of anti-capitalist. But this was nonsense for political effect. If anything, both Couzens and Roosevelt were pure capitalists, concerned with preserving the individual-enterprise system. In the thesis of Louis M. Hacker,[5] Couzens was the "industrial" capitalist, who viewed the "finance" capitalist, moving toward monopoly, as an enemy bent upon destroying the very system by which he had built his own fortune. Roosevelt, in the last analysis, was on his side, he believed.

2

So, for this campaign, a Republican who could not go along with Hoover, Couzens kept silent. When Roosevelt won, he was pleased.

He was not even sorry that Michigan, rock-ribbed Republican since the days of "Zach" Chandler, had gone completely Democratic, electing for governor William A. Comstock, the Democratic chairman who had called him "really a Democrat."

Among the Old Guard Republicans, Jim Watson went down, as did David A. Reed of Pennsylvania, one of those who had infuriated Couzens by praising dictatorships. So did George Moses, "the master parliamentarian" and coiner of the phrase, "Sons of the Wild Jackass." Like Watson, Moses had felt more than once the lash of Couzens' temper, notably after he had accused him of "personal animus" when Couzens had introduced the resolution for Mellon's resignation in 1928.[6]

It amused Couzens to recall that Moses had apologized for this remark after Couzens told him that unless he did, he would hear a speech on the Senate floor about certain aspects of his political career that Moses would prefer, he said, not to have mentioned.[7]

In 1926, Smoot of Utah had insisted that Couzens be removed from the Senate Finance Committee. Smoot had taken this drastic step because Couzens so frequently objected to his high tariff proposals.[8] A famous feud had gone on between them ever since. "I'd like to drive a golf ball through your head!" Couzens once had snapped at him.[9] Now Smoot was also gone.

"The election pleased me from a national point of view," Couzens wrote to Madeleine. "The most joy I had, of course, was the defeat of Moses, Smoot and Watson—a mean streak in me, no doubt."[10]

But his "joy," if that were the correct word, was to be short-lived.

For the 1932 election marked more than the end of the Hoover administration. It also marked the end of a whole era of American political and economic policy, and such turning points are usually accompanied by considerable agony for the leading actors in the drama. This, as he soon was to discover, would be true for Couzens, as well as for numerous other Americans.

BOOK FOUR

The Independent Man

CHAPTER XXXIII

THE BANK CRISIS

Roosevelt was not to take office until the following March 4, 1933, and Couzens like nearly everyone else believed the period between the election and inauguration would be a quiet time. But this calculation was rudely upset. New tremors in the banking system of the country occurred in Nevada, Maryland, Ohio, Pennsylvania, and Louisiana.

Then, on February 14, 1933, less than three weeks before the new administration was to take over, there occurred in Michigan the worst jolt of all: At the request of the bankers, Governor Comstock ordered all the financial institutions of the state closed for a "moratorium," or "banking holiday," because of an acute emergency involving the leading banks of Detroit.

In the words of Charles A. and Mary Beard, "The news from Michigan jangled the American System from center to periphery." If anything, this judgment was understatement. For the Detroit bank crisis proved the time bomb that temporarily toppled the whole American banking structure, bringing the closing of all the financial institutions in the land.[1] Possibly, in view of general economic conditions, the national banking system might have gone down regardless of the Detroit situation. Perhaps there were no resources, not even in the federal treasury, adequate to have averted the collapse, once the situation had gotten out of hand. But in the event, it was the Detroit crisis that touched off the national crisis.

2

Couzens played a certain role in the Detroit bank crisis, though it was not the role that many accounts of the situation assigned to him.[2] Indeed, he really had less to do with it than almost any of the

other actors. Yet the Detroit situation resulted for him in the most
violent controversy of his whole controversial career. He was blamed
for having closed the Detroit, and hence the Michigan, banks. Yet
his real involvement was in efforts to keep them open, and also, a
little later, to reveal why they were closed in the first place. As will
be seen, more than anyone else, his old partner, Henry Ford, touched
off the explosion, although the conditions in the banks themselves
were not of Henry Ford's doing.

In the larger sense, the Detroit banks crashed because they had
epitomized the whole fantastic financial pattern of the era. As a Senate
investigation demonstrated, one well summarized, it may be mentioned, by Federal Judge Ferdinand Pecora in his book *Wall Street
Under Oath,* no weird financial practice of the period was omitted—
from "window-dressing," pyramiding of resources for speculation
and the voting of unearned dividends, to the use of bank funds for
improper loans to officers and even minor employees.[3]

3

John T. Flynn, then a *New Republic* contributing editor, described the Michigan situation better than anyone else in an article
in *Harper's* for December, 1933, under the title "Michigan Magic":

> These Michigan magicians had invented something brand new
> in the way of banking. It was not so completely new, of course, as
> they supposed, for group banking has broken out in this country
> at intervals, and almost always with disastrous results. But this
> was group banking with more virulent tumescence and higher tem-
> perature and some new complications. It was a combination of unit
> banking and branch banking, security manufacture, real estate
> exploitation, and numerous other lines, including running a garage,
> and all brought together under the control of a holding company
> like a utility web or department store chain. There were, of course,
> holding companies running wild among banks in other places. But
> in Michigan two groups—two holding companies—set out to capture
> the entire banking resources of a whole state. . . .
>
> In other cities one bank might fail and the others, somewhat
> strained, might continue. But in Detroit, failure of one meant the
> failure of all. And they did fail. Not just two banks, but 178 banks
> closed their doors. A great industrial city and a rich industrial and
> agricultural state were left for months almost without money. It
> was the most comprehensive bank failure in our history, and it
> marked the crash of the kind of banking which these magicians
> gave Michigan.

4

But it is necessary to get a good deal of background:

The two banking groups were the Guardian Detroit Union Group, Inc., and the Detroit Bankers Group, Inc. The former was known, if not wholly accurately, as "the Ford group." Prominent in its affairs were Edsel B. Ford and his wife's brother-in-law, Ernest Kanzler, who also headed the then Ford-controlled Universal Credit Corporation. In fact, the Universal Credit Corporation was organized as a joint enterprise of the Ford Company and of the Guardian Detroit Group.[4]

Ironically, among the units of this group, as a consequence of a series of consolidations, were the two banks that Couzens himself had founded, the Highland Park State Bank and the Bank of Detroit, by then merged into a giant called the Guardian Union National Bank of Commerce.[5] Indeed, because of stock in those old banks that his father had given to him, Frank Couzens was a director of the Guardian Group, although he resigned in 1931, "not liking the looks of things." [6]

The second group was composed of most of the old-line bankers of Detroit and included in its units the city's biggest bank, the First National-Detroit. Its nominal head—"nominal" should be stressed —was aging E. D. Stair, then publisher of the *Detroit Free Press*.

It was in the so-called Ford group that the trouble first developed —specifically in the Union Guardian Trust Company. This was a successor to the Union Trust Company, which had barely escaped the panic of 1907, and which since 1927 was housed, apparently quite solidly, in a $12,000,000 elaborately ornamented skyscraper surmounted by a tower—of gilded bricks. Charles B. Warren, whom Couzens had helped to keep out of Coolidge's cabinet as Attorney General, shared in the planning of this strikingly garish "Aztec temple of finance," as it has been called.

As a matter of fact, Warren was generally credited with having also been the originator of the legal basis of the Michigan banking-group idea as a whole.

This trust company, as the former Union Trust Company, had been having trouble since 1926, mainly because of overactivity in real estate loans [7]—trouble that was a prime reason for the merger of the Union Trust, first with the National Bank of Commerce, and then with the Guardian Trust Company, to form the Union Guardian Trust Company.

By December 1931, if not before, the trust company's condition was such as to make necessary an emergency loan of $15,000,000 from the Bankers Trust Company of New York and the Continental Illinois Bank of Chicago. Before making this loan, these banks obtained personal endorsements, and the pledging of securities, from both Charles S. Mott, another leader in the group and a General Motors Corporation executive, and Edsel Ford.

By January 1, 1932, the Guardian Group owed to Edsel Ford, personally, a total of $8,500,000 in advances and endorsements.[8]

At the end of that year the Ford Company itself went to the aid of the trust company, advancing it $3,500,000, under an agreement which made the company, for all practical purposes, a Ford Company subsidiary. For it could then transact no major business without Ford Company approval.[9] Later it was revealed that, at this time, the trust company could not meet even routine cash withdrawals, except for overdrafts honored by the Guardian National Bank of Commerce, its own affiliate, and its possession of the welfare funds of the City of Detroit on deposit with it.[10]

5

When the Reconstruction Finance Corporation was established, the Union Guardian Trust Company applied for a loan almost instantly. By putting up its best collateral the company borrowed, on May 24, 1932, $4,250,000 from the RFC. In July 1932 it obtained an additional $8,733,000 from it.

Yet even then, the company "was in imminent danger of suspension," its officers advised the RFC, unless the RFC were willing to loan an additional $15,000,000.[11]

A stumbling block was the requirement in the original RFC law —later amended—that *loans could be made only on the basis of sound collateral,* a legal provision important to bear in mind. Also, the RFC board of directors at this time took the position that enough assistance had been supplied by the government. The Fords, they said, should make up the difference, in view of their involvement.[12]

It was after this that Henry Ford approved the $3,500,000 loan from the Ford Motor Company.

6

But this Ford Company loan was only additional and inadequate shoring, for the trust company still tottered. "Disclosures of the true facts to the public on December 31, 1932 probably would have resulted in its immediate suspension," one analysis summed up its condition.[13]

In cold figures, the trust company then (its trust accounts aside) had no more than $6,000,000 in convertible assets, as values then stood, against deposit liabilities and borrowings of approximately $20,000,000, *a shortage of at least $14,000,000.*[14]

A plan was discussed for saving the situation—to take the trust company entirely out of banking and investment activity, which had caused its trouble, transfer its deposit liabilities to the Guardian National Bank of Commerce, and keep its trust business only.[15] But to do this meant covering, somehow, the $14,000,000 deficit.

There was the rub—and the nub—of the Detroit crisis, in its first stage.

7

Certain leaders of the Guardian Group gathered at Kanzler's offices in the Universal Credit Corporation, for a private conference, on Sunday, January 15, 1933. To this meeting had been invited A. P. Leyburn, the chief national bank examiner, with headquarters in Chicago. Only a few weeks before, Leyburn had appeared before the board of the Guardian National Bank of Commerce to warn that this bank was in bad shape.[16] Now Leyburn heard Kanzler say:

"The trust company cannot hold up much longer. We have to get considerably more money or the whole group is going to collapse!" [17]

As later it became plain, the purpose of the meeting was to get Leyburn's cooperation to persuade the RFC to change its attitude toward the trust company. A new approach had been determined upon. Instead of going to the RFC for additional loans to the trust company *alone,* an application on behalf of the *entire* group would be filed. On being consulted, Edsel Ford approved. As he later said, "The whole matter was gone over with me by Mr. Kanzler. . . . I concurred . . . and steps were taken to proceed." [18]

At this meeting Kanzler informed Leyburn that Edsel Ford had told him that the Ford Motor Company would agree to subordinate its deposits of $7,500,000 in the trust company. At least, this was

Kanzler's understanding. In that event, the deficit in the trust company could be considered as being no more than $6,500,000. Edsel Ford later corroborated Kanzler's statement concerning the possibility of the Ford Company's freezing its deposits. "It was understood that the subordination would take place," he said.[19]

Leyburn fell in with the plan, but suggested refining it. Congress, only a short time before, had passed a little-publicized amendment to the RFC law which permitted loans to be made to banks through special corporations set up to receive such loans. On the basis of this, Leyburn suggested that the Guardian Group form such a corporation and apply for an RFC loan in its name. The suggestion was adopted, the Wolverine Mortgage Corporation was formed.

To the Wolverine Corporation, the group then did transfer numerous assets, totaling, in face value, $88,000,000.[20] With these as security, Kanzler went to Washington with Leyburn and presented to the RFC on January 26, 1933, a request for a loan of $65,000,000 (counting the earlier advances by the RFC to the trust company). In the meantime, affairs at the trust company were going from bad to worse. Nor was this merely in the natural course of events. As would be said in court, "Throughout the month of January 1933, the Group continued to withdraw as much as possible from the Trust Company." [21]

8

The RFC began immediately to process the $65,000,000 application. Its chief appraiser, John K. McKee (afterwards a member of the Federal Reserve Board) was sent to Detroit to check the Wolverine collateral.

"The various officers of the banks came in with their collateral in pouches, and we attempted, working day and night there, to prepare a schedule," McKee recalled.[22] But he was not happy over what he discovered.

To the RFC, on February 6, McKee reported that the $88,000,000 Wolverine assets were worth, for loan purposes, only $37,720,000, including the assets on which the RFC had made its earlier loans.

But Kanzler pleaded for special treatment.

> Mr. Kanzler admitted [the minutes of the meeting of the RFC for February 6 read] that there was a considerable gap between the value of the collateral which could be pledged, and the amount of the loan desired, but said that the Guardian Group situation in-

volved the imminent danger of financial disaster of major proportions affecting the State of Michigan and the country at large, and
that he and his associates, feeling that if possible something should
be done to avert this, had decided to lay the circumstances before
the directors of this corporation.[23]

The board members of the RFC shook their heads. A new administration was coming in. There had been widespread criticism of the
Dawes bank loan. Moreover, earlier loans to the trust company had
received unsavory publicity, John T. Flynn having written them
up, with the implication that Roy D. Chapin, of the Hudson Motor
Company, by then Secretary of Commerce in Hoover's cabinet (and
another of the founders of the Guardian Group) had used his "influence" with RFC.[24]

Besides, the Detroiters were asking something that was clearly
illegal. To accede would mean leaving the RFC board members
personally liable for any loss.

The RFC board refused to take such a risk.

As a solution, the board pointed to the Fords.

In view of the previous help by Edsel Ford and the Ford Motor
Company, the Fords actually were the leading creditors of the trust
company. If the RFC did grant a new loan, even if it were legal, in
effect this would have meant transferring the load from the Fords
to the federal government. Concerning the RFC board members'
views, Leyburn later recalled:

> They figured there was not enough security there. And they asked
> all the time, "Well, what will Mr. Ford do?" . . .
> Their idea was all the way through, or their thought was—and
> they did not hesitate to say so—"Why should we bail out Mr. Ford?"
> They figured that he should come to the rescue up there.[25]

Kanzler reminded them of the understanding that the Fords would
freeze their $7,500,000 in the trust company. But he was dubious
about the Fords doing more. To get them to put up an additional $6,-
500,000 was probably out of the question, he said.[26]

In the meantime, McKee telegraphed to Detroit to see if his RFC
assistants there could not dig up more assets. Kanzler finally agreed
that the application should be scaled down from $65,000,000 to $50,-
000,000.

"We revamped the application," McKee later said, "but there was
still a hole." He added, "We had just gone the limit." [27]

The "hole" in the trust company amounted to $6,000,000—provided the Ford Company stood by Edsel Ford's commitment of sub-ordinating its deposits. Otherwise, it would be larger.

Not emphasized at the time, but highly significant later in connection with Couzens, was one objection to the Wolverine Corporation plan in addition to its legal and political aspects. This was a moral objection. For the plan, in essence, called for using sound assets of *all* the units of the Guardian Group—banks outside as well as in Detroit—to bolster the shaky trust company. In short, innocent depositors in other banks were to have their funds jeopardized for the sake of the trust company, albeit the authors of the plan justified this, perhaps properly so, with the argument that failure of the trust company would also bring down the other banks.

In the event, the RFC flatly turned down the Wolverine scheme.[28] This should be noted in connection with allegations, repeated as late as 1952 by Herbert Hoover and reiterated still later by others, that it was Couzens who stopped the loan.[29] By design of the interested parties, as will be seen, he was not yet even in the picture.

CHAPTER XXXIV

THE WHITE HOUSE CONFERENCE

Two days later, February 8, 1933, Edsel Ford conferred in Washington on the situation with Ogden L. Mills, who had succeeded Mellon as Secretary of the Treasury. He also talked with Charles A. Miller of Utica, New York, who had succeeded Dawes as president of the RFC. Miller left a record of his conference with Edsel. "I . . . urged on him strongly the duty of himself and his father to come to the rescue of the situation [recalled Miller]. I gathered from him that he was entirely willing to do this, but that his father had other views and that influences other than his would have to be used to get his father to change his mind." [1]

There is no doubt that Edsel Ford was trying to be as helpful as possible, that he wished to avoid a disaster and wanted the Ford Company to help save the situation. But there also seems no doubt that he was meeting resistance from his father. As would be said by Roger Burlingame, Edsel's "life had always been more or less frustrated" [2] —mainly by Henry Ford, common knowledge in Detroit that Charles E. Sorensen amply confirmed in his memoirs published in 1956.

Edsel's remark about "influences other than his" suggested an idea to Miller. Why should not President Hoover personally request of Henry Ford himself that he save the situation? Miller's thought was that if the President invited Ford to the White House, Ford would not, could not, refuse. [3] Miller immediately called on Hoover and made that suggestion.

But Hoover, according to Miller, was reluctant to act on the proposal. "The President told me," Miller wrote, "that he was absolutely without influence so far as Mr. Ford was concerned, and to show that, he stated he had endeavored to obtain a contribution from Mr. Ford to the Republican campaign expense account, and had either been turned down entirely or had been offered some trivial amount, I've forgotten what, but I think about $500. Under these circumstances, he said he was entirely unwilling to ask any assistance in this matter from Mr. Ford." [4]

2

This was a strange attitude for Hoover to take, especially as Ford had spoken on the radio in behalf of his re-election, and in Ford Company plants all over America a pre-election notice had been posted, on October 17, which said:

> The Ford Motor Company is not interested in partisan politics. We do not seek to control any man's vote. [However] we are convinced that any break in [President Hoover's] program would hurt industry and employment. To prevent things from getting worse, and to help them to get better, President Hoover must be elected.[5]

Yet, apparently Hoover still did not feel he could appeal to Ford personally at this crucial time.

Of course, Hoover did honestly wish to save the situation. So in lieu of adopting Miller's suggestion, he decided to call a meeting at the White House for the evening of February 9th. To this conference he invited Secretary Mills, Miller, and Michigan's two senators— Couzens and Vandenberg.

It was this meeting that first brought Couzens directly into the picture.

3

Couzens had no idea as to the full nature of the Detroit banking situation until just two days before this White House conference. This had been because the representatives of the Guardian Group specifically had asked RFC officials not to let Couzens know of their application. Their later explanation was that they feared he would have "lectured them" on banking ethics.[6] Doubtless he would have. However, on February 7th, Jesse Jones and Harvey Couch, RFC directors, decided to tell Couzens. They did so, and also told him that there was no *legal* way for the RFC to accommodate the Guardian Group in the amount it had requested.[7]

Then, just before Senator Vandenberg advised Couzens that Hoover wanted both Michigan senators at the White House on the Detroit matter, Clifford Longley, a Ford attorney, and by then president of the Union Guardian Trust Company, and Colonel James Walsh, executive vice-president of the Guardian Group, called

Couzens to the anteroom of the Senate chambers, and gave him the details. At this same time they also requested his "support." (It was later testified that someone connected with the RFC had told them: "We want you to get Senator Couzens to recommend this loan to us.") [8]

Just then Couzens was a great deal more interested in some legislation he was sponsoring on the floor of the Senate than he was in any RFC matter. In the last weeks of the Hoover administration, his pet interest was to solve the problem of jobless, homeless boys and girls who, by the thousands, were roaming the highways of the nation in search of food and shelter. His solution, forerunner of the Citizens Civilian Conservation Corps (CCC camps of the Roosevelt administration), was to open Army forts in various parts of the country to homeless youths, who would work there on various projects, such as reforestation and flood control, for their board and shelter.[9]

The Senate was debating his proposal when a page boy advised him that two gentlemen from Detroit, Longley and Walsh, were waiting for him in the Senate anteroom. He went out to see them at once.

4

He did not give Longley and Walsh much of his time. When they began on the details of their application, he stopped them short. He knew all about the matter already, he said.[10] He commented acidly on the assets in the "Wolverine Corporation," asking pointedly if they included notes of a certain Detroiter, who, he said, he happened to know had been loaned a large sum and was notoriously unable to pay. The bankers ruefully admitted that these notes were included.[11]

There was some talk about the general problem of making RFC loans to banks. Finally he commented that as a matter of basic philosophy he was not at all certain that the RFC ought to save the banks. After the Dawes bank episode in Chicago, he had begun to have doubts about the soundness of the whole idea of the RFC, he said. In this, incidentally, he was not alone. Financiers as distinguished as Secretary of the Treasury Mills, Winthrop Aldrich of the Chase National Bank, and Melvin A. Traylor, president of Chicago's First National Bank, had voiced similar doubts as to whether unsound banks should be saved through government support.[12] Testimony about this interview was given later by Longley, in direct examination by Couzens himself.

> LONGLEY: You said you were in a quandary as to whether you should go one way in support of these institutions, or let things slide the other way and let them go. I have forgotten what your language was.
>
> COUZENS: I guess it was printable, was it not?
>
> LONGLEY: Oh yes, quite printable.

Longley and Walsh departed from the Senate feeling indignant.

5

Actually, this interview changed nothing. The decision was still up to the RFC, exclusively. No one as yet had devised any plan for meeting the objection that the Guardian collateral was not sufficient to permit a *legal* loan of more than $37,720,000, the McKee figure. This, as stated, was the nub.

That night Couzens went to the White House under a serious misapprehension as to the purpose Hoover had in mind. He believed that the conference was called to get approval of an *illegal* loan. If that were the case, he knew what he would do. He would voice opposition. He made this clear in a conversation with John Carson, his secretary, who drove him to the White House.

> Going to the White House that night [Carson recalled] I urged Couzens to take one position which might have been a cowardly one. I argued that the RFC had authority to make the loan, that he, as a senator, had no authority whatsoever in the matter, that if the RFC made the loan the RFC would divulge its action or keep it secret, that it was obvious the bankers and Hoover did not want to consult him until they felt compelled to do so, that therefore he would be justified in listening to the story and then saying that they had authority and responsibility and the facts and they should exercise their responsibility. His answer was that there was a critical situation and "you cannot run out on such situations." [13]

Actually, the White House conference was held, not for the purpose of putting through an RFC loan, certainly not in the case of the trust company, but to find a *substitute* for an RFC loan. As stated by Miller, later:

> Unless the directors of the RFC desired to take a really criminal responsibility, we could not have made the loan; and after we knew the facts and figures, none of us, I think, were in favor of making it, especially when Edsel Ford and the Ford Motor Company repre-

sented the large block of stock and held deposits there of an even larger amount.

The conference at the White House, therefore, was not held to discuss the possibility of the RFC making the loan as asked for, but was rather to find some feasible plan for coming to the assistance of this banking situation without violating our legal duty.[14]

President Hoover also made this clear—in 1933—in a communication to the later grand jury investigation of the crisis, saying:

> I was informed that the Guardian Trust Co. situation was such that, *even with the utmost of government assistance possible under the law, it would be insufficient without outside help* and reorganization internally. The request . . . was that I should endeavor to bring about cooperation from outside banks, private interests and leading depositors to reorganize the trust company and thus prevent a crisis. . . .[15]

6

The fateful conference was held in the Lincoln Room of the White House.

Unfortunately, it was opened by Miller in a way that contributed to Couzens' continued confusion as to its objective, as the RFC president realized later. For, instead of making clear at the outset, in his review of the situation, that the RFC could not make the requested loan, and had no intention of making it, Miller began the meeting by reading the *original* application for the $65,000,000 loan.

This convinced Couzens that the conferees were to be asked to give their approval to *that* application. His emotions began working when he heard Miller give his personal reasons why he, as RFC president, had rejected the loan—that the loan would be illegal and also immoral.

"Possibly I even overemphasized these reasons," Miller later recalled, "because my Washington experience had led me to expect that Senators and Representatives from a state where a loan was asked of the RFC were inclined to be very critical of any hesitation on our part to grant exactly the relief asked for, and were generally either ignorant or indifferent to the limitation of our powers under the act creating the RFC." [16]

If the RFC president expected the Michigan senators to act in accord with his "Washington experience"—that is, to insist that the loan be made—he got a surprise. "Senator Vandenberg made almost no comment on this occasion," wrote Miller.[17] As for Couzens,

Miller's use of the word "immoral" produced a predictable explosion.

If any such loan were made, he would "shout against it from the rooftops and on the floor of the Senate!" he said, a remark which, when lifted out of full context, was to get him into much trouble and also lead to much misrepresentation, unintentional or otherwise.[18]

7

But nobody else at the conference expressed any different views. Certainly no one expressed any disagreement with Couzens on his assertion.

President Hoover did not. It would have been strange if he had, inasmuch as in a speech in St. Louis, on the preceding November 4, he had gone out of his way to emphasize (concerning RFC loans) that "the law requires that they should be made on adequate security." [19]

In the words of Senator Vandenberg, all that Couzens had done was to be "particularly aggressive" in voicing his opinion.[20] It turned out later, however, that it would have been much better for Couzens had he not been so emphatic, for his explosion would be remembered and used against him.

After everyone had agreed that the RFC was estopped from helping the trust company, Hoover directed the conversation toward the real purpose of the conference. This, it turned out, was to induce Couzens personally to put up funds to help save the trust company.

As Hoover sketched the situation, the *status quo* in Detroit could be preserved if about $6,000,000 were raised privately. Hoover began this approach by saying that he had discussed the crisis with Alfred P. Sloan of General Motors and with Walter Chrysler, and that they had agreed to help, presumably assenting to advance $2,000,000 each. It should be noted that he did not then mention Ford. Hoover then asked Couzens if *he* would contribute $2,000,000.[21]

Still in an excited frame of mind, Couzens obviously was in no mood to have such a proposal made to him, especially not by Hoover. Also he resented hearing Hoover suggest to him his "duty" as a Detroiter. His reaction was told by Hoover: "He stormed that it was Ford's business." [22]

Hoover recalled:

I pointed out that Ford had previously put up $5,000,000 against assets of little value to help and was now proposing to take a further loss of $7,500,000.

The Senator showed great resentment to my pressing him, and I replied that if 5% of my fortune would save a panic in hundreds of banks with hundreds of thousands of small depositors and tens of thousands of people's jobs in my home town, they could have it tomorrow. He left in great heat.[23]

8

After Vandenberg, as well as Couzens, had departed from the White House conference, the decision was reached that someone ask Ford to put up additional cash. It was taken for granted, apparently, that the Ford Company would subordinate its deposits. Inasmuch as Hoover still elected not to talk with Ford personally, the discussion then came down to who would go to Detroit to get further Ford help. In view of Ford's personality, to select the right emissaries was all-important.

Here, if ever, was a case where the "personal equation" in a public matter needed to be reckoned with. If not Hoover, then Ogden L. Mills might have been a good choice. Ford might have been impressed by having the Secretary of the Treasury come to see him. But instead of Mills, Hoover suggested that Miller, hardly known outside of New York State, take the assignment. Miller begged off. He felt that he was needed in Washington to watch national developments. Besides, his wife was acutely ill.[24] So the suggestion was made that Secretary of Commerce Chapin and Arthur A. Ballantine, a Wall Street lawyer then serving as Undersecretary of the Treasury, go to Detroit on the errand.

This was to be the climax—and a worse-selected cast of characters could not have been imagined, if the play were to end happily.

CHAPTER XXXV

THE CLIMAX

CHAPIN and Ballantine arrived in Detroit on Saturday, February 11, 1933.[1] The date is important, for the next day, Sunday, February 12, was Lincoln's Birthday, making the following Monday a legal holiday; hence the banks would not be required to open. This meant that there was time until the following Tuesday morning, the fourteenth—an extra day—to make arrangements without the possibility of news of trouble in the trust company causing panic.

The interview with Ford was arranged for at Ford's estate at Dearborn. "Everything depended . . . on the result of the Ford interview,"[2] recalled President Miller.

Chapin and Ballantine kept their appointment promptly, but Ford allowed them to wait for more than an hour. He was out inspecting his fields, they were told.

This was not a good omen as to Ford's mood. Chapin and Ballantine were worried anyway by reports in Detroit that Henry Ford might not even permit Edsel to go through with his pledge of subordinating the Ford deposits in the trust company, that Ford was displeased with the whole picture and angry with Edsel and also Kanzler, whom he blamed for Edsel's involvement.

"Word came to us," Ballantine later testified, "that Mr. Ford did not want to make that subordination."[3] When Ford finally appeared, he made it immediately plain that new trouble was definitely ahead.

2

Indeed, the Chapin-Ballantine mission turned out to be worse than a failure; it was a disaster.

When Ford was asked to put up more money, he not only angrily refused this, but also then and there overruled the commitment that Edsel had made for subordinating the $7,500,000. He would not permit it, he said.

Ford delivered a "very vigorous diatribe against banks and bankers generally, and against the RFC in particular." He insisted that the RFC make a loan large enough to permit the trust company to pay off all deposits, including those of the Ford Motor Company.[4]

Ford said he was not impressed by the explanation that the RFC could not legally make such a loan. The RFC was organized to keep banks from closing. Therefore, it should save the Guardian institutions. His attitude was summed up later by one official biographer: "What was the RFC for, anyway, if not to assist in the stabilization of the banks?" [5]

3

Chapin and Ballantine attempted valiantly to get Ford to change his mind. They spoke of the possible consequences if the trust company failed. They "explained that the situation was so delicate throughout the whole country that the failure of the trust company, and with it a number of allied institutions, would almost certainly bring down the whole banking structure of the country and lead to distress and hardship, and even very likely to the failure of very many manufacturing and business institutions as well."

Ford said:

"Let them fail; let everybody fail! I made my fortune when I had nothing to start with, by myself and my own ideas. Let other people do the same thing. If I lose everything in the collapse of our financial structure, I will start in at the beginning and build it up again."

Chapin and Ballantine then appealed to Ford on the basis that "the country had benefited him and for him now to come to the assistance of the country and to save it was an opportunity that had never come to any businessman before." But this "only appeared to antagonize" Ford.

Ford then declared: "If the Reconstruction Finance Corporation does not make this loan promptly and immediately, I will have representatives at every Detroit bank the first thing Tuesday morning, when the banks open for business, and will draw my personal balances and the balances of the Ford Company from them without any further notice." [6]

4

This threat by Ford placed a wholly different complexion on the crisis. In addition to the $7,500,000 in the trust company, the Ford Company had deposits of nearly $32,000,000 in the Guardian National Bank of Commerce and more than $20,000,000 in the First National Bank-Detroit. Neither of those banks could have stood such a withdrawal. So now the crisis had spread from the trust company to the two leading banks of Detroit, the key institutions of both groups.

Whether or not Ford actually would have carried out his threat against all of the banks in Detroit—against the Detroit Bankers Group as well as the Guardian Group—cannot be known, of course. During the panic of 1907, it will be recalled, he had told Couzens that he believed he should withdraw all of his money from the banks then. Couzens commented years later, in 1927, that he believed Ford never gave up the idea of trying that. In 1914, Ford had withdrawn his funds from the Highland Park State Bank during the war panic—the incident that came close to causing Couzens to break with Ford at that time. In a book published in 1920, there is quoted this remark, seriously intended or not, by Ford: "I don't have to worry about banks—they have to worry about me." [7]

5

Worrying about Ford was precisely what banks were doing then. For in the meantime, an almost continuous meeting of bankers and other businessmen had been going on in the offices of the Union Guardian Trust Company. The original purpose was to raise what money the Fords might not supply. Kanzler had been zealously active in trying to get pledges. The most he could get totaled only $1,582,000, which included $619,000 from General Motors and $274,000 from Chrysler. [8] But Kanzler certainly was trying to save the situation in every possible way, once it had gotten out of hand.

It was a curious scene. Nearly all the financial wealth of Detroit was represented at the gathering. New York and Chicago bankers, including such important ones as Melvin Traylor, Eugene M. Stevens, and S. Sloane Colt, also were there. Everyone was aware that the whole banking structure of Detroit was in danger, and with it, that of the nation.

As far as they knew then, however, only $6,000,000 was needed.

Yet nothing like this amount was forthcoming. "Everyone talked, yet no one said anything; the meeting was pitiable," recalled one who was there.[9]

When Chapin and Ballantine appeared at this meeting with the report of their interview with Ford, the meeting went into a real panic. The first consequence was that General Motors and Chrysler bowed out altogether from their earlier offer to help. If Ford would not help, neither would they.[10]

How to prevent Ford from carrying out his threat then became all that occupied the minds of most of the conferees. Only two proposals emerged—induce Ford, somehow, to change his stand, or close the banks to keep him from drawing out his money.

With the latter solution in mind—a holiday such as Huey P. Long had proclaimed in Louisiana—the governor in Lansing was asked to hasten to Detroit.

New appeals were made to Ford to change his mind. Ballantine telephoned to Liebold, Ford's secretary. Liebold answered: Ford felt as before.[11] Ballantine notified President Hoover, but if Hoover did anything at precisely this time, the results are not on record.

Wilson Mills, chairman of the board of the First National Bank, a son-in-law of Pingree, by now really alarmed, tried to reason with Ford that it would be unfair to punish the First National Bank for a situation involving only the Guardian Union Trust Company. But Ford repeated his threat.

> Ford stated to me [Mills later related] that unless the Guardian were permitted to open the following day, he would come down and take his money, every cent of his funds, from us and from any other Detroit bank that was open. . . .
> I said, "Why is that, Mr. Ford?" He said, "I think it is up to the government to save these institutions by making them loans. They saved the Dawes bank."
> I asked him to play ball, told him what the situation was, told him we were applying for a loan from the RFC . . . and we hoped to secure one. [But] Mr. Ford made the remark that I have testified to.[12]

6

Then, in Washington, Couzens re-entered the picture, to try his hand at reversing Ford's attitude.

Contrary to later assertions, his personal relations at this time with Ford were good. They had long since become reconciled after

Couzens' attack on Ford's Presidential ambitions in 1923. In 1926 they had jointly issued a statement opposing the restitution of the death penalty for capital crime in Michigan. In 1927 Ford had presented to Couzens, to the accompaniment of a good deal of publicity, one of the first new-model Ford cars, as a token of "fond remembrance" of the days when they were associated in the Ford Company. And Couzens was "thrilled," he told Ford.[13]

Nothing had happened since to mar their truce. Thus, when Couzens was told of Ford's ultimatum, he did not hesitate to telephone to Ford.

He did so from the office of the RFC, to which he and Vandenberg had been summoned by the distressed Miller and Secretary Mills. Miller recalled:

> I was present during this telephone interview, but of course, I did not hear what Mr. Ford said. I gathered, however, from Senator Couzens' talk to him that Mr. Ford claimed that the whole crisis was brought about by the machinations of his competitors and that he again expressed his determination to draw all his deposits from the Detroit banks unless we made arrangements to enable the Guardian Union Trust Company to pay its depositors by the opening hour on the morrow.
>
> I will say, parenthetically, that if there were any errors during all these negotiations in handling Mr. Ford diplomatically, Senator Couzens was not responsible for them on this telephone call. He had apparently been willing almost to tear Mr. Ford limb from limb when he put in the call, and I have never witnessed so complete a change in language and manner as his when the call came through. During his entire conversation with Mr. Ford, the Senator dropped sweetness into the phone at every word and never suggested even a mild criticism of Mr. Ford's position.[14]

When Ford had thus spoken to him against the RFC and refused to withdraw his threat against the Detroit banks, Couzens still did not give up. He determined upon another approach and toward the end of his talk with Ford he asked him to have Clifford Longley, Ford's lawyer, get in touch with him by telephone. "I think we can arrange this thing for the Union Guardian Trust Company," he told Ford.[15] There was no use trying to discuss details with Ford, Couzens explained later.

<h2 style="text-align:center">7</h2>

Couzens was at dinner with Mrs. Couzens when Longley telephoned from Detroit shortly after 8 P.M. Of all the numerous telephone calls between Detroit and Washington that evening, this one was easily the most important. It was the one outstanding effort made by anyone to save the situation in Detroit.

To Longley, Couzens now emphasized what he had tried to get Ford to realize, that the RFC could not make a loan to the Guardian Union Trust Company unless more and adequate collateral were put up, but that it could make a loan if such collateral were made available. He then asked Longley to get over to Ford a message:

He, Couzens, would go fifty-fifty with Ford in putting up the collateral that would make possible an RFC loan to the trust company. "I asked him to ask Mr. Ford if he would join me in making a joint note to guarantee the RFC against any loss." [16]

In effect, that meant that Couzens was willing to risk at least $6,900,000 of his personal fortune to keep the banks open, if Ford would do likewise. He was willing, now that he saw the certain result of Ford's position, to do more than three times what Hoover had asked him to do the previous Thursday.

Longley called back. He had put Couzens' offer up to Ford, and Ford's answer was "No." Ford in fact was "annoyed" at the suggestion.[17] So there now disappeared the last chance of averting the bank panic in Detroit, and also of averting the bank holiday.

8

Governor Comstock, by then in Detroit, was not at all anxious to accept the responsibility of so drastic a step as to order a bank holiday. He was not certain as to the legality of the move. C. J. Huddleston, of Lacy, Anderson and Wilcox, among other lawyers, finally convinced him that he did have the power to keep the banks closed, although conceding that how to get them open again might present a different problem.[18]

Then there developed some dissension among the bankers as to whether or not a holiday *should* be proclaimed. The Guardian bankers were all for it, but the Detroit Bankers Group, feeling that their institutions were not involved except indirectly, tended to oppose the action, until they discovered that an RFC loan for them could not possibly be arranged in time.

Later, directors of the First National Bank-Detroit were to discover something just as appalling—that the First National's condition, with respect to liquidity, was not much better than that of the Guardian banks.[19]

Comstock finally said that if all the bankers agreed to sign a document asking him to proclaim the holiday, he probably would agree. The bankers signed. The federal government representatives, including Undersecretary Ballantine, also gave their approval.[20] Comstock still hesitated, but agreed to make up his mind in time to advise the bankers and the public before the hour of opening the banks on Tuesday morning. About midnight he left the meeting with Arthur J. Lacy to get a "breather."

"It was a cold, misty night. We strolled twice around the two blocks around the Union Trust Company and the Hammond building," Lacy later recalled. "We talked the problem over as we walked and as we dropped into a hot dog stand for a hot dog. Comstock asked me what I would do in his position. I told him that everybody at the meeting was agreed that a bank holiday was imperative and that if we didn't have one it would cause a nation-wide banking collapse.

"So we went back and Governor Comstock told the bankers and government men that he would call a holiday. . . ."[21]

At 1:32 Tuesday morning, February 14, 1933, in the gilded tower of the Guardian Union Trust Company, Comstock affixed his signature to a proclamation that closed the banks.[22]

At 2:00 A.M., Herbert R. Wilkin (a name to be remembered), one of many vice-presidents of the Guardian Group, called Ernest Kanzler on the telephone and gave him a message: "The jig is up!"[23]

CHAPTER XXXVI

"A HELL OF A MESS"

THE holiday served its major purpose of keeping any depositors, including Ford, from making withdrawals. But getting the banks open again was another matter.

Originally the holiday was supposed to last only eight days. Governor Comstock, however, was forced to extend it indefinitely at the request of the bankers themselves. For the federal bank officials took the position that the Guardian National Bank of Commerce as well as the First National Bank-Detroit, the leading Detroit banks, each head of its group, could not be reopened unless they were reorganized and more capital put into them. Otherwise, the banks would simply collapse under new runs that were bound to develop, they said. Their condition had been perilous, anyway, for months. In fact, the federal officials said, both banks were actually insolvent.[1] Chief Bank Examiner Leyburn summed up the situation: "Gentlemen, we are in a hell of a mess!" [2]

With its nationwide repercussions, the "mess" was complicated by the attitude adopted by nearly everyone concerned. For the efforts of solving the humpty-dumpty situation that had developed were carried on against a background of the most bitter kind of recrimination and misrepresentation.

Everybody apparently tried to place the blame on everybody else.

President Hoover and those close to him, blamed, at first, Governor Comstock.[3] The proclamation of the holiday was unnecessary; Comstock had yielded to panic, they said. As Theodore G. Joslin, one of Hoover's secretaries, even said later:

"I have always felt that the governor lost his head; if he had not become panicky, that catastrophe would have been averted." [4]

2

A defense of Hoover in the banking crisis—a book, *Prelude to Panic,* by Lawrence Sullivan—contained an amazingly inaccurate version.

> Secretary Mills . . . had been informed that the Detroit bankers, now in alarmed confusion, had called Governor William A. Comstock into consultation. A few hours later all the RFC plans were brought to an end by the sudden determination of the governor to proclaim a ten-day banking holiday throughout the entire State! This proclamation . . . was issued without consultation between Governor Comstock and the RFC, Treasury, or White House. By this single stroke all the ground was instantly cut from under the Washington rescue plans.[5]

3

Hoover also blamed Roosevelt. Here the argument was that the bank crisis would not have occurred had not Roosevelt undermined "public confidence," first, by failing to commit himself to Hoover's economic policies, and second, by failing to disavow certain advisers who suggested that it might be a good thing for the country to go off the gold standard.[6]

As for many of the bankers, they at first placed the blame, generally speaking, on "general conditions," ignoring evidence that some of them had been making unwise investments or extending unwise loans on the basis of unsound security, or that some bankers also had been motivated by "manipulation, greed, and dishonesty" (Couzens' words later) as they helped themselves, in the form of loans, to depositors' money in their custody. Later many bankers also echoed Hoover: "Roosevelt was at fault."

The Reverend Charles E. Coughlin, the "radio priest" of the Church of the Little Flower at Royal Oak, Michigan, was blamed—because of speeches he had made attacking the banking system in general and the Detroit Bankers Group in particular.

The *Detroit Times* was blamed—because it had been devoting a good deal of its space to the Coughlin speeches.

The RFC was blamed. Communists were blamed.[7] The Senate Finance Committee inquiry into Wall Street was blamed.[8]

Henry Ford came in at the outset for some slight criticism, for Governor Comstock issued a statement telling in part, although in a garbled way, the connection Ford had with the holiday. Later

Governor Comstock issued a repudiation of his revelation about the Ford role. "I misunderstood the facts," he said.[9] Even Couzens elected not to emphasize the part played by Ford in the disaster, not even in his own defense.

4

But of all the scapegoats, Couzens himself became Number One.

"You do not and cannot realize how unanimous the belief is that you are to blame for this bank situation!" Thomas A. Payne, an attorney who had managed Couzens' 1930 re-election campaign, and one of his most loyal friends, wrote to him. This was all too true.

Instantaneously there grew up a legend:

The Detroit banks could have been saved by an RFC loan, but "Senator Couzens blocked the loan," first, because he "hated Henry Ford," and, second, "because he hated all rich men in Detroit."

Unwittingly, perhaps, Hoover was in large part responsible for starting this legend. In talks by telephone with various Detroiters at the beginning of the crisis, he had spoken bitterly of Couzens' "non-cooperation" and mentioned, without proper interpretation, Couzens' threat of "shouting from the rooftops."[10] Editor Malcolm Bingay, who admittedly disliked Couzens, obtained Hoover's version. On the second day of the holiday, he published in the *Free Press* on its front page a story that set the pattern. The headlines were:

FORD-COUZENS CONFLICT
REVEALED AS A FACTOR
IN FINANCIAL STALEMATE

Senator Opposed RFC Loan to
Trust Firm, Saying Collateral
Was Not Sufficient

Insisted That Motor King Keep $7,100,000
on Deposit as "Frozen Asset"; Magnate
Refused to Sign Joint Note

and the article said:

> If it had not been for Senator Couzens' protests, the loan would have been granted.
> The RFC officials and other bankers held to the belief that this loan was necessary. There followed a bitter battle with Senator Couzens, who held that it was not a safe investment for the Government. He insisted that there should be more collateral. He was called to the White House and President Hoover pleaded with

him. He vowed he would go on the floor of the Senate and denounce the loan if it were made. . . .[11]

5

A more garbled version would be hard to imagine. But Couzens largely had himself to blame. For one thing, when it had leaked from the supposedly secret White House conference that he had made his "rooftops" threat, he readily confirmed that he had made the threat, but, like Hoover and Bingay, without making clear the circumstances.[12]

Later in the heat of controversy he voiced sentiments which made it look as if he himself confirmed Bingay's version or that he would have been glad if he had actually blocked the loan. For example:

"I did not stop the much disputed loan. . . . However, I'm glad to have the public think I stopped it, if the public wants to think that; because as it was presented to Washington, it was an illegal and a wicked loan." [13]

Moreover, just before the bank holiday, he had given to Jay Hayden a long interview on his views concerning RFC loans in general which made it appear that he was opposed to any kind of assistance to banks. This interview was unfortunately timed. It appeared in the *Detroit News* on Monday, February 13, the day before the holiday.

> Everybody is saying, "Let us ask the RFC for money." Now that, to my mind, raises the largest single issue facing the new administration. It is whether we shall open the treasury door to everyone or close it to everyone.
>
> I supported the RFC in its present form because I believed that, by aiding the railroads, the banks and other like industries, we would benefit the great body of bank depositors and borrowers, insurance policy holders and the like, and then stimulate recovery generally.
>
> But during the year that has elapsed, I have very carefully watched the operations of the RFC and the financial developments in the country and I have about reached the conclusion that the federal government either has to support the debt structure for all of the citizens or we have got to stop the rescue of any of them.[14]

To a good many people, later, as well as at the time, this article appeared to represent corroboration of the story in the *Free Press* two days later. Besides this, the newspapers then recalled that Couzens had denounced in the Senate an RFC loan of $12,800,000 to the

Missouri Pacific Railroad, because, as chairman of the Committee on Interstate Commerce, he was not satisfied that the way to solve the railroads' financial problems was through that procedure. He had sharply observed that the chief beneficiary would be, not the railroad, but J. P. Morgan and Company.[15] Also, he had raised questions about the Dawes Chicago bank loan in 1932, although in the end he approved that transaction when shown facts proving that if it had not been entered into, probably all of the banks in Chicago would have been forced to close. These protests, together with his sponsorship of a special Senate subcommittee to act as watchdog over all RFC loans, gave him the reputation of being irreconcilably anti-RFC as well as against helping the Detroit banks, although this was not at all his true position.[16] Even careful students of the crisis would be misled by published material about him on this point.

6

But there was still one more reason why the false version crystallized against Couzens. Usually over-quick to defend himself, he now determined that with the banks closed, it would be unpatriotic for him to stir up controversy over why the banks were in such a condition. To tell the facts, he would have to attack the bankers, and also to stress the part played by Ford. He decided not to do this. "Some day the history of all the events and personalities who played their parts, will be written, but now is not the time," he said.[17]

So, instead of devoting time to hitting back at accusations against himself, he concentrated on efforts for getting the Michigan banks reopened. "I am rushed to death with Michigan's bank troubles, plus all my own legislative work," he wrote Madeleine on February 20th.

His efforts, in which he was assisted by Vandenberg, bore fruit in the one plan that might have permitted the Guardian National and the First National to reopen. This was a proposal, embodied in a Joint Resolution, soon known as the "Couzens Resolution," which he presented to the Senate on the 20th. It authorized the Comptroller of the Currency to allow national banks, such as those in Detroit, to reopen and operate along the lines of a plan that already had been worked out in New York and in Iowa for state banks, permitting "frozen" banks to start from scratch after segregation of their non-liquid assets and obligations against them from current deposits and commitments, if state laws permitted. Disbursements would be permitted on a limited basis. In effect, this permitted insolvent banks to act as their own receivers, the while avoiding the stigma and penalties of failure.[18]

This resolution was adopted by the Senate in two days. The House concurred on February 25, and Hoover promptly signed the resolution.[19] Then, all that was needed to reopen the old banks—if the bankers so desired—was for the Michigan legislature to pass complementary legislation. Such legislation was introduced at Lansing, at Couzens' suggestion, with Kanzler acting as principal proponent.

7

Meantime the bankers and other businessmen in Detroit were working in other directions. They considered plan after plan. But each came to nothing because something that the First National directors might propose would be vetoed by the Guardian directors, and vice versa. Or cliques within the groups gave vent to expressions of rivalry and mistrust. Moreover, there was still reluctance on the part of the top financiers to put up any money.

The bankers' solution was to have one more merger, to consolidate the Guardian National and the First National. In this, they were encouraged by New York bankers and by the RFC itself. The theory was that if some $11,000,000 of new capital were subscribed for a consolidated bank, the RFC would extend a sizable loan to the new bank for unfreezing the frozen assets of the old banks. Then the Comptroller would authorize the new bank to take over the two old ones.

But an immediate hitch developed—again in the attitude of Henry Ford. As the leading depositor in both banks, his support was essential regardless of anyone else's. He was counted on to help supply the new capital—and Ford kept aloof.[20]

8

Indicative of the hysteria was a hastily written letter from Secretary of Commerce Chapin to Couzens. "I foresee by the first of the week," Chapin wrote on February 25th, "the possibility of very serious disorders. All sorts of threats are being made by depositors, and what they want—and that quick—is some form of relief. If it is not afforded, we shall have a riotous Detroit and a prostrate Michigan facing us." [21]

Two days later, the newspapers announced that the crisis was solved. Two new banks were to be established, as the bankers had urged, with Ford cooperation. The difference between this and earlier solutions was that the new institutions would be all Ford.

The Fords would put up, not some capital, but all of the capital, $11,000,000, and they would own all of the stock and designate the directors. The RFC would put up $135,000,000—$100,000,000 on First National assets and $35,000,000 on Guardian National assets. There would be an immediate payoff of 50 per cent to depositors.

At first, even by the bankers who were to be displaced, this Ford plan was greeted with hosannahs. A joint statement by the boards of directors of the First National and the Guardian National banks called it "generous and public-spirited." [22] The application for the $135,000,000 loan was rushed to the RFC. It was widely believed that the new banks would be operating in a few days.

Henry Ford gave out jubilant statements. He told newspaper reporters that he would evolve a new kind of banking system in the world. "Our policy will be an evolution," he said. Loans would be made only for "productive purposes." As for interest, it would be reduced or even "eliminated." [23] In Dearborn, Ford's town, a civic demonstration was staged, with three thousand persons parading the main street, bearing a banner that said: "BANK WITH HANK!" [24]

9

In Washington, Couzens was delighted, especially as he had been on the verge of offering to put up the capital himself for a new bank in Detroit, in answer to urgent pleas that "something had to be done" to get some kind of commercial banking going again. He had gone with Attorney Henry Bodman, prominent in the Detroit banking picture, to the office of the Comptroller to set his plan in motion.

He was greeted there by Acting Comptroller F. G. Awalt, who told him excitedly that the problem was settled. In Couzens' words later, "I, immediately, with considerable enthusiasm, said, 'Well, that lets me out!' I was glad to be out." [25]

But, almost immediately, came a great cooling off.

The fact was that almost no one, after reflection, was happy over the Ford solution, except those Detroiters whose sole interest was to get the promised 50 per cent payoff as quickly as possible.

The bankers were not happy. They did not look forward to being squeezed out of the banking business, or converted into operators on a new kind of Ford assembly line. They gagged over Ford's financial ideas.

Ford's business competitors were not happy.

A large number of outstate Michigan bankers immediately kicked up a rumpus. Under the leadership of Joseph H. Brewer, of Grand Rapids, president of the Michigan Clearinghouse Association, they began to bombard the RFC, the Comptroller, and all of the Michigan delegation in Congress, including Couzens, with telegrams opposing the granting of the $135,000,000 loans to the new Detroit banks. In the main, this was because of a ruling by the Comptroller that deposits of the outstate banks in the two Detroit banks, amounting to some $20,000,000, were not to be given a preferred status.[26]

10

Then Couzens himself set up some opposition. He took the position that it was against the national interest for the federal government to commit itself to a loan of $135,000,000 to the banks of one city, even his own city, when at that time similar crises were developing in other parts of the nation. Banks in Cleveland, Toledo, and Baltimore had just sent appeals to the RFC for large emergency loans. When this happened, even the RFC officials began to doubt whether they should grant the Detroit request.[27] That the federal treasury had the ability to bail out all banks was considered highly doubtful.

Couzens still did not at this time oppose all RFC help to the Detroit banks. A loan should be made, he said, but he suggested that it be limited to about $50,000,000. This would have enabled the banks to reopen, but would have reduced the amount of the initial payoff.[28] Couzens later explained:

> I thought it would establish a precedent for every city, county, and hamlet in the United States to call upon the federal government for its financial needs. The federal government must stand, regardless of what happens to states or their political sub-divisions. When the national credit is gone, there will be chaos, and regardless of what my constituents may think of my actions concerning their particular affairs, I am here to use every ounce of energy and effort to protect the federal government.[29]

11

In the end, it was the RFC itself, regardless of Couzens' position, which scaled down the Detroit loan. For, in the meantime, RFC appraisers had been burrowing into the records of both banks, and now came up with reports that neither bank had assets to justify the $135,000,000 loan. All that could be granted was $78,000,000. The RFC proceeded on that basis.[30]

Couzens raised no objections to the $78,000,000 figure; it represented, in his view, a reasonable compromise. He did ask that he be given the right to "represent" the RFC in the ultimate negotiations with the Detroiters, but this request was refused.

President Hoover ordered that he be "ignored," and the $78,000,000 loan be extended without delay in order to get the new Ford banks opened.[31] Again it was announced that the crisis was over.

12

Suddenly, all was confusion again. Two things had happened.

The Ford plan, also the RFC commitment, had been predicated on the willingness of the Central Hanover Bank in New York to renew loans totaling $20,000,000 made earlier to the First National Bank. It had been thought that the New York banks would agree, as a matter of course, to the renewals. Now came the news that legal objections had been raised by the bank's lawyers, objections supported by Stanley Reed, then counselor of the RFC, later an Associate Justice of the Supreme Court.[32] The $20,000,000 renewal was out.[33]

Then a revolt against the Ford plan developed in the ranks of the officers and shareholders of the First National Bank. At 11:45 P.M., Tuesday, February 28, McKee was handed a letter from Mills of the First National Bank, which read:

> At the conclusion of the board meeting today, I was instructed to telephone Mr. Edsel B. Ford and to state to him that the general opinion of the board is that it is inadvisable to go ahead under the proposed plan in which he and his father are interested. I might add, for your information, that this action of our board was unanimous. . . .
>
> Faithfully yours,
> WILSON W. MILLS,
> Chairman.[34]

As RFC President Miller remarked to Couzens, this was a "peculiar situation." For on the same day that James T. MacMillan, a prominent director of the First National, telephoned to him to ask that an additional $20,000,000 be granted to cover the New York bank item, Wilson Mills, the chairman of the board of the same bank, telephoned to ask that this $20,000,000 not be granted.[35]

In explanation, Mills later said that while he did not "block the Ford plan," he definitely was against it. "The bank was a profitable business and Ford's plan meant keeping all the profits for Ford, as Ford would not let anyone else hold any stock. . . . We felt that the depositors were entitled to [the profits]—not the stockholders and not any special interests, not Dearborn or New York, or anybody." [36]

What this "peculiar situation" added up to was that the bankers, in particular those of the First National, had by then decided that they wanted to operate on the basis of the proposal sponsored in the Senate by Couzens. As stated by Mills to the RFC on February 28, "If the $20,000,000 is not forthcoming, the bank will seek to operate under the Couzens Joint Resolution." [37]

13

Suddenly everyone concerned, in Washington as well as in Detroit, looked for salvation to the plan that Couzens had embodied in his resolution. Eugene Meyer, then Governor of the Federal Reserve Board, had written to Hoover on February 25th:

> Recently the Board, after giving the matter careful thought with these considerations in mind, approved the joint resolution regarding the powers of the Comptroller of the Currency introduced by Senator Couzens. . . . It felt that such a measure would be helpful in facilitating the working out of existing situations in various communities without creating undue disturbance.[38]

So, despite all the curses heaped upon him, Couzens now became the man of the hour. Requests poured in on him that he leave Washington immediately for Detroit to take the lead in putting the plan into effect there. Even Ford begged him to come.[39] So did Stair of the *Free Press*, who telegraphed: "Your presence in Detroit and your help on this banking situation greatly needed." [40] Mills of the First National twice telephoned him. Senator Vandenberg, whose responsibility to Michigan was equal to Couzens', but who cautiously stayed in the background, also urged him to go. Couzens went.

CHAPTER XXXVII

THE MISSION THAT FAILED

His overnight trip might well have been screen-titled: "Couzens to the Rescue." Its importance was well underlined in a memorandum that Vandenberg hastily typed on his portable in his Senate office and had delivered to Couzens at the Washington railroad station. "This stupendous journey" was how Vandenberg referred to Couzens' mission. "We have been in complete and constant touch. You know my views and I know yours . . . I am betting on you!" Vandenberg wrote.[1]

Then, for three days, following his arrival in Detroit on the morning of March 1, Couzens was the leading actor in the drama: "The Man with the Plan." For once even big business executives acted as if they esteemed him. His every word and action was reported in detail and with the greatest respect, even by Bingay. Couzens and Henry Ford met at Dearborn. With their sons, Frank Couzens and Edsel Ford, they posed for newspaper photographers. Said the Detroit *Times:*

> The Fords and the Couzens—father and son in two great families —were evolving a new solution of the banking problem of distressed Detroit today. Behind oaken doors . . . "Henry" and "Jim" talked over the most urgent problem of their twin careers, just as in years gone by they had charted the policies of the Ford Motor Company during the era of its greatest growth. . . .[2]

2

Actually, this was optimistic overstatement. Behind "the oaken doors," Couzens and Ford had lunch at a table that buzzed with the conversation of so many Ford executives that there was no chance to talk seriously about the banking crisis.

Then Ford asked Couzens to visit a laboratory to hear a dance orchestra, after which Ford said he had to depart, and did, without letting Couzens raise the question of the banks at all.[3]

But with others, Couzens made better headway, he thought. He was even praised now for having opposed the $135,000,000 loan because of national considerations. Wilson Mills, who later lashed out at him and blamed him for the closings on this very point, was one who hailed his stand.

FIRST NATIONAL BANK–DETROIT
DETROIT, MICHIGAN
March 3, 1933

DEAR SENATOR:

While I saw you only a short time during your visit to Detroit, I cannot let an hour go by after your departure without writing to thank you for coming and for what you have done. I think you made the way seem clear to everyone in Detroit, and I know we are all doing the right thing.

I also want to state to you here and now that last Saturday I could not understand your attitude in opposing a large loan by the Reconstruction Finance Corporation to the two Detroit banks. Of course, being so near to the grindstone, I was looking only at Detroit, and I am bound to say to you that now I think your attitude was the correct one, that is, the National Government and its solvency was, is, and must continue to be the primary consideration of every one of us.

Again my heartfelt thanks.

Faithfully yours,
WILSON M. MILLS

3

In such an atmosphere then, the leaders of the Guardian and the Detroit Bankers Groups finally agreed upon a simple plan. This was that the Michigan legislature should be asked to pass at once the legislation to permit limited operation of the old banks. Under that plan, the RFC would make loans to the old banks to permit a payoff of 15 per cent initially, with other payoffs to be made later. Governor Comstock and leaders of the legislature were consulted. The machinery was set in motion for the legislation to be passed when Couzens left Detroit on March 3 to be on hand in Washington for Roosevelt's inauguration.

He was confident that the situation in Detroit was now in hand. He apparently had succeeded in getting the various banking groups, shareholders, and depositors, the Fords and other business interests,

to subordinate their rivalries and thus agree on united action behind
his plan.

Everyone seemed grateful to him. An official statement by the
board of directors of the First National said, "The Senator has been
most helpful." [4]

Best of all, from the standpoint of the bankers, it appeared that
the verdict of insolvency for the Guardian National and the First
National banks would be escaped. There was general confidence
that within a matter of days, the old banks would be reopened.[5]

4

Everyone in Detroit, however, had failed to take into consideration
what was happening throughout the nation. In shocking succession,
state after state had gone into banking holidays, until, as of March
3, nearly thirty states were involved.[6]

Hoover seemed to clutch at straws. On February 17 he appealed
to President-elect Roosevelt for cooperation to bolster public confidence. He asked that Roosevelt join with him in a statement to
the public to the effect that under the new President "there will be
no tampering or inflation of the currency; that the budget unquestionably will be balanced, even if further taxation is necessary; that
the government credit will be maintained by refusal to exhaust it
in the issuance of securities." [7]

Roosevelt's reply was strangely delayed for twelve days. It was mis-
laid by a secretary, Roosevelt later explained. Regardless of that,
the President-elect made it plain that he would not have made the
kind of statement Hoover wished in any event. He considered
Hoover's request "cheeky." [8] It certainly was asking Roosevelt to
adopt Hooverian policies. As he explained politely, but firmly, to
Hoover, his thought was that the bank troubles were "so very deep-
seated that the fire is bound to spread in spite of anything that is
done by way of mere statements." [9]

Now, on the eve of disaster, Hoover turned to Roosevelt again.

Through William H. Woodin, Roosevelt's choice for Secretary
of the Treasury, Hoover asked that the President-elect at least "join
in a statement reiterating confidence in the fundamental soundness of American banks and appealing to depositors to stop withdrawing funds." Roosevelt refused to make this kind of statement
also. He "felt that a strong, positive, definite action should take the
place of appeals." [10] Hoover then asked if Roosevelt would join

him in sponsoring a special session of Congress for enactment of emergency legislation.[11] Again Roosevelt's answer was no. He did not feel that any action taken by him as "a private citizen" would be helpful.[12]

Hoover next considered two drastic, possible steps. Had he actually taken either one or both, the final result might not have been changed, but at least history might have revamped its view of him as a man incapable of bold action while President. First Hoover considered asking Congress, on his own initiative, for a government guarantee of bank deposits, at least temporarily. But before acting, he asked the Federal Reserve Board if it would support "some form of Federal guarantee of banking deposits." [13]

The Federal Reserve Board declined to support such an idea. "You are, of course, thoroughly familiar with the history of such experiments in some of the States and the inherent dangers in a proposal of this kind," Governor Meyer wrote him on March 2.[14] So Hoover backed away from the proposal, later adopted as part of the New Deal.

The other step was, by executive action, to close all of the banks in the country—a national holiday which, at least, would halt further withdrawals and maintain the *status quo*. From the first, Hoover was reluctant to take this action. His view was that "eighty per cent of the banks measured in deposits were still functioning." despite the numerous state holidays. But by then, with even the banks in New York City tottering, the Federal Reserve Board itself felt that drastic action was necessary. The Board urged Hoover to proclaim a national holiday.[15]

Was such action within the authority of the President? It had been suggested that the authority could be found in the Trading with the Enemy Act adopted in 1917 and never directly repealed, according to some lawyers.

Hoover asked the opinion of his Attorney General, then William D. Mitchell. Mitchell "advised that these war powers were so doubtful that they could be safely used only if it were certain that Congress would ratify the action." [16]

Pondering this equivocal opinion, Hoover again turned to Roosevelt, with the thought that if the new President would approve a national moratorium, ratification by Congress would be assured. But through Woodin, Hoover was told that Roosevelt took the position that "President Hoover was free to proceed as he thought best." [17] This was not, as has been represented, a refusal to approve the moratorium idea. But it certainly was another refusal by Roosevelt to join with Hoover in anything.

5

On the following day, March 3, Roosevelt, with his wife and son James, called at the White House for the traditional day-before-inauguration courtesy call. After tea, and the usual amenities, Hoover took the occasion to broach the moratorium idea to Roosevelt personally. Roosevelt said he believed the power was there, but suggested that if Hoover wanted to close the banks, he should do it, that "it made no difference who did it." [18]

Aside from the crisis, this tea was not a happy affair, either for Hoover or Roosevelt. Indeed, according to Roosevelt's secretary, Grace Tully, Hoover made one remark which caused Roosevelt to say later, "I hustled my family out of the room. I was sure Jimmy wanted to punch him in the eye." [19]

Such matters aside, it was plain that Hoover could not bring himself to act alone on a moratorium, but he was persistent with regard to Roosevelt. At 11:30 P.M., March 3, he put in a telephone call to Roosevelt at the Mayflower Hotel. There are conflicting versions as to precisely what Hoover said to Roosevelt and what Roosevelt said to Hoover at that eleventh-hour conference.[20] But the clear facts were that Hoover again asked Roosevelt to join him in proclaiming a national bank holiday, and that Roosevelt again insisted on taking no responsibility in the crisis until he had assumed the power of the Presidency.

The next morning, a matter of hours before the change in administrations, the final blow fell: In New York, the financial center of the nation, Governor Herbert Lehman proclaimed a banking holiday. Almost immediately, Governor Henry Horner of Illinois followed suit. So did ten other governors. By the time Roosevelt had taken the oath of office, nearly all of the banks of the nation were closed under state moratoria of one type or another.

Armed with an opinion by Attorney General Homer S. Cummings that the Enemy Trading Act was still valid, Roosevelt on Sunday evening, March 5, proclaimed a national holiday for all banks in the nation for four days, later extending it indefinitely. Under the terms of this proclamation, and of an emergency law adopted almost immediately afterward by Congress, no bank anywhere in the nation was to be open except under a special license issued by the Secretary of the Treasury.[21]

6

For Detroit, the result of Roosevelt's action was that even the Couzens Plan for reopening the Detroit banks had to be abandoned. The new banking legislation superseded and nullified the authority granted to the Comptroller under the Couzens Joint Resolution. The bankers there had delayed too long. The question of whether or not the Detroit banks were to be reopened at all then became a matter solely up to the new administration.

On March 12, when Roosevelt delivered the first of his "fireside chats," he emphasized over and over again that only *sound* banks were to receive licenses to reopen. Were the Detroit banks "sound?" Did "sound" mean "solvent?" These became the crucial questions.

For the emergency, Ballantine and Awalt had been retained in office by the new administration. Jesse Jones was slated to become chairman of the Reconstruction Finance Corporation. And these were the men upon whom the new Secretary of the Treasury, Woodin, relied for counsel. Their verdict was that the Detroit banks were not solvent.[22]

Couzens, who was to be denounced and slandered by the bankers and bank-stock owners, was almost the one official who tried to save the banks from this verdict.

On March 11, he protested vigorously to Secretary Woodin. Woodin called in Awalt and Ballantine and there occurred a heated scene.

"What is holding up these banks? Why don't you certify to their opening?" Couzens demanded of Awalt.

"I will not certify to the secretary that these banks are solvent," said Awalt.

And Ballantine said, "That is true. They cannot open up because they are insolvent." [23]

Couzens demanded proof as to the banks' insolvency. He threatened to "stay right here until the proof is forthcoming." He did not get proof, in facts or figures. Unfortunately for the banks, on the other hand, he was not able to present any facts to controvert the position of Awalt and Ballantine.

The Detroit bankers themselves, as he later pointed out, did not present any facts to offset the verdict of insolvency. Moreover, they were still entangled in their rivalries. They had been urged by the Treasury to take the initiative in forming a new bank. But they could not come to an agreement.

On March 14 Acting Comptroller Awalt, backed up by Secretary Woodin, let the sword fall. He named conservators for both the First National and the Guardian National. For those banks, as well as for the two groups of which they were the principal units, the action was the crack of doom. They were never allowed to reopen. Scores of investors had fortunes wiped out by this decision. Many of these then blamed Couzens, hating him fiercely to the end of his life because of this.

7

Yet, ironically, Couzens to the end had tried hard to avert the decision of insolvency. He went to Secretary Woodin and upbraided him in violent terms for having ruled that the banks could not be reopened.

Secretary Woodin—"Wee Willie Woodin," the press affectionately called him—was a likable personality, a big industrialist with a cherubic face, a financier whose hobby was music, and who had amazed most of his Wall Street associates by supporting Roosevelt and contributing heavily to the Democratic campaign funds.[24] But Couzens, characteristically, had been suspicious of him from the outset. Indeed, he had made an effort to hold up Woodin's confirmation as Secretary of the Treasury until the Senate could be informed about his "holdings." As president of the huge American Car and Foundry Company, Woodin had done much business with the railroads. On the floor of the Senate, Couzens raised a serious question. Wasn't it questionable "ethics" for a cabinet officer to be holding shares in a car and foundry company "when there is such close and obvious connection at this time between the railroads and government?" He wanted to be certain, Couzens said, that Roosevelt's Treasury head would not turn out to be another Mellon.[25]

Of course, with Roosevelt behind him, Woodin was confirmed promptly. But Couzens was never satisfied. Now he felt that Woodin was acting in the Detroit crisis in a way not at all in accord with the public interest, but more as any Wall Street banker would act. He scathingly reminded Woodin that he had been promised at a previous conference proof of the banks' insolvency before a final decision would be taken. He stormed at Woodin:

> You, during this conference, instructed your subordinates to satisfy me that the Detroit banks were insolvent, but up to this moment, not one word have I received from you or the Department. However, within an hour or so after I left, conservators

were appointed for both the Detroit banks, and I was not even done the courtesy of being notified.[26]

8

Couzens' protests, and those of the Detroit bankers, were in vain. Washington stood firm.

Then, and years later, there would be rumors that Wall Street, or the Federal Reserve Board, acting under the influence of New York interests, had played a part in this firmness. It would be alleged this was in accord with a longtime conspiracy to place the Ford Company under bankers' influence at last, though none of this was proved.

The fact was, the Treasury decision was not changed.

On March 21, the government itself, through the RFC, together with General Motors, established a new National Bank of Detroit to replace the two former institutions.[27]

On the following evening, James Watkins, police commissioner of Detroit, as spokesman for numerous Detroiters, went on the radio to accuse the government of having "played into the hands of Wall Streeters." Couzens commented in a letter to Madeleine:

"Police Commissioner Watkins raised Hell in his radio talk last night. . . . Over 10,000 telegrams reached Washington as a result. There's the Devil yet to pay over the Detroit bank problem. Wish I could have remained aloof." [28]

To which, it might be added, a better idea he never had . . . too late.

But the government went ahead. It was understood widely that Roosevelt himself had insisted that the Detroit crisis be cleanly and promptly ended. A little later there was established, also by the RFC, but with the Fords cooperating, the Manufacturers National Bank.[29] The First National and the Guardian National, with their holding companies, were gradually liquidated. In the history of Detroit finance, this was the end of an era. Almost all that remained of the wonderful group-banking idea in Michigan was the gilded tower of the ill-fated Union Guardian Trust Company, that monument to a fantastic financial era; and a seething mass of undeserved hatred toward Couzens, the one man who, though not financially involved, had tried, with willingness to make great personal sacrifice, to save the situation. And the story was not yet finished, for after an interlude, the whole thing was to flare up again.

CHAPTER XXXVIII

THE NEW DEAL ONLOOKER

ALL during these last bewildering days of the Detroit crisis, other events, equally tumultuous, had been transpiring in Washington. These were general developments in consequence of Roosevelt's inauguration and his calling of a special session of Congress the next day. With all his preoccupation with Detroit matters, Couzens tried his best to keep up with these events also.

He had liked Roosevelt's inaugural message. The ringing phrases which gave promise of driving "the money changers from the temple" and the pledges of direct federal action, if needed, to assist the "forgotten man" reinforced his earlier favorable impressions of Roosevelt. He would have agreed wholeheartedly with the comment of Karl Schriftgiesser: "Franklin Delano Roosevelt thus read the obituary of Normalcy" [1] of the Harding-Coolidge-Hoover era, against which Couzens' whole career in the Senate had been an angry protest.

The new President's inaugural speech, he told reporters, was "grand, grand!"

Indeed, in all his years as a senator, Roosevelt's message was the first of any President's he had felt like cheering.

He was pleased too by a gesture that Roosevelt made to him personally immediately after the inaugural exercises were closed. For the new President had sent word that he wished Couzens and Senator McNary to join him in an intimate gathering in "the President's Room" of the Capitol Building. When Couzens came in, Roosevelt gave him a warm handshake and his famous handsome smile.

That too was something new for Couzens from a President.

Roosevelt explained that he had sent for him and Senator McNary, who had stepped into defeated "Jim" Watson's shoes as Republican leader in the Senate, because he desired their cooperation in persuading the Senate, before adjourning, to confirm immediately certain emergency appointments without reference to committees.

Couzens liked the friendly, non-pompous way in which Roosevelt made the request to him. "You can take my word for it that these are good men!" [2]

Couzens went away from this, his first meeting with Roosevelt, with a sense of well-being he had not known for a long time. Roosevelt's whole manner, his seemingly utter calmness in face of general confusion, the ready smile, the magnetic personality that caused his crippled condition to be forgotten, all captivated him as no other personality in his whole life had done.

One of his senatorial colleagues commented, "Quite a change, eh?"

"Yes," said Couzens. "He's human!" [3]

2

To be sure, Couzens did not surrender to Roosevelt immediately, or ever, completely.

Being Couzens, his fingers were crossed. The old attitude, which back in his Ford Motor Company days caused him to be suspicious of the hale and hearty backslapping salesmen, persisted. Roosevelt seemed to measure up under his sharpest scrutiny, but he kept some reservations.[4] He had not forgotten that in 1928, except for his retention of Mellon, Hoover also had seemed good to him.

He did not even go along completely with Roosevelt on the request made at that first meeting. For one of his appointments Roosevelt wanted acted upon promptly was that of Woodin, and Couzens' protests in that connection represented the first opposition that Roosevelt encountered in Congress. Indeed, it was almost the only important opposition, save for the attacks on the new banking legislation by Senator Huey Long, that came in those very first days of the New Deal.

Yet, from the outset Couzens was one of Roosevelt's most fervent admirers. He even came close to wishing he were a Democrat. Now, with his rank on committees lowered, he considered that he would have to be more or less an onlooker on the New Deal that began with the special session called on March 5. "Most of the work is done by Democrats now," he wryly wrote to Madeleine.[5]

And to Clarence Wilcox: "We are having hectic days here and

making history. I have one regret, however, and that is that I am no part of it, because the Democratic administration is working perfectly." [6]

3

True, there were certain aspects of the Roosevelt beginning that troubled Couzens—the very ones, oddly, which caused so many other Republicans to cheer the new President. The Woodin appointment was one matter that caused him to wonder if there was to be a new deal after all. Another was Roosevelt's appointment of Dean G. Acheson as Undersecretary of the Treasury, to succeed Ballantine.

Couzens had checked Acheson's background and discovered readily that, like Ballantine, Acheson was a lawyer with Wall Street connections. For example, Acheson was a partner of George Rublee, a close associate of Dwight P. Morrow, partner of J. P. Morgan and Company. When Morrow ran for Senator in New Jersey in 1931, one of his ghost writers was none other than Acheson.[7] On May 17, 1933, Couzens rose in the Senate to oppose Acheson's confirmation.

"I know," he said, "that Mr. Woodin and Mr. Acheson are going to be just as much the agents of Morgan as anyone you could put there. . . . The Treasury now is being manned by men who, I believe, are unable, because of former connections, to serve the public properly." What kind of a New Deal is that? he asked. Was the New Deal intending to foist more Mellonism on the country? [8]

It was ironic, too, that just a few weeks later Roosevelt agreed with Couzens that Acheson was too conservative, and rather unceremoniously asked for his resignation when Acheson balked at Roosevelt's monetary policies.[9] It was more ironic that still later, this "too conservative" Acheson would be denounced as a "pro-Communist," after he became Secretary of State under Roosevelt's successor, President Harry S. Truman, with his friends recalling Couzens' opposition to his confirmation in 1933 as a defense.

4

Even more exasperating to Couzens was the so-called Economy Bill of 1933, sent to Congress by Roosevelt on March 10, which, in keeping with his pledges for cutting the costs of government, provided, among other things, for reducing war veterans' benefits.[10] To Couzens, this smacked too much of the old Hoover attitude, as he saw it, of causing the poor to bear the brunt of the depression.

He noted with distrust that Roosevelt's Economy Bill had the backing of all the Old Guard elements, in and out of Congress, that on this occasion at least, Big Business was solidly behind Roosevelt, as it had been behind Hoover. Indeed, Hoover in his heyday never received the plaudits of the conservative press with such unanimity as did Roosevelt at this time.[11]

In the Senate, with all his old-time directness Couzens stormed against this measure, going so far as to charge that members of Congress were threatened by White House "representatives" if they did not fall in line.[12] Indeed, on this occasion, he made one of the longest speeches of his career, a bitter attack on the administration, as bitter as any he had made on Hoover's.

At just this time, the Treasury had arranged to float a note issue of $800,000,000, and asked and obtained approval from Congress to pay to the purchasers a higher than usual rate of interest. Couzens contrasted this with the Economy Bill.

"I hope that any member of this body who has the nerve to walk out of this chamber after having voted for this iniquitous measure will hang his head in shame for having approved of an increase of 100 to 180 per cent in interest rates for the money lender, while he would take away from the veterans 45 to 50 per cent of their small allowances."

It was untenable, he said, for the "National Economy League, the big business organizations, and the Chambers of Commerce" to argue that the credit of the nation was in danger unless the Economy Bill were passed. The per capita debt of the nation, he pointed out, was only $160, whereas for Great Britain it was $800. To him this did not indicate that the United States was in desperate straits from the standpoint of debt.

"Yet it is said that the little man who is getting $30 or $40 a month because of the service he performed for the nation must have his compensation cut. Mr. President, I should hope to be stricken dead, if I walked out of this chamber after having voted for such an iniquitous measure to do such great injustice to the people who are least able to stand it."[13]

The Economy Bill was passed the next day, with twelve senators in addition to Couzens daring to vote against it. Considering Roosevelt's popularity and the strength of other forces behind the bill— even National American Legion Commander Louis A. Johnson (later rewarded with an office) supported the veterans' cuts—it was remarkable that a dozen senators sided with Couzens.[14] Curiously, as in the Acheson matter, Roosevelt later again came around to Couzens' view, for in a matter of weeks, he began issuing a series of executive orders ameliorating the effects of the Economy Bill and in the end almost all of the veterans' cuts were restored.[15]

5

Roosevelt in the meantime went forward with enough other legislation more in keeping with the general promises of the New Deal and Couzens' hopes for it. Especially was Couzens delighted that, either from emulation or by coincidence, Roosevelt had recommended to Congress a variation of his own idea for taking care of the jobless young people who had been roaming the highways. Like Couzens, Roosevelt insisted that these youngsters had to be provided for, and proposed the Civilian Conservation Corps program.

Couzens recalled with disgust how the Army had opposed his proposal in that regard because, as he angrily told the Senate, "the aristocracy of the Army did not wish to be annoyed" with "taking care of jobless and homeless boys." Some day, he said, this same "Army aristocracy" will want these boys as soldiers, to fight for their country. But now "it did not care what happened to them." This was a "shameful attitude," he declared.[16]

When told that his proposal would be expensive, involving an additional cost to the Army of some $88,000 a day, his answer was: "We appropriate millions for the problem of migratory birds and, though it is hard to believe, there is complaint now heard when we wish to appropriate money for the care of migratory boys."

For his part, he said, he "did not care what it cost." The question was, "What are we going to do about these boys?" [17]

"During the nearly eleven years that I have been a member of the Senate, I have seen almost every kind of legislation go through in the interest of business. I have not opposed these measures. I am not against the railroads or other business. I want to see their integrity maintained. But I also want to see maintained the integrity of the youth of our land, and I want to see them preserved.

"I have heard the words 'fundamental' and 'sound policies' and 'economy' and so on, until I am sick and tired. The whole United States ought to be sick and tired of the constant repetition of such words while millions and millions of our people are in distress." [18]

His proposal had been lost in the closing days of the last Hoover

Congress. Even a large number of Democrats had opposed him, joining in charges that his scheme was "demagogic." But now Roosevelt placed all his influence behind the CCC proposal. This time the Army, if it still had objections, suppressed them, and the plan was adopted.

It turned out that of all the New Deal projects, the CCC program, with its emphasis on reforestation, although of minor significance in the larger scheme of things, was the most popular. Although it would be stated that the idea for it was Roosevelt's "own," Couzens always felt that he was at least a co-parent of it. It was certainly an example of parallel thinking on his and Roosevelt's part. A specific problem, that of the jobless youth, existed; the way to meet it was to come up with a specific act. This appealed to Couzens. At last the government was ceasing to "play ostrich."

6

There was more, much more, in this first Roosevelt phase that satisfied Couzens beyond his expectations. Roosevelt easily pushed to adoption such changes in the banking laws as compulsory divorcement of investment affiliates from commercial banks, which in itself might have prevented the Detroit disaster. He caused Congress even more easily, without even waiting for the pledged repeal of the Eighteenth Amendment, to revise the Volstead Act to permit the sale of 3.2 beer. "I think this would be a good time for beer," Roosevelt said, and it was done.[19] Here also was personal vindication for Couzens—ten years after he had said, in opposition to Harding and the Anti-Saloon League, that the Volstead Act ought to be modified.

In breathtaking succession, came a new act for the small-home owners of the nation, a Home Owners Loan Corporation, which substantially met Couzens' objections to Hoover's Home Loan Bank act, for it provided direct aid to the home owners; and the Tennessee Valley Authority Act, which at long last decided the question of Muscle Shoals as Couzens as well as Norris and, of course, other progressives and liberals of both parties for years, had wanted it decided. As Couzens wrote to a protesting constituent, "My approval of TVA was the result of years and years of fighting here in Congress about what was to be done with Muscle Shoals."[20]

Then came an unemployment relief act, which willingly, rather than grudgingly, made federal funds available for direct relief to the needy as well as for providing jobs. Also an act for federal regulation of the sale of investment securities, which for the first time enacted into law, in so far as this field was concerned, a code of ethics which Couzens, along with such liberals as William O. Douglas, had always insisted ought to prevail among bankers; and an act for emergency railroad legislation that incorporated many of the views Couzens had fought for against Hoover, in his capacity as chairman of the Senate Committee on Interstate Commerce.

Indeed, as it began to take shape, the New Deal was in fact already an enactment of so many of the ideas Couzens, along with other independents and progressives, had been plumping for since the days of the elder La Follette, that it could properly, in a way, have been styled as much a Couzens program as a Roosevelt program. No wonder that Senator McNary—who had not long before got a laugh from Couzens by sending him a crate of prunes from his Oregon farm with a note, "These are of a new variety, thus somewhat radical"—observed:

"Couzens fell in love with the New Deal." [21]

7

This was true.

Toward the end of May, Roosevelt came up with the most sweeping of all his measures in his honeymoon period—the National Industrial Recovery Bill (NRA).

Couzens felt cause to be truly elated over this many-sided measure. Here in one package were recommendations in principle if not in exact detail which constituted implementation of most of the major positions he had championed ever since he had been in public life, a program harking back to his mayoralty, when Detroiters called him a "Bolshevik" for the way he took care of the unemployed during the depression of 1920–1922: prohibition of child labor; the right of working men to organize; shorter working hours to stagger employment with decent wage levels protected; and a gigantic public-works program precisely in line with that "fantastic" interview he had given to Ray Tucker back in 1931.

True, the NRA also involved some provisions, notably the "codes" permitting exemptions from the anti-monopoly laws, and also some omissions in the matter of wage rates on public-works projects, to which he would find himself in disagreement, or not certain of. But on the whole, the NRA, as it was first projected, appeared almost a millennial event from Couzens' point of view. On the basis of his past, this was precisely the kind of program he would have come up with, had he been President.

Taken with Roosevelt's boldness in going off the gold standard, which reversed the deflationary trend of the Hoover era, and the drastic farm-relief measures, which for once all the farmers' organizations agreed upon and practically drafted themselves, a fact that persuaded Couzens to vote for them, the NRA looked like a complete break with the Old Guard traditions in America, albeit even Hoover had been moving against his will in the same direction.[22]

As Frank Kent correctly observed at the time, the new Democratic administration had really taken over the program, not of the historic Democratic party, but of the Progressive insurgents in the Republican party, in which Couzens, if anywhere, actually belonged.[23] The "nice and decent revolution," forecast by William Allen White ten years earlier, almost to the day, had come to pass, apparently. To accomplish it, Roosevelt had supplied the needed cohesive force, which the Progressives, all intensely individualistic, never achieved.[24]

Moreover, Roosevelt's legislative assistants had on several occasions showed a marked disposition to do what the previous Republican administrations almost never did—consult with Couzens as well as other independent Republicans, on the drafting of legislation.

A case in point was the securities regulation bill. The New Deal historians Joseph Alsop and Robert Kintner would say that Couzens was responsible for the securities bill having been introduced and passed much earlier than Roosevelt had intended. "Prepared at the mere request of one of Ferdinand Pecora's assistant investigators, it was only introduced because Senator Jim Couzens suddenly decided the time was ripe for an exchange bill." [25] This was not the whole story, but there is enough truth in the statement to show how things had changed in his relations with the White House.

8

Yet after the first excitement over the Roosevelt approach had died down, Couzens was not really as happy as he had expected to be. Across the land, people hummed the New Deal theme song, "Happy Days Are Here Again!" There was a feeling that Roosevelt would take care of all the nation's ills. But Couzens still saw the heartbreaking effects of the continuing depression.

True, people no longer faced the danger of actual starvation amidst plenty. But there was still much hardship, and the basic causes remained.

"The misery I am going through here because of nationwide conditions is beyond telling in a letter," he wrote his brother Albert on May 26, 1933, nine days after Roosevelt sent the NRA bill to Congress.

This comment pointed up a facet of Couzens' nature that few people recognized. As with crippled children, he identified himself emotionally with victims of the depression. "He suffered physical pain that was real over the plight of the unemployed," Hiram Johnson observed.[26]

Each day's newspaper continued to emphasize millions of Americans still were without jobs, that relief rolls were still growing. For once, he even sympathized with some rich persons, whose investments had turned sour, especially in Detroit bank stocks. "I never expected to live to see the day when so very many even wealthy people are absolutely broke, when heretofore well-known rich people hardly know how to get a living," he told his brother.[27]

On top of this, all the aggravation of the bank crisis had taken from him a physical as well as mental toll. More than ever, he suffered from sleepless nights. He was desperately in need of a rest. But instead of relaxing, he plunged now, during that spring of Roosevelt's first period, with all his bulldog strength into an investigation of J. P. Morgan and Company, an activity not calculated to be a sedative for his nerves.

CHAPTER XXXIX

THE INVESTIGATOR AGAIN

THE inquisition of the House of Morgan began May 23, 1933, in the marble-floored conference room of the Senate Committee on Banking and Currency. In certain quarters it would be labeled a "circus," especially after the incident engineered by a press agent of having a midget suddenly plump himself on Mr. Morgan's lap.

But in truth this inquisition was one of the most important ever conducted by a Congressional committee in terms of its revelations as to the inner workings of interlocked finance and politics.

It was a continuation of the investigation into stock-market practices that the same committee had been conducting off and on for more than a year. In a large sense, it was also an extension of the investigation by the Senate Finance Committee two years earlier into the processes by which Americans had lost so heavily on Cuban, Peruvian, and other foreign bond issues. Taken together, the two inquiries furnished an especially candid picture of both domestic and foreign financial practices in the era of "wonderful nonsense."

Even before the House of Morgan was subjected to inquiry, the stock-market investigation, called off during the 1932 election campaign, already revealed enough to permit Charles and Mary Beard to summarize:

> Page after page of sworn testimony showed that mighty men among the Lords of Creation had formed "pools" for particular stocks and bonds, run up the price of securities, poisoned the news of financial columns by the bribery of reporters, drawn unwary sheep into the pens of bulls and bears and sheared them as the bottom fell out of liquid claims to wealth.[1]

While J. P. Morgan and Company had been mentioned now and then in some of these amazing transactions, and one of its prominent partners, Lamont, had been questioned by the earlier Senate Finance Committee inquiry into foreign loans, the impression had persisted that, on the whole, it had been above yielding to any challengeable practices. The House of Morgan, it was believed, was so strong and so circumspect that it had no need to adopt methods that could not stand senatorial scrutiny.

2

Now, however, the House of Morgan was subjected to its first thorough investigation since the Pujo inquiry of two decades before. It was understood that Roosevelt urged this personally, on the theory that the more adverse attention obtained by J. P. Morgan & Company, the more amenable Congress and the nation would be to New Deal legislation. In the words of Ernest K. Lindley, "To put the House of Morgan on the defensive immediately was to the Administration's advantage. To establish definitely and expose its position in the economic and political world was a necessity preliminary to reforms that would go far beyond the improvement of the banking system." [2]

In this inquiry, Couzens, even though now a minority member of the Banking and Currency Committee, played a prominent role. He was "merciless in his judgments and caustic of tongue," recalled Stokes.[3] Indeed, even though the committee finally retained Ferdinand Pecora, a hard-hitting New York City prosecutor, as counsel, it is doubtful if the House of Morgan investigation would have been so incisive if not for Couzens' participation.

A number of the other senators, including even the usually acid-tongued Senator Glass, seemed overawed by the prestige of this firm and especially of its head, J. P. Morgan himself. They reflected the attitude, reported on by Frank R. Kent in the *Baltimore Sun*, of "a number of people who talk about the 'terrible outrage' of a Senate committee dragging Mr. Morgan and his partners down here, cross-examining them like a lot of chicken thieves, and making it all a sort of Roman holiday." [4]

There was a tendency to handle Morgan with soft gloves, to show deference to him that was denied other bankers. Couzens put a stop to that. He had no more reverence for Morgan than he had possessed for Mellon. He agreed wholeheartedly with Frank R. Kent. "There should be nothing sacrosanct about the House of Morgan." [5]

At one point, Couzens engaged in a row with Senator Glass when the Virginian declared that Pecora should be more respectful and less barbed in his questioning of Morgan. "I insist that Mr. Morgan be treated like anyone else here!" snapped Couzens. He pounded the table. Glass backed down,[6] and from then on, Pecora, with Couzens' backing, went after Morgan without gloves.[7]

3

The results were startling enough to shake even a man so suspicious of other wealthy men as Couzens. The inquiry disclosed that J. P. Morgan and Company not only had engaged in many, if not all, of the practices common to the other firms already investigated, but, in one respect, had gone even further. Thus, while other firms had seduced mere newspaper editors and reporters to help win their cooperation for unloading inflated stocks on the public, the House of Morgan, it was now revealed, had apparently succeeded, by the device of so-called "preferred lists" in winning the influence, favor, or silence, of many of the most outstanding public figures of the nation. This seemed at least a fair inference when it was revealed that persons on the House of Morgan "preferred lists"—men permitted to purchase stocks in advance of the public sale at prices considerably lower than the public paid—included such public dignitaries as:

Former President Coolidge; Newton D. Baker, President Wilson's Secretary of War; Charles Francis Adams, Hoover's Secretary of the Navy; Charles D. Hilles and J. R. Nutt, officials of the Republican National Committee; Silas H. Strawn, former president of the United States Chamber of Commerce and law partner of Garrard Winston, Mellon's Undersecretary of the Treasury; Norman H. Davis, even then functioning as Roosevelt's ambassador-at-large in Europe on the question of war debts; John J. Raskob, former chairman of the Democratic National Committee; John W. Davis, 1924 Democratic Party nominee for President; General of the Army John J. Pershing; William G. McAdoo, Secretary of the Treasury under President Wilson and then Democratic Senator from California; and—most interesting of all to Couzens—William H. Woodin.[8]

It seemed obvious from this list that, in the game that was being played, the leaders of both parties were on equally good terms with the House of Morgan.

Couzens was among the first to comment pointedly on this bi-partisan financial policy of the nation's great. "When it comes to money," he told the press, "there are no Republicans or Democrats. Rich men never fight each other seriously. There is the finest coalition of all parties when it comes to control of the Treasury of the United States." [9]

This is what he had contended all his public life, and now evidence demonstrating his position had been produced.

The Morgan partners insisted that in most cases they did not even know the political affiliation or standing of their "preferred" clients and that "influence" was the last thing the firm had counted upon in letting these individuals in on chances to make gigantic killings in the stock market.[10] Probably some persons believed these disclaimers. Couzens was not among them.

Couzens questioned George Whitney, partner of J. P. Morgan and Company, also director in large corporations, on the motives behind the preferred lists. The banker protested, "perhaps too vehemently," he later conceded under questioning by Couzens,[11] that the lists were for purely business purposes, not for getting favors from high-placed individuals in politics and government.

It had been brought out, as one example, that J. P. Morgan & Company had distributed to the individuals on its preferred list shares of Johns-Manville Corporation at 47½ in June 1927, whereas when the stock was offered to the public a few weeks later, the stock sold at 79, "representing a potential combined profit to the members of the selected lists of $12,037,500.[12]

SENATOR COUZENS: You said the only object was that these men you distributed the stock to would make money?

MR. WHITNEY: I did not say our only object. I said we hoped they would.

SENATOR COUZENS: That was not the only object you had?

MR. WHITNEY: No sir.

SENATOR COUZENS: You hoped they would reciprocate?

MR. WHITNEY: No, really.

SENATOR COUZENS: You did not give them this price so that they would reciprocate and keep on good terms?

MR. WHITNEY: No, really. That is, of course, the suggestion that has been carried in the testimony yesterday, and in the papers, but I can only tell you that is not so.

SENATOR COUZENS: I never heard of anybody quite so altruistic in my life![13]

4

Nor did the Senate committee as a whole believe that altruism was the explanation, for it finally summed up:

The preferred lists strikingly illuminate the methods employed by bankers to extend their influence and control over individuals in high places. The persons upon whom princely favors were bestowed in this manner were . . . persons prominent in all the financial, industrial and political walks of our national life. The granting of these preferential participations . . . augured well for their mutual welfare and ill for that of the public.[14]

Of special interest to Couzens was testimony about certain taxation practices of the House of Morgan. This part of the inquisition produced unexpected corroboration of the significance of his investigation of Mellon and the Bureau of Internal Revenue almost a decade earlier. He had charged then that the Bureau, under Mellon, had favored wealthy individuals and corporations. The House of Morgan was not then involved. Now it was.

Mr. Morgan himself was forced to give testimony showing that the Bureau of Internal Revenue, during the period that Mellon was Secretary of the Treasury, exercised exceptional discreetness in matters in which the House of Morgan was concerned.

The committee later said in its report:

> Internal-revenue agents accepted without examination income-tax returns prepared by J. P. Morgan & Co. on the assumption that preparation by that firm *ipso facto* established the correctness of the returns. For example, the tax return of Mrs. Margaret Y. Newbold for the year 1928, prepared by J. P. Morgan & Co. bore the following legend:
>
> "Returned without examination for the reason that the return was prepared in the office of J. P. Morgan & Co., and it has been our experience that any schedule made by that office is correct. The books of the taxpayer are located in Philadelphia, and if necessary schedule C may be verified in that city. This office, however, recommends that the return be accepted as filed. C. M. SHEPPARD, Internal Revenue Agent."
>
> Many other returns, particularly of partners in large banking houses, were likewise exempted from adequate scrutiny. When examinations were made, the time devoted to them was comparatively short, in view of the wealth of the taxpayers and the complex nature of their transactions. Thus, in 1930, according to the Bureau's own records, 1 day was spent in checking the partnership return of J. P. Morgan & Co., and Drexel & Co.—the most powerful banking group in the world. This return was not subjected to any field examination, and apparently the agent's explanation was sufficient to satisfy the Internal Revenue Bureau that none was necessary.[15]

The Senate committee reported: "For the year 1930, 17 Morgan partners, including J. P. Morgan, paid no tax and 5 paid aggregate taxes of about $56,000. For the year 1931, not a single Morgan partner paid any tax. For the year 1932, not a single Morgan partner paid any tax." [16]

It was all dramatic vindication of Couzens' crusade against Mellon-ism, which Senators Moses and Watson, as well as others, including Mellon himself, characterized as merely a "private feud," or just a demonstration of Couzens' "terrible temper" and nothing more.[17]

5

There was still further personal vindication for Couzens in these hearings. He had been criticized back in the spring of 1932 for having opposed a loan of millions of dollars from the RFC to a rail-road because, he charged, the loan actually would go to J. P. Morgan & Company, which did not need it. The inquiry brought out that it was the House of Morgan that had suggested that the railroad apply for the loan and press it, over disapproval by the Interstate Commerce Commission, and that $5,850,000 of the government money promptly found its way into the coffers of the banking firm.[18]

Supremely corroborative as they were of much of Couzens' career in the Senate, such revelations did not, however, really please him as much as many persons supposed. Reporters and others took it for granted that the "Scab Millionaire," who preferred needling rich men to anything else, as it often was said of him, would be ecstatic over the House of Morgan inquisition. Actually, he was not. Such revelations merely added now to his painful frame of mind.

Coming on top of the Detroit bank episode, the findings of the Senate committee left him more acutely depressed than ever. He was being eaten up inwardly by suppressed hostility toward men like Morgan, who, he felt, ought to have behaved differently than he feared they had. He was not at all anxious to have it proved that the whole American business system, as it seemed to him, had been corrupt to the very highest pinnacle.

The day-after-day testimony to greed, irresponsibility, chicanery, and corruption, not of politicians and gangsters, but of the most respected persons in society, left him appalled. Former Governor James M. Cox of Ohio later had some conversations with him which caused Cox to conclude: "The world he was living in . . . gave him great concern, and he worried too much about it."[19]

This was all too true. He was more and more tense; more and more in need of a change of scene.

CHAPTER XL

THE DELEGATE TO LONDON

ROOSEVELT unexpectedly opened the way to his needed change of scene. Summoning him to the White House for a 9 A.M. meeting, but without telling him the purpose, Roosevelt had Couzens ushered into his private apartment. The President was still in bed, having breakfast and reading the newspapers, which informality (inconceivable with Coolidge or Hoover) so impressed Couzens that instead of setting down in his notebook the reason for the visit, he wrote: "Saw Roosevelt in his pajamas." Roosevelt promptly sprung on him the offer of an appointment as a delegate to the World Economic and Monetary Conference scheduled to open in London in June.

Roosevelt had been scouting around for a suitable Republican on an otherwise Democratic delegation, and Senator McNary mentioned Couzens' name to him. With certain other Republican progressives, McNary had begun hinting to Roosevelt that Couzens would be a good man in his cabinet as Secretary of the Treasury, if only because of his stand against Mellonism. The London assignment looked to McNary like a step in that direction. Besides, McNary was worried over Couzens' health and believed the trip would be good for him. Though wary of Couzens' independence, Roosevelt quickly fell in with the suggestion. He saw that Couzens fit exactly what he had in mind—a Republican who was sympathetic, openly so, toward the New Deal.[1]

With Mrs. Couzens, John Carson, and Jay Hayden, whom the *Detroit News* assigned to cover his activities, he sailed for England on June 6, 1933.

2

This was his fifth transatlantic crossing. His first, back in 1891, when he accompanied his father on a visit to London, was made just after he had begun his life in Detroit, still a Canadian. Oddly, in view of the purpose of this latest crossing—to help solve the deepest world monetary questions—his main impression of his first visit to London was the trouble he had experienced in keeping his American money straight in terms of pounds and shillings.[2]

The second and third trips abroad, in 1907 and 1909, had been in connection with the Ford Motor Company. Memories, some sharp, even poignant, naturally would be evoked from thinking of those days—of his early association with Ford, of Malcomson (dead ten years by 1933), of the Selden case, of the negotiations with Durant for selling the Ford company which, if they had gone through, would have left him one-fourth owner of General Motors (bigger than Ford now), of the five-dollar-a-day plan . . . of, indeed, the many phases of the whole Ford story.

Not all such memories were wholly pleasant. The break with Malcomson had not been pleasant. Nor the break with Ford. Then, too, there was the great sadness of his life, the death of that promising boy, Homer. Nobody else could ever know how deeply that tragedy had affected him, of what pleasure in life it had robbed him. Never had he ceased to reflect on the shining hopes of achievement he had held for Homer.[3]

True, his other son, Frank, had not done so bad. Indeed not! In 1933, Frank was the Mayor of Detroit. That had happened because Roosevelt, two weeks before he asked Couzens to go to London, appointed Mayor Frank Murphy as High Commissioner of the Philippines. As president of the Detroit Common Council, Frank Couzens succeeded to Murphy's job as Mayor. "I've lived pretty well, don't you think, to have raised a mayor?" Couzens said to reporters who interviewed him just before he left for London.[4]

Thoughts of Frank in his own former office in the grimy old Detroit City Hall were bound to bring to mind his own mayoralty, as well as his earlier term as police commissioner. How serene the world had appeared to most persons in that era! Possibly some remembered that on returning from his fourth visit abroad, in 1923, he had pointed to danger signals in Europe and suggested a receivership for Germany. These ideas were laughed at or denounced, and especially was this true of his assertion that the United States ought to play a more positive role in international affairs so as to help avoid another world war which he felt was brewing already in Germany. Now, ten years later, this conference, to which he was a delegate, had been called precisely because such warnings had been ignored. The economy of the whole world had gone to pot, just as the economy of the United States had gone to pot, and another world war would, in fact, be the result in six more years. In Germany Hitler was already in power.

Coolidge had been President when Couzens returned from that fourth trip. Just ten years ago—and it seemed centuries.

Poor Coolidge! Only the previous January 1933 he had died, heartbroken, it was said, because even to him it was plain that "Coolidge prosperity" had been built on sand. Coolidge had seemed so wise in saying, "The business of America is business," or when, on the international debt problem, he had commented, "They hired the money, didn't they?" Yet he lived long enough to realize that such "Yankee talk" was not so statesmanlike as he had supposed. The Coolidge world—Andy Mellon's too—had crashed utterly. Even the banks in Northampton, Massachusetts had closed.[5]

That the London conference, for which he was making this new trip to Europe as he was turning sixty-one, would help the world to recover economically was a hope that Couzens shared with many others. He had seldom talked in the Senate about foreign affairs, yet he had a greater awareness than most of his colleagues—certainly more than most of his fellow Middle Westerners, especially the other progressives—of the perilous position of the world and the impact of foreign conditions upon the United States, as witness his warning in 1923 to Coolidge about "Hiram Johnson's isolationism." He knew that the major powers, the United States included (with the Smoot-Hawley tariff act of 1932 especially), were engaged in a form of economic warfare. He hoped that the London conference might change this pattern and bring "economic disarmament" as a step for preventing the resort to military force. "On every side there are possibilities . . . more ominous than any since 1914," said James W. Angell, American member of the Preparatory Commission of the conference, in March 1933. And Couzens agreed as he sailed for England.[6]

3

Unhappily, the London conference proved unworthy of the hope it had inspired. It had been ill timed. It ought to have been held many months earlier, when first planned under Hoover, or not at all. For economic stabilization, as a condition precedent to the breaking down of barriers to international trade, was the principal goal, yet stabilization at that juncture was precisely what the Roosevelt New Deal was against. For stabilization then meant settling for the deflationary level of the depression. "Reflation," not stabilization, in the United States, was the Roosevelt goal, and he had flatly said in his inaugural that this must come ahead of international arrangements.

On arriving in London, Couzens found himself in an atmosphere of gloom because no one expected the meeting to succeed. "Everything within the delegation was all so riotously unhappy," recalled Herbert Feis, economic adviser to the United States State Department.[7] Nor were matters helped by the British. It had been specifically agreed, or so it was thought, that the question of war debts would not be brought up. Yet Prime Minister Ramsay MacDonald in his opening address, seconded by Neville Chamberlain, then the Chancellor of the Exchequer, brought up precisely this question.[8] Then, just after Couzens arrived, the conference faced a kind of sit-down strike. No monetary stabilization, no action on anything else that the agenda provided, such as toning down tariffs, exclusive trade agreements, dumping, and the other impediments to free trade in the world—such was the tacit position of France. It was no wonder that Couzens later said he was under "a terrific strain" there "trying to be diplomatic." [9] Frustration engulfed everyone.

4

He was appointed to the monetary and financial commission. It was there that the struggle over stabilization centered. As always, he took his responsibility seriously and worked hard at it. Mrs. Couzens wrote to Madeleine, "Daddy's hours are from 9:30 in the morning until 7:30 in the evening, sometimes later. . . . He is quite tired." [10] But he was not long in discovering that the conference was involved in an irreconcilable conflict: nationalism versus internationalism.

On June 19 he expressed himself candidly to the conference on this impasse. "The nations have not suffered enough to be willing to meet in complete humility. . . . Most nations are still rather cocky about their nationalism and feel confident that they can paddle their own canoes, whether anything comes out of the conference or not." [11]

Of all the utterances at the gathering, this most bluntly exposed the impasse. The *Times* of London placed over it a headline that showed that in one statement he had been capable of making in

London the same impression for which he was most noted in Washington: "PLAIN SPEAKING."

5

Not even the American delegation was in agreement within itself on a program. There were some in the delegation who wanted to agree to currency stabilization after all, in spite of Roosevelt. A resolution to that effect was drawn up, but word came from Roosevelt that he was against it. "The whole conference very nearly broke up in disorder," recalled young James P. Warburg, one of the advisers to the American delegation.[12] Couzens sided with Roosevelt. "We must work together," he said in a statement showing that he was shelving his mild internationalist views, at least temporarily, to embrace fully Roosevelt's program of "First things first." [13]

But unity remained the one thing the delegation could not achieve. "On one day at the conference," recalled Raymond Moley, then a confidant of Roosevelt and Assistant Secretary of State, "Senator Couzens spoke against tariff reductions and, on the next, Representative McReynolds asserted that lower tariffs were necessary to recovery. To complete the impression created by this episode, McReynolds denounced the Republican party as though he were making a speech on the floor of the House." [14] This was typical.

When it was suggested at a meeting of the American delegation that no one speak for publication without the approval of Secretary of State Cordell Hull, the delegation chairman, Couzens refused to be bound by such a rule. He "intended to voice his opinions to the press on all matters at any time," he said.[15]

His insistence on his independence did not endear him to Hull, who later asked Moley to convey to Roosevelt a pointed message. The President should "not give Progressive Republicans too prominent a place in the administration, since they didn't seem capable of working with anybody." [16] Roosevelt of course knew that Couzens in London was more in line with "the administration" than was Hull, for Hull did not believe that economic recovery in the United States could come from domestic action alone.[17] After a row with Hull, one of several, Couzens threatened to resign.[18] Mrs. Couzens expressed his feelings when she wrote to Madeleine: "If the policy of this conference does not change and get a little more pep and sense into it, I am sure Daddy will pack up and get out of it all. This crowd is going around in circles." [19]

Only Hull's pleas that Couzens' resignation would prove a serious embarrassment and that he should at least stand by until the expected arrival from Washington of Moley, caused Couzens to stay on. But after this, he devoted himself mainly to championing aggressively the Roosevelt program for increasing employment in the United States through public works and to urging all other nations to do likewise. "I am enthusiastic about what President Roosevelt is accomplishing, if press reports are correct," he wrote to Tom Payne concerning news about the NRA, which went into effect on June 16. In the same vein, during a formal speech before the monetary and financial commission, he argued that the nationalistic Roosevelt program be made international, that all the nations do as the New Deal was doing—an idea that Roosevelt, cruising on a destroyer off the Atlantic coast, almost at the same moment was expressing to Moley.[20] Thus did Couzens try personally, albeit naively, to bridge the unbridgeable gap that then existed between nationalism and internationalism.

6

When Moley arrived in London on the next day, he immediately took the spotlight as one who had recently been with Roosevelt. Would Moley be able to break the deadlock on the question of monetary stabilization? He tried his hand. At the American embassy, during a secret meeting which Couzens attended, he drafted the text of a suggested resolution which was forwarded to Roosevelt. It committed no nation to anything except a desire to return to the gold standard when it was deemed proper to do so. Couzens sensed that Roosevelt would not approve even this innocuous resolution.

Thoroughly disgusted by then—the more so since Hull had raised objections because he had been in on the embassy meeting, whereas Hull had known nothing of it—Couzens informed Moley that he wished to resign forthwith.[21] But again yielding to an appeal not to bring into the open the pitiful division within the delegation, he agreed to remain at least until Roosevelt responded to the resolution forwarded by Moley.[22] "If this conference does not come to some understanding soon, poor Daddy will blow up," Mrs. Couzens wrote to Madeleine.[23]

When Roosevelt responded on July 3, his message said that the conference should not "allow itself to be diverted by the proposal of a purely artificial and temporary experiment affecting the monetary exchange of a few nations only. . . ." [24] Whatever was Roosevelt's intent, the effect of his pronouncement was to bring the conference to an end for all practical purposes.[25] Again there was talk of resignation, this time not by Couzens, but by Hull.[26] Indeed, it was Couzens, in the unusual role of pacifier, who stood out among those who tried to save the conference from wreckage. He made a speech attempting to explain America's position and urged: "The conference must go on with the work for which it was summoned." [27] But almost no one shared his view that anything still could be accomplished, and his heart was really not in the effort.

7

After this, the conference became just an occasion for social gatherings. These were interesting, of course. At one of them Mrs. Couzens met "the lady that the Prince of Wales is so devoted to, and had a charming visit with her." But soon even the parties grew boring to everyone. London's weather turned uncommonly hot. "Poor Daddy will be a wreck—it is so hot," Mrs. Couzens informed Madeleine on July 7. "Besides, everyone of our delegates is very unhappy over the turn affairs have taken and are undecided what to do." [28]

But Couzens knew what he intended to do. He made reservations to sail for home without waiting for the official adjournment. He did not, however, get away before being involved in one more irritating incident. Roosevelt had asked Moley to send him a confidential estimate of the American delegation. In complying, Moley deprecated in frank terms all the delegates except Senator Pittman. He had marked the message "Secret from Moley, to the President Alone and Exclusively." But an embassy employee showed a copy to Ambassador Robert Bingham, who showed it to Hull, who saw to it that Couzens, among the others mentioned, read the Moley comments. Especially wrathful because just previously Moley had "particularly praised him to his face," Couzens gave Moley a tongue lashing. No wonder John Franklin Carter summed up the whole conference as a "diplomatic bedroom farce." [29]

Thus at the end as at the start, this interlude, "a Donnybrook Fair," as Moley accurately called it, proved a poor sedative.[30] Especially was this so in view of still another eruption, one occurring in Detroit, that disturbed Couzens as much as the frustrations in London, indeed even more.

CHAPTER XLI

THE SMEAR

THE Detroit bank case had re-exploded.

Couzens first learned of this development between sessions in London when Jay Hayden showed him a cable from his newspaper, the *Detroit News*. The cable asked Hayden to get Couzens' comments on testimony given before a one-man grand jury that day by Clifford Longley, the Ford attorney and the latest president of the defunct Union Guardian Trust Company.[1]

Asked why the original RFC loan to the Guardian Group did not go through, Longley had said, "There was considerable opposition in Washington."

"Why and by whom?"

Longley had paused for a moment. He laced his fingers together, and smiled. "Well, I think the largest single opposition to the loan in the amount we were asking came from Senator Couzens." Couzens "was very antagonistic," he said.

He "gathered" that "Couzens was very much put out because of our not coming to him in the first place." He "gathered" that "Couzens opposed the loan very strongly." He "gathered" that "Couzens' opposition stopped the loan."[2] All of which was reason enough for most of the Detroit and Michigan newspapers to carry banner lines on one theme:

COUZENS BLOCKED LOAN FOR BANKS!

2

It was soon apparent that this grand-jury investigation, presided over by Judge Harry B. Keidan, supposedly called to reveal the facts behind the bank crisis, actually was maneuvered from the beginning into an elaborate device for pinning the blame for the whole tragedy on Couzens personally.

At first, Couzens was not overly disturbed. Not even when a cable reached him from his lawyer-friend, Tom Payne, asking his permission for Payne to go before Judge Keidan to ask that the inquiry not be adjourned until after Couzens had testified. Couzens cabled the permission, and also dictated to Hayden a rejoinder to the Longley testimony to be published in Hayden's paper.

His answer to Longley was a notably calm statement, wholly devoid of acrimony. In it he reviewed briefly the Guardian Group loan application of January 1933. He pointed out that none of the RFC directors had approved the loan application, and that this was also true of those who attended the White House conference. Recalling that Senator Vandenberg attended the White House meeting, he suggested that Vandenberg be "consulted for details." [3]

The *News* did query Vandenberg. From Grand Rapids, he issued a statement which, while cautious, fully upheld Couzens.

"There is no question," Vandenberg said, "that Senator Couzens is correct when he says that at the initial conference no one felt, on the basis of the figures submitted by the RFC, that the program could be put through as originally requested. This included Ogden L. Mills, Secretary of the Treasury, Charles A. Miller, president of the RFC, and President Hoover himself." [4]

3

That seemed to take care of matters very well. On June 22, Couzens wrote to Payne, "Do not hesitate to make any expense to keep me informed and to protect my name, because I have nothing to hide and no financial interest to protect or to hazard." [5] Then he placed the matter pretty much out of his mind as he concentrated on the problems of the conference. But in the following week came news from Detroit that was more of a "bombshell" to him than was President Roosevelt's July 3 rebuke to the gold-bloc nations of the conference.

This concerned some fantastically irresponsible testimony. For H. R. Wilkin, a vice-president of the Guardian National Bank, later convicted of fraud in connection with operations of one of the group units, had implied that Mrs. Couzens had made a "smart money" withdrawal from the Union Guardian Trust Company just before the bank holiday.

Illustrating the careless manner in which the grand jury investigation was conducted, Wilkin had injected Mrs. Couzens' name into the hearing knowing, as his testimony itself shows, that his assertions were based on hearsay, a knowledge that also was shared by everyone else concerned.

Wilkin was being questioned at the time by Harry S. Toy, then Wayne County prosecutor. Toy had asked Wilkin to comment on reports that certain large withdrawals had been made from the Union Guardian Trust Company prior to the holiday. Wilkin mentioned that a bank in Houston, Texas, the bailiwick of Jesse Jones, the RFC board member, had withdrawn about $165,000 between February 8 and 11. Then:

Q—Were there any other large withdrawals made prior to the holiday?

A—Not to my knowledge.

Q—What do you mean to your knowledge? Did someone tell you about them?

A—Yes. One of the officers of the bank told me Mrs. Couzens had withdrawn nearly all her balance the Saturday before the holiday.

Q—How much did she withdraw?

A—I don't know.

Q—Did you ever try to find out?

A—Yes, I saw the ledger card and it showed a pretty scant balance. Later I tried to find out from the receiver of the bank, (B. C.) Schram, and he told me he could not divulge the amount of the withdrawal without permission of the comptroller of currency.

Q—You say this withdrawal was made the Saturday before the holiday?

A—Yes.

Q—When was this withdrawal cleared through the Detroit Clearing House?

A—The clearing house cleared approximately $4,000,000 on the fifteenth. . . .

Q—Would the check of the average depositor have been cleared the same as the check of Mrs. Couzens?

A—Yes, I think so.[6]

That was all there was to this line of testimony. But it was enough to inspire headlines and stories all over the world which, if they did not say so directly, gave the impression that Mrs. Couzens had made a "smart money" withdrawal of a really substantial amount.

The facts? Mrs. Couzens had made a withdrawal from a personal account in the Union Guardian Trust Company. It was for approximately $5,000, which she requested transferred around February 6 to the Riggs National Bank in Washington, to be used by her for customary contributions to charities in which she was interested.[7]

Obviously this was not a "smart money" withdrawal, nor was it important in any respect to the fate of the trust company.

However, as a result of the way the Wilkin testimony was presented, Couzens, in London, experienced the jolt of his life when he saw on the front page of the Paris edition of the *New York Herald* the headline:

SENATOR'S WIFE BLAMED
FOR WRECKING MICHIGAN BANKS
BY SMART MONEY WITHDRAWALS

4

He turned red—and he saw red. Ever afterward, he could never recall this incident without feeling anger. "I was stabbed in the back, and my dear wife's name was dragged into this mess. I'll never rest until I get even with them," he was later quoted as saying.[8] Whether or not he used precisely those words, this was certainly how he felt. In this mood he returned to the United States, an angry man, determined to go before the Keidan grand jury and at last tell all he knew about the bank crash.

There was no longer any reason anyway, he concluded, to hold back the facts. He needed certain documents to back up what he had learned—reports and letters in the possession of the Comptroller of the Currency. So, before going to Detroit, he made it a point to call on President Roosevelt to report personally on the London conference, and obtained from the President permission to have access to the Comptroller's records of the Detroit banks, including copies of confidential reports filed by various bank examiners.[9]

5

Couzens appeared as a witness before Judge Keidan on August 17, 1933. Up to then, the investigation had proved worthless as a fact-finding process. Even State Attorney General Patrick O'Brien, who had initiated the inquiry, had become disgusted. "We are getting nothing but speeches," he said. However, after Couzens had been on the stand for two days, the Attorney General changed his mind. "I am satisfied to go on," he said. "Now we are getting facts." [10]

The kind of material that Couzens now presented was illustrated by a report drawn up in May 1931 by the examining committee of the Guardian National Bank of Commerce. This report, written by officers of the bank itself, said:

The committee finds in the list of bad loans many loans that obviously have no other purpose than speculation on the stock market. The makers of these loans had only limited earnings and no prospects of the payment of the loan otherwise than the rise in stock prices. They were made to clerks, stenographers, bank officers, and bank clerks, salesmen and others whose incomes were not sufficient to warrant any substantial credit. . . .

The committee also finds in the list of bad loans, loans to officers in other banks which were clearly made to assist or further stock market operations. . . .

We find on the list of loans a substantial number of individuals who have been recommended by directors of the banks for such loans, loans to associates of directors in business, and loans to concerns in which the directors are interested or in which they were officers.[11]

If this document, and others of similar import, reflected fairly how the Detroit banks were being operated, what remained of charges that Couzens, Mrs. Couzens, or any other outsider—even the RFC, let alone "radicals"—had wrecked the banks?

6

But no one connected with the grand jury was happy over this kind of evidence. Prosecutor Toy, presumably intent upon getting the facts, proceeded to badger Couzens. The *Free Press* under Bingay carried articles to the effect that up to then the inquiry had been proceeding properly, but Couzens, by "casting a spell," because of his position in public life, had changed the course of the inquiry into undesirable paths. Editorials by Bingay in the *Free Press* chided the prosecutor for being "awed" by Couzens. Prosecutor Toy should break through the "spell" by getting tougher, the editorials said.[12]

Toy obviously sought to comply. He subjected Couzens to a good deal of harassment. However, it was plain that Couzens had transformed the hearing into a true fact-finding inquiry, not by any "spell," but through the force of facts.

Indeed, he furnished a classic example of the explosive nature of Truth in a controversy, of how it shatters the most carefully constructed alibis and melts through the layers of the most expertly contrived makeups.

7

At times, his anger betrayed him into a too-sweeping indictment of bankers in general. He included some individuals who apparently were blameless, notably certain directors of the First National Bank. This left him open to some equally anger-inspired counterblasts, such as one from James O. Murfin, a First National director, who said: "I can shorten this testimony by saying every time Jim Couzens mentioned my name, he lied!" [13]

Then, Longley returned to the stand to say "Couzens didn't know anything about the [Guardian] assets at the White House. He didn't know anything about them when he testified here. I don't think he knows anything about them now." [14] The press featured these blasts, and Couzens was placed on the defensive.

His recital of why the banks failed also suffered at times from disorganized presentation of his material. This was not wholly his fault, although his emotional tenseness tripped him up in this respect. To reconstruct properly the whole story, months, even years, would be needed. Moreover, all the facts—the minutes of the RFC for example—were not then open to him or anyone else. His presentation suffered too, because he still chose to play down the part played in the whole episode by the Fords. But these flaws and errors were really matters of minor detail. The fact was, as a result of his appearance in five sessions scattered through August and September, Detroit really began to see for the first time what had happened to its banks.

8

Yet, the effect of Couzens' presentation was not at all what should have been expected. Judge Keidan was strangely impatient with Couzens. Concerning Couzens' declarations that the banks were undoubtedly insolvent, the judge demanded to know how this could have been the case inasmuch as the federal government permitted the banks to continue to operate until the holiday.

Was it not the law that the Comptroller of the Currency must close insolvent banks?

As the Comptroller did not act, was that not sufficient evidence that the banks were in fact solvent?

Such questions had logic in them. But Couzens answered them with some amazing evidence. He produced documents to show that the Comptroller of the Currency, J. W. Pole, had adopted a policy of extraordinary leniency with the nation's banks. One such document read as follows:

October 6, 1931

A. P. Leyburn,
Chief National Bank Examiner,
164 West Jackson Boulevard, Chicago, Ill.

Please instruct all examiners to exercise extraordinary discretion in their work and to use every effort to encourage and sustain the morale in banks examined.

Leniency consistent with proper regard for public interest should be extended. Present conditions demand sympathetic treatment on the part of this office, and examiners can in important measure contribute to the alleviation of the difficult problems with which we are temporarily faced.

J. W. POLE, Comptroller.[15]

Couzens showed that later the Comptroller reiterated such instructions for "leniency." In the following December, all national bank examiners were instructed by Pole that in cases of greatly depreciated securities held by banks, the examiner "should discuss the situation with the directors and urge recourse to methods by which the bank may be strengthened, *but should make no mandatory demands.*" [16] In July 1932 the Comptroller had circularized all chief national bank examiners with a communication that criticized examiners for being too strict in their appraisals of securities.[17]

Couzens quoted a statement made in the Senate on May 1, 1933, by the "father of the federal reserve system," Senator Glass:

> For the last 12 or 14 years there has been no espionage on the weak national banks. The comptroller of the currency admits that if he had enforced the law he would have closed half the national banks of the country. This means that the comptroller's office has not done its duty. It has allowed banks to engage in irregular and illicit practices. It has endangered the whole banking community. . . .[18]

Judge Keidan wanted to know why the federal government adopted such a policy. "On the theory," Couzens answered, "that prosperity was just around the corner. Public officials, from the President down, were holding out that hope to the people." [19]

He then made a point that later drew a vigorous protest from Hoover, who felt that it was a reflection upon his administration.[20] Couzens said:

"Your Honor must remember that there was a political campaign on and that there was undoubtedly a disposition on the part of the powers that be not to cause a bank collapse or bank difficulties while a political campaign was on." [21]

9

Of course there was another side to this picture. Strict enforcement of the banking laws would have hastened the closing of many more banks than were closed, and nobody could be sure that this was correct national policy. But Couzens' purpose was not to question the policy, rather to show what the banking situation had been.

In this, he not only received little cooperation from the judge, but more antagonism from County Prosecutor Toy. His statement that the political campaign influenced officials to be soft toward actually insolvent banks was hooted at, though he had merely anticipated the verdict of a well-known banking student, Professor Westerfield of Yale, who later wrote: "Most of the banks had portfolios choked with immobile and worthless loans and investments; banking supervisors had been restrained for political and other reasons from exacting obedience to bank law and had ceased to require banks to write off losses." [22]

A good deal of the material that Couzens presented was from so-called "yellow sheets." These were letters that bank examiners had sent to Washington as supplements to their regular reports. They were confidential letters, designed only for the eyes of the Comptroller—letters in which the examiners told exactly what they thought about the banks they had examined, in which they set down comments which, for reasons of policy, were not included in the regular reports.

Because of their nature, these "yellow sheets" often were more revealing than the official "white sheets," and especially so during the period of Pole's "leniency."

But because they were not "official," Prosecutor Toy, backed up by Judge Keidan, proceeded to develop the theory that they were unreliable. The prosecutor scoffed at them. Who had ever heard of the "yellow sheets," he asked, in effect. Why, no one had! This was precisely the point about them—that they were confidential. But to the prosecutor that vital point was enough to damn them as evidence.

Couzens asked that the bankers be recalled to the stand. They were. It was soon obvious that they were summoned not to be questioned on the records and the transactions he had mentioned, but to give them an opportunity to heap denunciation upon him. This they did in full measure. Indeed, the proceedings then became, rather than an investigation of the banks, a forum from which witness after witness assailed Couzens.

Even former Governor Groesbeck, Couzens' original sponsor for the Senate, now receiver for the Guardian Union Detroit Company, joined in the attack. So also did aging Judge Connolly, whom Couzens had defeated for mayor back in 1919, now receiver for the Detroit Bankers Company.[23] Once again, almost all that was heard in Judge Keidan's court was the refrain: "Couzens wrecked the banks!"

10

There was much cruelty in the way he was attacked, both in and out of the courtroom. Frederic L. Smith, who had become an admirer of Couzens since the days back in 1903 when Couzens had defied Smith's Selden patent association, wrote him that the easiest way to start a row in the Detroit Club to which both belonged, was for someone to make a remark in his defense. "I tried this," said Smith, "and ran the risk of being thrown out."[24]

How this group of Detroiters felt about him was made clear to Couzens in an experience of his own. On his going to his accustomed table for lunch at the Detroit Club, several of the men who had shared that table with him for years stiffly rose and carried their plates to another location.[25] Ever since he had joined the club many of the members had tolerated his general criticisms of the economic system by which they had become the industrial and financial leaders of Detroit. But now that he had become specific, and worse, had declared open war upon the most respected leaders of the city, the bankers and bank directors, they felt that he had put himself beyond the pale of polite society. Even for a "scab million-aire," he had gone too far, they decided.

This bitterness toward him was more intense than any he had generated during his entire previous career, greater than that caused by his fight for M.O., his attack on the Mellon tax plan, or his opposition to Warren for Attorney General. Not since the 1890's, when Mayor Hazen S. Pingree was expelled from his clubs and his church for advocating the reforms in municipal politics that Couzens was to carry out, had Detroit seen anything like it.

The whole atmosphere was distinctly that of a pack, snapping and snarling. The furor surpassed even the anger he had aroused back in 1914, when he had denounced the Board of Commerce members' labor policies, the incident that had evoked a description of him in the *Detroit Journal* as a "commercial Savonarola." This newspaper, now long out of existence, had said: "Society has an unpleasant way of crucifying those who tell it the truth one generation too soon. And woe to Couzens for his truth indulgences were he less strong in this community! For banks can crush and capital can ostracize." [26]

In the hot summer of 1933, those passages in the editorial printed in the long-ago winter of 1914 must have seemed highly prophetic to Couzens. He probably remembered them, for during the height of the storming, he once wryly remarked, "I'll be lucky not to be hanged in person, not merely in effigy." [27]

II

But Couzens was neither crushed nor silenced. Because he had not been able to present before Judge Keidan all of his material gleaned from the government documents and, concluding from the judge's attitude that he would not be permitted to do so, he attempted to proceed through direct action. He invited Prosecutor Toy and members of the prosecuting staff to come to his office in Birmingham. There he laid before them a mass of records, with the hope that they would make use of the material on their own. The prosecutors were strangely unprosecutorlike. They did nothing. Couzens then offered the material directly to the newspapers. The newspapers were decidedly cautious, perhaps for good reasons, in their view.

Indeed, almost the only result of this move was that, on September 14, he became involved in a furious argument with Malcolm Bingay when that journalist, instead of welcoming the material, proceeded to upbraid Couzens for "keeping up this endless argument and flinging of personalities." [28]

There was still Judge Keidan's court. It was only right that Couzens should have the opportunity to testify there again, especially in view of the assaults made upon him. So he made ready to present new material to the grand-jury investigation. Day and night, "and Sundays included," in his office in the Wabeek Building in Birmingham, he labored over the reports and figures. On September 15 he wrote to Judge Keidan that he had "considerable new evidence concerning the Guardian Detroit Union Group" and asked the judge to advise him when he might be permitted to testify again.[29]

Before his letter could reach the judge, Couzens heard incredible news—Judge Keidan planned to adjourn the inquiry immediately, without hearing him. He promptly telephoned the judge, who agreed to meet him the following morning at Frank Couzens' home. "Judge Keidan . . . argued against my again appearing on the witness stand for the reason that I might introduce new evidence, which would cause the bankers to again request a chance to be heard and further delay the conclusion of the grand jury," Couzens later related. Finally the judge grudgingly consented to let him testify once more, on a condition: Couzens was to confine himself to answering the attacks made on him. Under no circumstances, said the judge, was he to bring up anything new.[30]

With respect to influencing the findings of Judge Keidan, Couzens might well have saved himself that final three-hour exertion at the grand jury session. For as soon as Couzens finished, the judge ruled that the inquiry was over, and at once produced a previously pre-pared document setting forth his findings. This gave the bankers and the banks a clean bill of health.

12

Judge Keidan had enjoyed the reputation of being one of the most judicial of judges on the bench in Detroit and an honorable man. Couzens had esteemed him, at one time considered recommending him for a place in the federal judiciary. No breath of scandal or of venality of any kind had ever touched him. But it was clear from his conduct throughout the grand jury, and especially from his statement of findings, that Judge Keidan, for whatever reason, had no stomach for exposing any wrongdoing on the part of the bankers. He, at least, was no Savonarola.

The judge revealed clearly in his statement that his major con-cern was to have the grand jury create public pressure which would cause the federal government to come through quickly with money for paying off the depositors. He wrote: "In the final analysis, the public is interested in this help. Criminations and recriminations are futile." [31]

In short, Judge Keidan's view was to let sleeping dogs lie. The thing to do was to thaw out the frozen assets. He wanted no part of Couzens' program of getting the causes of the banking crisis pre-sented to the public.

13

Couzens then took to the speaking platform. At a meeting of depositors at the Northwestern High School Auditorium in Detroit, he gave a fiery two-hour speech. "I am satisfied," he told this audience, "that a determined effort to get at all the transactions of the bank holding companies and their subsidiaries will convict somebody of a crime." [32] He was angry; no doubt about that.

However, he soon decided that such meetings would really get him nowhere. Obviously speeches were no weapons in the war that quickly opened up between him and Bingay of the *Free Press*, which then—this was before the *Free Press* came under a new and more objective management, that of the Knight Newspapers—was openly feuding with him. That he was at a disadvantage in this feud was brought home to Couzens when that newspaper devoted nearly three columns of its front page to an article which carried these headlines:

COUZENS ADMITS REVENGE
SPURS HIM ON IN ATTACK
UPON BANKS OF DETROIT

Says He Is Moved
By Personal Hate

Feels Safe Because
of Wealth and Office [33]

14

Malcolm Bingay had written the article on the basis of the argument that they had engaged in on September 14. It was printed, said the *Free Press*, because "the strange attitude of Senator Couzens requires explanation"; because "it is necessary now for the people of Detroit and Michigan who have for so many years honored James Couzens to know his mental attitude." As summed up by Bingay, there was nothing to Couzens' efforts to bring out the facts in the bank situation except hatred of the bankers and a desire for revenge. Bingay shored up his thesis by quoting utterances by Couzens made in the heat of their personal argument in Couzens' office in Birmingham.

After the heat of the bank controversy died down, it was plain what Bingay had done. He had goaded Couzens into a personal argument, knowing how easily Couzens lost his temper, and then had printed the result as if it were an "interview."

True, Couzens had asked for this treatment. He had flown off the handle with a newspaperman. His ingrained outspokenness and anger had betrayed him into making remarks he obviously would not have made had he believed he were being interviewed for publication. A calmer man would never have let himself get into such a position.

To friends, he pretended that he was not bothered by Bingay's article. Actually he was a good deal upset over it.[34] He promptly called off any further speaking engagements on the bank situation. He felt keenly that the public had been poisoned against him, that most Detroiters really believed that he had been responsible for wrecking the banks. He talked moodily with intimates about how his reward for twenty years and more of public service was that he had become an object of scorn. "I went through Hell," he told Tom Payne.[35]

15

Actually, it had been a mistake, from any angle, for him to participate in the Keidan grand jury investigation. As a Senator, he had at hand the most effective medium in the country for producing facts—a Senate investigation.

As early as the previous March, various persons had suggested that the Senate Committee on Banking and Currency, still probing into the New York Exchange and other financial institutions, might well turn its attention to the Detroit affair. In June, the City Council of Detroit adopted a resolution asking that the Senate committee "come to Detroit and conduct a thorough and public investigation." [36]

As a member of that committee, Couzens was not then convinced that the Detroit situation warranted a full-dress Senate inquiry, especially as new banking legislation already had been adopted, presumably for making impossible a repetition of the Detroit bank organizational defects.[37]

However, after the Keidan investigation fiasco, he changed his mind. Besides, his spirits were now considerably elevated, in consequence of a special mayoral election held in Detroit at just this time that resulted in Frank Couzens' being elected mayor by a handsome majority.

"I guess that shows that I haven't ruined the family reputation after all!" Couzens exclaimed.

He was ready to fight again.

When he returned to Washington on October 1, he discussed with Pecora, still counsel to the Senate Banking and Currency Committee, the possibilities of a fruitful inquiry by that committee into the Detroit banking mess.[38] Soon after, the full committee, of which Senator Duncan U. Fletcher of Florida was chairman, voted to conduct such an inquiry.

This Senate investigation of the Detroit banks, which began in Washington on December 19, 1933, was decidedly different from the Keidan grand jury investigation. It laid bare in minutest detail the full story of the Michigan bank holiday, its causes and its aftermath. Almost everyone who had anything to do with the banks and the holiday was called to testify and subjected to searching examination by the expert cross-examiner, Pecora. Edsel Ford was called, though not Henry Ford, and from Edsel the role of the Fords was brought out clearly.

There were no "speeches" at this investigation, and no hearsay. Only facts. The facts filled 1,647 closely printed pages in the four volumes published by the Senate.[39]

A study of those volumes leaves no doubt as to where the fault lay for the holiday, nor for the conditions which led up to it. The bankers themselves had wrecked their banks, albeit, the final Senate report in words approved by Couzens, rather obliquely put it: "Nor can the failure of these companies be attributed *solely* to the constituency, competency, or honesty of the persons controlling these institutions.[40]

True, some of the truly shocking actions laid bare had been forced on them by the depression and represented desperate efforts to prevent the crash. But careful and honest banking, rather than recklessness and speculation and worse, obviously would have avoided the full extent of the crash. Moreover, it was unquestionably established that Couzens had nothing to do with the refusal of the RFC assistance asked for in the beginning, nor even with the scaling down of the ultimate loan granted.

If any one person had forced the bank holiday, this person was, not Couzens, but Henry Ford.

All this was placed on the record.[41] That record constitutes more than a defense of the accusations against Couzens; it is a detailed description of the Michigan banking "magic" which turned out to be, not magic, but financial buccaneering on a scale beyond ordinary comprehension.

Studied efforts were made to discredit this Senate investigation. It was dubbed solely a "Couzens affair." [42] The truth was precisely the opposite, as even a cursory examination of the record shows. But angry men will say many things; Couzens did, and so did those who opposed him for one reason or another.

16

The Senate investigation came to an end exactly on the anniversary of the White House conference on the bank crisis. "We concluded our Detroit bank hearings at five o'clock tonight, and, I feel, with a blaze of glory, because today's testimony was quite corroborative of my position," Couzens wrote to Tom Payne.[43]

He did not exaggerate. On that day the committee had heard Ballantine, Leyburn, and Awalt. Their combined testimony underlined emphatically what was plain to anyone who bothered to follow the hearing—that the bankers themselves, by the type of banking they had developed, had been at fault. There could be no doubt of that.

Frederic L. Smith, who, like Couzens, had lived through the panics of 1893, 1907, and 1921–1922, and had observed such Congressional investigations as the Pujo inquiry into the "money trust," wrote to Couzens: "Your investigations have been more truly constructive, timely, and, I believe, ultimately 'curative' than those of any government-run investigations since I began to take notice. . . . They have opened the eyes of the man on the street."

Couzens answered that, while he was "distressed" over the disclosures as to how the banks were operated, he was satisfied "they had to be made in the public interest. . . . What I wanted was for the Senate and the country to know." [44] This he had accomplished.

He had shown, among other things, that so far from having been "responsible" for the closing of the Detroit banks, he had tried to do more than almost anyone else to keep them open, having gone to the length of offering a good slice of his personal fortune to save the situation, even though he had no stock in any of the banks and very little other personal financial interest. He had shown, too, that his objections to an "immoral" RFC loan were not at all a factor in the crisis—that no one else in the government approved the original loan requested after the facts were known. His statement about "shouting from the rooftops" was not at all a "cause" of the crisis. It had been torn out of context and used to misrepresent his position, also to make of him the scapegoat for the crisis brought about by others.

He had shown that the Detroit crisis was not something that had developed suddenly, but was long in the making, in large part because of "general conditions" and some unwise mergers, and also because of unsound and in some cases immoral as well as illegal banking practices. He had established also that whereas the Fords were involved in the crisis, his own relationship with the Fords, friendlier then than at other periods, was not a factor. Above all, he had shown that had the bankers as a class followed the safe, sane, and strictly ethical principles which he himself, when a banker, had epitomized, the situation might not have developed, certainly not so critically. Having established a record showing all this, he had good reason to be satisfied with the verdict of history.

17

On August 1, 1934, largely in consequence of the revelations at the Senate investigation, the Department of Justice obtained federal grand jury indictments against twenty-eight of the leading bankers in both groups on charges of technical violations of the federal banking laws.[45] Complicated cases brought some complicated results. In 1935 three bankers in the First National group were acquitted. But in 1936 three others of the same group were found guilty and fined, though the verdict in the case of one was later set aside. In 1937 all of the cases were dismissed after still another trio entered pleas of *nolo contendere* and were fined $1,000 each.[46]

One banker did get a prison sentence on criminal-count conviction in a state court. This was Wilkin, the witness who had brought Mrs. Couzens' name into the controversy before Judge Keidan. He was held responsible for "window-dressing" of the Union Industrial Bank of Flint, a unit of the Guardian Group.[47]

As for Couzens, after the Senate investigation was over, he was content to let the bank matter pass into history. His principal interest after this was in the further unfolding of Roosevelt's New Deal. And to this he devoted himself with much of his old-time zeal.

CHAPTER XLII

THE NEW DEAL REPUBLICAN

By THEN, in 1934, Roosevelt's honeymoon was over. As the banks stayed open and business indices rose, as everyone began to feel better about the state of the nation, the earlier fear disappeared. Then many stand-patters turned on the new President and there occurred, with Couzens playing a part, increasingly bitter debate over the policies of the new administration.

In August 1934, on the occasion of his sixty-second birthday, Couzens was interviewed by the North American Newspaper Alliance. He took the occasion to rebuke those who, without offering an alternative, criticized the New Deal, saying: "This is not the time for mere words. The country is in the fifth year of depression, and action, rather than words, is needed." [1]

In the following November, he told the Detroit Optimist Club:

> The thing to do is for everyone to show a continued faith in President Roosevelt's policies. . . . There is no light in the future of America unless we get away from the idea of "rugged individualism" which means, I believe, that a few can become wealthy at the expense of the many. . . .[2]

No one was more disgusted than he with the propaganda line of New Deal opponents which pictured certain Roosevelt advisers, notably Professor Rexford G. Tugwell, then of Columbia University, later of the University of Chicago, as "communists" bent on undermining the nation.[3] He told Madeleine: "Most of these yarns about communism, dictatorship, etc. are smoke screens, or evidence of fear that someone's money may be lost." [4] When one of his constituents in Detroit wrote him to urge that he try to get rid of Tugwell before America was "sovietized," Couzens answered:

"I am unwilling to sit by and see millions of our people in distress because they are unable to secure work, and if that is what Professor Tugwell is driving at, then I am for it." [5]

2

By no means, however, was he always on Roosevelt's side.

He was still Couzens, still the individualist who stubbornly hoed his own row; still the natural critic. Hence, he often let loose blasts at the Roosevelt administration as trenchant and resounding as any set off by the "Stop Roosevelt" bloc then active. A case in point occurred when Secretary Woodin, because of illness, resigned from the Treasury, and Henry Morgenthau, Jr., was named his successor. Couzens did not object to Morgenthau; rather, he approved.[6] But he did object to Morgenthau's plan to retain in the Treasury department as a principal assistant Earl Baillie, member of J. & W. Seligman & Company. In Couzens' view, this was "another Acheson type of appointment." Baillie's banking firm was one of those involved in the foreign-loan scandals unearthed by the Senate Finance Committee. Indeed, it was the very firm that had floated the discredited Peruvian loan of unpleasant memory. Couzens let it be known that unless Baillie went, he would conduct a fight against the confirmation of Morgenthau. He "laid down the law," and Baillie resigned.[7]

3

Certain New Deal projects went wholly against Couzens' grain. The public housing program was one. As did the remaining stalwart Republicans and conservative Democrats, including a new and inconspicuous senator from Missouri, Harry S. Truman, he voted against the bill establishing the United States Housing Authority.[8] His general opposition to public housing was that it represented a subsidy to employers. "I never quite understood the theory of some people," he wrote, "that the taxpayers should supply houses for certain low income wage workers to enable private employers to get these workers at low wages." [9] His attitude seemed an about-face from his own stand as Mayor of Detroit, when he proposed a municipal bond issue to build homes because of the wartime housing shortage. But he viewed his proposal as different from the New Deal program of raising the standards of homes that existed.

As in the days when he suggested the five-dollar-a-day plan at the Ford Company, he held to the view that it was up to the industry to pay wages high enough so that workers could arrange for their own housing. Or, he maintained, let employers pay the whole bill in higher corporation taxes, rather than assess the cost to the general taxpayer.[10]

One phase of New Deal housing, the subsistence homestead projects, had his sympathy for these represented fruition of an idea that he and Ford had toyed with back in the days of the five-dollar plan. The concept was that factory workers would also be small farmers. Couzens was glad to see the New Deal experiment in that direction. But here he felt that the approach was wrong, in that the first such projects were located in areas that lacked factories, notably the so-called Red House project in West Virginia.

With Roosevelt, and also with Harry Hopkins, relief administrator, Couzens carried on an extended argument over this. It was foolish, he told them, "to go out in a field and build some houses under the assumption that eventually some industry would come in. . . . He felt that it was far more sensible to build the houses somewhere adjacent to where industries already were established." The New Dealers, he said, were "cockeyed" in their approach.[11]

Curiously enough, as a result of this discussion, he found himself sponsoring a housing project, even though he was opposed to the general idea.

"How much did the Red House project cost?" he asked Hopkins.

Hopkins guessed that the cost was $550,000.

"All right," said Couzens. "I'll put up $550,000 for a project to show that I am right. But if the Red House project cost more, and I think it did, you put up the balance." [12]

The Red House project cost $850,000. So the arrangement was made for Couzens to donate $550,000 to the State of Michigan, to which the federal government added $300,000, and there was born the non-profit "Oakland Housing, Inc.," for building West Acres, a community of 150 six-room homes located on a 1,000-acre tract nine miles west of Pontiac, in close proximity to the automobile industry.[13] There, low-income families who were subject to the seasonal unemployment then characteristic of the automobile industry, were permitted to acquire on easy terms homes on sufficient land to enable them to fill in their income through raising garden products.

But he was sorry that he had made this housing gift almost as soon as he had made it. His doubts about it were clearly revealed in the announcement that was made to the public.

> This project is not economically sound if there is any fundamental soundness in our capitalistic system. It is merely a bridge. . . . Our fundamental job is to readjust national income, wages, and working conditions so as to provide more of these men with a living income. . . .[14]

4

This ambivalence, well-founded, regarding West Acres really reflected his basic attitude toward the way the New Deal was being administered. Roosevelt himself admitted that he often considered himself "a quarterback" who followed one line and then another, depending on how the game was going.[15] Couzens noted this, was disturbed, and complained. He frankly told Roosevelt that good laws were being ruined by "abominable administration." In one such talk with Roosevelt he said, "Do you know what's wrong with your administration? You haven't anyone in it who ever earned a dollar. That's what's wrong!" [16]

To Dr. Freund he wrote: "While I have a very definite conviction that where the President wants to go is right, I am not always sure that he is on the right road and neither can anyone else be." [17]

In the following spring he complained to a friend in London: "Things are in a terrible turmoil, and I haven't the slightest idea where the New Deal is going. . . ." [18]

Yet it was always apparent that his criticisms of the New Deal were those of a friend who wanted a new program to succeed. Often the fault he found with the New Deal was that it was not liberal enough.

5

In April 1934 he drew upon himself much of the abuse generally reserved for Roosevelt, when he initiated an amendment to an appropriation bill for increasing surtaxes on large incomes by a flat 10 per cent as the most equitable way to pay the cost of unemployment relief.

It was his old fight on Mellonism over again.

In San Simeon, California, Publisher Hearst was enraged by Couzens' tax plan. The Hearst papers soon campaigned against it in 120-point type. Hearst was especially bitter, it appeared, because Hiram Johnson had endorsed Couzens' amendment, thus, for once in this period, taking a non-Hearstian stand.

"Hearst called his editors in a violent wrath in the dead of night and ordered them to crucify Johnson and Couzens with him. . . . Hearst screamed: 'That man Couzens has all the money he wants and now he's trying to feather his political nest by appearing to help the people. We'll have to throw Couzens out. His money has turned Johnson's head!' " So one Hearst editor recalled.[19]

B. C. Forbes, in earlier years author of several articles friendly toward Couzens, sent nationwide a bitter attack on Couzens. "The foremost 'Soak the Rich' advocate in America is a rich man, a very rich man, a multi-millionaire," wrote Forbes. "This extremely wealthy soaker of the rich has placed himself largely beyond the reach of the kind of soaking he vehemently urges for others, for his fortune is in tax-exempt bonds." Not patriotism but demagoguery motivated Couzens, Forbes said.[20]

In the Senate, although not in the House, Couzens obtained passage of his proposal.[21] Then he delivered an attack on Hearst, referring to him scornfully as a "yellow journalist."[22] Hearst stood for "soaking the poor," he said. He sarcastically noted that Hearst had finally changed his slogan against his plan from "Soaking the Rich" to "Soaking the Thrifty" because "somebody must have tipped him off to the absurdity of the 'soak the rich' slogan, as there isn't anybody else to soak." He reminded the Senate that Hearst was the foremost supporter of a general sales tax. "I compliment the American Congress," he said, "for never having fallen for the stupid and unscrupulous general sales tax, in spite of the years and years of propaganda for it by Mr. Hearst."[23]

His main purpose in answering the Hearst attacks, he said, was to comment on a more important and dangerous propaganda line then prominent in Hearst editorials. This was that England, then under a Tory government, had staged a greater recovery from the depression than had the United States, by balancing her budget and planning to lower taxes. If England had indeed balanced her budget, went on Couzens, she had done so by postponing payment of her debt to the United States.

"We could balance our budget and reduce our income taxes if we repudiated all of the money we borrowed from our citizens to loan to Great Britain and other countries."[24]

6

Not long after that he again rubbed persons of wealth the wrong way when, as in the Mellon days, he plumped for publicity on income tax payments, holding that "secrecy . . . breeds favoritism, corruption, dishonesty, graft and maladministration." As he wrote to an editor of the *Detroit News:* "If the income tax returns had been matters of public record, Congress long ago would have discovered the means of evasion adopted by the Morgans, Mitchells, and others to avoid all taxation for the years 1930 and on. . . ."[25]

He conceded that one argument against the publicity proposal was valid: gossip would be encouraged. But, he declared, "there are many things in a democratic society which have to be done to maintain our country." [26]

In this battle, one that stirred up a great heat, much abuse was directed at Couzens. Bingay devoted a column to the old charge that Couzens wanted to embarrass other rich men, whereas "Jim has $60,000,000 in tax exempt bonds." [27] A few weeks later, the *Chicago Tribune* published a long magazine-section article under the headings:

'SWAT THE RICH' IS COUZENS' CRY
$30,000,000 SENATOR HAS TAX-FREE FORTUNE [28]

However, the real complaint against Couzens by staunch Republican organs was more fundamental than mere outrage over his views on taxation. He was now looked upon, with Norris, young La Follette, and Hiram Johnson, as a real threat to the continued existence of the Republican party. His evident friendliness toward the New Deal was interpreted as playing into the hands of a Rooseveltian scheme to bring about a new political alignment in the United States, by which the old parties would give way to a Liberal and a Conservative party. The inclusion in Roosevelt's cabinet of two Republicans, Henry A. Wallace and Harold L. Ickes, was seen as one step in this direction. Another would be the winning permanently of the allegiance of the old Republican insurgents.

So Couzens was now anathematized in the conservative Republican papers as a "New Deal Republican" or, worse, a "Roosevelt New Dealer," who had turned traitor to his own party and class. "Party wheelhorses are taking the position that anything that could be done to discredit Couzens would be to the Republican advantage," Jay Hayden wrote.[29]

7

But Couzens did not at all resent the New Deal label. More than ever, he was convinced that not just recovery, but a new deal in fact, was needed in America. It would be stupid, he felt, to go back to the old order, and thus merely assure a repetition of the Great Depression. Until a better new deal was produced, he would support Roosevelt's, regardless of partisan considerations.

Temperamentally, this decision meant disciplining his trait of independence. It would have been easier on his emotions to let this trait now take him along the path followed, for example, by Senator Borah. For by 1935 Borah, once denounced as a dangerous radical, had become, strangely, a hero of the conservative Republicans. He had decided that the whole New Deal was "unconstitutional," its tax program, in particular, a "spread the poverty" scheme that would lead to "dictatorship." [30] In effect, Borah had committed insurgency against himself. With him on his circuitous route, Borah took along an oldtime admirer, Vandenberg. For a time Vandenberg had surprised Couzens, and, perhaps, even himself, by standing for certain New Deal proposals and even going further than Roosevelt wished, as in sponsorship of federal insurance of bank deposits. Now, like Borah, Vandenberg was declaiming against the New Deal as a threat to American institutions. His slogan was: "Roosevelt must be stopped." [31]

To Couzens, Borah's position was illogical—opposition to the New Deal for mere opposition's sake, something of which he himself had been often accused. If Borah were motivated by a desire to preserve the old party labels—perhaps to get the Presidency in 1936— Couzens was even less sympathetic. During the crisis, he was for postponing all partisan activity. Thus in December 1934 he turned down an invitation to participate in a conference of Republican leaders, even when the meeting was ostensibly to be held for the purpose of reorganizing the Republican party along liberal lines.[32]

A few months later, he still held to this position even to the extent of creating a new breach between himself and the Republican leadership in Michigan. Howard C. Lawrence, state chairman, had asked him to send a message to the regular Republican state convention, scheduled to be held in Lansing in March 1935. A mere greeting would have served. Couzens declined even this. He bluntly informed the state chairman that he did not believe a political convention should be held at that time, in view of the critical problems which the nation faced. It was "inopportune" to discuss "partisan politics" in such a crisis, he said.[33] Of course, the party leaders were offended, retaliating at the convention by passing a resolution praising Senator Vandenberg but pointedly ignoring Couzens. It was 1924 all over again.[34] It was also a forecast that if Couzens were forced to choose between Republicanism and Roosevelt, Roosevelt probably would win.

CHAPTER XLIII

THE UNBOWED HEAD

THAT spring Roosevelt sent to Congress a request for an emergency public-works program to cost $4,800,000,000. It was a measure, one which made possible not only big public works, but also the WPA projects of "made work," the National Youth Administration, and other agencies to supply jobs for the unemployed, that sent the conservative opposition into a kind of frenzy. Such an expenditure, though only a fraction of the size of federal appropriations some of them lived to see and even approve, would "wreck the nation," they declared.

Vandenberg, now often mentioned as a Republican candidate for President in 1936, took this line, and delivered a lengthy oration in the Senate on the theme that so vast a project must lead first to bankruptcy, then to a dictatorship.

Couzens naturally favored the public-works program. It had been his own idea also. Yet he also took part in this furious debate as critic, as well as defender, of Roosevelt. He agreed with Vandenberg that the bill, as originally drafted, gave too much power to the President in determining what projects were to be undertaken.[1] His most vigorous objection, however, was not at all a conservative one. It was against a provision that workers on the projects were to be paid a so-called "security wage," averaging about fifty dollars a month, or less than half of the prevailing rates. He told the Senate:

"The industry that supplies the lumber has no limitations on its prices at all, but the most defenseless group of our citizens is told, 'You will take what you are given and you will perform a day's work for half what any other citizen gets for performing the same work.' "[2]

This, he insisted, was unjust and ought not to be tolerated by the New Deal, not for economy reasons, not even to placate Southern leaders, who feared high wage scales for Negroes. When an amendment was adopted which met Couzens' objections to the "security wage," he quite happily voted for the bill.[3] He did not think much of Vandenberg's fears that a $4,800,000,000 outlay to put men to work could "bankrupt America."

2

Up to then, Roosevelt's program in the main had concentrated on relief and recovery. Now the New Deal moved more in the direction of reform, with the Social Security Bill, the Wagner Labor Relations Act, the Public Utility Holding Company Act, and the first major New Deal tax program imposing higher income tax rates as well as greatly increased levies on inheritances and gifts.[4] Couzens favored all of these proposals, especially the tax program.[5] In a sense this was his real victory at last in the battle he had waged for progressive principles on taxation when Mellon was in office.

Even before this, it was obvious that he was almost always in Roosevelt's camp when the chips were down, more so, in fact, than many members of Roosevelt's own party. He stood with Roosevelt for adherence to the World Court, in face of an unprecedented barrage of letters in opposition generated by Father Coughlin and the Hearst papers, thousands of which descended upon him from Michigan.[6]

He likewise stood with Roosevelt against the Patman Bill for immediate payment of the soldiers' bonus, which Roosevelt vetoed. He was bitterly denounced as a "turncoat" by veterans' groups for that vote, for he had been a bonus advocate during the Coolidge and Hoover regimes, and he had opposed Roosevelt's veterans' cuts in March 1933. But he now agreed with Roosevelt that, with all the relief provided by the New Deal, the war veterans did not need special treatment.[7]

3

Two other measures with wide popular support, the Townsend Old Age Plan, and the McLeod Bill for having the federal government make a payment of 50 per cent to all depositors in closed banks, likewise found him standing with the administration, whereas there were wide defections from Roosevelt within his own party on these issues. For Couzens, like Roosevelt, opposed these popular measures.

Even Borah, then the "constitutionalist," supported the McLeod

Bill, which the Hearst press advocated. It was a popular measure, especially in Couzens' home state, with all its closed banks.

Among thousands of others, Couzens' own brother, Homer, urged that he support it. "For the love of Mike," begged Homer, "get behind the McLeod Bill . . . so I can pay off on our new home." [8] But Couzens told Homer what he wrote to others. The McLeod Bill was "stupid." For the government to pay off closed bank depositors out of government funds perhaps looked like relief to the average citizen, but actually meant pouring billions into the coffers of a few corporations and wealthy persons, who owned the bulk of bank deposits in closed or open banks. He told the Senate that "anyone so lacking in judgment as to endorse the so-called McLeod Bill is not entitled, in my judgment, to vote on the floor of the Senate." [9] In particular, he meant Borah, now in his view a fallen idol of progressivism and independence.[10]

4

However, the big fight was on Roosevelt's reform measures. Against these the Republican Old Guard, conservative Democrats, Borah, Vandenberg, the Hearst press, and a newly formed, supposedly nonpartisan, American Liberty League (of which Alfred E. Smith, John W. Davis, and John J. Raskob were leaders) began a tremendous campaign on the theme that the New Deal was intent on tearing down "the American system."

Of this American Liberty League, Couzens was scornful. It might have been nonpartisan, he said in an interview, but this was only true with regard to the formal political affiliations of the members. The leaders were all rich men, Democratic as well as Republican, so there was no question in his mind that they represented "the same convictions." The nonpartisan claim was "humorous" to him, he said.[11]

When the great debate opened, the tension heightened by Supreme Court decisions that held invalid certain portions of the NRA and the Agricultural Adjustment Act, Couzens prepared to participate prominently.

In particular, he planned to defend the Roosevelt tax program against the attacks on it by Hearst, Borah, and Vandenberg.[12] Roosevelt supporters were delighted with the prospect of his aid, for his status as a multimillionaire defending the New Deal seemed in itself a refutation of the charge that the New Deal was a "communistic plot." This debate had only begun, when, just as had happened to him in 1924, at the crisis of his Mellon fight, he had to leave the arena because of a new siege of illness.

5

"I am tired. . . . I am tired. . . ." For some months there had appeared in his letters to friends and family this warning phrase. In March 1935 he told Madeleine that his "very conflictual" mail from constituents had become enormous, and that keeping up with it was wearing on him.[13] His sister, Rosetta, suggested that he take at least a year off. But he could not see himself doing that. "When I am unoccupied, I have a great deal of mental distress," he said.[14]

So he continued to drive himself, although obviously suffering from acute fatigue. He began to lose weight noticeably. He complained of a peculiar numbness. Dr. Freund came from Detroit to see him, and arranged immediately for a medical conference with several Washington doctors. The discovery was made that he was a victim of diabetes. He was ordered to be hospitalized at once, not in Washington, but at Harper Hospital in Detroit.

"What the Senator needs is a good long rest," Dr. Freund said in a public announcement.[15] Actually, Dr. Freund knew that his patient needed that and a good deal more.

When he had been at Harper for ten days, there came worse news. The old bladder condition had become acute again,[16] so acute that it was decided to rush him to the Mayo Clinic at Rochester, Minnesota. At Rochester he underwent two major operations, and remained there for seventy-eight days.

6

For weeks he was a man in torture. The pain that he suffered was monumental. Once he exclaimed to Dr. Freund, "I've given twelve million dollars for the Children's Fund. I'd give another twelve million dollars if you could find a way to end pain!"[17]

Yet by November 1935 he was well enough, he thought, to go with Mrs. Couzens to Phoenix, Arizona. His stay there, at the beautiful Arizona Biltmore, did not turn out nearly so well as he had expected. For one thing, on top of all else, he now developed sinus trouble. Spells of pain returned. He suffered from a peculiar weakness which showed up in all his movements. On November 11, 1935, he wrote to his friend, Senator McNary, in a shaky script:

"My legs seem to be in about as desperate a condition as the Republican party; they wobble like Hell. This is the most unsatisfactory period I have ever had to go through."

What added to his physical distress was the old protest against inactivity. "Just sitting around" a hotel depressed him. In December, he wrote to Madeleine, "I think I am about through with active business and work." [18] Soon, however, he began talking about cutting short his stay at the winter resort to return to the Senate.

His doctors argued against this, but on December 15 he and Mrs. Couzens were on a special train, Washington-bound. And when the Seventy-fifth Congress convened, January 3, 1936, he was there, applauding Roosevelt's State of the Union message in which the President, concerning the New Deal, declared: "I recommend to the Congress that we advance; that we do not retreat." [19]

Just hearing Roosevelt again was a tonic for Couzens. He was glad he had defied his doctors and returned to work. To his colleagues, he insisted that he felt "just fine," though he didn't. But he stayed on the job, wracked but unbowed by the massive pain that so often attacked him. Jay Hayden once found him writhing on the desk of his office in the Senate Office Building because of pain—because he refused to call a doctor, which, in his view, would have been a sign of giving up.[20]

CHAPTER XLIV

THE POLITICAL DILEMMA

HE WAS never to feel really "fine" again. The incisions were slow in healing. He had to have injections of insulin. The attacks of terrible pain recurred. He was disappointed and depressed over his physical condition, he wrote to John C. Manning, nephew of Mrs. Couzens. But for the most part, his mood was to rise above his physical distress and carry on.

He certainly demonstrated very early in the new Congress that he still had plenty of fight left in him. For he took the lead in opposing, as did Roosevelt, a new soldiers' bonus bill. When Roosevelt vetoed the "new veterans grab," as it was called, Couzens was among only nineteen senators to vote to sustain the veto.[1]

To Madeleine's husband, William R. Yaw, of whom he had become very fond, he commented: "By this time you will have seen how much in the minority I was when I voted against the payment now of the adjusted compensation certificates for veterans. That vote undoubtedly will lose me votes. However, I do not suppose I will ever have the courage to quit and so it may be to my own interest to be defeated. Whatever happens will satisfy me."[2]

2

Then, in February 1936, he conducted a vigorous one-man campaign against what seemed to him to be an especially flagrant abuse of patronage power by the administration. His target was Walter C. Cummings, a Des Moines and Chicago streetcar manufacturer, who had been introduced into the administration as Assistant Secretary of the Treasury by Woodin.

Couzens pointed out to the Senate that Cummings received some unusual patronage plums, unusual in salary and in number. Cummings was installed, through the RFC, as chairman of the huge Continental Illinois National Bank and Trust Company of Chicago, at a salary of $75,000, as trustee of the Chicago, Milwaukee, St. Paul and Pacific Railroad, at another salary of $15,000, and, also through the RFC, as board member of a large insurance company, the Maryland Casualty Company. Undoubtedly, Cummings was an exceptionally able man, and Couzens did not deny this, nor did he question his integrity.

But what compounded the case, in Couzens' view, was that Cummings was then also the treasurer of the Democratic National Committee. He denounced what he described as "the possibility of interlocking directorates, political appointments, the tying in of politics with business and the tying in of railroads with bankers, and so on down the line," all apparently personified in Cummings.[3] Not long after this, Cummings resigned as treasurer of the national committee, though he still headed the big Chicago bank.

3

This episode, which, the *Chicago Tribune* said, "gave Democratic party leaders the jitters," [4] did not mean that he had by any means deserted Roosevelt. It merely meant that, as before, he reserved the right to criticize the Roosevelt administration, even while supporting it. On this point, referring to the position Cummings was in, to solicit, if he desired, campaign contributions from corporations with which he did business in his various financial posts, Couzens told the Senate:

"I happen to know that during the Republican administrations . . . millions of dollars [in campaign funds] were collected from parties who had income tax claims pending before the bureau of internal revenue. So my complaint now is in no sense political or partisan. It involves a question which I have vigorously fought here for some thirteen or fourteen years, and I intend to continue to find fault, regardless of what administration may be in power." [5]

4

As 1936 wore on, his affinity for the New Deal caused considerable concern to certain of his political well-wishers. That was the year he was up for re-election, if he wished to remain in the Senate. They worried especially over the problem of how he could expect to win a Republican nomination, in a Republican primary, if he stuck by his New Dealism with no organization of his own.

He had become quite friendly with George Averill, editor of *The Eccentric*, the local newspaper in Birmingham, Michigan. Averill sketched quite early to him a plan to solve his dilemma. He suggested that Couzens adopt the view that while he supported the Roosevelt program "in principle," he had decided that the Republican party could do a better job and therefore Roosevelt ought to be defeated in 1936. If he adopted that position, said Averill, he could be re-elected easily.[6]

Essentially, this was how Vandenberg had won his re-election in 1934. Couzens rejected such advice offhand. His record of supporting Roosevelt, as well as Roosevelt's principles, was made, and he could not repudiate it. He would not "stultify" himself, he told John Manning.[7]

5

The primary was the critical hurdle. In the general election itself, he could expect, as before, the support of voters of all parties, including especially the followers of Roosevelt. Not so in the primary. Roosevelt's very popularity had set up an additional obstacle to Couzens there. He saw this new situation clearly:

> Until 1932 there was practically no Democratic party in Michigan and so nearly everybody (in the primary) went in and asked for a Republican ballot, and in that case my sledding was easy. Now, however, they have a Democratic party in Michigan and all of the Democrats and Roosevelt supporters will undoubtedly go in and ask for a Democratic ballot. My name will not be on that ballot and so I will not be able to get their vote.[8]

This meant that, in the Republican primary, his candidacy more than ever would be at the mercy of the organization politicians of the Republican party.

There was not much doubt but that those elements, as before, would be against him. Already they were lining up behind young Wilbur J. Brucker, who had been governor and who in 1955 was to be Secretary of the Army in the Eisenhower administration, as the candidate in place of Couzens. At the state Republican convention in March 1935, at which Couzens had been snubbed, Brucker, then an Old Guard type of lawyer with a flair for oratory, was ostentatiously idolized along with Vandenberg. It was plain that Brucker would be run against Couzens, with the support of the whole Republican organization of the state.

In 1924, Couzens had overcome with ease the opposition of the organization Republicans. But 1936, obviously, would not be 1924.

As he himself said, "I am not under-rating the many enemies I have accumulated during the past five years. When you frankly oppose the payment of the soldiers' bonus, the Townsend Old Age Pension Plan and other crazy schemes (like the McLeod Bill), you obviously collect a bunch of enemies, in addition to those I have accumulated through the misrepresentation about the bank closing." [9]

6

Back in February 1935, former Mayor Frank Murphy, then Governor-General of the Philippines, later Governor of Michigan and named by Roosevelt to the Supreme Court, had a conversation with John Manning which pointed to an interesting solution of Couzens' problem. Couzens should change parties, Murphy said, and seek the Democratic nomination for senator.

Coming from Murphy, then emerging as the leading Democrat of the state, this suggestion was by no means mere conversation, especially as Murphy then was preparing to run for governor on the Democratic ticket in 1936. If Couzens would agree to seek the Democratic nomination, said Murphy, the Democratic organization would not put up a candidate against him.

"I know I can manage it," Murphy told Manning. "Connolly and some of the Old Guard Democrats would fume, but they are done; their power is gone." [10]

Murphy told Manning that this idea came to him after a group of wealthy Detroiters had approached him with the offer of backing him for senator against Couzens. As related to Couzens by Manning:

"Three friends of Ed Stair actually met Murphy in Honolulu and tried to sell him. . . . Murphy asked why they were approaching him—a Democrat and fully as radical as you—instead of grooming one of their conservative Republicans. . . . He considered it an . . . illustration of the extent of their hatred for you, that in their desperation they would go to a man like him to run against you." [11]

Murphy declined the suggestion. "Senator Couzens stands for the same things in government that I do. He is for the people. He is head and shoulders above every other man in the Senate in integrity and independence and unswerving devotion to the interests of the great mass of people. We need men like him in our government. His way should be made smooth rather than hampered." [12]

Murphy later added to this: "They offered me a half million dollars for a campaign fund. They considered Couzens a traitor to his class. They wanted to beat him, desperately." [13]

In Washington a few days after his talk with Manning, Murphy called on Couzens himself and made the same suggestion to him directly, that Couzens seek the Democratic nomination.[14] "Your position in the Republican party is untenable," he said. "You never have voted with the Republicans. You belong in the Democratic party. You can't win as a Republican. You can win as a Democrat." [15]

Couzens protested on this occasion that he had "started as a Republican and wanted to stay a Republican." [16] But he did not close the door tight against Murphy's suggestion. There was yet time to decide, he said.

Could he do as Henry Ford had done in 1918, and run as both Republican and Democrat? Hiram Johnson had done that in California, and had run on a third-party ticket to boot.

He asked Senator Vandenberg to obtain a formal opinion from Harry S. Toy, by then the Attorney General of Michigan, on this point. Toy's opinion was that it was legal to be a candidate on both tickets, but that in the general election he would have to designate himself as either a Democrat or Republican. This meant that if he entered both primaries and won only in the Democratic primary, he would have to call himself a Democrat.[17] He shied from that, and postponed a definite decision.

7

In November 1935 still another overture from the Democrats was made to Couzens. G. Hall Roosevelt of Detroit, brother of Mrs. Franklin D. Roosevelt and a close political associate of Frank Murphy, called on Frank Couzens. He told Frank that the Democratic party in the state "might" endorse Senator Couzens for re-election, but wanted to be certain beforehand that the Senator would not "slap back at them." [18] He asked Frank to sound out his father in secret. Couzens' response to Frank was:

"I think I told you that numerous prominent Democrats had talked to me along the same lines . . . but on each occasion I was silent or at least noncommittal. I would not, under any circumstances, make any private arrangements with anybody. Whatever I do with respect to my campaign, will be done publicly." [19]

But what would he do? He did not know.

8

Apparently with the idea of coaxing him to accept the Democratic overtures, certain Democrats began feeding newspaper writers "inside information" that he would run as a Democrat. Among other publications, the *Free Press* said that there had been a deal: Postmaster Farley was backing Couzens. In the *Review of Reviews,* there appeared an item that said:

> The real political fight looming in Michigan will be an effort by the now thoroughly entrenched Republicans to oust Senator Couzens as an independent Republican New Dealer. The violent-tempered multimillionaire is Farley's only hope in Michigan.[20]

Publicly, Couzens ignored these assertions. But to Tom Payne, he wrote, "I can say to you, in confidence, of course, that no such offer was ever made to me by Mr. Farley." [21] He also denied the Farley reports in private correspondence with Governor Frank D. Fitzgerald, who had announced that he, at least, among leading Republicans, favored his renomination as against Brucker. To Governor Fitzgerald, he added:

> While the necessity of filing petitions and the primaries are somewhat in the distance, I know of no reason why I should not run on the Republican ticket, unless it be that the party again comes under the standpat and reactionary leaders who have heretofore had control of the party.[22]

9

Which way the wind was blowing in the Republican party appeared to be well indicated by the sentiment at a dinner held in Detroit in February 1936 by the Wayne County Republican Party. A headline on February 21 told the story:

JAMES COUZENS' NAME
BOOED AT G.O.P. DINNER

In April, Brucker formally announced his candidacy for the Senate on a typically Old Guard platform: anti-Roosevelt and anti-Couzens.

Couzens' friends now urged that he also announce. "Every day you lose in making clear your stand will require at least two days of vigorous work . . . to win back the support you seem to be losing," wrote George Averill.[23] That was all too true. But he still hesitated.

In May he told Tom Payne, "I think finally it will be my decision to enter the Republican primaries." Then, only a week later, he asked Payne to find out if he could legally run as an independent. Shortly after he inquired of Payne: "How would we go about organizing another party?" [24] That same month, the Democratic party in Michigan, without consulting him, adopted a resolution endorsing him for re-election on the Democratic ticket, if he chose to accept.

Would he accept? He declined to say.

10

"There is no doubt that Senator Couzens seriously considered running on the Democratic ticket," Prentiss M. Brown, then Democratic Congressman from Michigan (later Couzens' successor in the Senate) recalled. Brown himself, among other Democratic Congressmen, urged that Couzens head the Democratic ticket in Michigan. He was also "authorized from a much higher authority to express the hope that the Senator would run," said Brown.[25] But an affirmative answer could not be pried from Couzens.

One reason for his indecision was that, at times, he considered not running at all. His secretary, Carson, had in fact urged that decision upon him. Carson felt that the prospects for victory were too slim, and, besides, that Couzens was not in good enough physical condition to undertake another campaign. He discussed with Couzens the possibility of his accepting some worthwhile appointment from Roosevelt. "Without actually committing him, I got him to say that he would accept an appointment," Carson recalled.

So Carson began consulting with certain men close to Roosevelt. His own hope, he later said, was that Roosevelt might offer Couzens the post of Secretary of the Interior, in place of Ickes, albeit this was only a hope on the part of Carson, who did not like Ickes. Among others, Prentiss Brown was interested in Carson's efforts.

Slated to be the Democratic candidate for Senator, Brown was only too glad to avoid the possibility of a contest between himself and Couzens. He agreed to talk with Roosevelt about Carson's proposal.[26] But Brown encountered delay in seeing the President. Couzens himself did nothing to press the matter.

11

In June, he was forced by the political calendar to make a decision one way or another. Democratic friends, including Murphy and Brown, continued to press him to accept a Democratic nomination. He finally turned that down. He told Murphy that to run as a Democrat, would mean he would be called "a turncoat," and he could not "tolerate" that.[27]

To Brown he gave yet another excuse. His son Frank, by the kind of administration he was giving Detroit as mayor, was now launched on a promising political career. "If I became a turncoat, it would harm Frank's political future," he told Brown. He did not wish to do that.[28]

Actually, there was a deeper reason for his rejection of the Democratic nomination. He had made a career of being an independent man. Now, in his last years, how could he most clearly demonstrate his independence? By seeking refuge in another party? Or by insisting that he was a Republican even though the Republicans denied it?

His answer to that was inevitable. On June 15, he announced that he would be a candidate for the Republican nomination. "I am," he said, definitely, "a Republican." [29]

Three days later, while he was packing to leave Washington for Detroit, Congressman Brown received the long-awaited message from the White House to confer with Roosevelt on "the Couzens matter." Couzens was already at the railroad station when Brown later reported to Carson on his talk with Roosevelt. The President had indicated to Brown that he was ready to make a worthwhile offer to Couzens. There was a distinct possibility that Farley might retire temporarily, for the duration of the campaign, as Postmaster General, Roosevelt indicated. Politically, this seemed an expedient thing, as the Republicans appeared intent on making a serious campaign issue out of "Farleyism." Even Senator Norris had been stirring up sentiment against the administration over Farley's handling of patronage.

Roosevelt would be glad to have Couzens become Postmaster General for that period, with the understanding that another post would be found for him after the election.[30]

Carson hurried to the station to tell Couzens. "We walked up and down the station and talked it out," Carson related. The offer had come too late, Couzens finally said. Had it come earlier, before he had announced his candidacy, he might have accepted. "To take the offer at that hour would make it look as if he had been bought off. He could not take it." [31] So he entrained for Detroit for his third campaign for the Senate.

CHAPTER XLV

THE INDEPENDENT MAN

In truth, there was no campaign. He still had no organization with which to make one, a price he paid for having eschewed patronage in politics.

After fourteen years as a Senator, he was in the pitiful position of a political leader unable to count on more than a dozen men in the whole state to serve as the nucleus of a strong campaign committee. Then, too, he declined to give the signal for the start of any kind of real effort to get his story to the public.

He made only one speech, a talk to the Detroit Optimist Club, in which he scarcely referred to his candidacy. "I will be entirely content," he said, "if the people of Michigan say I am through, if they are dissatisfied with my work."

Most of the time during this appearance, he spent in answering questions concerning his attitude toward the Roosevelt administration.

"Was Roosevelt bankrupting the nation?" he was asked.

"Certainly not," he answered. "I have been disgusted with this constant talk about balancing the federal budget. How could anybody have balanced it?"

Did he expect a "Red government" in Washington as a result of Roosevelt?

"Absurd," he said. "All three branches of our government, the legislative, executive, and judicial are functioning."

He made no reference to Brucker, his opponent. Nor did he mention Alf M. Landon, the Republican nominee for President.

2

Whereas by all the rules, with his opponent going up and down across the state, he ought to have been out on the hustings himself, he instead chartered, from Leon Mandel of the Chicago department store, a yacht, the *Buccaneer,* and spent most of his time cruising with Frank, William J. Norton, and others on the Great Lakes. It would be said that he was a man "sulking on his yacht," because of chagrin over the impossibility of being renominated. If so, his sulking was a most agreeable kind, for friends who joined him on the *Buccaneer* from time to time found him more relaxed and amiable than they had ever known him. He had, as he wrote to Senator Vandenberg, "a most delightful and restful summer and, of course, time to think and think and think." [1]

He did a great deal of fishing. He told stories. One night he held his guests "enthralled past midnight as he told the true story of the founding of the Ford Motor Company."

He talked of his lost boy, Homer. As he recalled that boy, he wept openly for the first time. Apparently, somewhere in him an emotional dam had broken. He felt all the better for this, and was able at last, after twenty-two years, to speak of Homer without bitter regret over his death.[2]

Once while the yacht was on Lake Superior, someone pointed to the Canadian shore and commented: "If you had not been born over there, in Chatham, you might have been President." He laughed. This was very nearly the same comment he had made to his mother fifty years before.[3]

3

His friends kept pressing him, as the summer wore on, to let some kind of campaign be put up for him. But he delayed giving his approval. He put them off usually with the assertion that the people knew his record, so the usual activity was unnecessary.

His real reason was something else. He could not envision himself making an appeal for renomination without making his stand clear on the one big issue—Roosevelt. Obviously, he was for Roosevelt. But should he say so? And when?

His opponent, Brucker, was demanding that he declare himself. On August 5, at Petoskey, Michigan, Brucker, who twenty years later would find himself defending Republican President Eisenhower against the charge of "New Dealism" and "socialism," asked, "How can the Republican Party put up a united front against President Roosevelt and his socialistic doctrine, if the head of the federal ticket in Michigan is a New Dealer?"

At Cadillac, Brucker said, "I dare Couzens to tell the people of this

state whether he is supporting Alf M. Landon, the Republican nominee for President, or President Roosevelt." [4]

At Detroit, in a radio broadcast, Brucker said: "Mr. Couzens has
utterly failed . . . to say whether he supports Landon or Roosevelt. . . . The people are entitled to know. . . . Why isn't Senator
Couzens out working for Landon's election? Senator Vandenberg
is out on the stump for Landon, while Mr. Couzens won't even declare himself." [5]

4

The politically wise advice to Couzens was to refrain from answering Brucker. To state openly that he favored Roosevelt's re-election
could not possibly help his own cause in the Republican primary.
On the contrary, such a statement could only harm his already slim
chances of winning, if not cinch his defeat. If he insisted on coming
out for Roosevelt, he should hold off until after the primary.

On the yacht, Couzens pondered that problem. The primary was
set for September 15. Early in August, Bill Yaw, his son-in-law, began pressing him to approve an advertising budget for a campaign
keyed to two themes—that Couzens was a Republican and that a
big Republican vote was desirable. Henry T. Ewald, the advertising-
agency head, had prepared the campaign. Radio time had to be reserved.

On the afternoon of August 12, as the *Buccaneer* was off St. Ignace
Island, Couzens reached his decision. On a radiogram blank he wrote
out a message to Yaw:

> I intend to announce myself as desiring Roosevelt's election.
> Therefore tell Ewald and Carson all plans cancelled. . . . Also tell
> Ewald I do not desire any radio reservations and am unconcerned
> about plan of getting Republicans out to vote. . . . [6]

He handed the message to John P. Frazer, a friend of Frank's who
was on the yacht, and asked that he send it. Frazer read the message
and blanched. He argued with Couzens that he should "wait."
Couzens said no, he had "decided."

"I won't send it!" said Frazer.

"If you don't, I'll get it on the radio myself," Couzens replied.

Frazer pleaded some more. But it was no use. The radiogram was
sent. [7]

5

Efforts were made by Bill Yaw, Tom Payne, and others to get him
to change his mind. All they succeeded in doing was to get him to hold

up for awhile public announcement of his decision. Maybe something would turn up, they hoped. They knew that for a Republican candidate for Senator to come out openly for Roosevelt would doom even a slight chance of winning in the Republican primary. It just could not be done—not in 1936.

Couzens insisted that it would be "dishonest" not to make known, before the primary, clearly and unequivocally his decision. He recalled that back in 1924, Brookhart had been accused of "fraud and deception" because he favored La Follette, but did not say so until after he had won the Republican party nomination in Iowa. That was one of the reasons the Old Guard in the Senate gave for refusing to let Brookhart take his seat.[8]

Couzens would not lay himself open to that kind of thing. He would not "stultify" himself, he repeated. The Republican voters had a right to know.

Madeleine Yaw tried her hand at getting him to change his mind, when he visited her in Harper Hospital, where she was expecting her fourth child—Couzens' twelfth grandchild.

"Well, Pete," he greeted her. "I won't be re-nominated."

"Why not?" Madeleine demanded.

"Because I am coming out for Roosevelt."

"But you don't *have* to do that."

"Yes, I do. That's the honest thing."

Madeleine agreed in her heart. But she felt it was not "good" for him to be defeated. So she kept on arguing with him. But it was no use.[9]

On Sunday, August 23, three days before his sixty-fourth birthday, the newspapers all over the nation carried his statement:

> Believing as I do that the most important matter confronting the nation is the re-election of President Roosevelt, I intend to support him.
> The outcome of my own candidacy is neither important to the nation nor to me, but I do believe it is important that my many loyal supporters in Michigan be advised in advance of the primary. . . .

This was the real end of his campaign, such as it was, for re-election. It was clear immediately that his senatorial career was over, ended in the way he had started it, by an affirmation of what had been his greatest aim—to be Couzens, the independent man.

CHAPTER XLVI

THE TRIUMPHANT DEFEAT

HE KNEW only too well the consequences. "I have written myself out of the Senate," he wrote to Senator McNary.[1] Friends said, "Too bad, too bad." His response was, "Not at all. The important thing is that the New Deal, what it stands for, be firmly entrenched. That means another term for Roosevelt is necessary. Otherwise the country will swing back. What happens to me is not important, next to that consideration."[2]

Vandenberg was dismayed and suggested to Couzens that he had yielded to impulse while "mentally disturbed." "That is not the fact," Couzens told him. "On the boat, I had days and days to consider the future of my adopted country."[3]

"The odd thing about it," said Senator McNary, who got to know Couzens perhaps better than anyone else, "was that Couzens meant it when he said he acted solely from his view of the good of the country."[4]

2

The chief beneficiary of his announcement, Roosevelt, was then on a tour of Western states. Roosevelt was both elated and surprised, all the more as he knew that Couzens had turned down a chance to run as a Democrat in place of Prentiss Brown.

THE WHITE HOUSE
    Washington

September 8, 1936
DEAR JIM:
    It is one of the fine things about public life that every once in a while the usual rules of the political game are not followed! Your announcement is not only fine in itself but it is especially so because it came without solicitation or suggestion on my part or on that of any member of the Democratic organization.
    Frankly, I was just as much taken by surprise as, I imagine, Brother

Landon was. I want you to know that I appreciate not alone what you have said and done but also your manner of doing it—for you have shown a very deep courage based on conviction and may lose your Primary as a result.

Perhaps you have not seen this typical vile editorial in the Chicago *Tribune* which came to me the other day. I do not give a continental under which party label you or I may happen to enroll ourselves but I do know that very fundamentally you and I have the same ethical standards.

Always sincerely,
FRANKLIN D. ROOSEVELT [5]

3

The "vile editorial" to which the President referred was an example of the anger Couzens' announcement had provoked. His support of Roosevelt was part of a conspiracy between him and Roosevelt of long standing, the *Tribune* said. "It is established now that he [Couzens] helped in creating a hero role for Mr. Roosevelt in 1933." Had he not caused the nation-wide bank crisis by "blocking" the RFC loan to the Detroit banks? And had not Roosevelt, too, opposed aid to the Detroit banks? It was all now clear. They had purposely set the stage for Roosevelt to win acclaim for saving the financial system that they themselves had "wrecked." "Now the people of Michigan will have an opportunity to wreak their vengeance upon the two men primarily responsible for that state's worst calamity." [6]

Loyal Tom Payne also received a letter—typical of the reaction of certain war veterans who resented Roosevelt's and Couzens' attitude on the latest bonus proposal.

> This . . . written against the man you are working for politically, Senator James Couzens. . . . He has deserted the honest, the upright, the noble, for the degrading position of a bootlicker to the most dangerous, damaging demagogue that ever sat in the President's chair. No good can ever come from a turncoat. . . .

4

After docking at Detroit for the day to make his announcement, Couzens promptly sailed away again on the *Buccaneer*, to be gone, except for one short visit to Wabeek in the interim, until primary day. He did not share the gloom of his associates. Indeed, he was now noticeably in especially good spirits. He was like a man who had cast off a great load. He had followed his conscience. As expected, he was badly defeated. The surprising thing was that he still received 199,204 Republican votes against the 328,560 for Brucker.[7]

5

Three days after the primary, G. Hall Roosevelt arrived in Detroit with a confidential letter from the President.

THE WHITE HOUSE
Washington

September 17, 1936

Personal

DEAR JIM:

Hall has been with me here in Washington while the returns were coming in. I need not tell you that you were a good sport because you were a lot more than that—you lived up to your own ideals. Actually, your run was a feat unprecedented in political history and will always be remembered.

What I want to convey to you in very simple terms is that you and your ideals and ability must not, because of a political system be lost to the country. As you are aware, one of the most difficult problems before us is that of American shipping. Ever since the mail subsidies of the eighteen forties, when the Merchant Marine legislation was first passed, shipping has gone through ups and downs but always more or less the victim of party politics or of shipping lobbies.

Today I am confronted with constituting a Maritime Commission under the new bill, which, although not perfect, is very definitely a step in the right direction, giving powers to this independent Commission which are far greater than any previously granted. In fact, this new Commission *can* put our sea borne trade back on its feet in an honest way. . . .

What I need and what the country needs is a fearless Chairman of this Maritime Commission, who will take the responsibility in setting up and putting through a new and permanent Mercantile Marine policy. Experts on engineering, ship design, ship management, etc., can be hired, but a Chairman with the capacity and the courage I seek cannot be hired; he must be drafted. That is why I want you on the first of January to undertake the task of heading the Maritime Commission. . . .

In sending you this note by Hall, I can only reiterate that irrespective of party affiliations the country needs you in public service, and I cannot conceive of any higher or more important duty than getting the Maritime Commission started under real leadership and under auspices that will be considered neither political nor tinged with any special interest. I have emphasized courage because it will take courage to end many abuses which have grown up in the shipping industry in the past. You have that courage.

My warm regards,
Faithfully yours,
FRANKLIN D. ROOSEVELT [8]

6

This letter pleased Couzens, but he was not certain that he wanted to accept the chairmanship of the Maritime Commission. "I do not know the first thing about water shipping, naval construction or design, yet . . . I would have to assume the responsibility of the decision of your so-called experts," he replied to Roosevelt. He did not, however, reject the offer flatly. He left the matter open until he would return to Washington, "probably about election time."

The more immediate thing, he told Roosevelt, was the election. He wrote to him:

> I want . . . to emphasize . . . that the election is not won and I think there is a lot of work to be done. Great headway could be made . . . by pointing [up] your Good Neighbor policy and your endeavor to keep us out of foreign conflict. . . . Some simplified form has to be adopted for ridiculing our national debt. I told Hall that I wanted to be helpful in your campaign and I still do.[9]

7

From Vandenberg, he received an interesting testament.

> The returns are in—and it appears that we are "parting company" as Senate colleagues. Under the circumstances, I cannot refrain from this reminiscent note. I cannot explain my very real affection for you —but I have it—and there it is.
>
> Many times in the last eight years you have made me "mad as Hell" and I know that I have had the same effect on you. But most of the time we have travelled comfortably in double harness and I have deeply cherished the privilege of knowing you with an intimacy denied to most other men.
>
> I know that my legislative association with you has been distinctly and usefully tempering to what was originally too "conservative" a view on my part, and you have had much to do with instilling in me a sense of "social responsibility" which I hope I may never lose.[10]

Grateful for this from Vandenberg, he yet could not resist the urge to take advantage of the opportunity to tell Vandenberg that he believed him wrong for supporting Landon, even for the sake of party regularity.

> Let me say to you, Arthur, that if the great mass of our people who live on an economic precipice ever get the idea back in their minds that their government has no interest in them and that their government is only interested in the "big boys," we will never be

able to stop the growth of communism and the other isms that are being propagandized in our country. That is one of the reasons I do not want Mr. Landon elected. I think it would be a setback. . . .

Nor did he resist telling Vandenberg that he hoped he would not have Brucker as a colleague. He frankly asserted that Prentiss Brown should be elected, "in the interest of Michigan and our country." He noted that Vandenberg had told him that his advice would continue to be welcomed.

> This leaves me free to be as candid with you in the future as I have been in the past and I think that over the years I probably will be availing myself of it. You know we still have a Washington house and I am going down there after the election to spend some considerable time. . . .[11]

8

What he expressed there was only a hope. For within a week after the primary his health took another bad turn. Just after his talk with Hall Roosevelt on September 18, in his office in Birmingham, he felt so weak and feverish that he went home early in the afternoon and to bed. Feeling the need for more air in the room, he got out of bed to open a window. He came close to collapsing from the sudden pain caused by the exertion—and it was found that he had injured his sacroiliac.[12]

Five days later he was ordered to Harper Hospital in Detroit "for treatment," as he himself recorded in his notebook, "for jaundice, diabetes, and sacroiliac." [13]

A postscript to his letter to Vandenberg told the story:

> I am signing this in the hospital, so forget the errors. I am feeling very rotten. JIM.

Bill Yaw visited him on October 1. That afternoon he wrote to Carson:

> Frankly, I am quite concerned about the Senator's health. . . . I am not at all pleased about his general condition. . . . I have an idea that he really feels his defeat more than he thought he would, although I am sure that he has no regrets that he was unwilling to compromise his convictions.

On October 2 Couzens decided to leave the hospital. The old rebellion against being inactive returned. As a compromise, he took a suite at the Book-Cadillac Hotel, where Dr. Freund could be closer to him. He had "things to do," he insisted, like preparing to help

the Roosevelt campaign and also for paying a visit to Madeleine and
her new baby, a boy, James John Yaw, born on August 28, two days
after his own birthday. He felt so well that during the next few days
he took Mrs. Couzens to several shows, including a performance of
Romeo and Juliet. They even drove out to Wabeek.

On October 7 Marvin McIntyre, one of Roosevelt's secretaries,
called from Washington to ask him if he would be in Detroit on
October 15, when Roosevelt was to make a campaign visit there.
The President wanted to see him on that occasion.[14] Couzens said
that he would, and that certainly he would be glad to see Roosevelt.
On the 10th a letter from Roosevelt himself arrived. It said:

> . . . You are right about the campaign not yet being won. I
> expect to spend one day—October fifteenth—in Michigan, and I
> hope that I shall see you at that time, if only for a few minutes. It
> would help me if you were seen with me! [15]

9

He accepted the position of honorary chairman of the committee
in charge of the Detroit reception for Roosevelt.[16] On Monday, October 12, he invited Arthur Krock, Washington correspondent of
the New York *Times,* out to Wabeek for an interview on the political
situation. He predicted that Roosevelt would sweep Michigan.[17]

He seemed then to be in fairly good shape. But on Wednesday,
October 14, Dr. Freund ordered him back to Harper Hospital when
he developed a stomach disorder that prevented him from keeping
down any food. So he was at the hospital in Detroit when Roosevelt
came into Michigan from Chicago on a special train.

At Flint, Frank Murphy, campaigning for governor, told Roosevelt of Couzens' new illness. The President said he would go to
see Couzens at the hospital. But Couzens would not "stand for it."
"It wasn't right for the President to come to him." [18] He said he would
keep his date with the President, if he were at all able.

So, in the late afternoon of the 15th, he left his bed at Harper and
went by automobile to the Grand Trunk Railway yards in Highland
Park to greet Roosevelt in his campaign car.

While waiting for the President's train to be switched into place,
he talked with a local Democratic leader about his own political position. "Some people have asked me why, if I would not join the
Democratic Party, did I not lead a third party in Michigan. The
answer is that I am too ill for anything like that."

He did not have to emphasize that he was ill. It showed in his face and in his posture. He had had no nourishment for two days. In the President's car he was to have dined with Roosevelt. He joined the President, but all he took was a glass of milk.[19]

10

He stayed with Roosevelt through the whole strenuous evening. He was in the parade through the city. He stood with the President at a rally in Hamtramck Stadium, built by the PWA. At a great mass meeting that night in front of the Detroit City Hall, he was there, ill as he was.

Detroit had never before seen such a turnout for any candidate. But that mass meeting was really for Couzens as well as for Roosevelt. For when he was introduced to the throng, a "thunderous cheer" went up for him.[20]

He was pleased by the speech Roosevelt gave that night. The President talked of the importance of building up mass purchasing power. He spoke of the need for more security for labor—and got down to cases with mention of the automobile industry. "It is my belief that the manufacturers of automobiles and the manufacturers of many other necessary commodities must, by planning, do far more than they have done to date to increase the yearly earnings of those who work for them." [21]

This was almost precisely what Couzens had in mind nearly twenty-two years before when, just a few blocks away, he had addressed the Board of Commerce on the responsibility of Detroit's employers to their employees.

He had been called names for having made that speech in 1914. He had been denounced for the five-dollar-a-day plan. And now here was the President of the United States enunciating those views as government policy. So this night was one of triumph for him, triumph despite his personal defeat. He might be out of the Senate, but Roosevelt would be re-elected, he felt, despite a *Literary Digest* poll that forecast an overwhelming Republican landslide.

Thus his own policies would be carried on.

Roosevelt gave him a warm handshake in thanks for his having come out that night.

"Take good care of your father," said Roosevelt to Frank, who, as Mayor, was the President's official host. "We need him." [22]

CHAPTER XLVII

"THE END OF THE ROAD"

WHETHER or not the exertion of being with Roosevelt that night had harmed him, none could say. He was obviously exhausted. Frank and Bill Yaw escorted him from the Roosevelt meeting to the Book-Cadillac Hotel, where Dr. Freund was waiting to take him back to the hospital.

Dr. Freund saw that he was over-fatigued. "Was it worth it?" he asked, after they were settled in an automobile on the way to Harper.

"Yes. Definitely," Couzens answered.

"Just why do you think it's so important to re-elect Roosevelt?"

"Here's something I have never told anyone," Couzens said. "The President has told me that he is afraid that war is coming. It may come from Japan. If that happens, all this opposition to the New Deal will not mean anything. I think Roosevelt is the one man to be our leader if we have a war. That's one reason I feel he must be re-elected even though I am a Republican." [1]

2

He was glad to get into bed at the hospital. "I'll never be back with you at Wabeek," he told Madeleine. [2]

On October 20, his condition was such that his daughters Margo and Betty were called from Washington to be at his bedside, along with Madeleine, Frank, and Mrs. Couzens. By then Dr. Freund and consulting physicians had determined that he was a victim of uremic poisoning. on top of all the other ailments. Through Carson, Roosevelt was advised that Couzens' condition was desperate. The President sent a telegraph message which, he hoped, would help rally Couzens' spirit.

I KNOW THAT YOU LIKE A FIGHT AND I AM PUTTING ALL MY FAITH IN THAT DOGGED DETERMINATION OF YOURS. IT HAS WON MORE THAN ONE

FIGHT FOR YOU AND IT IS STILL OUR BEST BET. I HOPE YOU WILL BE
YOURSELF AGAIN VERY SOON. I NEED YOU AND SO DOES THE COUNTRY.
FRANKLIN D. ROOSEVELT.[3]

He did seem to rally. On the 21st, Dr Freund said that he believed
he was gaining. "The pulse and temperature are normal." [4] But on
the following afternoon his temperature went up again. A medical
consultation was held. Then Dr. Freund said to him: "Senator, we
are not satisfied with the way you are getting along." Dr. Freund
decided that another operation was necessary.

3

He had been through this before—seven, eight, nine, even more
times—too often to count accurately. Each time before, he had put
up some kind of protest. But not now. The old spirit was ebbing.
"All right. It's all right with me." [5]
Frank, who had sat in on the medical consultation, expressed
dismay that another operation was ordered. But his father smiled
at him. "Don't worry." he said. "They can't kill an old dog like me."
Mrs. Couzens was permitted to see him for a moment before he was
wheeled from the room. He held out his hand to her and she clasped
it. "I'll see you later, Mother. Don't worry."
They operated at 3:00 and he was brought back to his room at
4:00. Dr. Freund said to Mrs. Couzens, as they waited his awakening
from the anaesthetic, "It was the only thing to do. It was the end of
the road." [6] So it was—October 22, 1936. He did not wake up.

4

Death is the Great Biographer.
For some time, the attacks on James Couzens in the conservative
press and by the politicians, notably in connection with the bank
case, had obscured the esteem with which he was held by the people.
Likewise, they had obscured his truly remarkable career.
Now, suddenly, on every side, it was remembered that he had been
more than a man in politics. Suddenly, it was remembered that he
he had been one of the great builders of American industry, starting
from scratch; that he had struck mighty blows for the workingmen
while still an industrialist; that, after making millions, he had retired not to leisure, but to public service; that he had been a great
and constructive mayor before he had become an outstanding senator;
that he had been a benefactor of children through philanthropy

equaled by few; that he was that rare thing, an honest man in politics. In the words of a writer in the *New Republic,* he was the "perfect example of the honest man in politics . . . the most intellectually honest man . . . in Washington." [7]

5

Even men and women who had been taught to dislike him, suddenly realized that a great void had been caused by his passing, that a man of uncommon strength had been among them. All this was reflected in the honors that were paid to him, by adversaries as well as admirers, now that he was gone. Never in the history of his city and his state was any man so honored in death as was this man who had come there forty-six years before—a youth from a small town in neighboring Canada.

The city government of Detroit asked that his body lie in state in the City Hall, the resolution for that being introduced in the Common Council by Councilman John Lodge, with whom Couzens had had one of his celebrated "rows" as mayor. The flags of all public buildings in the city were ordered kept at half-staff for thirty days. Long was the line that passed by the coffin in the City Hall, a line composed almost wholly of wage-earners. Perhaps never had a millionaire been mourned so sincerely by so many from the common ranks of a community. Their outpouring emphasized the strangest and also strongest aspect of his life, that with all his great wealth he made himself a symbol of opposition to arrogant wealth and a champion of those who lacked any wealth at all.

At Bath, Michigan, the children in a school that he had erected there to replace one wrecked by a maniac in 1927, spontaneously contributed pennies for a floral tribute. There was sadness among the attendants at the Children's Hospital of Michigan. They remembered that the work they were doing for their crippled charges had largely been made possible by his generous giving. There was sadness in the hearts of countless fathers and mothers of the poor who knew that their children's lives had been enriched because he had established the Children's Fund of Michigan, then in its sixth year. They would not have understood the comments of certain politicians and industrialists to the effect that he was a "cold man."

6

Tributes poured in from all over the nation, for the man who had been the boy in Canada who made himself not just a Detroiter and a Michigander, but an American "of unique renown," [8] For once all the tributes were honest, as if his candid—often too candid—spirit controlled them. There were no false notes, no generalities to fit any public man.

Roosevelt interrupted a speaking tour in Connecticut to say:

> In the death of Senator Couzens the Senate of the United States and the people of Michigan and the Nation have lost a leader whose convictions were a part of the best that America aspires for and whose courage was a match for his idealism.
>
> Senator Couzens did not enter public life because he sought either fame or power, but rather because of a service he believed he could render to the cause of progressive thought and political uprightness. He was a party member. But his prior obligation was to the well-being of the people whom he served. He never hesitated in that service.
>
> The death of Senator Couzens to me is a great loss. But, more than that, it is a great loss to the multitudes of Americans whose needs and problems were always in the forefront of his thought and action. [9]

All city and county offices in Detroit were closed for the funeral on October 26. Recalling that he had established the municipally owned transportation lines, the Detroit Street Railway brought every streetcar and bus in Detroit to a halt for a minute at the hour the body was placed in the mausoleum in Woodlawn cemetery.

Recalling his services as commissioner of police, nearly all of the city's policemen lined the highway of the funeral procession from Wabeek to the cemetery.

More than two thousand persons were present at the interment. The honorary pallbearers were men who had known him or had been associated with him in all the phases of his career—Ernest C. Kern, Joseph Mack, Clarence H. Booth, William O'Leary, Dr. Freund, William J. Norton, John P. Frazer, C. H. Haberkorn, Jr., Thomas Payne, George B. Judson, Clarence E. Wilcox, and Henry Ford.

7

In the week after the funeral, there was held at Traverse City, Michigan, where only that previous June his Children's Fund had dedicated the Central Michigan Children's Clinic, a spontaneous community-inspired memorial service. There, William J. Norton, the director of the Fund, gave a nearly perfect tribute, an honest appraisal.

This man was a rugged and dauntless fighter. He was no molly-coddle. He was a warrior's captain. . . . He fought always on the side of justice and human rights. His sword was never drawn in the cause of special privilege. Mistakes of the mind he no doubt made in some of the causes he espoused, for he was intensely human, but mistakes of ethical purpose—never.

His conscience held the most finely etched pattern as a guide for his own conduct that I have ever seen in any man of wealth or dominance. Simple honesty, complete integrity, a sense of great responsibility, cold-blooded objective justice, perfect faith in the democratic ideal, and a love for gentle charity were all burned clearly and distinctly into that ethical pattern that acted as his sole governor in all of his public relations. . . . Those ethical mandates were the only masters he acknowledged. . . .

On the first anniversary of his death, Edgar DeWitt Jones, the minister, in a nationwide radio broadcast, came close to voicing in seven words the complete epitaph: "He preserved his individuality to the end."

In a large sense, to do this had been his career.

Appendices

NOTES

BIBLIOGRAPHY

INDEX

NOTES

PROLOGUE: *October 12, 1915*

1. The scene between Couzens and Ford is based on the transcript of an interview given by Couzens to Judge Neil, a magazine writer, on July 27, 1926, and approved by Couzens as authentic. Copy in Couzens' papers. The interview, in substance, was published in *Real America*, April 1934. John C. Lodge's comment was made to author, 1941. See his book, *I Remember Detroit*, in collaboration with M. M. Quaife, 1949.
2. Before U.S. Board of Tax Appeals, 1927, *Transcript*.
3. Milo M. Quaife, *The Life of John Wendell Anderson*, p. 140; also in U.S. Board of Tax Appeals, 1927, *Transcript*.

CHAPTER I. *The Beginning*

1. Homer Couzens, brother of James Couzens, interview in Detroit, 1940.
2. "Historical Chatham," supplement with *The Planet Souvenir* of Chatham, Ontario, 1904.
3. Homer Couzens, interview; and Alice Couzens Lund to author, September 23, 1941.
4. Mrs. James Couzens, interview.

CHAPTER II. *The Canadian Boy*

1. Homer Couzens, interview.
2. Alice Couzens Lund, a sister, in a letter of September 23, 1941.
3. Ross Schram, an unpublished story of James Couzens' life to about 1920, in Couzens' papers. A Detroit newspaperman, Schram had served Couzens temporarily as secretary.
4. *Detroit Journal*, January 26, 1915.
5. Homer Couzens, interview.
6. *Detroit Journal*, January 26, 1915.
7. Alice Couzens Lund, letter, April 18, 1940.
8. John Carson, secretary to Couzens, to author, 1941.

CHAPTER III. *The Money-Making Machine, I*

1. Interviews in Chatham: William Mann, Frank Baxter, Charles Donovan, *et al.*, 1941.
2. James Couzens, article in *Nation's Business*, December 1926.
3. Charles Donovan, memorandum for author, 1941.
4. Victor Lauriston, Chatham, unpublished article loaned to author, 1941.
5. Albert L. Couzens, letter, September 23, 1941.
6. Alice C. Lund, letter to author, September 7, 1940.
7. *Pipp's Weekly*, June 16, 1922.
8. Charles Donovan of Chatham, letter to author, October 1940.
9. Homer Couzens, interview.
10. Arthur Stringer, Canadian novelist, boyhood friend of James Couzens in

Chatham, author of the book about a Chatham boyhood, *Lonely O'Malley;* letter to author, December 19, 1940.

11. William Mann and Frank Baxter, boyhood friends of Couzens in Chatham, interviews, February 7, 1941.

12. Interview with Bill Turtle in Chatham, February 6, 1941.

13. *New York Times*, December 20, 1922, and Detroit papers—stories based on interviews with James Couzens after his appointment to the U.S. Senate; also *Detroit Journal*, January 26, 1915, a basic item on his youth.

CHAPTER IV. *The New Detroiter*

1. Homer Couzens, interview: also Daniel Hackett, fellow worker at the Michigan Central Railroad and the late mayor of Jackson, Michigan, interview, 1940.

2. Schram, unfinished study of Couzens, *op. cit.;* also Catlin, *The Story of Detroit*, and the works of Milo M. Quaife.

Concerning the automobile industry and its founders, the most recent study, also the fullest and no doubt the best, with certain reservations as to interpretations, is by Allan Nevins, in collaboration with Frank Ernest Hill and others of Columbia University, published in 1954 under the title *Ford: The Times, The Man, The Company*. It is cited here as Nevins, *Ford, I*. A second volume of this important study, entitled *Ford: Expansion and Challenge 1915–1933*, was published in 1957, and is cited here as Nevins, *Ford, II*.

For readers who may be curious about certain similarities between that study and this book with respect to the treatment of James Couzens and his role in the Ford Motor Company from its founding to 1915, the explanation is that, as a matter of academic cooperation, the typescript of this work, before it was put in final form, was made available to Professor Nevins, as courteously acknowledged in the Nevins study. The typescript of the unfinished version of this book is cited in the Nevins study as "Harry Barnard, *James Couzens of Detroit*," which was the working title of this book. For an especially excellent though short study of Henry Ford and the company see Roger Burlingame's *Henry Ford: A Great Life in Brief*, 1955.

3. Sidney Glazer, in Quaife and Glazer, *Michigan, From Primitive Wilderness to Industrial Commonwealth*, pp. 247 and 281.

4. Catlin, *op. cit.*, pp. 586–606.

5. Couzens to Daniel Kiefer, March 5, 1917.

6. Daniel Hackett.

7. A. T. Dempster, a Michigan Central employee, interview.

8. *Ibid.*, and *Detroit News*, April 13, 1924.

9. Arthur J. Lacy, Detroit attorney, whose firm, Anderson, Wilcox and Lacy, handled Couzens' legal affairs over a long period, interviews, 1940.

10. A. C. Goodson of the Michigan Central, in *Detroit News-Tribune*, October 27, 1915.

11. Daniel Hackett, memorandum for author, 1940.

12. Daniel Hackett, *op. cit.*

13. Michigan Central Railroad records, copy prepared for author.

CHAPTER V. *The Coal Clerk*

1. John Gunther, *Inside U.S.A.*, p. 403. Mr. Gunther did, as he wrote, find out that Malcomson was an original stockholder in the Ford Motor Company, owning an amount of shares equal to Ford's. He said, "Ford must, of course, have bought him out many years ago, as he bought out Couzens." But it is no wonder that Mr. Gunther did not come out with the full story about Malcomson. Until recently, most accounts of the Ford company left Malcomson out, or included him only glancingly, especially the stories supposedly authored by Ford.

2. *Detroit Journal*, October 27, 1902.

3. A. R. Malcomson, interview, 1942.

4. *Detroit Free Press*, April 1, 1903; see also Jere C. Hutchins, *A Personal Story*, pp. 283–84.

5. A. R. Malcomson, interview; also comments by Helen Malcomson Gore, his daughter, in a letter to the author dated July 25, 1942.

6. Ross Schram, *op. cit.*

7. *Ibid.*

CHAPTER VI. *The Family Man*

1. Mrs. James Couzens, interview, 1940.

2. *Ibid.*

3. *Ibid.*

4. Frank Couzens, interview, February 13, 1941.

5. Mrs. James Couzens, *ibid.*

6. Couzens to his daughter, Madeleine C. Yaw, November 14, 1933.

7. Mrs. David Huffman, letter to author, August 27, 1941.

8. Jay G. Hayden of the *Detroit News*, interview, April 17, 1940.

9. Mrs. James Couzens, interview.

CHAPTER VII. *The Ford Motor Company*

1. In *My Life and Work*, 1922, p. 36, actually written by Samuel Crowther, a work to be read with great caution. See Burlingame, *Henry Ford*, p. 185, for pertinent comments. Data about Malcomson and Ford, based on interviews with various persons who knew them both, including A. R. Malcomson and Mrs. Couzens, and also Schram's work.

2. McManus and Beasley, *Men, Money, and Motors*, p. 1. This work is exceptionally well authenticated, for many principals read it over before publication, and it rates as a primary source on Ford and others. It is cited hereafter as "McManus."

3. McManus, *op. cit.*, pp. 1ff.; see also Nevins, *Ford I, op. cit.*, p. 185.

4. McManus, *op. cit*, p. 2; see also Glasscock, *The Gasoline Age*, pp. 50–52, and Doolittle, *The Romance of the Automobile Industry*, 1916.

5. McManus, *op. cit.*

6. *Detroit News*, July 11, 1919; Nevins, *Ford, I,* includes an extended account of the Henry Ford Company, pp. 206ff.

7. Burlingame, *Henry Ford*, p. 29; also interviews in Detroit by author.

8. Charles B. King, *Psychic Reminiscences*, pp. 18–19.

9. John W. Anderson, testimony, in *Dodge, et al., v. Commissioner of Internal Revenue, U.S. Board of Tax Appeals, 1927* (known as the tax case brought against Couzens by Secretary of the Treasury Andrew W. Mellon; see *infra.*), *Transcript*, pp. 1270–72. Hereafter the record of this case will be cited as *Board of Tax Appeals, Transcript* See also Nevins, *Ford, I,* pp. 226ff.

10. Quaife, *The Life of John Wendell Anderson*, privately printed in 1950, pp. 89ff. A copy of this book was courteously loaned to the author by Milo M. Quaife.

11. *Ibid.,* p. 107; also interviews by author.

12. Schram, *op. cit.*

13. Schram, *op. cit.* Schram's account is based upon talks with Couzens himself.

14. Benson, *The New Henry Ford*, p. 103. Benson talked with Couzens as well as Ford.

15. *Ibid.*

16. J. C. Long, *Roy D. Chapin*, 1945, p. 35, concerning the Dodges' work for Olds. Chapin, who became head of Hudson Motor, started with Olds.

17. Benson, *op. cit.*, p. 103.

18. John W. Anderson to his father, Dr. Wendell A. Anderson of LaCrosse, Wisconsin, June 4, 1903. This letter is a primary source of exceptional value on the founding of the Ford Motor Company. A copy was made available by Anderson's associates. Quaife, in his *Life of Anderson*, publishes it in full, pp. 94ff, and also it is in Schram, *op. cit.*

19. *Ibid.*

20. *Ibid.*

21. John W. Anderson, *Transcript, op. cit.*, 1273.

22. *Philadelphia Evening Public Ledger*, interview, December 4, 1922.

23. McManus, *op. cit.*, p. 28.

24. Charles T. Bennett, president of the Daisy Air Rifle Company, interview with author, July 11, 1941. Bennett put $5,000 into the Ford Motor Company, but sold out later.

25. McManus, *op. cit.*, p. 29.

26. *Detroit Free Press*, April 1, 1903.

27. Benson, *op. cit.*, p. 115.

28. McManus, p. 31. Couzens also tried to enlist share buyers, but from book to book, a story has been printed, as in Simonds, *Henry Ford*, 1943, to the effect that, once after failing, Couzens sat on a street curb and burst into tears, which sidelight on him may be dismissed as incredible.

29. Quaife, *Anderson, op. cit.*, p. 102.

30. Merle Crowell, in *American Magazine*, February 1923.

31. McManus, *op. cit.*, and others.

32. Anderson letter, *op. cit.*

33. Mrs. James Couzens, interview, June 27, 1941.

34. *Ibid.*

35. *Detroit News*, January 20, 1927. Several books erroneously refer to Couzens' sister Rosetta as having taught school in Detroit. It was in Chatham.

36. Schram, *op. cit.*, and interviews.

37. *Ibid.*

38. Minutes of the Ford Motor Company, in *Board and Tax Appeals Transcript*, p. 425.

39. *Ibid.*

40. A. R. Malcomson, interview, June 23, 1941; also Mrs. James Couzens, interviews.

41. Anderson, *op. cit.*

CHAPTER VIII. *The Business Manager*

1. *Detroit Times*, December 3, 1922.

2. See Nevins, *Ford, I*, p. 229, for example, concerning Ford's appreciation of C. Harold Wills' "severity"; also Marquis' *Henry Ford, An Interpretation* (1923), in many ways perhaps still the best study of Ford the man. Pertinent, too, of course, is the relationship between Ford and Harry Bennett, among others, after Couzens left. See Bennett's remarkable story, *We Never Called Him Henry*. Also Robert Coghlan's superlative piece in *Life*, February 28, 1955.

3. See Nevins, *Ford, I*, p. 503; also Marquis.

4. B. C. Forbes, "Why Multimillionnaire Couzens Quit Business," in *Forbes Magazine*, December 1922.

5. Couzens interview, *Philadelphia Public Ledger*, December 4, 1922, and Forbes, *op. cit.*

6. Vernon Fry, interview with author, June 1941.

7. *My Life and Work*, p. 56.

8. Anderson, *op. cit.*

9. *Ford Times*, July 1, 1908, p. 8; in Nevins, *Ford, I*, p. 214.

10. Stipulation on Ford history, *Board of Tax Appeals, Transcript*, pp. 424–25.

11. *New York Times*, October 14, 1915.

12. McManus, *op. cit.*, p. 20.

13. Quaife, *op. cit.*, p. 105.

14. Couzens to J. W. Anderson, "Statement of Business, October 1, 1903."

15. *Detroit News*, January 23, 1937.

16. McManus, *op. cit.*, p. 20.

17. Stipulation, *Board of Tax Appeals Transcript*, pp. 425 and 435; also Nevins, *op. cit.*, p. 262.

18. McManus, *op. cit.*, p. 25; also B. C. Forbes interview; see also Garet Garrett, *The Wild Wheel*, 1952, p. 113, among the most perceptive works on Ford, although quite subjective.

19. Testimony of P. E. Martin, *Transcript*, pp. 846–50.

20. Stipulation, *Transcript*, p. 426.
21. Norval Hawkins, *Transcript*, p. 1610.
22. *Ford Times*, July 1, 1908, p. 8.
23. Garrett, *The Wild Wheel*, p. 113. See also, for Couzens' role in the company, Charles E. Sorensen, *My Forty Years with Ford*, pp. 36, 43, 84, 86–88, and 153.

CHAPTER IX. *The Cloud*

1. *Ford Times*, July, 1908.
2. Couzens notebook, 1906.
3. Bennett, interview, *op. cit.*
4. *Detroit News Tribune*, October 19, 1915.
5. James Couzens, "What I Learned About Business From Ford," *System* magazine, September 1921, p. 261.
6. *Ibid.*
7. *Ibid.*
8. *Ford Times*, September 15, 1908.
9. Couzens, *op. cit.*, p. 262.
10. Schram, *op. cit.*, p. 252.
11. Article by Oscar E. Hewitt, in the *Chicago Herald*, October 23, 1916.
12. Milton R. McRae, *Forty Years of Newspaperdom*.
13. *Detroit News*, October 19, 1915.
14. Ida M. Tarbell, manuscript of planned book on Ford Motor Company, loaned to author, 1942.
15. *Transcript*, p. 1281.
16. George D. Selden, in *Rochester Alumni-Alumnae Review*, February–March 1940, p. 16.
17. *Ibid.*
18. Patent No. 549,160, U.S. Patent Office.
19. George Byers, in *The Patent Office Journal*, October 1940, p. 725.
20. See Nevins, *Ford, I,* 98n. and 284ff., and other sections, for a superb description and analysis of the Selden patent matter, the best and most complete ever done. For the text of the licensing agreement, a curious document, see appendix of Epstein, *The Automobile Industry*.
21. Quaife, *op. cit.*, p. 116.
22. Anderson testimony, *Board of Tax Appeals, Transcript*, pp. 643–44.
23. *Transcript*, pp. 643–44.
24. In *Detroit Saturday Night*, quoted by Glasscock, p. 141.
25. *Transcript*, p. 1284; also Glasscock, p. 78.
26. Glasscock, *op. cit.*
27. McManus, *op. cit.*, p. 56. It should be noted that nearly everyone who writes about the decision to fight the Selden patent gives credit for the decision to a different person. Quaife, in *Anderson*, seems to give it to Anderson. Nevins, in *Ford*, seems to give it to Ford and Ralzemond A. Parker. Burlingame is quite neutral on this point. The McManus and Beasley account is used here as most objective, based, in the author's judgment, on the best sources. The final decision, of course, was a cooperative one.

CHAPTER X. *The Realignment*

1. Anderson testimony, *Transcript*, p. 1284.
2. *American Encyclopedia of the Automobile*, pp. 176–77.
3. Frederic R. Coudert, one of the attorneys, letter to author; and Mrs. James Couzens, interview. For watching carefully the expenses of some of the lawyers, Couzens not surprisingly incurred the antipathy of one or two, as witness the slurring comments about his role in the patent case attributed to a son of one lawyer, in Nevins, *Ford, I,* p. 424n.
4. *The Automobile Review and Automobile News*, October 15, 1903, p. 156.
5. *Transcript*, pp. 674–76.
6. Appel, *The Business Biography of John Wanamaker*, p. 155.

7. Couzens article in *System, op. cit.,* p. 263.
8. *Harper's,* March 16, 1907.
9. *Ford Times,* June 15, 1908.
10. *Transcript,* p. 755.
11. Rackham testimony, *Transcript.*
12. A. R. Malcomson, interview, June 23, 1941.
13. McManus, *op. cit.,* p. 20.
14. Couzens to Madeleine C. Yaw, January 30, 1928, quoting Ford.
15. Mrs. James Couzens, interview, June 27, 1941; also A. R. Malcomson, June 23, 1941.
16. A. R. Malcomson, interview, June 23, 1941; also C. H. Bennett, interview.
17. McRae, *Forty Years in Newspaperdom,* p. 393.
18. *Detroit News,* May 23, 1917.
19. *Ibid.*
20. Benson, *op. cit.,* p. 116.
21. Minutes, Ford Motor Company, September 9, 1905, in *Transcript.*
22. Board of Tax Appeals, *Petitioner's Statement of Facts,* p. 47.
23. *Ford Times,* August 17, 1904.
24. McManus, *op. cit.,* p. 144. There is a suggestion, in Nevins, *Ford, I,* p. 247, that there was some basis for dissatisfaction over the quality of work done by the Dodge brothers, implying that this was a factor in the Ford Manufacturing Co. scheme. This is certainly debatable, as the Dodge Brothers, then as later, were universally known to be dependable manufacturers. They would be criticized, but not for the quality of their products.
25. Vernon Fry, interview; See also testimony by Norval Hawkins, *Transcript,* pp. 1960–61, and Sorensen, *My Forty Years with Ford,* pp. 72–78.
26. Minutes of the Ford Motor Company, November 17, 1905.
27. Michigan Corporations and Securities Commission records, November 29, 1905.
28. *Ibid.*
29. Malcomson's letter in minutes of Ford Motor Company, December 22, 1905; also in *Detroit News,* February 22, 1927.
30. Minutes for December 22, 1905.
31. *Automobile Magazine,* May 1906, p. 354.
32. Sinsabaugh, *Who Me?,* p. 222.
33. A. R. Malcomson, interview, June 23, 1941.
34. See Nevins, *Ford, I,* pp. 278 and 330.
35. Minutes of Ford Motor Company, quoted in *Detroit News,* February 22, 1937; also interview of Fry by author, July 8, 1941.
36. In 1955, the Ford Motor Company, under Henry Ford II, and in connection with the Ford Foundation, for the first time became a public corporation, with Ford shares available to the public.
37. Ford to Couzens, cablegram, November 19, 1906, in Couzens papers.
38. Couzens to Judge Neil, interview, July 27, 1926.
39. Mrs. Couzens, interview; see also Nevins, *Ford, I,* generally.
40. *System, op. cit.,* p. 262.
41. See Sorensen, *My Forty Years with Ford,* pp. 36, 43–44, 86–88.

CHAPTER XI. *The Money-Making Machine, II*

1. Gibbons, *John Wanamaker,* II, pp. 122 and 128.
2. Testimony, Frank W. Blair, president, Union Trust Co., in U.S. Senate Committee on Banking and Currency, *Transcript of Hearings, 73d Congress, 2d Sess.,* p. 4766.
3. *Ford Times,* December 1, 1908.
4. See Sward, *The Legend of Henry Ford,* pp. 22ff.
5. *Ford Times,* October 15, 1908, p. 10.
6. *Ibid.,* 14.
7. *Ibid.,* September 15, 1908.
8. Crowther interview of Couzens, *System, op. cit.,* p. 264.

9. Minutes of April 22, 1907.

10. *Transcript,* U.S. Board of Tax Appeals, pp. 430 and 440.

11. Fred H. Colvin, *Sixty Years With Men and Machines,* p. 131.

12. *Electric Vehicle Co., et al., v. C. A. Duerr & Co., et al.,* 172 Fed. 923, 1909.

13. *Ibid,* 935.

14. *Columbia Motor Car Co., et al., v. C. A. Duerr & Co., et al.,* 184 Fed. 893, 1911.

15. Board of Tax Appeals, *Transcript,* pp. 430 and 440.

16. *Petition on Appeal,* Board of Tax Appeals, p. 34.

17. *Ibid.*

18. *Transcript,* p. 1156; also see Sward, *op. cit.,* p. 44.

19. *Transcript,* pp. 819 and 1705.

20. See Burlingame, *Backgrounds of Power,* p. 256.

21. *Detroit News,* November 22, 1913.

22. Testimony before Judge Harry B. Keidan, August 22, 1933, in one-man grand-jury investigation of the Detroit bank crisis.

23. Couzens to A. E. Stilwell, March 1, 1911.

24. *Toronto Daily News,* October 21, 1915.

CHAPTER XII. *The Crisis*

1. Frank L. Klingensmith, interview. Klingensmith became vice-president of the company in 1915.

2. Transcript of Couzens' interview with Neil, *op. cit.*

3. See Seltzer, *A Financial History of the American Automobile Industry,* pp. 34–35; McManus, *op. cit.,* p. 68; Epstein, *op. cit.,* p. 225; Pound, *The Turning Wheel, A History of General Motors;* Kennedy, *op. cit.,* p. 49; Glasscock, p. 136; Briscoe, in *The Detroit Saturday Night,* June 1908; Richards, *The Last Billionaire,* and Simonds, *op. cit.,* pp. 114 and 123. The facts about the contemplated sale of the Ford Motor Company are corroborated by William C. Durant, in material from his memoirs, loaned to the author; and by Herbert L. Satterlee in letters to the author, 1942. The references cited in the Ford biography by Simonds, a Ford publicist, may be accepted as confirmation finally coming from Henry Ford himself, in 1943.

4. Herbert L. Satterlee to author, letter, March 12, 1942. He later helped organize General Motors for Durant.

5. Durant memorandum, *op. cit.*

6. Couzens notebook, 1908.

7. Satterlee and also Seltzer, *A Financial History of the American Automobile Industry,* pp. 34–35.

8. Durant, *Memoirs,* excerpt, *op. cit.*

9. Concerning W. C. Durant, for a good though short account, see David L. Cohen, *Combustion on Wheels,* pp. 112ff.

10. McManus, *op. cit.,* p. 72.

11. Durant, *Memoirs,* excerpt, *op. cit.*

12. *Ibid.*

13. Couzens notebook, October 5, 1909.

14. Durant, *Memoirs, op. cit.*

15. William C. Richards, *The Last Billionaire,* New York, 1948, p. 350.

16. Durant, *Memoirs, op. cit.*

17. *Ibid.*

18. Richards, *The Last Billionaire,* p. 350. Richards, an associate editor of the *Detroit Free Press,* was quite friendly with Henry Ford.

19. Minutes of the General Motors Corporation, quoted by Seltzer, *op. cit.,* p. 36.

20. *Ibid.*

21. Couzens notebook, October 24, 1909.

22. McManus, *op. cit.,* p. 72.

23. Durant, *Memoirs, op. cit.*

24. Harry B. Harper, interview, November 23, 1940.

25. Player to Couzens, December 24, 1934, and Hay, interview.

26. T. J. Hay interview, August 13, 1940.

27. See Keith Sward, *The Legend of Henry Ford*, pp. 43ff.

28. Malcolm Bingay, for example, in *Saturday Evening Post*, June 29, 1940.

29. Mrs. W. R. Yaw (Madeleine Couzens) to author, interview.

30. Couzens to Madeleine Couzens, May 11, 1925.

31. *Ibid.*, April 1, 1925.

32. *Ibid.*

33. Couzens to Edward W. Alexander, December 7, 1915.

34. Neil interview, *op. cit.*

35. Couzens to R. L. Jobling, October 12, 1912.

36. See Fay L. Faurote, "The New Ford Line-up," *Engineering Magazine*, January 16, 1916.

37. Garet Garrett, in *Everybody's Magazine*, April 1914.

38. Nevins, *Ford, I*, p. 573.

39. John C. Lodge, interview, July 3, 1941.

40. Couzens to J. H. Neil, interview, *op. cit.*; Frank L. Klingensmith, interview with author, June 30, 1941. Mrs. Ford's attitude toward Couzens is confirmed in Sorensen, *op. cit.*, p. 15.

41. Frank L. Klingensmith, interview.

42. Nevins, *Ford, I, op. cit.*

43. Couzens interview with Judge Neil, *op. cit.*

44. *Ibid.*

45. *Ibid.*

46. *Ibid.*, also Richards, *The Last Billionaire*, pp. 244–45.

47. Charles W. Duke, in *Philadelphia Public Ledger*, July 2, 1933.

48. B. C. Forbes, *op. cit.*

49. See *Reply Brief on Behalf of James Couzens*, U.S. Board of Tax Appeals, May 12, 1927, prepared by Arthur J. Lacy and Clarence Wilcox, pp. 66–67. Subjoined to the statements quoted from this brief was the following significant comment: "Eliminating Henry Ford, it is reasonable to believe that this program (of expansion) would have been carried out exactly as planned. Henry Ford was not in charge of that expansion program, although he agreed with the rest as to its desirability. The minutes show that it was projected and effectuated by James Couzens and others acted under his direction."

50. *Detroit News*, December 30, 1921.

CHAPTER XIII. *The Five-Dollar-A-Day Plan*

1. Mrs. James Couzens, letter to author, July 24, 1942.

2. Couzens to Edward W. Alexander, December 29, 1912.

3. Couzens notebook, entry for July 24, 1912.

4. Nevins, *Ford, I*, 581n.

5. Couzens to Chapin, December 18 and December 31, 1912, and January 10, 1913. Excerpts in J. C. Long, *Roy D. Chapin*, pp. 109ff.

6. Jay G. Hayden, a history of the Detroit railway commission, in mss., loaned to author.

7. Hayden, mss.; *Detroit Free Press*, August 4, 1913.

8. Forbes, *op. cit.*

9. Villard, "The Unique Millionaire," *Forum Magazine*, January 1937.

10. Belle C. and Fola La Follette, *Robert M. La Follette*, p. 352.

11. Gibbons, *op. cit.*, p. 258.

12. Board of Commerce *Minutes*, 1912.

13. *Chicago Tribune*, June 2, 1935, article by Willard Edwards.

14. Mrs. Couzens, interview; and Keith Sward, *op. cit.*, p. 50.

15. *Highland Park Times*, October 6, 1916.

16. From a stenographic copy of Miss Tarbell's notes, as dictated on a record for John S. Phillips, editor of *The American Magazine*, May 28, 1915. Loaned to author by Miss Tarbell, March 20, 1942. Also her manuscript of chapter III of unfinished book, "Making Men and Fords," loaned to author, 1941.

17. James Couzens, article in *Michigan Manufacturer and Financial Record*, October 26, 1918.

18. John R. Lee, "The So-called Profit Sharing System in the Ford Plant," *The Annals of the American Academy of Political and Social Science,* May 1916, Vol. LXI, p. 299.

19. *Ibid.*

20. Tarbell, *op. cit.*

21. *Ibid.*

22. Tarbell, *op. cit.,* also *Detroit News,* November 25, 1914; also McManus, *op. cit.,* p. 154.

23. B. C. Forbes, "Multimillionaire Couzens Tells Why He Quit Business," *Forbes Magazine,* December 22, 1922.

24. Tarbell, *op. cit.*

25. McManus, *op. cit.,* p. 156.

26. *Chicago Tribune,* June 2, 1935.

27. Interview with Henry Nimmo, *Detroit Saturday Night,* December, 1914.

28. Margaret Moors Marshall in *New York Evening World,* December 4, 1922, quoting Couzens.

29. Tarbell, *op. cit.,* and McManus, *op. cit.;* also *Chicago Tribune,* June 2, 1935.

30. See Simonds, *op. cit.,* p. 138.

31. Theodore McManus and Norman Beasley, *Men, Money and Motors,* pp. 157–58. Frank L. Klingensmith, vice-president of the Ford Motor Company, to author, March 5, 1942: "*Men, Money and Motors,* by McManus and Beasley, is an absolutely authenticated book, every word in it having been proofread and approved by representatives of the various companies mentioned. While the incident of the wage raise is told in narrative form, the facts are there and I will stand by every word that Beasley wrote. When it was written (1929) the time had not been so long, and the facts were fresh in our minds, and I personally O.K.'d the article. I don't care what Stidger (author of *Henry Ford; The Man and His Motives,* 1923) or anyone else says!" Ordway Tead, editor of Harper & Brothers economics books, who published *Men, Money and Motors,* to author, October 7, 1942: "I never saw or heard of it being challenged."

32. Couzens to *New York World,* December 4, 1922; and Ida M. Tarbell, notes.

33. Tarbell notes; also McManus, *op. cit.,* p. 158; Forbes, *op. cit.;* also Sward, *op. cit.,* p. 51.

34. Pipp, *Henry Ford, Both Sides of Him,* p. 48. Pipp quotes Ford as having said that he (Ford) first had the idea of increasing wages in order to step up production, to increase profits, and that he finally decided to make the basic scale $4.84, when Couzens suggested the five-dollar rate.

35. McManus, *op. cit.,* p. 158. In the lawsuit of *Henry Ford v. The Tribune Company, et al* (1919), Transcript of Record, pp. 2713–2716, John R. Lee, first head of the Ford "sociological department," testified under oath: "Mr. Couzens, as I remember it, finally mentioned the $5-a-day and Mr. Ford readily agreed with him." He also testified: "Mr. Couzens had been urging him (Ford) largely; I think it was a result of his urging that Mr. Ford came to this profit-sharing idea." John Dodge, in the same law suit, agreed. Transcript kindly loaned to author by the *Chicago Tribune's* law firm in Chicago, Kirkland, Fleming, Green, Martin, and Ellis, October, 1942.

36. *Minutes of Ford Motor Company,* for January 5, 1915, quoted in Board of Tax Appeals, *Transcript.*

37. Flynn Wayne, "Couzens: A Master Builder in Business Efficiency," *National Magazine,* September 1915.

38. Garrett, "Henry Ford's Experiment in Good Will," *Everybody's,* April 1914, p. 462.

39. Excerpts from pamphlet by Ford Motor Company, "Helpful Hints and Advice to Employees," in 1915.

40. See Sward, *op. cit.,* pp. 58ff.

41. *Detroit Saturday Night,* January 1916.

42. Sward, *op. cit.,* p. 52.

43. Couzens to William Robins, February 23, 1916.

44. Couzens to William Robins, November 15, 1915; Sward, *op. cit.,* p. 51.

45. A great many versions of the birth of the five-dollar-a-day plan have been published, some of them cited in the footnotes, but most are unreliable. The author is

satisfied that the version here given—one backed by sworn testimony in several court proceedings, is the correct one. Couzens, of course, explained the differing versions when he said that it was the Ford company policy, in which he had participated, that Ford was to get the credit exclusively as a matter of company advertising and public relations. In all probability, this particular Ford myth will never die. Two books on Ford published in 1954, Burlingame's *Henry Ford* and Nevins' *Ford, I,* may help dispel the myth. Nevins, in a footnote on page 532, makes an interesting comment: "After the lapse of forty years, the precise facts about this fateful conference (when the wage scale was adopted) are irrecoverable." In 1956 Charles E. Sorensen, in *My Forty Years with Ford,* presented a version giving the full credit to Henry Ford, pp. 5 and 136–40, but it suffers from defects common to other versions based upon one perspective.

CHAPTER XIV. *The Final Break*

1. Klingensmith to Couzens, February 6, 1914.
2. *Ibid.,* March 27, 1914.
3. See Sward, *op. cit.,* pp. 54–55.
4. Garet Garrett, "A World That Was," *Saturday Evening Post,* June 8, 1940.
5. Alfred P. Sloan, "Adventures of A White Collar Man," *Saturday Evening Post,* August 31, 1940.
6. Garrett, *The Wild Wheel,* p. 9.
7. Garrett, *Saturday Evening Post,* June 8, 1940.
8. McManus, *op. cit.,* p. 164.
9. Couzens to E. D. Stair, January 8, 1914.
10. *Ibid.*
11. *Detroit Times and Tribune,* December 22, 1914.
12. *Detroit Labor News,* November 1, 1918.
13. *Detroit News,* November 25, 1914.
14. Simonds, *op. cit.,* p. 147.
15. Henry S. Morgan, interview; also letter to author, August 21, 1942; see Richards, *The Last Billionaire,* p. 244.
16. Copy in Couzens' papers.
17. Morgan, interview.
18. Mrs. James Couzens, interview.
19. Klingensmith, interview.
20. *Chicago Tribune,* June 7, 1919. See also Nevins, *Ford, II,* pp. 26ff., for Ford's peace views and anti-war activities.
21. *Toronto Daily News,* October 21, 1915.
22. Couzens to Glenn Frank, May 2, 1917.
23. McRae to Couzens, November 14, 1911; Couzens to McRae, October 19, 1915; November 19, 1915. Also, McRae, *Forty Years of Newspaperdom,* p. 394.
24. Klingensmith, interview, June 30, 1941.
25. Jay G. Hayden, interview, April 17, 1940.
26. Couzens to Louis B. Block, October 14, 1915.
27. Pipp, *Henry Ford, Both Sides of Him,* pp. 14–15; see also Sward, *op. cit.,* pp. 64–65, Richards, *op. cit.,* pp. 70–71; and Nevins, *Ford, II,* pp. 10–11, 23–24.

CHAPTER XV. *The Job-Seeker Again*

1. *Toronto Evening Record,* December 6, 1915.
2. Hutchins, *op. cit.,* p. 244.
3. Catlin, *The Story of Detroit,* pp. 633–72.
4. *Detroit News-Tribune,* Oct. 31, 1915.
5. Catlin, *op. cit.*
6. Jay G. Hayden, manuscript, *op. cit.*
7. Couzens to McRae, May 6, 1929.
8. Couzens to Townsend, June 15, 1916.
9. Couzens to Warren, September 27, 1916.
10. *Detroit News-Tribune,* June 11, 1916.
11. William J. Norton, address at Memorial Services for James Couzens, Traverse

City, November 1, 1936. Published by the Kiwanis Club, Traverse City; also Catlin, *The Story of Detroit*, pp. 672–73.

12. *Detroit News*, December 22, 1924.
13. *Ibid.*, September 28, 1916; also Catlin, pp. 673.

CHAPTER XVI. *The Police Commissioner*

1. *The Story of Detroit*, p. 673.
2. *Detroit News*, October 2, 1916.
3. *Detroit Saturday Night*, October 9, 1916.
4. *Detroit Times*, October 6, 1916.
5. *Grand Rapids News*, September 30, 1916.
6. *Detroit News*, November 6, 1924.
7. *Ibid.*, October 13, 1916.
8. Charles W. Wood, "He Had Millions but Wanted a Job," *Collier's*, August 5, 1922.
9. *Detroit Free Press*, May 19, 1917.
10. *Detroit News*, March 27, 1917.
11. *Detroit Free Press*, April 17, 1917.
12. Barry, *The Outlook*, December 20, 1923.
13. Hard, William, "Coming: Couzens of Detroit," *Hearst's International*, May 1922.
14. William J. Norton, interview.
15. Frank Couzens, interview.
16. *Detroit Times*, December 5, 1916.
17. *Detroit Journal*, March 23, 1917.
18. *New York Times*, June 2, 1917.
19. *Detroit News*, June 2, 1917.
20. See Ray Tucker, *Sons of the Wild Jackass*, pp. 239–40.
21. *Detroit News*, February 25, 1918.
22. *New York Sun*, March 2, 1918.
23. *Ibid.*; also see Richards, *The Last Billionaire*, pp. 71–72.
24. *Detroit Free Press*, February 20, 1918.
25 *Detroit News*, February 20, 1918.

CHAPTER XVII. *The Odd Candidate*

1. McRae to Couzens, November 10, 1916. In Malcolm Bingay's *Of Me I Sing* (1948) there is a prejudiced but interesting sketch of McRae. See McRae's own biography, *Forty Years in Newspaperdom* (1924).
2. Couzens to McRae, November 16, 1916.
3. *Ibid.*, March 5, 1918.
4. *Detroit News*, April 1, 1918.
5. William Alden Smith to Couzens, April 5, 1918.
6. *Detroit News*, June 4, 1918. Concerning Ford's candidacy for U.S. Senator, *see* Nevins, *Ford, II*, pp. 114–124.
7. See Catlin, *op. cit.*, also Leo Donovan of the *Detroit Free Press* in *Our Fair City* (ed. by Robert S. Allen), p. 153.
8. Mrs. E. Roy Pelletier, interview, July 10, 1941.
9. *Detroit News*, December 22, 1922.
10. *Ibid.*, July 16, 1918.
11. *Detroit News*, July 9, 1918.
12. *Detroit Free Press*, December 14, 1895, quoted by O'Geran, *A History of the Detroit Street Railways*, pp. 153–55.
13. Detroit papers, August 14, 1918.
14. *Detroit News*, August 14, 1918.

CHAPTER XVIII. *The Strong Mayor*

1. Couzens to Gertrude Beeks, May 4, 1915.
2. C. H. Haberkorn, Jr., interview.
3. Couzens to Dr. Hugo A. Freund, December 3, 1924.

4. *New York Times,* December 10, 1922.
5. William Alden Smith to Couzens, September 3, 1919; Couzens to Smith, September 9, 1919.
6. William Hard, *op. cit.*
7. Mabel Ford, his secretary, interview, July 2, 1941.
8. William Hard, *op. cit.*
9. *Detroit Times,* March 30, 1921; *New York Times,* March 31, 1921.
10. *Detroit News,* January 31, 1922.
11. *Detroit News,* June 21, 1919.
12. *New York Times,* December 4 and December 8, 1921.
13. Couzens to James Schermerhorn, June 23, 1919.
14. *The Detroiter,* December 4, 1922.
15. Miss Mabel Ford, interview, July 2, 1941.
16. George W. Engel, interview.
17. H. S. Campbell, interview, February 19, 1941.
18. See *Detroit's Government, Report by the Common Council and the Mayor of the City of Detroit,* 1922, p. 73.
19. *Ibid.,* p. 74, and *Detroit News,* October 26, 1921.
20. See Leo Donovan, in *Our Fair City, op. cit.,* pp. 153ff.
21. Angus McSween to Couzens, April 19, 1920.

CHAPTER XIX. *The People's Man*

1. Lloyd Wendt and Herman Kogan, *Big Bill of Chicago,* 1953.
2. See Frederick Lewis Allen, *Since Yesterday,* and Walter Johnson, *William Allen White's America.*
3. *Detroit News,* September 19, 1922.
4. *Detroit News,* September 19, 1922.
5. *New York World,* December 3, 1922.
6. See Frederic L. Paxson, *Postwar Years, Normalcy, 1918–1923,* pp. 229 and 266.
7. Ray Lyman Wilbur and Arthur Mastick Hyde, *The Hoover Policies,* pp. 370–71.
8. Henry S. Morgan, interview.
9. Associated Press Story, Detroit, November 21, 1919.
10. *Detroit News,* November 21, 1919.
11. See F. L. Allen, *Only Yesterday,* and C. Vann Woodward, *Tom Watson, Agrarian Rebel,* for good accounts of the Palmer raids. Also Beard, *Rise of American Civilization,* II, p. 671.
12. Beard, *op. cit.,* II; p. 671.
13. *Detroit News,* January 7, 1920.
14. *Detroit Saturday Night,* January 10, 1920.
15. See Johnson, *William Allen White's America,* p. 323.
16. *Detroit Free Press,* January 15, 1919.

CHAPTER XX. *The Battle For M.O.*

1. Jay G. Hayden, Mss., *op. cit.*
2. E. T. Fitzgerald, interview, July 12, 1941.
3. Jay G. Hayden, Mss., *op. cit.;* Clarence E. Wilcox, then Detroit's Corporation Counsel, interview. The commissioners were Abner Larned, Sidney D. Waldon, and Francis C. McMath.
4. J. Hutchins, *op. cit.,* p. 274.
5. *Detroit News,* October 13, 1915.
6. Original in Couzens papers.
7. Pipp, *Henry Ford, Both Sides of Him,* p. 20.
8. *Detroit News,* April 3, 1919.
9. Hayden, *op. cit.;* see also Sorensen, *op. cit.,* p. 188–89 for Sorensen's side.
10. "Senator Couzens' Metamorphosis from Business Man to Politician," December 30, 1922.
11. *Detroit News,* April 4, 1919.
12. *New York Times,* April 8, 1919.
13. *Detroit News,* June 7, 1919.

14. *New York Times*, June 8, 1919.
15. *Detroit News* and *New York Times*, June 10, 1919.
16. *Detroit News* and *New York Times*, June 12, 1919.
17. *Detroit News*, December 26, 1919, and March 3, 1920.
18. *Ibid.*, March 14, 1920.
19. Clarence E. Wilcox, interview, *op. cit.*, also Hayden, *op. cit.*
20. *Detroit News*, January 6, 1920.
21. Hayden, *op. cit.*
22. *Ibid.*
23. *Ibid.*
24. Couzens to Clarence E. Wilcox, January 17, 1927. See also Garrett, *The Wild Wheel*, p. 120; Burlingame, *Henry Ford*, p. 98; and Quaife, *Anderson*, pp. 139ff.
25. Quaife, *Anderson*, p. 140; also Couzens to Walter H. Bennett, and *New York Times*, September 24, 1918.
26. *Detroit Saturday Night*, November 8, 1919.
27. *Detroit News*, April 7, 1920; see also Catlin, *op. cit.*, pp. 633–34; and Ross C. Schram, "How Detroit Came to Run Its Own Street Cars," a pamphlet.

CHAPTER XXI. *"The Damnable Outrage"*

1. Hayden, *op. cit.*
2. *Detroit Times*, August 17, 1920.
3. *Detroit Times*, January 10, 1921; Hayden, *op. cit.*; also Tucker, pp. 241–42.
4. *Detroit Free Press*, January 27, 1921.
5. *Detroit United Railway, Appt., v. City of Detroit, et al.*, 255 U.S. 171, 1921.
6. *Detroit News*, March 4, 1921.
7. *Ibid.*, August 5, 1921.
8. *Detroit News*, January 2, 1922.
9. *Detroit News*, December 7, 1920.
10. Henry S. Morgan, interview; also Hayden, *op. cit.*
11. *Detroit News*, April 18, 1922.
12. See Catlin, *op. cit.*, pp. 621ff.; an obviously prejudiced and antagonistic view is given by Malcolm W. Bingay in *Detroit Is My Own Home Town* (1946). Bingay and Couzens, once friendly, were engaged in an almost constant feud. With respect to Couzens, Bingay was seldom reliable.

CHAPTER XXII. *The Reward*

1. Charles W. Duke, in *Philadelphia Public Ledger*, June 18, 1922.
2. *Detroit News*, July 27, 1925.
3. *Newberry v. United States*, 256 U.S. 58, 1920; see also Spencer Ervin, *Henry Ford v. Truman Newberry* and Nevins, *Ford*, II, pp. 114–124.
4. George W. Norris, *Fighting Liberal*, pp. 216ff.
5. Spencer Ervin, *op. cit.*; also Paxson, *Postwar Years*, p. 271.
6. Hayden interview.
7. B. C. Forbes, *Forbes Magazine*, December 22, 1922.
8. Charles W. Wood, "He Had Millions, But Wanted a Job," *Collier's*, August 5, 1922.
9. *Detroit News*, June 10, 1922.
10. Forbes, *op. cit.*, December 22, 1922.
11. See Norris, *op. cit.*, p. 216; and Pat Harrison, "Keynote Address, Democratic Convention, 1924," in William A. White, *Politics the Citizen's Business*, p. 246.
12. Couzens to Fred W. Upham, May 16, 1918.
13. *Detroit Times*, November 22, 1922.
14. Ross Schram, Mss., *op. cit.*
15. Couzens to Madeleine Couzens, November 11, 1922.

CHAPTER XXIII. *The One-Man Bloc*

1. NEA News Service, December 26, 1922.
2. See Frederic L. Paxson, *Postwar Years, Normalcy, 1918–1923*, p. 319.
3. *Detroit Times*, December 9, 1922.

4. Senator Arthur Capper, interview.

5. Charles P. Stewart, NEA syndicate story, June 14, 1926.

6. Jay G. Hayden, interview, April 17, 1940.

7. See Charles A. and Mary R. Beard, *America in Midpassage;* also Paxon, *op. cit.;* and Karl Schriftgiesser, *The Gentleman from Massachusetts, Henry Cabot Lodge.*

8. Cordell Hull, *Memoirs,* p. 113. Mr. Hull was then chairman of the Democratic National Committee.

9. See Beard, *op. cit.,* II, pp. 692–93.

10. Norris, *op. cit.,* p. 215.

11. *Literary Digest,* November 23, 1929; also Tucker, *op. cit.*

12. See Samuel Hopkins Adams, *Incredible Era, The Life and Times of Warren Gamaliel Harding;* also William Allen White, *Autobiography,* and his *A Puritan in Babylon, the Story of Calvin Coolidge,* pp. 260–63.

13. *New York Tribune,* March 11, 1923.

14. *Detroit Free Press,* December 8, 1922.

15. *Detroit Times,* March 18, 1923.

16. *St. Louis Censor,* January 4, 1923.

17. Beard, *op. cit.,* II, p. 694. For a good, though colored summary of the Ship Subsidy Bill, see Senator Pat Harrison's keynote speech at the Democratic National Convention, 1924, reprinted in William Allen White, *Politics: The Citizen's Business,* p. 242. See also Paxon, *op. cit.,* pp. 351–53.

18. Norris, *op. cit.,* pp. 328ff.

19. December 12, 1922.

20. December 14, 1922.

21. Norris, *op. cit.,* p. 261; also Alfred Lief, *Democracy's Norris;* Simonds, *op. cit.,* pp. 197–98; Keith Sward, *op. cit.,* pp. 127–31, and Nevins, *Ford, II,* pp. 305–311.

22. Claudius O. Johnson, "George William Norris," in *The American Politician* (J. Salter, ed.), p. 103.

23. C. H. Haberkorn, Jr., interview.

24. *Detroit Free Press,* December 7, 1922; see also Norris, *op. cit.,* p. 249.

25. Couzens to Malcolm Stewart, June 5, 1925.

26. *Detroit Free Press,* December 7, 1922.

27. Charles P. Stewart, February 13, 1930.

28. Richard Barry, "Newberry's Successor; A Study of Senator Couzens," *The Outlook,* December 10, 1922.

29. *Congressional Record,* Vol. 64, p. 2905.

30. *Ibid.*

31. John P. Frank, *Mr. Justice Black, The Man and His Opinions,* p. 48.

32. *Congressional Record,* Vol. 64, pp. 2911–15; also newspapers, February 3, 1923.

33. *Congressional Record,* Vol. 64, pp. 2914–16.

34. February 3, 1923.

35. *Labor,* January 12, 1923; also *New York Tribune,* January 13, 1923.

36. Associated Press story, January 27, 1923.

37. *New York Times,* January 27, 1923.

38. *Kansas City Star,* January 30, 1923.

39. *Detroit Times,* March 18, 1923.

40. Senator George W. Norris, interview with author, April 12, 1940; also see La Follette, *op. cit.,* p. 1090.

41. White, *A Puritan in Babylon,* p. 230; see Samuel G. Blythe, "A Calm Review of a Calm Man," *Saturday Evening Post,* July 28, 1923; and Will Irwin, *The Making of a Reporter,* pp. 386–405.

42. Mrs. James Couzens, interview.

43. Walter L. Dunham, Detroit banker, interview, July 1941.

44. Couzens' notebook, February 7, 1923; also *Philadelphia Record,* February 5, 1923.

45. Harding to Couzens, February 26, 1923.

46. Couzens to Harding, February 27, 1923.

47. Warren G. Harding to Couzens, March 1, 1923.

48. White, *op. cit.*, p. 295.
49. *Detroit News*, March 5, 1923.
50. *Detroit News*, July 17, 1923.
51. James B. Morrow, "Couzens, Radical—and Rich," *Nation's Business*, June, 1923.
52. Anon., "Who's Who—and Why—Serious and Frivolous Facts About the Great and Near Great," *Saturday Evening Post*, April 21, 1923.

CHAPTER XXIV. *The Plain-Speaking Statesman*

1. Garrett, in *The Wild Wheel*, gives an interesting account of the Ford Presidential boom, pp. 159ff. See also Burlingame, *Henry Ford*, p. 123, and especially Nevins, *Ford, II*, pp. 300–305.
2. *New York Times*, October 28, 1923.
3. Norris, *op. cit.*, pp. 256ff.
4. *Detroit Times*, June 25, 1923.
5. See Mark Sullivan, *Our Times, The Twenties*, p. 246; Adams, *Incredible Era*, p. 369; Pringle, *Taft*, p. 982.
6. *Detroit News*, July 8, 1923.
7. *Detroit News*, July 25, 1923.
8. *New York Times*, July 10, 1923; *New York Herald*, July 4, 1923.
9. *Christian Science Monitor*, July 7, 1923.
10. *New York Post*, October 13, 1923.
11. *Ibid.*
12. Couzens to Calvin Coolidge, November 23, 1923.
13. See Claude Bowers, *Beveridge and the Progressive Era;* and Pringle, *op. cit.*, pp. 1012ff. and 1060.
14. *New York Evening Post*, October 13, 1923.
15. Couzens to Vandenberg, June 11, 1924.
16. Vandenberg to Couzens, June 2, 8, and 12, 1923.
17. About a year later, Couzens did drop his support of the proposed La Follette amendment, but was never happy over the old arrangement. Couzens to Vandenberg, July 22, 1924.
18. Couzens to Willis J. Abbott, November 21, 1923.
19. *Detroit Times*, November 1, 1923.
20. Couzens' notebook, October 29, 1923.
21. C. Bascom Slemp, *The Mind of the President*, p. 227, and Garrett, *The Wild Wheel*, p. 167.
22. Garrett, *op. cit.*, concerning Coolidge on Muscle Shoals and also Ford's plan; see C. Herman Pritchett, *The Tennessee Valley Authority*, pp. 8ff., and also Nevins, *Ford, II*, pp. 305–311.

CHAPTER XXV. *The Millionaires' War*

1. Quoted by Couzens in a letter to *New York Times*, November 13, 1923.
2. *Ibid.*
3. *Detroit News*, November 3, 1923.
4. Paul Kerns in *The American Politician* (edited by Salter), p. 10; see Thomas L. Stokes, *Chip Off My Shoulder*, p. 177.
5. White, *Politics: The Citizen's Business*, p. 36.
6. See Harvey T. O'Connor, *Mellon's Millions, a Biography of a Fortune;* also Philip Love, *Andrew Mellon*.
7. Mellon to Couzens, January 5, 1923, in *New York Times*, January 6, 1923.
8. Couzens to Vandenberg, August 1924.
9. David Lawrence, column, April 14, 1924.
10. *New York Herald Tribune*, March 19, 1925.
11. *Ibid.*
12. Couzens to Mellon, January 10, 1923.
13. Mellon to Couzens, in *New York Times*, January 9, 1923.
14. Couzens to Charles L. Brownell, May 17, 1923.

15. *Congressional Record*, May 27, 1936, p. 8005.
16. *New York Times*, January 13 and 19, 1924.
17. Couzens to Mellon, January 12, 1924, in *New York Times*, January 13, 1924.
18. Walter R. Dorsey, interview, April 1940.
19. Jay C. Hayden, interview, April 1940.
20. *Congressional Record*, February 21, 1924.
21. Frank Kent, "Couzens of Michigan," *American Mercury*, May 1927.
22. *Congressional Record*, March 12, 1924.
23. See *Congressional Record*, March 22, 1928, pp. 5148ff; and Kent, *op. cit.*, pp. 52ff.
24. Mrs. James Couzens, interview, 1943.
25. *New York Times*, April 11, 1924, *passim;* see also George H. Haynes, *The Senate of the United States, Its History and Practice*, p. 561. Concerning Heney, see La Follette, *Robert M. La Follette.*
26. Gifford Pinchot, interview with author in Washington, 1941.
27. *New York Times*, April 8, 1924.
28. *Ibid.*, April 15, 1924.
29. *Congressional Record*, April 12, 1924.
30. *Congressional Record*, April 12, 1924.
31. *Ibid.*, p. 6194; also *New York Times*, April 12, 1924; Stokes, *op. cit.*, pp. 175–77; and Tucker, *op. cit.*, pp. 231–32.
32. Pringle, *Taft, op. cit.*, p. 1020.
33. *Congressional Record*, pp. 6194–95; also George H. Haynes, *The Senate of the United States*, p. 982.
34. See Rixey Smith and Norman Beasley, *Carter Glass, a Biography*, pp. 252–57.
35. Couzens' notebook, March 25, 1924, and *passim.*
36. Syndicated column, April 16, 1924.
37. Earl Davis of Detroit was substituted for Heney.
38. Senate Report 27, 69th Congress, 1st Session, 3 parts, "*Investigation of Bureau of Internal Revenue, Pursuant to Senate Resolution 68*," 1926. See also *Congressional Record*, March 22, 1929, pp. 5149ff., for Couzens' comments on reports.
39. See *New York Times*, December 11, 1925.
40. *Ibid.*, January 13, 1925.
41. *Ibid.*, and Oliver Clarkson and Ernest Sutherland Bates, *Hearst, Lord of San Simeon*, p. 299; also see *Congressional Record*, March 22, 1928, p. 5149, concerning the case of William Boyce Thompson, Republican leader.
42. Wilbur and Hyde, *The Hoover Policies*, p. 536; see also Kent, *op. cit.*, pp. 176–77.
43. See George Haynes, *The Senate of the United States*, pp. 313–15; and Tucker, *op. cit.*, p. 234.
44. See *Congressional Record*, March 9, 1925, pp. 59ff. and Thomas L. Stokes, *op. cit.*, pp. 176–77.
45. *New York Herald Tribune*, February 11, 1927. Senator Watson denied this in a letter to author, October 11, 1940, but the facts are against him. See also Kent in *American Mercury*, May 1927, pp. 50–51, and Quaife, *Anderson*, iii, ff. and p. 137.
46. See statement by Joseph E. Davies, U.S. Board of Tax Appeals, *Transcript*, I, pp. 23–24; also *New York Herald Tribune*, February 11, 1927; and *Detroit Free Press*, February 13, 1927.
47. See *Transcript*, U.S. Board of Appeals, pp. 2662–65; pp. 2690–91.
48. See *New York Times*, May 9, 1929; *Detroit News*, May 8, 1928.
49. Tucker, *op. cit.*, pp. 232–33.

CHAPTER XXVI. *"The La Folletteite!"*

1. *Detroit News*, March 18, 1931.
2. Couzens to Alfred Sleight, Sturgis, Michigan, August 26, 1924.
3. *Saginaw News Courier*, August 4, 1924.
4. James Couzens, address, "La Follette, The Greatest American of the Age," in *Brotherhood of Locomotive Firemen and Enginemen's Magazine*, September 1925, pp.

216ff.; see also, for an estimate of La Follette, William B. Hesseltine, "Robert Marion La Follette and the Principles of Americanism," in *Wisconsin Magazine of History*, Vol. XXXI, March 1948, pp. 261ff. See also W. A. White's contemporary estimate, *Politics: The Citizen's Business*, pp. 122ff. Also Bela and Fola La Follette's biography, *op. cit.*

5. *Detroit Times*, June 5, 1924.
6. Vandenberg to Couzens, July 7, 1924; Couzens to Vandenberg, July 8, 1924.
7. *Detroit News*, July 5, 1924.
8. Norris to Couzens, July 12, 1924.
9. Johnson to Couzens, July 10, 1924.
10. Johnson to Couzens, July 12, 1924.
11. July 19, 1924.
12. Couzens to Vandenberg, July 8, 1924; *Detroit News*, July 7, 1924.
13. James H. Shideler, "The La Follette Progressive Party Campaign of 1924," *Wisconsin Magazine of History*, Vol. XXXIII, June 1950, p. 450; also White, *op. cit.*, p. 307.
14. Couzens to Vandenberg, September 5, 1924; also Couzens' notation, "Telephoned him September 5th saying not an issue and could not say now what I would do," on Vandenberg-to-Morgan telegram, September 5, 1924.
15. Vandenberg to Couzens, September 6, 1924.
16. Couzens to Vandenberg, September 5, 1924.
17. Couzens to Vandenberg, September 8, 1924.
18. *Detroit News*, August 21, 1924.
19. Couzens to Vandenberg, September 12, 1924.

CHAPTER XXVII. *The Critic of Coolidge*

1. Couzens to Vandenberg, August 29, 1924.
2. Text in *Brotherhood of Locomotive Firemen's and Enginemen's Magazine*, September 1925.
3. For the text of Chief Justice Warren's address on La Follette, see *Madison Capital-Times*, June 20, 1955; also story in *New York Times* and other newspapers, same date.
4. Walter Johnson, *William Allen White's America*, p. 398.
5. Norris, *Fighting Liberal*, p. 221.
6. *Congressional Record*, March 7, 1925, pp. 24–31, and pp. 79ff., see also White, *A Puritan in Babylon*, pp. 319ff., and Leif, *Democracy's Norris*, pp. 280ff.
7. *Congressional Record*, March 7, 1925, pp. 18–19.
8. White, *op. cit.*
9. Thomas Sugrue and Edmund W. Starling, *Starling of the White House*, p. 228.
10. White, *op. cit.*, p. 321.
11. *Ibid.*
12. February 21, 1925.
13. *Detroit News*, March 11, 1925.
14. For a good account, see Senator James Watson, *As I Knew Them*, pp. 242–44.
15. *Congressional Record*, March 9, 1925, p. 50.
16. *Ibid.*, pp. 59ff.
17. *Congressional Record*, March 13, 1925, pp. 215ff.
18. *Ibid.*, March 9, 1925, p. 50; also see Kent, *American Mercury, op. cit.*, p. 51.
19. *Detroit Times*, October 23, 1936.
20. Mark Sullivan, *Our Times, The Twenties*, p. 631.
21. *Detroit News*, October 14, 1925; Emile Gauvreau and Lester Cohen, *Billy Mitchell, a Biography*.
22. *Grand Rapids Herald*, September 27, 1925, for a good account of this.
23. Couzens to William J. Norton, December 29, 1926; also Norton interview, February 12, 1941.
24. *Detroit News*, March 21, 1928.
25. *Congressional Record*, March 22, 1928, pp. 5146–51.
26. Galbraith, *The Great Crash, 1929*, p. 114.
27. Couzens to Madeleine Yaw, December 2, 1929.

CHAPTER XXVIII. *The Restless Statesman*

1. Mss. fragment in Couzens papers.
2. Couzens to Vandenberg, July 22, 1924.
3. John P. Frazer, interview.
4. Couzens to Madeleine Yaw, January 30, 1928.
5. Charles L. McNary, Arthur A. Ballantine, etc., interviews with author.
6. See Mary Earhart Dillon, *Wendell Willkie,* concerning McNary.
7. Joseph P. Tumulty to Couzens, May 22, August 10 and 12, and September 21, 1924.
8. Couzens to Clarence Wilcox, February 22 and March 4, 1935; also *Lima Trust Company, as Trustee for Creditors of Couzens Ice Machine Company v. Charles F. Carroll, et al.,* Common Pleas Court, Auglaize County, Ohio, No. 11481.
9. Couzens, James, "The Installment Buyer Worries Me," *Nation's Business,* December 1926, p. 36.
10. Clarence Wilcox interview, February 9, 1941.
11. Couzens to Madeleine, October 1, 1929. For Frank Couzens' career, see obituary articles in *Detroit Free Press, News,* and *Times,* October 31 and November 1, 1950.
12. Frank Couzens, interview.

CHAPTER XXIX. *The Magnificent Gift*

1. Couzens to Gordon McGregor, December 23, 1915.
2. Gitchell interview, October 24–25, 1942.
3. *Ibid.*
4. Norton interview and others; also his talk, "The Saga of a Foundation Executive," before Prismatic Club of Detroit, November 6, 1954.
5. *Detroit News,* October 22, 1919.
6. Henry S. Morgan, interview.
7. Trust instrument, March 26, 1924.
8. Lacy memorandum to author, May 2, 1940.
9. Couzens to Madeleine Yaw, March 3, 1929.
10. Children's Fund of Michigan, *Reports;* also Norton to author, February 10, 1955, and Norton's Prismatic Club talk, *op. cit.* For a full report on the Children's Fund of Michigan and a good account of Couzens' philanthropies, see the book published in 1957 by the Fund—*Biography of a Foundation, The Story of the Children's Fund of Michigan,* by William C. Richards and William J. Norton.
11. Children's Fund of Michigan, *Sixth Annual Report.*
12. Dr. Stewart Hamilton to author, October 29, 1942.
13. Couzens to Ralph Stone, December 15, 1926.
14. Couzens to Martin H. Carmody, December 2, 1924.
15. Norton, Prismatic Club talk, *op. cit.,* and interviews.
16. See Children's Fund of Michigan, *Twelfth Annual Report,* 1940–41, 6.
17. Children's Fund of Michigan, *Seventh Annual Report,* 1935, 5.
18. William J. Norton, memorandum for author, 1941.
19. Couzens to Mrs. Yaw, May 14, 1929.
20. *Ibid.,* June 18, 1929.

CHAPTER XXX. *The "Dangerous Man"*

1. Herbert Hoover, address at Palo Alto, August 11, 1928, in Wilbur and Hyde, *The Hoover Policies,* p. 2.
2. Couzens to C. H. Haberkorn, Jr., June 5, 1925.
3. Couzens to Norton, November 8, 1926.
4. Couzens to Frank Couzens, February 21, 1928.
5. Couzens before Keidan grand jury, Detroit, testimony on August 18, 1933.
6. *New York Times,* June 5, 1929.
7. *The Causes of Unemployment,* U.S. Senate, 70th Congress, Senate Report No. 219, published in March 1929.
8. *Ibid.,* pp. iv–vi.

9. *Ibid.*, p. xv.

10. Couzens to Leon F. Whitney, May 13, 1929.

11. Couzens to George W. Johnson, July 23, 1929.

12. Frederick Lewis Allen, *Since Yesterday*, New York, 1939, p. 26.

13. Myers and Newton, *The Hoover Administration*, p. 23.

14. See Dixon Wecter, *The Age of the Great Depression, 1929–41;* also Charles A. and Mary R. Beard, *America in Midpassage*, pp. 55ff.; Allen, *Since Yesterday* and Galbraith, *The Great Crash, 1929*, which are among the best works on this.

15. *Literary Digest*, November 9, 1929.

16. Arthur Pound, *Detroit, Dynamic City*, New York, 1940, p. 316.

17. Galbraith, *op. cit.*, discusses the causes in an impressive way. It is interesting how close were Couzens' views at the time with those expressed by Galbraith in 1955 in his book, *The Great Crash, 1929.*

18. Arthur H. Vandenberg to author, letter, August 18, 1941.

19. *Literary Digest*, March 30, 1929.

20. Frank R. Kent, *Without Grease*, p. 274.

21. See Tucker, *Sons of the Wild Jackass*, pp. 14–17, and p. 242; also Watson, *As I Knew Them*, pp. 164–66.

22. Charles P. Stewart, Washington column, February 14, 1930.

23. Thomas L. Stokes, *Chip Off My Shoulder*, p. 79.

24. *New York Times*, January 13, 1931; see Stokes, *op. cit.*, p. 354.

25. *New York Times*, April 15, 1931.

26. Richard Hofstadter, *The American Political Tradition and the Men Who Made It*, p. 286, an incisive analysis of Herbert Hoover.

27. Leif, *Democracy's Norris*, p. 256; Couzens to Mrs. Yaw, February 13, 1929.

28. Couzens to Hoover, January 18, 1930.

29. See Stokes, *op. cit.*, pp. 257ff., 293ff.

30. *Detroit Times*, August 13, 1933.

CHAPTER XXXI. *The Crusader Again*

1. The Beards, *America in Midpassage*, pp. 42ff.; also Pritchett, *The Tennessee Valley Authority, op. cit.*, pp. 12ff.

2. Myers and Newton, *The Hoover Administration*, p. 470.

3. The Beards, *op. cit.*, p. 62.

4. Myers and Newton, p. 60.

5. *Ibid.*, and *New York Times*, January 1, 1931.

6. Myers and Newton, p. 61; see also *Literary Digest*, January 17, 1931.

7. Couzens to Mrs. Yaw, May 29, 1930.

8. *Congressional Record*, February 3, 1931, p. 3833.

9. *Ibid.*

10. *Ibid.*, Part 6, February 26, 1931, p. 6230.

11. Hoover Message to Congress, December 6, 1932, in Wilbur and Hyde, *op. cit.*, p. 463. See also Stokes, *op. cit.*, p. 326.

12. Couzens to William Timberlake, May 8, 1936.

13. *New York Times*, August 5, 1931; also Bates, *The Story of Congress*, p. 415.

14. Couzens to Arthur J. Lacy, May 23, 1932.

15. See Stokes, *op. cit.*, p. 280; *Literary Digest*, February 14, 1931; Wilbur and Hyde, *op. cit.*, pp. 399ff.

16. Ernest Sutherland Bates, *The Story of Congress*, p. 415.

17. Myers and Newton, *op. cit.*, p. 85.

18. Justice Frank Murphy, interview with author; *New York Times*, August 23, 1931.

19. Couzens radio speech, November 1, 1931, typescript.

20. Wilbur and Hyde, *op. cit.*, pp. 422ff.

21. Frederick Lewis Allen, *op. cit.*, p. 75, and Galbraith, *op. cit.*, pp. 98, 137.

22. Allen, p. 86. See also Dexter Perkins, *The New Age of Franklin Roosevelt*, p. 4ff.

23. Wilbur and Hyde, p. 434.

24. Simonds, *Henry Ford*, p. 224.

25. *Ibid.,* p. 230.
26. Lindley, *Halfway with Roosevelt,* p. 6, and *Literary Digest,* August 13, 1932.
27. Harold Nicolson, *Dwight Morrow,* p. 395.
28. The Beards, *America in Midpassage,* p. 81.
29. *Ibid.,* p. 70.
30. *Ibid.,* pp. 74–82.
31. Frederick Lewis Allen, *Since Yesterday,* p. 100; Stokes, *op. cit.,* p. 356.
32. *Ibid.*
33. The Beards, *America in Midpassage,* pp. 177–78.
34. *Congressional Record,* July 11, 1932, p. 14986; see also Watson, *op. cit.,* pp. 267ff.
35. *Literary Digest,* January 21, 1933; Frederick Lewis Allen, *op. cit.,* pp. 90–91.
36. Couzens to Sidney T. Miller, February 23, 1917.
37. Couzens to C. G. Marshall, May 23, 1934.
38. June 16, 1933, and June 20, 1933.
39. Ray Tucker, to author, May 5, 1951.
40. *Ibid.*

CHAPTER XXXII. *The End of An Era*

1. Sugrue and Starling, *Starling of the White House,* p. 299.
2. Stokes, *Chip Off My Shoulder,* p. 305.
3. *Congressional Record,* May 28, 1932; see also Ernest K. Lindley, *The Roosevelt Revolution,* p. 26.
4. See Mauritz H. Hallgren, *The Gay Reformer, Profits Before Plenty Under Franklin D. Roosevelt,* pp. 30ff., 220ff., 253ff., and 310 and Dexter Perkins, *op. cit.,* p. 5ff.
5. Louis M. Hacker, *The Triumph of American Capitalism.*
6. *Congressional Record,* March 22, 1928, p. 5148.
7. Pearson and Allen, *More Washington Merry-Go-Round,* p. 340.
8. Ray Tucker, *op. cit.,* p. 235.
9. *Detroit Times,* February 10, 1926.
10. Couzens to Mrs. Yaw, November 16, 1932.

CHAPTER XXXIII. *The Bank Crisis*

1. *America in Midpassage, op. cit.,* p. 155. In C. C. Holt and N. S. Keith, *28 Days, A History of the Banking Crisis,* will be found a good circumstantial summary of the national banking picture in connection with the "holidays." Also see, for good, though brief accounts, F. Cyril James, *The Growth of the Chicago Banks,* and Marquis James and Bessie R. James, *Biography of a Bank, The Story of the Bank of America* (1954), and Jesse H. Jones with Edward Angly, *Fifty Billion Dollars.* But to get the full story it is necessary to study, as was done for the account in this book, the thousands of pages of testimony in *Report and Hearings Before the Committee on Banking and Currency,* U.S. Senate, 73rd Congress, Second Session, 1934, among other official sources, for which see footnotes.
2. In particular in Malcolm W. Bingay, *Detroit Is My Own Home Town* (1946) and Lawrence Sullivan, *Prelude to Panic* (1936), both quite unreliable. It is a curious thing that Herbert Hoover, in his *Memoirs,* Vol. III, *The Great Depression,* includes, p. 207, a long excerpt from Bingay's account, as if this were really substantiation of his own version. The "curiousness" of this, as Alice in Wonderland might say, will become apparent as the story unfolds.
3. See *Report and Hearings Before the Committee on Banking and Currency,* U.S. Senate, 73rd Congress, Second Session, Part 10, 1934; hereafter cited as *Senate Report* or *Senate Hearings;* also Ferdinand Pecora, *Wall Street Under Oath,* and *Transcript of Hearings Before Judge Harry B. Keidan,* of Detroit, who conducted a one-man grand jury investigation, 1933. Basic is *Senate Report.*
4. Edsel B. Ford testimony, in *Senate Hearings,* pp. 4677–84; also testimony of Kanzler, Longley, and letter of A. P. Leyburn, chief federal bank examiner to the Comptroller of the Currency, June 14, 1932, in *Senate Hearings,* p. 4639. For pertinent, if biased, comments on Kanzler, concerning Edsel Ford, see Sorensen, *op. cit.,* pp. 307 and 310–11.

5. Robert O. Lord testimony, *Senate Hearings*, p. 4210.

6. Frank Couzens, interview, also letter to his father, 1931. For the connection of the Universal Credit Corporation with the Guardian Group, and also the roles of Edsel Ford and Kanzler in this respect, together with the relationship of the Ford Motor Company, see the interesting material in Nevins, *Ford, II,* 465.

7. Frank W. Blair, former president of the trust company, testimony, *Senate Hearings,* pp. 4803 and 4806.

8. Edsel B. Ford testimony, *Senate Hearings,* pp. 4677–84; also pp. 4681ff.

9. *Senate Hearings,* p. 4685.

10. *Senate Hearings,* p. 4808, testimony of Longley; also *Times Publishing Company and the Union Guardian Trust Company v. Harvey C. Emery, Liquidating Trustee, Brief for Appellees,* by Butzel, Levin and Winston, in the Supreme Court of Michigan, No. 40472, which goes into detail on the condition of the trust company.

11. *Senate Hearings,* p. 4810, minutes of the RFC, June 28, 1932, *ibid.*

12. Minutes of the RFC, July 5, 1932, *ibid.,* also Leyburn to Comptroller, June 14, 1932, *ibid.,* p. 4639.

13. *Brief of Appellees, Times Publishing Company, et al., v. Emery, op. cit.,* p. 35.

14. *Ibid.*

15. *Senate Hearings,* p. 4733.

16. *Senate Hearings,* p. 4516.

17. Leyburn testimony, *Senate Hearings,* pp. 4638–39.

18. Edsel Ford testimony, *Senate Hearings,* p. 4687.

19. *Ibid.,* p. 4692.

20. Kanzler testimony, *Senate Hearings,* p. 4755.

21. *Brief for Appellees, op. cit.,* p. 59.

22. *Senate Hearings,* p. 4725.

23. RFC minutes, February 6, 1933, in *Senate Hearings,* pp. 4562–63.

24. *Harper's Magazine,* January 1933.

25. Leyburn testimony, *Senate Hearings,* p. 4627; also Pecora, *Wall Street Under Oath, op. cit.,* p. 256.

26. Minutes of the RFC, February 6, 1933, in *Senate Hearings,* p. 4693.

27. McKee testimony, *Senate Hearings,* pp. 4728 and 4735.

28. Minutes of the RFC, February 6, 1933, *op. cit.*

29. For example, Hoover, *Memoirs,* III, pp. 206–07.

CHAPTER XXXIV. *The White House Conference*

1. Charles A. Miller, memorandum, March 27, 1942.

2. Burlingame, *Henry Ford, op. cit.,* p. 158; and see Edsel Ford testimony, *Senate Hearings.*

3. See Leyburn testimony, *Senate Hearings,* p. 4627.

4. Miller memorandum, p. 4; also Longley testimony, *Senate Hearings,* p. 4627. Hoover did call Ford *after* the bank holiday. C. C. Holt and N. S. Keith, *28 Days, A History of the Banking Crisis,* p. 8. In correspondence with the author, Hoover stated that he asked Ford's assistance and that Ford was always willing. But this clearly referred to a later time. In his *Memoirs,* p. 207, Mr. Hoover says: "Together with Secretary Mills and Under-Secretary Ballantine, I made great efforts to secure local support to that key bank which would make it eligible for RFC loans even on any definition of legal security. Henry Ford has $7,000,000 on deposit in this bank. I persuaded him to subordinate to the RFC loan any claim he might have on its assets. . . ." This was true, *except* that this occurred at a later time, after the crisis had gotten out of hand, as will be seen. Perhaps the explanation pertinent is that matters developed so rapidly and hectically, as will be seen, that Mr. Hoover is not to be blamed for getting some things mixed up in recollection, especially as he continued to be angry with Couzens, as his *Memoirs,* published almost thirty years after the events, show.

Incidentally, Henry Ford was not the only wealthy person Hoover had called for campaign funds in 1932, and found himself turned down. Another such call was made to A. P. Giannini of the Bank of America in California, as told in Marquis and Bessie R. James, *Biography of a Bank, op. cit.,* pp. 361–62.

5. *Literary Digest*, November 5, 1932.

6. Wilson Mills, chairman of the First National Bank, Detroit, interview, 1941.

7. James Couzens, "Michigan Banking Events," a memorandum prepared for the Keidan one-man grand jury, 1933. Also his notebook, February 7, 1933; *Detroit News*, June 20, 1933.

8. *Senate Hearings*, p. 4627.

9. See *Unemployment Relief Act (Public No. 5, S. 598)*, approved March 1933, described in Beard and Smith, *The Future Comes*, p. 123; also *Detroit News*, February 14, 1933; *Congressional Record*, February 9, 1933, p. 3706.

10. John Carson to author, October 25, 1931; Longley testimony, Keidan grand jury.

11. Couzens memorandum, "Michigan Banking Events," *op. cit.*

12. C. C. Colt and N. S. Keith, *op. cit.*, p. 24. For an account of the Dawes bank matter (the $90,000,000 loan was repaid), from Dawes' view, see Timmons, *Portrait of an American; Charles G. Dawes* (1952), p. 316.

13. Carson to author, October 25, 1941.

14. Miller memorandum for author, *op. cit.*, p. 9.

15. Hoover telegram to Harry S. Toy, Prosecuting Attorney of Wayne County, Michigan, in *Detroit News*, August 23, 1933. Mr. Hoover does not make all this so clear in his *Memoirs*, *op. cit.*, in 1952. His statements there must be read very carefully, though they are true as far as they go in most frames of reference.

16. Charles A. Miller to author, March 27, 1942.

17. Miller memorandum, p. 6. Vandenberg corroborated this in public statements, see *infra*.

18. For examples, see Bingay, *op. cit.*, and Hoover, *op. cit.*, as well as Arthur Ballantine, "When All the Banks Closed," in *Harvard Business Review*, March 1948, pp. 129ff. The article by Mr. Ballantine, who was in a position to know the facts and who testified objectively in the Senate investigation, is strangely unsatisfactory as a piece of history, though presented as such. While valuable as an eyewitness account, for its facts, this article is likely to mislead students of the Detroit bank crisis when Mr. Ballantine expresses some subjective conclusions that incorporate several myths, such as the myth that Couzens and Ford were then feuding and also that Couzens' "rooftops" remark and his attitude toward RFC loans were factors in the closing of the banks. Mr. Ballantine, of course, was then a member of the Hoover administration.

19. *New York Times*, November 5, 1932.

20. *Detroit News*, June 20, 1933; see also Sward, *Legend of Henry Ford*, p. 249.

21. Herbert Hoover, to author, September 14, 1941.

22. *Ibid.*

23. *Ibid.* See also Hoover, *Memoirs*, p. 207, substantially the same, but with the added comment: "As Senator Vandenberg was a witness to this scene, it rankled in Couzens' mind until he died. The Detroit banks closed."

24. Miller, memorandum, p. 7.

CHAPTER XXXV. *The Climax*

1. Ballantine testimony, *Senate Hearings*, p. 5793.

2. Miller memorandum, p. 10.

3. Ballantine testimony, *Senate Hearings*, p. 5793.

4. This and other data in this section is based on Miller's memorandum, testimony of Edsel Ford and Arthur A. Ballantine in *Senate Hearings*, and conversation between the author and Mr. Ballantine, July 30, 1946.

5. Simonds, *op. cit.*, p. 233.

6. Henry Ford's threat to draw out all Ford deposits was fully corroborated later at the Senate hearing by Edsel Ford. "Mr. Henry Ford made that statement." (p. 4695) Also by Arthur Ballantine in his testimony, (p. 5796) and in personal interview, July 30, 1946. It was also recorded in the minutes of the RFC for February 13, 1933, *Senate Hearings*, p. 4695. The quotes in the text are from Mr. Miller's memorandum, but in almost identical language they are also in the record of the Senate hearings. Mr. Ballantine also tells of Ford's threat in his article in the *Harvard Business Review*, *op. cit.* But his conclusions as to the causes of the Detroit crisis and why the original RFC

loan was not made should be read with great caution. He accepts the scapegoat role for Couzens. See note 18, Chapter XXXIV.

7. Edwin Wildman, *Famous Leaders of Industry*, p. 131. Concerning Henry Ford's way of thinking, see also Nevins, *Ford*, for example pp. 576 and 582; also Coghlan in *Life* Magazine.

8. Carson memorandum to Couzens.

9. *Detroit News*, June 17, 1933.

10. Arthur Ballantine testimony, *Senate Hearings*, p. 5796.

11. *Senate Hearings*, p. 5797.

12. Wills testimony, *Senate Hearings*, p. 5511.

13. Couzens to Henry Ford, December 5, 1927; also to Edsel B. Ford, December 7, 1927.

14. Miller Memorandum, pp. 16–17.

15. Couzens testimony, Keidan grand jury, August 17, 1933.

16. Couzens memorandum; also testimony before Keidan grand jury, August 17, 1933. Mr. Longley confirmed this in his testimony before the Keidan grand jury, September 15, 1933; see *Detroit Free Press*, September 16, 1933; also letter of Wilson W. Mills to Couzens, August 3, 1933. Mills confirmed this in an interview with author, February 11, 1941.

17. Couzens testimony, Keidan grand jury, *op. cit.*

18. Huddleston interview, February 11, 1941.

19. See *Senate Hearings*, Part 12, Leyburn testimony, p. 5762.

20. *Ibid.*

21. Lacy testimony, Keidan grand jury, August 29, 1933; *Detroit Times*, August 29.

22. Comstock proclamation in Detroit papers, February 14, 1933.

23. Wilkin testimony, Keidan grand jury, June 25, 1933.

CHAPTER XXXVI. *"The Hell of a Mess"*

1. Leyburn testimony, *Senate Hearings*, p. 5656.

2. *Ibid.*, and *Detroit Free Press*, August 16, 1933; see also Frederick L. Allen, *Since Yesterday*, pp. 99–100; and Lindley, *The Roosevelt Revolution*, p. 73.

3. Hoover to Harry S. Toy, telegram, August 23, 1933, in *Detroit News*, same date.

4. Joslin, Theodore G., *Hoover Off the Record.*

5. Sullivan, p. 86.

6. Wilbur and Hyde, *The Hoover Policies*, p. 530.

7. F. Cyril James, *The Growth of Chicago Banks*, II, p. 1054. This book contains one of the best published accounts of the general banking crisis of 1933.

8. Lindley, *op. cit.*, p. 73.

9. *Literary Digest*, February 25, 1933; see also Simonds, *op. cit.*, p. 232. On the bank crisis, this book by a Ford publicist is almost completely unreliable. Cf. Colt and Keith, p. 8, and Sward, pp. 242ff.

10. Among others, Wilson Mills was told by Hoover that Couzens was to blame, interview, July 11, 1941.

11. *Detroit Free Press*, February 15, 1933. On the morning before, Bingay printed a similar, but less "pepped up" version. This same story, almost without change, was reproduced thirteen years later in *Detroit Is My Own Home Town*, by Bingay, even though the *Free Press* in the interim had carried much corrective material. See Hoover, *op. cit.*

12. See *Detroit News*, March 3, 1933.

13. Keidan grand jury testimony, August 22, 1933; in *Detroit Times*, same date.

14. *Detroit News*, February 13, 1933.

15. See Pearson and Allen, *More Washington Merry-Go-Round*, p. 147.

16. *Ibid.*, pp. 147–48 and 479.

17. *Detroit News*, March 3, 1933.

18. See *Annual Report of the Secretary of the Treasury on the State of Finances for Fiscal Year Ended June 30, 1933*, pp. 23 and 187ff.; also Beard and Smith, *The Future Comes*, pp. 17ff.; and *Literary Digest*, March 11, 1933, p. 9.

19. Sullivan, *Prelude to Panic, op. cit.*, p. 98; see also Colt and Keith, pp. 18 and 29.

20. Statement issued by the Ford Motor Company, *Detroit Times,* February 27, 1933.
21. Roy D. Chapin to Couzens, February 25, 1933.
22. *Detroit Times,* February 27, 1933.
23. *New York Times,* February 27, 1933.
24. Sward, *op. cit.,* p. 252; also *Literary Digest,* March 11, 1933, p. 10.
25. Miller memorandum, *op. cit.;* Couzens' statement, "Michigan Banking Events"; also Detroit papers, March 3, 1933.
26. Couzens' statement, *op. cit.*
27. See RFC minutes for February 22, 1933, *Senate Hearings,* Part 10, p. 4748.
28. Couzens telegram to Charles A. Miller, February 25, 1933; in *Detroit Times,* February 27, 1933; Jesse H. Jones to author, April 30, 1946.
29. Couzens to Don R. Carrigan, letter, February 23, 1933.
30. RFC minutes of February 26, 1933, in *Senate Hearings,* p. 4752.
31. Miller memorandum, *op. cit.,* and Sullivan, p. 102.
32. Miller memorandum, *op. cit.*
33. See Wilson Mills testimony, Keidan grand jury, August 17, 1933.
34. *Senate Hearings,* Part 10, p. 4753.
35. Couzens testimony, Keidan grand jury, August 18, 1933.
36. Mills testimony, Keidan grand jury, August 17, 1933.
37. Mills to the RFC, telegram, *op. cit.*
38. Eugene Meyer to Herbert Hoover, February 25, 1933, in Myers and Newton, *op. cit.,* p. 357.
39. Couzens notebook, February 28, 1933.
40. E. D. Stair to Couzens, February 28, 1933.

CHAPTER XXXVII. *The Mission That Failed*

1. Vandenberg to Couzens, memorandum, "Memo to Senator Couzens from Senator Vandenberg," in Couzens papers.
2. *Detroit Times,* March 2, 1933.
3. *Detroit Times,* March 1, 1933.
4. *Detroit Free Press,* March 3, 1933.
5. Couzens to C. L. Cardwell, March 4, 1933.
6. See Beard and Smith, *The Future Comes,* pp. 1–3; Wecter, *The Age of the Great Depression,* pp. 62–63; and C. F. James, *op. cit.*
7. Hoover to Roosevelt, February 17, 1933, in Myers and Newton, p. 340.
8. Grace Tully, *F.D.R., My Boss,* p. 63.
9. Roosevelt to Hoover, February 28, 1933, *ibid.*
10. Franklin D. Roosevelt, *Public Papers and Addresses,* I, p. 871.
11. Myers and Newton, p. 361.
12. Roosevelt, *Public Papers and Addresses,* I, p. 871.
13. Myers and Newton, p. 359.
14. *Ibid.,* p. 362.
15. Myers and Newton, pp. 365–66.
16. *Ibid.,* p. 364.
17. Raymond Moley, *After Seven Years,* p. 144.
18. *Ibid.,* p. 146; also Roosevelt, *Public Papers, op. cit.,* p. 870; also Ernest K. Lindley, *The Roosevelt Revolution,* p. 74.
19. Grace Tully, p. 64.
20. See Myers and Newton, p. 366; Roosevelt, *Public Papers,* p. 870; Raymond Moley, *After Seven Years,* p. 147; and Smith and Beasley, *Carter Glass,* pp. 340–42.
21. See Roosevelt, *On Our Way,* p. 24; also *Public Papers, op. cit.,* pp. 868–71; also for all texts, *Annual Report of the Secretary of the Treasury on the State of the Finances for Fiscal Year Ended June 30, 1933,* pp. 187–202.
22. See Jesse Jones' version in his *Fifty Billion Dollars,* pp. 66ff.
23. Couzens' testimony, Keidan grand jury, September 18, 1833; see also Ballantine testimony, *Senate Hearings,* p. 5803.
24. See Lindley, *The Roosevelt Revolution,* pp. 56 and 285ff; and the Beards, *America in Midpassage,* p. 146.

25. *Congressional Record*, March 5, 1933, pp. 6–7. See Rexford G. Tugwell, *The Democratic Roosevelt*, p. 264, for a sympathetic portrait of Secretary Woodin.

26. Couzens to Woodin, March 27, 1933.

27. Detroit papers, March 21, 1933; also statement by Jesse Jones, July 13, 1933.

28. Couzens to Madeleine Yaw, March 23, 1933.

29. Detroit papers, July 14, 1933.

CHAPTER XXXVIII. *The New Deal Onlooker*

1. Karl Schriftgiesser, *This Was Normalcy*, p. 296.

2. *Literary Digest*, March 18, 1933, quoting Ray Tucker.

3. *Ibid.*, also Lindley, *The Roosevelt Revolution*, p. 80.

4. John Carson to W. R. Yaw, April 1940.

5. Couzens to Madeleine Yaw, March 23, 1933.

6. Couzens to Clarence E. Wilcox, May 1, 1933.

7. Harold Nicolson, *Dwight Morrow*, p. 378.

8. *Congressional Record*, May 17, 1933.

9. John Carter Franklin, *The New Dealers*, p. 121; Grace Tully, *F.D.R., My Boss*, pp. 177–78.

10. Lindley, *The Roosevelt Revolution*, pp. 88–91.

11. See *Literary Digest*, March 18 and 25, 1933.

12. *Congressional Record*, March 14, 1933, p. 347.

13. *Congressional Record*, March 14, 1933, p. 346; *Literary Digest*, March 25, 1933, p. 6.

14. *Congressional Record*, March 15, 1933; *Literary Digest*, March 25, 1933.

15. Franklin D. Roosevelt, *op. cit.*, pp. 53–54, 219–21; also Lindley, p. 163.

16. *Congressional Record*, February 11, 1933, p. 3858.

17. *Ibid.*, p. 3841.

18. *Congressional Record*, February 11, 1933, pp. 3841 and 3858.

19. Lindley, p. 91.

20. *Ibid.*, p. 100.

21. McNary interview, April 15, 1940.

22. See Beard and Smith, *The Future Comes, A Study of The New Deal*, viii; also pp. 42ff. and 165; Stokes, *op. cit.*, pp. 369ff.; Saul Alinsky, *John L. Lewis*; cf. Mauritz A. Hallgren, *The Gay Reformer* and Dexter Perkins, *op. cit.*, pp. 15ff. and pp. 71ff.

23. See Frank Kent, *Without Gloves*, p. 25, and *Without Grease*, pp. 10–11. See also James E. Watson, *op. cit.*, p. 297; and Stokes, *op. cit.*, pp. 457–58.

24. See Pearson and Allen, *Washington Merry-Go-Round*, pp. 184ff. for an incisive analysis of the Progressives' inherent weaknesses.

25. *Men Around the President*, pp. 69–70; see also Lindley, *The Roosevelt Revolution*, pp. 105ff.

26. Johnson, interview, April 22, 1940.

27. Couzens to Albert Couzens, May 26, 1933.

CHAPTER XXXIX. *The Investigator Again*

1. The Beards, *America in Midpassage*, p. 161.

2. Lindley, *The Roosevelt Revolution*, p. 139.

3. Stokes, p. 348; see also Kent, *Without Gloves*, pp. 70–72; and Rodney Dutcher column, June 1, 1933.

4. Frank R. Kent, *Without Gloves*, p. 22; also Lindley, p. 143.

5. Kent, p. 24.

6. *New York Times*, May 27, 1933.

7. *Literary Digest*, June 10, 1933.

8. *Senate Hearings*, *op. cit.*, part 2, pp. 150–52; also the Beards, *America in Midpassage*, pp. 166–67, and Galbraith, *The Great Crash, 1929*, p. 56.

9. Rodney Dutcher, syndicated column, June 1, 1933.

10. Beards, *op. cit.*, pp. 167–68.

11. *Senate Hearings, Stock Market Practices*, Part 1, pp. 172–73.

12. *Ibid.*, p. 254; also Part 2, pp. 882–84.

13. *Ibid.,* Part 1, pp. 172–73; also *Literary Digest,* June 10, 1933.
14. *Senate Report, Stock Market Practices,* pp. 109–10.
15. *Senate Report, Stock Exchange Practices,* pp. 331.
16. *Senate Report, op. cit.,* p. 321.
17. *Congressional Record,* March 22, 1928, p. 5151.
18. *Senate Report, op. cit.,* pp. 380–81.
19. James M. Cox to author, November 13, 1945.

CHAPTER XL. *The Delegate to London*

1. Senator McNary, interview, April 11, 1940; also Rodney Dutcher, column, June 6, 1933. Concerning the conference, see Jeannette P. Nichols, "Roosevelt's Monetary Diplomacy in 1933," *American Historical Review,* Vol. LVI, No. 2 (January 1951), p. 308.
2. Daniel Hackett, interview.
3. Mrs. Couzens, interview.
4. Frank Couzens died October 31, 1950. Ford's son, Edsel, died in 1943.
5. White, *Puritan in Babylon, op. cit.,* p. 431ff.
6. Angell, James W., *Program for the World Economic Conference,* 15.
7. Herbert Feis, letter to author.
8. Cordell Hull, *Memoirs,* p. 256.
9. *Detroit News,* July 29, 1933.
10. Mrs. James Couzens to Madeleine Yaw, June 22, 1933.
11. *Times* of London, June 20, 1933.
12. Warburg, *The Money Muddle,* p. 114.
13. *Detroit News,* June 20, 1933.
14. Raymond Moley, *After Seven Years,* p. 239.
15. Moley, *op. cit.,* p. 239n.
16. *Ibid.,* p. 267.
17. Hull, *op. cit.,* p. 256.
18. Couzens notebook, June 22, 1933; also Moley, *op. cit.,* p. 254.
19. Mrs. James Couzens to Madeleine Yaw, June 24, 1933.
20. Associated Press, June 26, 1933.
21. Moley, *op. cit.,* pp. 249 and 253–54.
22. Couzens notebook, July 2, 1933.
23. June 30, 1933.
24. Roosevelt, *Public Papers and Addresses,* II, pp. 264–65.
25. See Lindley, *Half Way with Roosevelt,* p. 493.
26. Lindley, *The Roosevelt Revolution,* p. 216.
27. *New York Times,* July 8, 1933.
28. Mrs. Couzens to Madeleine Yaw, July 4 and 7, 1933.
29. John Franklin Carter (The Unofficial Observer), *The New Dealers,* p. 263.
30. Moley, *After Seven Years, op. cit.,* p. 217. Concerning the confusion at monetary conference, see also Tugwell, *The Democratic Roosevelt,* pp. 314–318 and 323–325, for a discussion from the Roosevelt point of view, and Dexter Perkins, *op. cit.,* pp. 92–94, 165.

CHAPTER XLI. *The Smear*

1. Jay G. Hayden, interview.
2. *Detroit News,* June 20, 1933.
3. *Ibid.*
4. *Detroit News,* June 20, 1933.
5. Couzens to Payne, June 22, 1933.
6. *Detroit Times,* June 26, 1933.
7. Statement by Arthur J. Lacy, in behalf of Mrs. Couzens, to Keidan grand jury, June 29, 1933; Couzens testimony, August 18, 1933.
8. *Detroit Free Press,* September 28, 1933.
9. Couzens memorandum, "Michigan Banking Events," and C. J. Huddleston, interview.
10. *Detroit News,* August 21, 1933.
11. *Senate Hearings,* pp. 4494–95.

12. August 19, 1933.

13. Keidan grand jury, transcript, August 23, 1933.

14. Keidan grand jury, transcript, September 18, 1933.

15. *Senate Hearings*, Part 10, p. 4641.

16. *Ibid.*, p. 4644.

17. *Ibid.*

18. Testimony, Keidan grand jury, August 18, 1933.

19. *Ibid.*

20. Hoover to Couzens, September 5, 1933.

21. Keidan grand jury testimony, August 18, 1933.

22. Ray B. Westerfield, "National Versus State Banks," *Annals of the American Academy*, January 1934, "Banking and Transportation Problems," p. 21.

23. *Detroit News*, September 18, 1933.

24. Frederic L. Smith, to Couzens, January 14, 1934.

25. Wilson W. Mills, interview, July 11, 1941.

26. December 29, 1914.

27. Frederic L. Smith to Couzens, *op. cit.*

28. *Detroit Free Press*, September 28, 1933.

29. Couzens to Keidan, letter, in *Detroit News*, September 20, 1933.

30. Couzens' statement, *Detroit News*, September 20, 1933.

31. Findings of Judge Harry B. Keidan, September 18, 1933; in *Detroit Free Press*, September 19, 1933.

32. Associated Press, September 26, 1933.

33. September 28, 1933.

34. Mrs. Couzens, interview.

35. Couzens to Payne, January 4, 1934.

36. *Detroit Free Press*, June 7, 1933.

37. See *Detroit News*, June 5, 1933.

38. Couzens notebook, October 2, 1933.

39. *Senate Hearings, Stock Market Practices*, Parts 9, 10, 11, and 12.

40. *Senate Report, op. cit.*, p. 231.

41. *Senate Hearings*, Part 10, pp. 4677–99 and Part 12, pp. 5791 and 5807.

42. *Detroit Free Press*, October 23, 1936.

43. Couzens to Payne, February 9, 1933.

44. Frederic L. Smith to Couzens, January 16, 1934; Couzens to Smith, January 22, 1934.

45. *Detroit News*, August 1, 1934.

46. *Detroit News*, June 9, 1937.

47. *Senate Report, op. cit.*, pp. 266–68.

CHAPTER XLII. *The New Deal Republican*

1. *New York Times*, August 26, 1934.

2. *Ibid.*

3. See Lindley, *The Roosevelt Revolution*, pp. 305–07; also Stokes, p. 384.

4. Couzens to Madeleine Yaw, January 31, 1935.

5. Letter, January 2, 1934.

6. Couzens notebook, November 20, 1933.

7. *The New Dealers, op. cit.*, p. 118. See also Galbraith, *The Great Crash, 1929*, p. 186.

8. *Congressional Record*, June 16, 1936, p. 9565.

9. Couzens to Mary Kingsbury Simkhovitch, January 4, 1936.

10. *Congressional Record*, June 15, 1936, p. 9346.

11. William R. Yaw to author, February 26, 1940.

12. W. J. Norton, interview, June 22, 1941.

13. *New York Times*, June 20, 1935.

14. *Ibid.*

15. Lindley, *op. cit.*, p. 280.

16. Couzens to George R. Averill, February 20, 1936; and Jay G. Hayden, interview, April 17, 1940.

17. Couzens to Dr. Freund, December 28, 1934.
18. Couzens to Lord Ashfield, May 10, 1935.
19. Carlson and Bates, *Hearst, Lord of San Simeon*, p. 247.
20. B. C. Forbes column, April 10, 1934.
21. *Congressional Record*, May 3, 1934, p. 7977.
22. Carlson and Bates, *Hearst*, pp. 220ff.; Norris, *Fighting Liberal*, p. 375; Leif, *Democracy's Norris*, pp. 297ff.
23. *Congressional Record*, May 3, 1934, p. 7977.
24. *Ibid.*
25. Couzens to W. S. Gilmore, March 13, 1935.
26. Couzens to C. T. Bach, December 18, 1934.
27. *Detroit Free Press*, April 7, 1935.
28. *Chicago Tribune*, June 2, 1935.
29. *Detroit News*, August 23, 1933.
30. See *Literary Digest*, August 3, 1935.
31. Stokes, *op. cit.*, p. 456.
32. Couzens to Walter L. Bouve, Jr., December 4, 1934.
33. Couzens to Howard C. Lawrence, February 23, 1935.
34. *Detroit Free Press*, March 2, 1935.

Chapter XLIII. *The Unbowed Head*

1. *Congressional Record*, February 18, 1935, pp. 2075–76.
2. *Ibid.*
3. *Ibid.*, pp. 2284–85.
4. *Literary Digest*, August 31, 1935.
5. Couzens to George R. Averill, February 20, 1936.
6. *Literary Digest*, February 9, 1935.
7. *Ibid.*, June 1, 1935.
8. Homer Couzens to Couzens, April 24, 1934.
9. *Congressional Record*, May 14, 1934.
10. *Ibid.*
11. *New York Times*, August 26, 1934.
12. Carlson and Bates, *Hearst*, pp. 268–69; *Literary Digest*, June 29, July 13, and September 28, 1935.
13. Couzens to Madeleine Yaw, March 23, 1935.
14. Couzens to Rosetta Hauss, March 30, 1935.
15. *Detroit News*, June 11, 1935.
16. Dr. Freund to Carson, July 4, 1935.
17. Dr. Freund, interview, February 14, 1941.
18. Couzens to Madeleine, December 10, 1935.
19. Franklin D. Roosevelt, *op. cit.*, 1936, p. 17.
20. Jay G. Hayden, interview.

Chapter XLIV. *The Political Dilemma*

1. Couzens to John C. Manning, January 31, 1936.
2. Couzens to W. R. Yaw, January 21, 1936.
3. Couzens to Chairman Jesse H. Jones of the RFC, April 2, 1935; also *New York Times*, February 25, 1936.
4. March 8, 1936.
5. *Congressional Record*, February 24, 1936.
6. George Averill to Couzens, February 15, 1936; Couzens to Averill, February 20, 1936.
7. May 5, 1936.
8. Couzens to John C. Manning, January 31, 1936.
9. Couzens to *ibid.*, March 30, 1935.
10. Manning to Couzens, February 23, 1935.
11. *Ibid.*
12. Manning to Couzens, February 23, 1935.

13. Justice Frank Murphy, interview, April 19, 1940.
14. Couzens to Manning, March 5, 1935.
15. Justice Frank Murphy, interview, April 19, 1940.
16. *Ibid.*
17. Attorney General Harry S. Toy to Vandenberg, June 4, 1935.
18. Frank Couzens to James Couzens, November 29, 1935.
19. Couzens to Frank Couzens, December 20, 1935.
20. February 1, 1936, p. 45.
21. Couzens to Payne, January 8, 1936.
22. Couzens to Frank D. Fitzgerald, February 4, 1936.
23. Averill to Couzens, May 21, 1936.
24. Couzens to Payne, May 21 and 28, 1936.
25. Prentiss M. Brown, letter to author, September 6, 1941.
26. John Carson, letter-memorandum to William R. Yaw, August 26, 1943; Prentiss Brown to author, September 6, 1941, and interview, June 1946.
27. Justice Murphy, interview, *op. cit.*
28. Prentiss M. Brown, interview, *op. cit.*
29. *Detroit News,* June 16, 1936.
30. Prentiss Brown confirmed this in interview, June 1946.
31. Carson memorandum to Yaw, *op. cit.* In Couzens' notebook for June 19, 1936, the day he entrained for Detroit, there appears this: "Carson at train—talked about Farley leaving PMG." Mr. Farley has commented: "Certainly it was never discussed with me by President Roosevelt. . . . I'm inclined to think there wasn't anything to it. It might have been some other place in the Cabinet, but not the Postmaster General." Letter to author, January 29, 1946.

CHAPTER XLV. *The Independent Man*

1. Couzens to Vandenberg, September 1, 1936.
2. John P. Frazer, interview.
3. W. J. Norton, interview, February 12, 1941.
4. *Detroit News,* August 5 and 7, 1936.
5. Radio address, Station WJR, August 21, 1936.
6. Couzens to W. R. Yaw, radiogram from yacht *Buccaneer,* August 12, 1936.
7. John P. Frazer, interview, September 26, 1943.
8. Ray Tucker, *Sons of the Wild Jackass, op. cit.,* p. 365.
9. Madeleine C. Yaw, interview, June 1946.

CHAPTER XLVI. *The Triumphant Defeat*

1. Couzens to McNary, August 24, 1936.
2. W. J. Norton to author, interview, *op. cit.*
3. Couzens to Vandenberg, September 24, 1936.
4. Senator McNary, interview, *op. cit.*
5. In Couzens papers; also in Grace Tully, *F.D.R., My Boss,* pp. 215–16.
6. August 27, 1936.
7. *Detroit News,* October 23, 1936.
8. In Couzens papers. The text, in part, of this letter was released by the White House on October 16, 1936, *New York Times,* October 27, 1936.
9. Couzens to Roosevelt, September 25, 1936.
10. Vandenberg to Couzens, September 16, 1936, dated "Wednesday afternoon, Lakewood Farm."
11. Couzens to Vandenberg, September 24, 1936.
12. Couzens' notebook, September 19, 1936.
13. *Ibid.,* September 24.
14. *Ibid.,* October 7, 1936.
15. Roosevelt to Couzens, October 7, 1936.
16. Couzens' notebook, October 11, 1936.
17. Arthur Krock, letter to author, February 26, 1946.
18. Justice Murphy, interview, *op. cit.*

19. *Detroit News,* October 23, 1936.
20. *Ibid.,* October 16.
21. Roosevelt, *Public Papers,* 1936, pp. 495-99.
22. W. R. Yaw, interview, June 1946.

CHAPTER XLVII. *"The End of the Road"*

1. Dr. Freund, interview, June 1946; see also Children's Fund *Report,* 1942-43, p. 3.
2. Madeleine C. Yaw, interview, June 1946.
3. In Couzens papers.
4. *Detroit News,* October 21, 1936.
5. *Ibid.,* October 23, 1936.
6. Madeleine C. Yaw, interview, June 1946.
7. *New Republic,* September 30, 1936.
8. *Detroit News,* October 23, 1936.
9. Roosevelt, *Public Papers, op. cit.,* 1936, p. 531.

BIBLIOGRAPHY

Adams, Samuel Hopkins, *Incredible Era, The Life and Times of Warren Gamaliel Harding*, Boston, 1939.
Alinsky, Saul, *John L. Lewis*, New York, 1949.
Allen, Frederick Lewis, *Lords of Creation*, New York, 1939.
——, *Only Yesterday*, New York, 1931.
——, *Since Yesterday*, New York, 1940.
Allen, Robert S., ed., *Our Fair City*, New York, 1947.
Alsop, Joseph, and Catledge, Turner, *The 168 Days*, New York, 1938.
——, and Kintner, Robert, *Men Around the President*, New York, 1939.
American Encyclopedia of the Automobile.
American Mercury.
Angell, James W., *Program for the World Economic Conference*, Boston, 1933.
Annals of the American Academy of Political and Social Science.
Anon., "Who's Who and Why—Serious and Frivolous Facts About the Great and the Near Great," *Saturday Evening Post*, April 21, 1923.
Appel, Joseph H., *The Business Biography of John Wanamaker*, New York, 1930.
Arnold, Thurman, "Must 1929 Repeat Itself," *Harvard Business Review*, January, 1949.
Automobile Magazine.
Automobile Review and Automobile News.
Ballantine, Arthur A., "When All The Banks Closed," *Harvard Business Review*, March, 1948.
Baltimore Sun.
Barber, H. L., *The Story of the Automobile, Its History and Development from 1760 to 1917*, Chicago, 1917.
Barkley, Alben W., *That Reminds Me*, New York, 1954.
Barron, Clarence W., *They Told Barron*, ed. by Arthur Pound and S. T. Moore, New York, 1930.
Barron's Magazine.
Barry, Richard, "Newberry's Successor: A Study of Senator Couzens," *The Outlook*, December 20, 1923.
Bates, Ernest Sutherland, *The Story of Congress, 1789–1935*, New York, 1936.
Beals, Carleton, *The Story of Huey P. Long*, Philadelphia, 1935.
Beard, Charles A. and Mary R., *The Rise of American Civilization*, New York, 1930, 1939.
——, and Smith, George E. H., *The Future Comes, A Study of the New Deal*, New York, 1933.
Beasley, Norman, *Knudsen, a Biography*, New York, 1947.
Bennett, Harry, as told to Paul Marcus, *We Never Called Him Henry*, New York, 1951.
Benson, Allan, "The Bombshell That Henry Ford Fired," *Pearson's Magazine*, April 1915.
——, *The New Henry Ford*, New York, 1923.
Bingay, Malcolm, *Detroit Is My Own Home Town*, Indianapolis, 1946.
——, "Get A Horse," *Saturday Evening Post*, June 29, 1940.
——, "The Motor Boys in Action," *Saturday Evening Post*, July 6, 1940.

Bingay, Malcolm, obituary article on James Couzens, *Detroit Free Press*, October 22, 1936.

——, *Of Me I Sing*, Indianapolis, 1948.

Blythe, Samuel G., "A Calm Review of a Calm Man" [Warren G. Harding], *Saturday Evening Post*, July 18, 1923.

Borth, Christy, *Masters of Mass Production*, Indianapolis, 1945.

Bowers, Claude, *Beveridge and the Progressive Era*, Boston, 1932.

Bradford, Gamaliel, *The Quick and the Dead*, Boston, 1929.

Briscoe, Benjamin, "The Inside Story of General Motors," *Detroit Saturday Night*, June 22, 1927.

Burck, Gilbert, and Silberman, Charles E., "Why the Depression Lasted So Long," *Fortune*, March 1955.

Burlingame, Roger, *Backgrounds of Power*, New York, 1949.

——, *Henry Ford*, New York, 1954.

Burns, James M., *The Lion and the Fox—Roosevelt*, New York, 1956.

Busch, Niven, Jr., *21 Americans*, New York, 1930.

Bushnell, Sarah T., *The Truth About Henry Ford*, Chicago, 1922.

Butler, Nicholas Murray, *Across the Busy Years*, New York, 1936.

Byers, George, "The Selden Patent Case," *Patent Office Journal*, October 1940.

Carlson, Oliver, and Bates, Ernest Sutherland, *Hearst, Lord of San Simeon*, New York, 1936.

Carter, John Franklin (The Unofficial Observer), *The New Dealers*, New York, 1934.

Catlin, George B., *The Story of Detroit*, Detroit, 1926.

"Causes of Employment," Hearings Before the Committee on Education and Labor, United States Senate, 70th Congress, 2nd Session, United States Senate Investigation, 1928.

Chatham (Ontario) *Planet*.

Chicago Tribune.

Children's Fund of Michigan, *Reports*.

Coghlan, Robert, "Co-Captains in Ford's Battle for Supremacy," *Life*, February 28, 1955.

Cohn, David L., *Combustion on Wheels, An Informal History of the Automobile Age*, / Boston, 1944.

Colt, C. C., and Keith, N. S., *28 Days, A History of the Banking Crisis*, New York, 1933.

Columbia Motor Car Co., et al., v. C. A. Duerr and Co., et al. 184 Fed. 893, 1911. The second Selden patent case.

Commercial and Financial Chronicle.

Congressional Digest.

Congressional Record.

Connally, Tom, *My Name Is Tom Connally*, New York, 1954.

Couzens, James, "American Industry and the Social Good," *Printer's Ink*, July 1934.

——, "The Installment Buyer Worries Me," *Nation's Business*, December 1926.

——, "Why I Believe in High Wages," *World's Work*, April 1916.

——, "Providing for the Depreciation of Human Earning Power," *Michigan Manufacturer and Financial Record*, October 26, 1918.

——, Report of Detroit Police Department, Detroit, 1918.

——, "Senator La Follette—The Greatest American of Our Age," *Brotherhood of Locomotive Firemen and Enginemen's Magazine*, September 1925.

——, "Wages," *Survey*, April 11, 1930.

——, "What I Learned About Business from Ford," *System*, September 1921.

Cox, James M., *Journey Through My Years, An Autobiography*, New York, 1946.

Crowell, Merle, "Would You Be Happier If You Were Worth Millions?," *American Magazine*, February 1923.

Cuncannon, Paul M., "Arthur H. Vandenberg," in *The American Politician*, ed. by J. T. Salter, New York, 1938.

Cycle and Automobile Trade Journal.

Current History.

Davies, Joseph E., *Mission to Moscow*, New York, 1941.

Dearborn Independent.

Detroit Common Council Proceedings.
Detroit Free Press.
Detroit Journal.
Detroit Labor News.
Detroit News.
Detroit News Tribune, "The Wonder Plant and the Man Who Guides It," August 29, 1915.
Detroit Saturday Night.
Detroit Times.
Detroit Times and Tribune.
Detroit United Railway Appt. v. City of Detroit, et al., 255 U.S. 171, 1920.
Detroiter.
"Detroit's Government," Report by the Common Council and the Mayor of the City of Detroit, Detroit, 1922.
Dillon, Mary Earhart, *Wendell Willkie,* Philadelphia and New York, 1952.
Dodge, John and Horace, v. Ford Motor Co., Michigan Supreme Court, 1919, 170 Northwestern Reporter, 669.
Donovan, Leo, "Detroit," in *Our Fair City,* ed. by Robert S. Allen, New York, 1947.
Doolittle, James F., *Romance of the Automobile Industry,* Chicago, 1916.
Electric Vehicle Co., et al., v. C. A. Duerr & Co., et al., 172 Fed. 923, 1909.
Engineering Magazine.
Epstein, Ralph, *The Automobile Industry,* Chicago and New York, 1927.
Ervin, Spencer, *Henry Ford vs. Truman H. Newberry,* New York, 1935.
Everybody's Magazine.
Farley, James A., *Behind the Ballots,* New York, 1938.
———, with Walter Trohan, *Jim Farley's Story,* New York, 1948.
Faurote, Fay Leone, "The New Ford Line-up," *Engineering Magazine,* January 16, 1916.
———, and Arnold, H. L., *Ford Methods and the Ford Shops,* New York, 1915.
Fay, Charles Norman, *Social Justice, The Moral of the Henry Ford Fortune,* Cambridge, Mass., 1926.
Filler, Louis, *Crusaders for American Liberalism,* New York, 1939.
Flynn, John T., "Detroit Business Men Cheer Couzens' Defeat," *New Republic,* September 30, 1936.
———, "Inside the RFC," *Harpers,* January 1933.
———, "Michigan Magic—The Detroit Bank Scandal," *Harpers,* December 1933.
Forbes, B. C., "Why Multimillionaire Couzens Quit Business," *Forbes Magazine,* December 1922.
———, and Foster, O. D., *Automotive Giants of America,* New York, 1926.
Forbes Magazine.
Ford, Henry, *My Life and Work,* New York, 1922.
———, with Samuel Crowther, *Today and Tomorrow,* New York, 1926.
———, with Samuel Crowther, *Moving Forward,* New York, 1931.
Ford Times.
Foreign Policy Reports.
Fortune.
Frank, John P., *Mr. Justice Black, The Man and His Opinions,* New York, 1949.
Freidel, Frank, *Franklin D. Roosevelt,* 3 vols., Boston, 1952, 1954, 1956.
Fuess, Claude M., *Calvin Coolidge, The Man from Vermont,* New York, 1940.
Galbraith, John Kenneth, *The Great Crash, 1929,* Boston, 1955.
Garrett, Garet, "Henry Ford's Experiment in Good Will," *Everybody's,* April 1914.
———, *The Wild Wheel,* New York, 1952.
———, "A World That Was," *Saturday Evening Post,* June 8, 1940.
Gauvreau, Emile, and Cohen, Lester, *Billy Mitchell, a Biography,* New York, 1942.
Gibbons, Herbert Adams, *John Wanamaker,* New York, 1926.
Gilbert, Clinton W., *Mirrors of Washington,* New York, 1921.
Ginger, Ray, *The Bending Cross, a Biography of Eugene Victor Debs,* New Brunswick, 1949.
Glasscock, G. B., *The Gasoline Age, The Story of the Men Who Made It,* Indianapolis, 1937.

Grand Rapids [Michigan] *News.*

Graves, Ralph H., *The Triumph of an Idea,* New York, 1935.

Green, James F., "Great Britain's Foreign Trade Policy," *Foreign Policy Reports,* January 15, 1938.

Gunther, John, *Inside U.S.A.,* New York, 1948.

Hacker, Louis M., *The Triumph of American Capitalism,* New York, 1940.

Hallgren, Mauritz A., *The Gay Reformer, Profits Before Plenty under Franklin D. Roosevelt,* New York, 1935.

Hamilton, James de Roulhac, *Henry Ford, the Man, the Worker, the Citizen,* New York, 1927.

Hard, William, "Coming: Couzens of Detroit," *Hearst's International,* May 1922.

Harpers.

Harrod, R. F., *The Life of John Maynard Keynes,* New York, 1951.

Hatch, Louis C., and Shoup, Earl, *A History of the Vice Presidency of the United States,* New York, 1943.

Hayden, Jay G., "A History of the Detroit Railway Commission" in manuscript.

Haynes, George H., *The Senate of the United States, Its History and Practice,* Boston, 1938.

Hendrick, Burton J., *Age of Big Business,* Cambridge, 1927.

Hesseltine, William B., "Robert Marion La Follette and the Principles of Americanism," *Wisconsin Magazine of History,* Vol. XXXI, No. 261, March 1948.

Hewitt, Oscar, articles in the *Chicago Herald,* October 1923.

High, Low Washington, anonymous, New York, 1932.

Hinshaw, David, *Herbert Hoover, American Quaker,* New York, 1950.

Hinton, Harold B., *Cordell Hull, A Biography,* New York, 1942.

"Historical Chatham," *Chatham Planet Souvenir,* Chatham, Ontario, 1904.

Hofstadter, Richard, *The Age of Reform, from Bryan to F.D.R.,* New York, 1955.

————, *The American Political Tradition and the Men Who Made It,* New York, 1948.

Hoover, Herbert, *Memoirs,* New York, 1951 and 1952.

Howe, Irving, and Widick, B. J., *The UAW and Walter Reuther,* New York, 1949.

Hull, Cordell, *Memoirs,* New York, 1948.

Hutchins, Jere C., *A Personal Story,* Detroit, 1938.

Hutchinson, William T., *Lowden of Illinois,* Chicago, 1957.

Ickes, Harold L., *Autobiography of a Curmudgeon,* New York, 1943.

————, *The Secret Diary of Harold L. Ickes, The First Thousand Days, 1933–36,* New York, 1953.

Irwin, Will, *The Making of a Reporter,* New York, 1942.

James, F. Cyril, *The Growth of Chicago Banks,* New York, 1938.

————, ed., "Reforming the American Banking System," *The Annals of the American Academy of Political and Social Science,* January 1934.

James, Marquis and Bessie R., *Biography of a Bank, The Story of the Bank of America,* New York, 1954.

Johnson, Claudius O., *Borah of Idaho,* New York, 1934.

————, "George William Norris," in *The American Politician,* ed. by J. T. Salter, New York, 1938.

Johnson, Walter, *William Allen White's America,* New York, 1947.

Jones, Jesse H., with Edward Angly, *Fifty Billion Dollars, My Thirteen Years with the RFC 1932–1945,* New York, 1951.

Kennedy, E. D., *The Automobile Industry,* New York, 1941.

Kennedy, John F., *Profiles in Courage,* New York, 1956.

Kent, Frank R., "Couzens of Michigan," *American Mercury,* May 1927.

————, *Without Gloves,* New York, 1934.

————, *Without Grease,* New York, 1936.

Kern, Paul J., "Fiorello H. La Guardia," in *The American Politician,* ed. by J. T. Salter, New York, 1938.

King, Charles B., *Psychic Remembrances,* New York, 1939.

Labor.

La Follette, Bella Case and Fola, *Robert M. La Follette,* New York, 1953.

La Follette's Magazine.
Lane, Rosa Wilder, *Henry Ford's Own Story*, New York, 1917.
Lansing [Michigan] *News.*
Laski, Harold J., *The American Democracy*, New York, 1948.
Lauriston, Victor, *Arthur Stringer, An Appreciation*, Indianapolis, 1940.
——, *Postscript to a Poet, Off the Record Tales About Arthur Stringer*, Chatham, Ontario, 1941.
Leach, Paul R., *That Man Dawes*, Chicago, 1930.
League of Nations, *Journal of the Monetary and Economic Conference*, No. 4, London, 1933.
Lee, John R., "The So-called Profit-Sharing System in the Ford Plant," *The Annals of the American Academy of Political and Social Science*, May 1916.
Leonard, Jonathan Norton, *Tragedy of Henry Ford*, New York, 1932.
Levine, Isaac Don, *Mitchell, Apostle of Air Power*, New York, 1943.
Lief, Alfred, *Democracy's Norris*, New York, 1939.
Life.
Lindley, Ernest K., *Half Way with Roosevelt*, New York, 1936.
——, *The Roosevelt Revolution*, New York, 1933.
Lippmann, Walter, *Interpretations*, selected and edited by Allan Nevins, New York, 1936.
Literary Digest.
Littell, Robert, *Read America First*, New York, 1926.
Lochner, Louis P., *Henry Ford*, New York, 1925.
Lodge, John C., with Milo Quaife, *I Remember Detroit*, Detroit, 1949.
London Daily Herald.
Long, Huey P., *Every Man a King*, New Orleans, 1933.
Long, J. C., *Roy D. Chapin*, Detroit, 1945.
Love, Philip, *Andrew W. Mellon*, New York, 1930.
Lyons, Eugene, *Our Unknown President, A Portrait of Herbert Hoover*, New York, 1949.
Mackay, Kenneth Campbell, *The Progressive Movement of 1924*, New York, 1947.
Madison (Wisconsin) *Capital-Times.*
McManus, Theodore F., *The Sword Arm of Business*, New York, 1927.
——, *They Told Barron*, New York, 1927.
——, with Norman Beasley, *Men, Money, and Motors, The Drama of the Automobile*, New York, 1929.
McRae, Milton A., *Forty Years in Newspaperdom*, New York, 1924.
Marquis, S. S., *Henry Ford, An Interpretation*, Boston, 1923.
Marshall, Margaret Mooers, interview, *New York World*, December 1, 1922.
Mason, Alpheus Thomas, *Harlan Fiske Stone, Pillar of the Law*, New York, 1956.
Mertz, Charles, *And Then Came Ford*, New York, 1929.
Michigan, A Guide to the Wolverine State, compiled by WPA writers of the State of Michigan, 1941.
Michigan Manufacturer & Financial Record.
Miller, James M., *The Amazing Story of Henry Ford*, Chicago, 1922.
Moley, Raymond, *After Seven Years*, New York, 1939.
Morrow, James B., "Couzens, Radical—and Rich," *Nation's Business*, June 1923.
Motor World.
Myers, William Starr, and Newton, Walter H., *The Hoover Administration*, New York, 1936.
Nadler, Marcus, and Bogen, Jules I., *The Banking Crisis*, New York, 1933.
Nation.
National Magazine.
Nation's Business.
Neil, Judge Henry, "Senator Couzens Tells Why He Broke With Henry Ford," *Real America Magazine*, April 1934.
Neuberger, Richard L., "A Politician Unafraid" [George W. Norris], *Harpers*, October 1936.

Neuberger, Richard L., and Kahn, George, *Integrity—George W. Norris*, New York, 1936.
Nevins, Allan, *John D. Rockefeller*, New York, 1932.
——, with Hill, Frank Ernest, *Ford, The Times, The Man, The Company*, New York, 1954.
——, and Frank Ernest Hill, *Ford, Expansion and Challenge*, New York, 1957.
Newberry v. United States, 256 U.S. 58, 1920.
New Republic.
New York Herald Tribune.
New York Post.
New York Sun.
New York Times.
New York World.
Nichols, Jeannette P., "Roosevelt's Monetary Diplomacy in 1933," *American Historical Review*, Vol. LVI, No. 2, January 1951.
Nicolson, Harold, *Dwight Morrow*, New York, 1935.
Norris, George W., *Fighting Liberal*, New York, 1945.
Norton, William J., address at memorial services for James Couzens, Traverse City, Michigan, November 1, 1936, published by the Kiwanis Club of Traverse City.
——, "The Saga of a Foundation Executive," address before Prismatic Club, 1954.
Norwood, Edwin P., *Ford Men and Methods*, New York, 1931.
O'Connor, Harvey, *Mellon's Millions, The Biography of a Fortune*, New York, 1933.
O'Geran, Graeme, *A History of the Detroit Street Railways*, Detroit, 1931.
Outlook.
Parker, Read L., article in *Fort Wayne* [Indiana] *Journal*, November 15, 1914.
Paxson, Frederic L., *Postwar Years, Normalcy, 1918-23*, Berkeley and Los Angeles, 1948.
Pearson, Drew, and Allen, Robert S., *More Washington Merry Go Round*, New York, 1932.
——, and Allen, Robert S., *Washington Merry Go Round*, New York, 1931.
——, and Brown, Constantine, *The American Political Game*, New York, 1935.
Pecora, Ferdinand, *Wall Street Under Oath*, New York, 1939.
Pepper, George Wharton, *Men and Issues*, New York, 1924.
——, *Philadelphia Lawyer*, New York, 1924.
Perkins, Dexter, *Charles Evans Hughes and American Statesmanship*, Boston, 1956.
——, *The New Age of Franklin Roosevelt, 1932-1945*, Chicago, 1957.
Perkins, Frances, *The Roosevelt I Knew*, New York, 1946.
Philadelphia Public Ledger.
Pipp, E. G., *Henry Ford, Both Sides of Him*, Detroit, 1926.
Pipp's Weekly.
Pound, Arthur, *Detroit, Dynamic City*, New York, 1940.
——, "The Ford Myth," *Atlantic Monthly*, January 1924.
——, *The Iron Man in Industry*, Boston, 1922.
——, *The Turning Wheel*, New York, 1934.
Pringle, Henry F., *Life and Times of William Howard Taft*, New York, 1939.
——, *Theodore Roosevelt*, New York, 1931.
Pritchett, C. Herman, *The Tennessee Valley Authority, A Study in Public Administration*, Chapel Hill, 1943.
Pusey, Merlo J., *Charles Evans Hughes*, 2 vols., New York, 1950.
Quaife, Milo M., *The Life of John Wendell Anderson*, Detroit, 1950.
Report on Motor Vehicle Industry, House Document No. 468, Federal Trade Commission, Government Printing Office, Washington, D.C.
Richards, William C., *The Last Billionaire*, New York, 1948.
——, and Norton, William J., *Biography of a Foundation, The Story of the Children's Fund of Michigan*, Detroit, 1957.
Rogers, Lindsay, *The American Senate*, New York, 1926.
Roosevelt, Elliott, ed., *F.D.R., His Personal Letters*, 2 vols., New York, 1950.
Roosevelt, Franklin Delano, *On Our Way*, New York, 1934.
——, *Public Papers and Addresses*, New York, 1938.
Roosevelt, Theodore, *Autobiography*, New York, 1926.

Ross, Martin, *Shipstead of Minnesota*, Chicago, 1940.

Saginaw [Michigan] *News Courier.*

Salter, J. T., ed., *The American Politician*, Chapel Hill, 1938.

Saturday Evening Post.

Schlesinger, Arthur, Jr., *The Age of Roosevelt*, Boston, 1957.

Schram, Ross C., "How Detroit Came to Run Its Own Street Cars," pamphlet, City of Detroit, 1922.

Schriftgiesser, Karl, *The Gentleman from Massachusetts, Henry Cabot Lodge,* Boston, 1944.

———, *This Was Normalcy*, Boston, 1948.

Schuman, Frederick L., *Europe on the Eve*, New York, 1939.

Secretary of the Treasury, *Annual Report, 1933*, Washington, 1933.

Selden, George D., "The Selden Patent," *Rochester Alumni-Alumnae Review*, February–March 1940.

Seltzer, L. H., *A Financial History of the American Automobile Industry*, Boston, 1928.

Sherwood, Robert E., *Roosevelt and Hopkins, An Intimate History*, New York, 1948.

Shideler, James H., "The La Follette Progressive Party Campaign of 1924," *Wisconsin Magazine of History*, June 1950.

Simonds, William A., *Henry Ford, His Life, His Work, His Genius*, Indianapolis, 1943.

———, *Henry Ford, Motor Genius*, New York, 1929.

Sinsabaugh, Chris, *Who Me?*, Detroit, 1940.

Slemp, C. Bascom, *The Mind of the President* [Calvin Coolidge], New York, 1926.

Sloan, Alfred P., "Adventures of a White Collar Man," New York, 1941.

Smith, Rixey, and Beasley, Norman, *Carter Glass, A Biography*, New York, 1939.

Sorensen, Charles E., *My Forty Years with Ford*, New York, 1956.

Steffens, Lincoln, *Autobiography*, New York, 1931.

Stern, Philip Van Doren, *The Tin Lizzie*, New York, 1954.

Stewart, Maxwell S., "The Work of the London Economic Conference," *Foreign Policy Reports*, November 8, 1933.

Stidger, William L., *Henry Ford, the Man and His Motives*, New York, 1923.

———, *The Human Side of Greatness*, New York, 1940.

Stiles, Lela, *The Man Behind Roosevelt, The Story of Lewis McHenry Howe*, Cleveland and New York, 1954.

"Stock Exchange Practices," United States Senate Report No. 1455, Report of the Committee on Banking and Currency, 73rd Congress, 2d Session, Washington, 1934.

Stokes, Thomas L., *Chip Off My Shoulder*, Princeton, 1940.

Stone, Irving, *Clarence Darrow for the Defense*, New York, 1941.

———, *They Also Ran*, New York, 1944.

Street, Julian, "Dynamic Detroit," *Colliers*, July 4, 1914.

Stringer, Arthur, *Lonely O'Malley*, Indianapolis, 1920. A novel about Chatham, Ontario.

Sullivan, Lawrence, *Prelude to Panic*, Washington, 1936.

Sullivan, Mark, *The Education of an American*, New York, 1938.

———, *Our Times—the 20's*, New York, 1936.

Sward, Keith, *The Legend of Henry Ford*, New York, 1948.

Time.

Times, The (London).

Timmons, Bascom N., *Jesse H. Jones, The Man and the Statesman*, New York, 1956.

———, *Portrait of an American, Charles G. Dawes*, New York, 1953.

Toronto Border Cities Star.

Toronto Daily News.

Tucker, Ray, and Barkley, Frederick R., *Sons of the Wild Jackass*, Boston, 1932.

Tugwell, Rexford G., *The Democratic Roosevelt*, New York, 1957.

Tully, Grace, *FDR, My Boss*, New York, 1949.

Upham, Cyril B., and Lanke, Edwin, *Closed and Distressed Banks*, Washington, 1934.

Upson, Lent D., *A Quarter-Century of Citizen Concern with Government*, a preface and a bibliography of the Detroit Bureau of Governmental Research, 1916–1941.

Vandenberg, Arthur H., Jr., and Morris, Joe Alex, eds., *The Private Papers of Senator Vandenberg*, Boston, 1952.

"Vanishing Millions, The Story of the Detroit Bank Crash," a series in *Detroit Times*, March–April 1933.
Viereck, George Sylvester, *Glimpses of the Great*, New York, 1930.
Villard, Oswald Garrison, "The Unique Millionaire—A Weak Heart Made James Couzens Great," *Forum Magazine*, January 1937.
Wallis, J. H., *The Politician*, New York, 1935.
Warburg, J. P., "Monetary Policy of the United States," *The Annals of the American Academy of Political and Social Science*, January 1934.
————, *The Money Muddle*, New York, 1934.
Watson, James, *As I Knew Them*, Indianapolis, 1936.
Wayne, Flynn, "A Master Builder of Efficiency," *National Magazine*, September 1915.
Wecter, Dixon, *The Age of the Great Depression*, New York, 1949.
Wendt, Lloyd, and Kogan, Herman, *Big Bill of Chicago*, Indianapolis, 1953.
White, William Allen, *Autobiography*, New York, 1946.
————, *Calvin Coolidge*, New York, 1925.
————, *Masks in a Pageant*, New York, 1928.
————, *Politics: The Citizen's Business*, New York, 1924.
————, *Puritan in Babylon*, New York, 1939.
White, William S., *Citadel, The Story of the U.S. Senate*, New York, 1956.
Wilbur, Ray Lyman, and Hyde, Arthur Mastic, *The Hoover Policies*, New York, 1937.
Wildman, Edwin, *Famous Leaders of Industry*, Boston, 1920.
Wood, Charles W., "He Had Millions But Wanted a Job," *Colliers*, August 5, 1922.
Woodward, C. Vann, *Tom Watson, Agrarian Rebel*, New York, 1938.
World's Work.
Young, William P., *A Ford Dealer's Thirty Year Ride*, Pittsburgh, 1932.
U.S. Senate Report 27, "Investigation of Bureau of Internal Revenue Pursuant to Senate Resolution 68," 69th Congress, 1st session, Washington, 1926.
U.S. Department of State, *Foreign Relations of United States, 1933*, I, Washington, 1950.

UNPUBLISHED SOURCE MATERIAL

Couzens, James, general letters, notebooks, addresses, and clippings, 1903–1936, Library of Congress.
Couzens, James, "The Michigan Banking Crisis," a memorandum, 1933.
Detroit Board of Commerce, Minute Books, 1911–1914.
Durant, W. C., Memoirs, a manuscript extract.
Ford, Henry vs. The Chicago Tribune, Transcript of Testimony.
Hayden, Jay G., a history of Detroit politics.
Hoover, Herbert, a memorandum on the Detroit bank crisis.
Jones, Edgar Dewitt, radio address on anniversary of James Couzens' death.
Lauriston, Victor, "When Senator Jim Couzens Peddled Soap in Chatham," unpublished article on James Couzens in Chatham.
League of Nations mimeographed bulletins on the World Monetary and Economic Conference, London, 1933.
Miller, Charles A., memorandum on the Detroit bank case, 1942.
Neil, J. H., notes on interview with James Couzens, 1924.
Pratt, John S., special assistant to the U.S. Attorney General, Memorandum to Assistant Attorney General Keenan, "Re: Detroit Banking Situation," March 22, 1934.

INTERVIEWS AND CORRESPONDENCE

Among others:
Herbert Hoover, Charles G. Dawes, John N. Garner, Hiram Johnson, Charles L. McNary, Robert M. La Follette, Jr., George W. Norris, Frederic W. Hale, Pat Harrison, James E. Watson, Key Pittman, Arthur H. Vandenberg, Prentiss M. Brown, Arthur W. Capper, Cordell Hull, William C. Bullitt, William Comstock, Alex J. Groesbeck, James M. Cox, Gifford Pinchot, Frank Murphy, Henry Morgenthau, Jr., James A. Farley, Bernard M. Baruch, Herbert Bayard Swope, James P. Warburg, Samuel S. Marquis, Samuel Crowther, Jay G. Hayden, Charles A. Miller, Arthur A. Ballantine, Edward Keating, Thomas L. Stokes, Ray Tucker, John Carson, Frank L. Klingensmith,

Harry B. Harper, Edward G. Liebold, Herbert Feis, Raymond Moley, Edward T. Fitzgerald, Theodore C. Joslin, Charles T. Bennett, Ida M. Tarbell, Arthur J. Lacy, Clarence Wilcox, C. J. Huddleston, Ross C. Schram, Henry A. Morgan, Joseph E. Davies, Abner Larned, Wilson W. Mills, W. L. Dunham, Daniel J. Hackett, Mrs. Roy Pelletier, Dorothy Dunn, Walter R. Dorsey, Garet Garrett, Victor Lauriston, Arthur Stringer, William Mann, Charles Donovan, A. E. Couzens, Homer Couzens, Frank Couzens, Mrs. Alice Couzens Lund, Mrs. Rosetta Couzens Hauss, Mrs. James Couzens, Mrs. Madeleine Couzens Yaw, William R. Yaw, William J. Norton, MacPherson Browning, A. R. Malcomson, William C. Durant, Charles B. King, Charles T. Bennett, Vernon Fry, Herbert L. Satterlee, John C. Lodge, John P. Frazier, Harvey Campbell, Byers H. Gitchell, C. H. Haberkorn Jr., Henry T. Ewald, Dr. Hugo A. Freund, Mabel Ford, George W. Engel, A. C. Studer, Dr. Miles Griffin, Thomas W. Payne, William J. Twohey, John C. Manning, Helen Malcomson Gore, George Judson.

PERSONAL ACKNOWLEDGMENTS

To a number of persons, in addition to those named, gratitude is felt for various helps and encouragements in the fruition of this work, in particular, though not all-exclusively, to Wayne Andrews, for much valued guidance as well as a colleague's inspiration; to Allan Nevins, for having suggested that this work be done; to Judith B. Papier, for the index and other aids; to Stephen A. Mitchell and Bertram B. Moss, for crucial advice; and, foremost, though last here, to Ruth E. Barnard, my wife, who, through it all, was what God doubtless intended a wife to be in all respects—strong, comforting, and endlessly patient.

H. B.

INDEX

Acheson, Dean G., 255
Adams, Charles Francis, 264
Addams, Jane, 86
Aero Co., 61, 63, 66
Aldrich, Winthrop, 223
Alsop, Joseph, 260
Altgeld, John P., 25, 26, 125
Aluminum Corporation of America, 165
American Legion, 124
American Liberty League, 300
American Motor Car Manufacturers' Association, 56, 57
American Red Cross, 203
Amos House, 22, 23
Anderson, John W., 7, 36, 40-41, 43, 46, 52-53, 54, 60, 61, 62, 64, 130
Anderson, Paul Y., 141
Anderson, Wendell, Dr., 41, 47
Angell, James W., 270
Anti-Saloon League, 153, 168
"Association of Licensed Automobile Manufacturers," 52, 53-55, 56-59
Atlanta (Ga.), 95
Automobile Magazine, 49
Averill, George, 305, 308
Awalt, F. G., 241, 250, 251, 289

Baillie, Earl, 292
Baker, Newton D., 264
Ballantine, Arthur A., 227-229, 231, 234, 250, 289, 350
Baltimore (Md.), 164, 242
Baltimore Sun, 145, 197, 263
Bank of Detroit, 105, 146, 215
Bankers Trust Company of New York, 216
Bank Holiday, 213-252, 275-290
Barkley, Alben W., 178
Barron's, 7
Bath (Mich.), 324
Beard, Charles and Mary, 174, 213, 262

Beasley, Norman, 331
Belle Isle, 31, 131
Bennett, Charles T., 40, 49-50, 62, 64
Bennett, Harry, 332
Benson, Allan, 152
Bethlehem Steel Company, 165
Beveridge, Albert J., 155
Bingay, Malcolm, 237, 238, 279, 284, 286, 296, 341, 351
Bingham, Robert, 274
Birmingham *Eccentric*, The, 305
Birmingham (Mich.), 185, 286
Block, Louis B., 50, 100
Bodman, Henry, 241
Book-Cadillac Hotel, 319
Booth, Clarence H., 325
Booth, Ralph, 137
Borah, William E., 143, 154, 199, 297; 299-300
Boston (Mass.), 49
Boston University, 156
Brandeis, Louis D., 86, 125
Breitmeyer, Philip, 110
Brewer, Joseph H., 242
Brisbane, Arthur, 137, 179
Briscoe, Ben, 72, 73
Brookhart, Smith, 143, 145, 149, 177, 199, 314
Brown, Blanche Leuven, 186-187
Brown, Prentiss M., 309-310, 315, 319, 357
Brownell, Charles A., 4, 99
Browning, McPherson, 190
Bruce, King, 87
Brucker, Wilbur J., 305-306, 308, 311, 312-313, 316, 319
Bryan, Charles W., 172
Bryan, William Jennings, 86, 172
Buick Company, 50, 72
Buccaneer, 312ff
Buffalo (N.Y.), 46, 49

Printed in the USA
CPSIA information can be obtained
at www.ICGtesting.com
LVHW021230040124
767087LV00016B/443